EVALUATING EDUCATIONAL PROGRAMS AND PRODUCTS

EVALUATING EDUCATIONAL PROGRAMS AND PRODUCTS

GARY D. BORICH, Editor
University of Texas at Austin

Educational Technology Publications
Englewood Cliffs, NJ 07632

Library of Congress Cataloging in Publication Data

Borich, Gary D
    Evaluating educational programs and products.

    1. Educational accountability. 2. Teaching--Aids
and devices. I. Title.
LB2805.B67   379´.15   74-1298
ISBN 0-87778-070-6

Printed in the United States of America.

Library of Congress Catalog Card Number:
74-1298.

International Standard Book Number:
0-87778-070-6.

First Printing: May, 1974.

PREFACE

This book is about educational programs and products—how to develop them and how to evaluate them. The reader will notice that this book is not a textbook or collection of articles but an especially prepared *guide and handbook* for planners, developers, and evaluators of educational programs and products. For this reason readers will find this book different from others in that it is neither a theoretical work that goes beyond proven practice nor a collection of techniques that have yet to be tried and tested. To the contrary, the purpose of this book is to provide practical insights that are immediately applicable to planning and executing effective program and product evaluations.

Organization

This book divides the evaluator's work into three important activities: *establishing perspective, planning the evaluation,* and *analyzing the data.* The first activity is completed when the evaluator chooses an appropriate role for the context in which he will work; the second when he chooses an appropriate model or strategy for planning the evaluation; and the third when he selects appropriate methods and techniques for analyzing the data. The key to each of these activities is the word "appropriate." The task of this book is to identify for the reader specific procedures that *are* appropriate to each of these activities. The organization of this book, therefore, is divided into *Roles and Contexts, Models and Strategies,* and *Methods and Techniques* for evaluating educational programs and products.

In Part One, *Roles and Contexts*, the various settings in which the evaluator commonly works and the many roles he performs are identified. Five chapters have been prepared by evaluators who have distinguished themselves by writing about and conceptualizing the role of the evaluator as it applies to different contexts. Each author has chosen to develop a specific aspect of the overall problem of defining what the evaluator's responsibilities should be as he pursues his activities in the context of programs, products, and curricula.

After the evaluator chooses an appropriate role in relation to the context in which he will work, he must decide upon a model or strategy to guide his evaluation. This content is covered in Part Two, *Models and Strategies.* Here, five chapters have been prepared by evaluators who have distinguished themselves in developing evaluation models applicable in specific contexts. These authors and their work represent major research and development centers and laboratories across the nation that have supported the development of these models and now act as field sites for testing and implementation. The models presented are applicable to various settings—some chapters deal with evaluation models for large-scale research and development agencies, while others present strategies for the evaluation of specific educational programs and products.

Part Three of this book, *Methods and Techniques*, deals with the problem of collecting and analyzing evaluation data. Here, specific methods and techniques are presented dealing with six different problems in evaluation methodology. Three of these problems customarily occur in the formative context (selecting instruments and measures, evaluating component parts of a program, and evaluating the program in an ongoing setting) and three in the summative context (sampling and design, choosing the unit of analysis, and selecting an analysis strategy).

Each of the book's three parts is preceded by an introduction which, on a broad scale, places the general topic to be considered in perspective with current developments. These introductions acquaint readers with basic concepts and arguments as a means of providing background for the chapters that lie ahead. Introductions relate chapter content with trends and developments in roles and contexts (Part One), models and strategies (Part Two), and methods and techniques (Part Three). At the conclusion of each introduction, major concepts are summarized and key points emphasized for each chapter.

The Prologue and Epilogue to this volume are of special note. Prepared by two innovative educators, Michael Scriven and Kenneth Komoski, these contributions depict the nature of standards for program and product evaluation as they should be today (Prologue) and as they very well may be in the future (Epilogue). Both authors have long been noted for their contributions to evaluation—Scriven for his rich conceptualization of evaluation methodology which is now commonplace in evaluation practice, and Komoski for his practical implementation of evaluation methods and techniques for reporting product effectiveness data to the educational consumer. Both men bring longstanding insight into their respective contributions that, on the one hand, prepares us for the chapters that lie ahead and, on the other, prepares us for trends that will mark the future.

Goals

The goals of this book are threefold. They are (1) to help the evaluator see himself in perspective, i.e., in relation to his formative and summative role and in the context of products, programs, and curricula; (2) to help the evaluator plan an evaluation by presenting models and strategies from which he can choose concepts for constructing an appropriate model in his own settings; and (3) to acquaint the evaluator with important considerations for the collection and analysis of evaluation data. The following chapters attempt to provide instruction in these areas. For readers whose interests are largely within only one of these areas or whose interests are highly specific but run across all three of the areas, the *reader's guide* which follows the Table of Contents will be helpful in establishing reading priorities. In the guide, readings are divided according to the reader's occupational role, and a sequence of chapters is designated as either of primary, secondary, or peripheral importance. The former designation represents chapters which the reader will want to study closely and perhaps reread, while the latter encompasses chapters to be read after the primary readings have been completed. Together the chapters represent a complete sequence of activities for planning and executing an evaluation study.

The Procedure

Bringing together in one volume the work of so many respected and experienced evaluators has spanned the better part of two years. The impetus to prepare such a volume came from a national evaluation conference funded by the U.S. Office of Education which brought evaluators together from across the nation to identify and seek solutions to many of the problems treated in this book. Much of the substantive activity of this conference has been documented in its proceedings, *Problems and potentials of educational R&D evaluation,** and continues to be carried out by the Association for Educational Research and Development Evaluators, operating as a special interest group under the auspices of the American Educational Research Association.

It was early in the development of this group that authors were selected to begin preparing chapters according to general guidelines. First drafts of proposed chapters were completed in the fall of 1972. On October 30th of that year, authors met in Berkeley, California, to discuss their first draft manuscripts and ways in which to organize and structure the volume. At this meeting, many authors made valuable suggestions which eventually found their way into the final version of this book. Subsequent to the Berkeley meeting, first drafts of each chapter were submitted to the reviewers (listed on the following pages) for their critical comments and suggestions. These reviewers played an important role in shaping the structure of the individual chapters and indirectly the entire volume. In many cases, they are known to have spent long hours reading and rereading their respective assignments in an effort to provide useful suggestions to the author for revising or expanding his or her chapter. Subsequent to the critiques, the editor prepared his own comments on each manuscript, dealing with macrocosmic concerns, i.e., is the chapter comprehensive, how well does it fit with others in its division, and does it communicate clearly and effectively? Final manuscripts were prepared from both the editor's and reviewers' comments in the Spring of 1973, and final draft manuscripts were submitted to the editor the following Summer. At that time, introductory sections were prepared by the editor for each of the three divisions of the book. Therefore, the development of this volume has been slow and deliberate, not only to allow authors ample time to carefully prepare their manuscripts but also to seek the greatest amount of input from reviewers and other interested persons for guiding the nature of this book.

Acknowledgments

This work has relied upon the help and cooperation of a great many persons in addition to those who have contributed chapters. In

*H. Poynor (Ed.) Problems and potentials of educational R & D evaluation. Austin, Texas: Southwest Educational Development Laboratory, 1974.

particular I would like to thank Rosemary Gordon, for her excellent help in typing the volume; Betsy Munson, for her assistance with editing the manuscripts; and Bob Prestwood and Dave Wilson, for their help in preparing the graphics. I would like to acknowledge the Research and Development Center for Teacher Education at The University of Texas at Austin, which has in spirit supported the preparation of this volume over the past two years, and especially the co-directors of the Center, Dr. Robert F. Peck and Dr. Oliver H. Bown, who provided the atmosphere necessary for completing this work.

I would be remiss without mentioning in this regard my family which, I am afraid, bore the greatest burden during the preparation of this book. I owe a great deal to my wife Kathy for her help and encouragement and to my daughter Brandy, who I hope will now get to see her daddy on the weekends.

Gary D. Borich
The University of Texas at Austin

CONTRIBUTORS

MARVIN C. ALKIN is Director of the Center for the Study of Evaluation, University of California at Los Angeles.

EVA L. BAKER is a member of the School of Education, University of California at Los Angeles.

KATHERINE A. BEMIS is Director of Evaluation at Southwest Research Associates, Albuquerque, New Mexico.

CHARLES L. BERTRAM is Director of Research and Evaluation at the Appalachia Educational Laboratory, Inc., Charleston, West Virginia.

GARY D. BORICH is Director of Evaluation at the Research and Development Center for Teacher Education, The University of Texas at Austin.

BARBARA J. BRANDES is currently an Evaluation Specialist at the Research, Planning, Development and Evaluation Component of the State Superintendent's Office, Helena, Montana.

JEAN W. BUTMAN is an Evaluation Specialist at the Northwest Regional Educational Laboratory, Portland, Oregon.

THOMAS R. CHIBUCOS is with the National Institute of Education, Washington, D.C.

ROBERT D. CHILDERS is Deputy Director of the Appalachia Educational Laboratory, Inc., Charleston, West Virginia.

DONALD J. CUNNINGHAM is a member of the School of Education, Indiana University.

STAN F. DREZEK is Research Associate at the Research and Development Center for Teacher Education, The University of Texas at Austin.

KEITH J. EDWARDS is a member of the Rosemead Graduate School of Psychology, Rosemead, California.

R. TONY EICHELBERGER is Evaluation Project Leader at the Learning Research and Development Center, University of Pittsburgh.

ARLENE FINK is a member of the Center for the Study of Evaluation, University of California at Los Angeles.

JERRY L. FLETCHER is Director of Research and Evaluation in the Rural Education Program, Northwest Regional Educational Laboratory, Portland, Oregon.

ROBERT J. HESS is Evaluation Specialist at CEMREL, Inc., St. Louis, Missouri.

DOUGLAS S. KATZ is Research Assistant at the Center for Occupational Education, North Carolina State University at Raleigh.

M. FRANCES KLEIN is in the Research and Development Division of IDEA, Inc., Los Angeles, California.

P. KENNETH KOMOSKI is Executive Director of the Educational Products Information Exchange, New York City.

MAX LUFT is Executive Director of the Southwest Research Associates, Albuquerque, New Mexico.

JANICE LUJAN is Director of Quality Assurance at Southwest Research Associates, Albuquerque, New Mexico.

ROBERT L. MORGAN is Research Associate at the Center for Occupational Education, North Carolina State University at Raleigh.

ANDREW C. PORTER is Director of the Office of Research Consultation, School of Education, Michigan State University.

HUGH POYNOR is Associate Director of Educational Systems Associates, Austin, Texas.

JAMES R. SANDERS is currently Senior Research Associate at the Northwest Regional Educational Laboratory, Portland, Oregon.

MICHAEL SCRIVEN is a member of the Department of Philosophy, University of California at Berkeley.

LOUISE L. TYLER is a member of the School of Education, University of California at Los Angeles.

JERRY P. WALKER is Associate Director for Evaluation at the Center for Vocational and Technical Education, The Ohio State University.

WILLIAM J. WRIGHT is Director of Evaluation at CEMREL, Inc., St. Louis, Missouri.

REVIEWERS*

(1) Frederick Mulhauser, Research and Development Specialist, Experimental Schools Program, Northwest Regional Educational Laboratory

(2) W. James Popham, Graduate School of Education, University of California at Los Angeles

(3) Frederick B. Davis, Director, Center for Research in Evaluation and Measurement, University of Pennsylvania

(4) Richard McCann, Practicum for Instructional Development, University of California at Los Angeles

(5) William B. Michael, School of Education, University of Southern California

(6) George F. Madaus, Director of Research, Center for Field Research and School Services, Boston College

(7) Desmond L. Cook, Director, Educational Program Management Center, The Ohio State University

(8) John L. Wasik, Research Associate, Center for Occupational Education, North Carolina State University

(9) Daniel L. Stufflebeam, Department of Educational Leadership, Western Michigan University

*Chapters for which reviewers were responsible appear in parentheses.

(10) Ida S. Carrillo, Director, Teacher Training, Southwestern Cooperative Educational Laboratory

(11) Blaine R. Worthen, Director of Research and Evaluation, Northwest Regional Educational Laboratory

(12) Barak Rosenshine, Bureau of Educational Research, University of Illinois

(13) William W. Cooley, Co-director, Learning Research and Development Center, University of Pittsburgh

(14) David L. DeVries, Center for the Social Organization of Schools, The Johns Hopkins University

(15) Donald J. Veldman, Department of Educational Psychology, The University of Texas at Austin

(16) William A. Mehrens, Department of Counseling, Personnel Services, and Educational Psychology, Michigan State University

TABLE OF CONTENTS

READER'S GUIDE

Focus of Chapter Content in Relation to Reader's Occupational Role

Roles	Primary (Study)	Secondary (Read)	Peripheral (Scan)
Educational administrator (program or project director)	1, 2, 3, 4, 5, 6,	7, 8, 9, 11, 12, 13	10, 14, 15, 16
Curriculum specialist	1, 2, 3, 5, 6, 7, 10	4, 9, 11, 12, 13	8, 14, 15, 16
Formative evaluator	1, 2, 5, 8, 10, 11, 12, 13	3, 6, 7, 14, 15, 16	4, 9
Summative evaluator	3, 4, 14, 15, 16	1, 2, 6, 7, 11, 12, 13	5, 8, 9, 10
Educational planner/developer	1, 2, 3, 5, 8, 9	6, 7, 10, 11, 12, 13	4, 14, 15, 16
Quantitative specialist, methodologist	11, 12, 13, 14, 15, 16	2, 6, 7, 8, 9, 10	1, 3, 4, 5
Systems analyst	6, 7, 8, 9	1, 2, 10, 11, 12, 13	3, 4, 5, 14, 15, 16
General educator (college, university, public school)	1, 2, 3, 4, 5	6, 7, 8, 9, 10, 11, 12, 13	14, 15, 16

Note: Prologue and Epilogue are "primary" for all occupational roles.

EVALUATING EDUCATIONAL PROGRAMS AND PRODUCTS

PROLOGUE

PROLOGUE:

STANDARDS FOR THE EVALUATION OF EDUCATIONAL PROGRAMS AND PRODUCTS

Michael Scriven
University of California at Berkeley

I think one of the most important functions I can perform in introducing this volume is to provide a set of suggested standards for program and product evaluation, something which the individual evaluator may have inadequate time or budget to provide on his or her own. A public stand on the matter of standards as appears in this Prologue and indeed throughout the chapters that follow could represent a very real element in improving the decision-making of a recalcitrant project manager. By "recalcitrant" I mean "unwilling to plan or fund adequate evaluation of the appropriate kind, despite demonstration of its necessity."

Although the standards suggested herein are not in first draft form (they have been developed from minimum standards set out by the Master Panel in their report on the lab and center review of summer 1972 and have been reworked a good deal as we progressed through the 90-odd products that were reviewed), they have not yet been subjected to the most important feedback—that from field evaluators and producers who are most likely to use them. In my view, the work involved in developing standards is as great as that involved in writing a book or a substantial slice of new curricula materials—and perhaps even more important. And, like these tasks, the following standards can profit from feedback and revision. I hope, therefore, that readers will examine the standards carefully and provide me with suggestions for improving them.

Introduction
The following standards and accompanying checklist can be used as key items in the evaluation of programs and products of almost any kind. Specifically, they can be used in each of the following ways:

a.   as an instrument for evaluating programs and products;

b.   as an instrument for evaluating producers in the "pay-off" dimension, i.e., without considering matters such as personnel policy, community impacts, potentiality, etc.;

c.   as an instrument for evaluating evaluation proposals focused on programs, products, or producers;

d.   as an instrument for evaluating production proposals, since any competent producer should incorporate plans for achieving each of these standards and establishing that these standards have been achieved; and

e.   as an instrument for evaluating evaluators of programs, products, producers, etc., since it is argued that competent evaluation must cover each of these points.

It will thus be seen that the checklist provides a remarkably versatile instrument for assessing the quality of all kinds of educational activities and products; the more so because the concept of "Program and Product," as here used, is a very broad one, covering processes and institutions as well as typical products such as technical devices.

So much for applicability in principle. What about application in practice? In my view, no educational program or product has ever been produced that met all of the following standards prior to production, and only a handful have ever been produced that met enough of them to justify confidence in the merit of the product. It must be made clear that satisfactory achievement of all of these standards is not the only criterion for funding a project. Exploratory, or research, or realistic field trial projects are all defensible, even when the chances against meeting all of these standards are quite long. But they should be conceived as *no more than* exploratory, etc., projects, funded as such, and only moved into a production phase when these standards (or enough of them to make a very convincing case) *are* met. The application of this "hard-line" would not only greatly reduce the costs of educational research and development activity, which should have only a short-term effect, but it would transform the conception of satisfactory quality in education. And the long-term positive results of that are far more significant and beneficial than those of dropping a few substandard projects at the moment.

Given that the use of this checklist is potentially extremely lethal, prospective users deserve to know something about its reliability. The following three comments are offered, under that heading. First, every checkpoint on the checklist has a clear *a priori* rationale, in almost all cases so obvious that elaboration is not needed. That is, a straightforward argument could be constructed that the failure to meet any one of the checkpoints immediately leaves open a significant possibility that the product (for example) is simply not of good quality. Second, medical and industrial products routinely pass every checkpoint. Third, the checklist has been developed out of the most intensive systematic and large-scale product evaluation activities with which I am familiar— the Product Review Panels of 1971-72 and 72-73 done for the National Center for Educational Communication, on subcontract to the Educational Testing Service. The 15 experienced evaluators and educators that worked on these panels provided the raw material in their detailed assessment procedures from which I extracted the first eight versions of this checklist. It has since been further refined, as a result of interaction with other groups, notably the Educational Products Information Exchange.

I believe, therefore, that its credentials are extremely good, in that they have been based on a proper rather than superficial use of the R & D iterative cycle, which alone would make this as a product superior to almost all that are currently available. As an educational product itself, the checklist is, of course, self-referent, and a study of this introduction with the checklist in mind will show that there are still substantial gaps in the evidence that the checklist is worthwhile. Some of these will be closed if every reader and particularly every user of the checklist will accept part of the responsibility for the improvement of educational quality that I believe we all share, and provide whatever criticisms and alternatives he or she can. They will be acknowledged and incorporated as appropriate. For my part, I believe that I have a responsibility to convince evaluators, developers, and funding organizations, including legislatures, of the crucial importance of using this checklist. Since I have already had some success with this, it is particularly important that errors or shortcomings in it be identified as soon as possible. I have every confidence in the R & D process, and consequently great confidence that such errors exist, even in this twelfth iteration.

The Product Evaluation Checklist

A preliminary note on the status of the checkpoints themselves is in order. Rod Stephens, one of the most brilliant yacht designers of the twentieth century, recently published a 100-item checklist to be used in the evaluation of racing and cruising yachts. The status of every item in that checklist can be expressed by saying that each is a *desideratum*. But the items in the following checklist are *not*— except in the one case noted—*desiderata*; they are *necessitata*. One or two of them are relevant only to certain types of programs and products; those are neither desiderata nor necessitata for other types of programs and products, but they are necessitata for the relevant types of programs and products. So—unless there are deficiencies in the argument—each of these conditions must be met in order that one should have impeccable grounds for a conclusion of merit for an educational program or product. Now there are often occasions in which a decision must be made, where it will be impossible to find anything that meets all these standards. For example, a course may be planned and the arrangements be such that it must be given, so that some materials must be collected for it. We may not be able to determine whether materials selected are really much good; but it would be desirable to determine whether the ones we select are the *best available*. In such a case, one may be able to guess two or three of the items on which one has no direct evidence, and this may be an acceptable procedure. But it should not be forgotten that the cost in time spent on materials of dubious value is very high; it is nearly always possible to rearrange a curriculum or training institute, etc., so that something of proven value can be done. After all, we do *know* that French courses do teach *some* French, and that calculus courses do teach *some* calculus; there is no possibility that these subjects are being acquired in some other way—by the vast majority of students, at least. Nevertheless, there may be cases where a product can be defensibly used without all the checkpoints being met. But the reader should treat those cases as unusual; that is, the reader should treat each item in this list as a claimed necessity. With that challenge in mind, it is more likely that he or she will uncover errors.

It is suggested that the following items be marked on a five-point high/low scale. This should be expanded verbally as illustrated for the first checkpoint, and on the full form that follows.

1. *Need (justification)*. Good evidence that the product fills a *genuine need* or—a weaker alternative—a *defensible want*.

This is not covered by market research data showing the product is saleable; so is snake oil. True needs assessments involve establishing that the product actually facilitates survival, health, or some other defensible end *that is not now adequately serviced*; it may involve moral, social, and/or environmental impact considerations.

This item is listed first because most proposed products fail to pass even this requirement.

The five-point scale for Need might look like this:

Maximum priority	4
Great importance	3
Probably significant need	2
Possibly significant need	1
No real evidence of need	0

In scoring need, the following should be taken into account: number of people affected, social significance of the need (compensatory justice, etc.), absence of substitutes, urgency of the matter, possible multiplicative effects (e.g., the need for tool skills is not just a function of their immediate utility but of the dependence of other accomplishments on them). Cost level may or may not be part of the need specifications; it *should* be, but if not, this checkpoint has to be restudied (as does checkpoint 2) after cost data on a particular product is in.

It is undesirable to use "selected expert" judgments to establish need, if there is any chance another selection would deny it. (But many important innovative projects can do no better.) It is better to quote actual statistics on, e.g., illiteracy of the kind that this type of program or product has satisfactorily handled in field trials.

2. *Market (dissemination).* Many needed products (especially educational ones) are unsaleable by ordinary means (e.g., automobile safety belts). It is only possible to argue for developing them if there is a special, preferably tested, plan for getting them used (e.g., subsidy, legislation, agents), or if there *probably* will be such a plan, or if there is high "stand-by" value (e.g., civil defense pamphlets). For this reason, dissemination plans should *antedate* detailed product development plans. Checkpoint 2 requires that there be dissemination plans that *ensure* a market: it is scored on the size *and* importance of the *demonstrably reachable* market. It is, if you like, the pragmatic aspect of Need. The dissemination plan (or procedure, if already operative) needs to be clear, feasible in terms of available resources, expert and ingenious in its use of those resources, and keyed to the need(s).

3. *Performance—true field trials.* The first of several "performance criteria"—actually criteria for the kind of evidence about performance—

stresses the necessity for field trial data that refer (a) to the *final* version; (b) to *typical* users who are (c) operating without producer (or other special) assistance; in (d) a typical setting/time frame. It is very tempting to think one can extrapolate from field trials with volunteer schools who get the materials and phone-consulting free, or from the penultimate edition of the materials, but it has frequently turned out to be unsound. Of course, the Research-Development-Diffusion-Evaluation model makes this point quite clear; but, in actual practice, deadlines, overcommitment, and underfinancing combine to render almost all products deficient on this checkpoint.

4. *Performance—true consumer.* The concept of "the consumer" is a free variable in the RDD&E model, and it tends to be interpreted differently by different participants. Inservice teacher training materials, for example, will be "consumed" by: (a) superintendents or assistant superintendents in charge of staff development programs, (b) teacher trainers, (c) teachers, (d) students, and (e) taxpayers. To decide what data one needs with regard to which of these groups requires a very clear sense of the function of the evaluation itself; which audiences it is addressed to, commissioned by, and—regardless of those two considerations—responsible to. The result of such considerations indicts a great deal of evaluation; for example, in the case just described, it is common to run the tests on teachers. This would be entirely adequate if we had the research base to connect specific changes in teacher behavior with increased learning (or joy, etc.) on the part of the students. We have no such connection, and consequently we cannot justify heavy expenditures aimed at changing teaching behavior. Perhaps some modest costs for a project responsive to teachers' requests could be tossed in as a fringe benefit, but otherwise we are simply doing idle experiments with public money.

Quite often, there will be several groups of consumers of a given program or product, each interested in different aspects of it: all should be treated independently and only summed under No. 11 below.

5. *Performance—crucial comparisons.* There are few if any useful evaluations which can avoid the necessity to present data on the comparative performance of the *critically* competitive programs and products. All too often, the data refer to some pre-established standards of merit, and the reader has no idea whether one can do better for less, or twice as well for five percent more, etc.—which is typically what a consumer wants to know. Where comparisons *are* done, the results are

sometimes useless because the competitor is so chosen as to give a false impression. The worst example of this is the use of a single "no-treatment" or "last year's treatment" control group. It is not too thrilling to discover that an injection of 100K worth of computer assisted instruction can improve the math performance of a school by 15 percent, if there is a possibility that 15K of programmed texts would do as well or better. There are few points where good evaluators distinguish themselves more clearly than in their choice of critical competitors. Sometimes they must be created, e.g., by converting the program from computer assisted to a programmed text.

6. *Performance—long-term.* A follow-up is almost always desirable, usually crucial—since certain undesirable side effects often take quite a while to surface, and good results fade fast.

7. *Performance—side effects.* There should be a *systematic, skilled, independent* search for side effects *during, at the end of,* and *after* the "treatment." Project staff are peculiarly handicapped in such a search, by goal-oriented tunnel vision (here the outside evaluator operating in the goal-free mode is particularly helpful).

8. *Performance—process.* Process observation is relevant for three reasons. It may substantiate or invalidate (a) certain descriptions of the product, (b) the causal claims involved in evaluation (that the gains were due to this treatment), and (c) it may bear on moral questions that have preemptive force in any social interaction such as education.

For example, a product called an Inquiry Skills kit may not deserve the title, either because of its content or because of the way it is or is not implemented in the classroom. (In extreme cases, one is not actually evaluating the product at all, but the teachers.) Again, the dimensions of injustice, unhappiness, cruelty—and their converses—should be independently observed. (They are not side *effects* since they may be part of the treatment itself, not residues from it.)

9. *Performance—causation.* One way or another, it must be shown that the "effects" reported could not reasonably be attributed to something other than the treatment. No way of doing this compares well with the fully controlled experiment, and ingenuity can expand its use into most situations. But there are good alternatives to it, as well as bad ones, and the best possible must be used: in fact the best possible *combination*, since *modus operandi* checks should be done in most designs, as insurance. (It is for picking up *modus operandi* data that the process observation is sometimes useful.)

10. *Performance—statistical significance.* This requires no elaboration and is frequently the only mark of sophistication in an evaluation design. It is worthless without, but rarely accompanied by, the next item.

11. *Performance—educational significance.* Statistical significance is a necessity but it is all too easily obtained without the results having any *educational* significance, especially (a) by using the magnifying power of a large *n*, and (b) by using instruments that test mere vocabulary gains, or (c) nongeneralizable gains (where they should be generalizable). The evaluator needs to look at raw score gains, displayed by item; then he or she needs independent expert judgment that gains of that size on those items represent an educationally significant result. The raw scores need not be reported in the evaluation, but the grounds for thinking them important must be reported; *and* a congruence check must be done to establish relevance to the needs assessment which provides the basic justification. For example, an English-as-a-second-language course for the Portuguese minority in New Bedford, Massachusetts, might show statistically very significant gains. To rule out possibilities (a) and (b) above, one would normally use the judgment of independent experts on English learning by native speakers of Portuguese at the appropriate age level. *They* would of course have to look at raw scores and item analyses. But the congruence check would still be necessary to ensure that their judgment of educational significance relates to the ESL need and not to, e.g., the need for cultural identity or pride by Portuguese minority groups in the U.S. If the latter *is* the main basis for the judgment of gain (or an important element in it), then we do not have evidence that the one need we have carefully validated is being met. We may of course *also* be able to validate the (generally acknowledged) need to which the "side effect" does speak. But we shall have to do so as a separate task and the evaluation is in limbo until we do. There should be no suggestion that late-discovered dimensions of educational significance are illicit; any development process must search for them and hope for them—but then there must be a recycyling of the needs assessment.

12. *Costs and cost-effectiveness.* Cost data must be:

a. *Comprehensive.* That means covering maintenance as well as capital costs, psychic as well as dollar costs, "weaning" costs, and costs of in-service updating of needed helpers, as well as direct costs, etc. There should be some consideration of opportunity costs other than those covered previously under critical competitors (e.g., what else could the *district* or the *state* have done with the funds?), and a pass should be made at cost-effectiveness analysis where possible.

b. *Verified*. Cost estimates and real costs should be verified independently. It is really not satisfactory to treat cost data as if they are immune to bias. Performance data should also have some independent certification, and the procedures outlined above involve this at several points. The cost data require this for reasons that have not thus far been generally recognized. Costing is an extremely difficult business, requiring technical skills that at the moment are not part of the training of evaluators. As a matter of fact, there are plenty of CPA's who are quite incompetent at estimation of costs of educational products of a rather nonstandard kind. Nevertheless, the advice of one or more CPA's is certainly required in costing large projects; one should also get advice from inexperienced businessmen. Here, as in other aspects of evaluation, there are great advantages to employing more than one consultant, working independently, in order to obtain some check on reliability. (This is what Stake thinks of as "desirable redundancy"; it might be more precisely described as "reliability estimation.")

c. *For each program or product compared*. Costs must of course be provided for the critical competitors, something which would be covered by the admonition to include opportunity costs, given under (a) above. But it may perhaps be worth independently stressing the need to provide rather careful cost estimates for the *artificial* competitors that the ingenious evaluator should *create* as part of his or her analysis. Strictly speaking, these too should be part of a decent opportunity cost analysis, but I believe this has not been part of the tradition of opportunity cost analysis. Hence this separate itemization.

The preceding considerations bear on the quality of the cost *data*. But this checkpoint is not treated as merely a methodological one. Since one already has the judgment of educational significance, and since the cost data are for comparable products, one can here score cost-effectiveness, i.e., (roughly) the justifiability of the expenditure.

The cost-effectiveness rating stands to Educational Significance rather as Market does to Need; the first is the pragmatic incorporation of the second.

13. *Extended support.* Here is an item that can at the moment be regarded as desirable rather than necessary, but it is to be hoped that this state of affairs will change in the near future. In the educational field, unlike—for example—the pharmaceutical or automobile field, the responsibility for the product is all too frequently supposed to terminate upon the commencement of production. If it should subsequently transpire that important improvements could be made in the program or product, they may or may not get made, depending upon commercial considerations. This is scarcely a service to the consumer. It should be regarded, therefore, as a strong plus for a program or product if there exists or will exist a systematic procedure for updating and upgrading it in the light of post-marketing field experience—and, of course, this implies the necessity for a systematic continuing procedure for collecting field data. One of the types of data that ought to be collected is data on new critical competitors; and one of the decisions that ought to be arranged for is the decision to cease production even if it is commercially profitable to continue, when the evidence clearly indicates the existence of a superior program or product that can reasonably be expected to take over the market in question if it is left free for the takeover. An important kind of "improvement" is covered by this checkpoint—it might also be described as an extension of the use of the program or product; for example, its use in new circumstances or in conjunction with new auxiliary products needs new evaluation and explanations in the handbooks, etc. The provision of user-training, itself subject to progressive cycles of improvement, should be assessed as a desideratum; and possible procedures for cost reduction by means of format change or implementation "tricks" are other items that deserve recognition—eventually, indeed, deserve to be treated as reasonable expectations from responsible producers.

The Upgrading Phase

Given that few programs and products meet these requirements (actually, few programs and products meet *even half* of them), what can reasonably be done at the moment?

I believe it should be stressed that the appropriate interim policy is *not* to treat those programs and products that meet the largest number of these requirements as deserving of full support. *No* program or product that fails to meet checkpoints 1-13 deserves full support, for the very good reason that we do not have good grounds for supposing that such a program or product is really worthwhile. Nevertheless, we may well have grounds that justify further investigation in order to fill the gaps in the evaluation checklist. And, as mentioned before, we may indeed have enough grounds to support the tentative use of such a program or product pending the further investigations.

I would like to conclude by describing what I believe is a realistic and responsible policy for producer certification. Funding that is available should, according to this plan, be allocated in the following way. It should be made rather easy to obtain small production grants, suitable for producing a module of curriculum materials or a small product, when there is some rather persuasive *a priori* evidence that supports the *possibility* that this product will provide a substantial breakthrough. Producers that succeed in establishing, by use of the preceding checklist (or improved successors), that their mini-project has really been successful, then become eligible—and nobody else does—for major product development grants. A producer can receive several of the mini-grants, up to the point where the selection panel thinks they have evidence of his incompetence, because these are—like most experiments in education—very long shots. But absolutely nobody can get even one maxi-grant without success with a mini-grant. (In addition, management skills are required; these can also be exhibited by a management performance with mini-grant subsidy, as well as otherwise.) The cost of this approach is that it rules out synergistic pay-off unless this can be approached step-wise, which may well not be possible in some important cases. But, at the present stage of our experience, I believe *that* cost is trivial compared to the costs of the present policy which constantly results in funding poor-quality enterprises. We now turn to the checklist itself (see the following page).

PROGRAM AND PRODUCT EVALUATION CHECKLIST

1. *Need*

Consider and check   *Rate and circle*

... Number affected   4   Maximum priority
... Social significance   3   Great importance
... Absence of substitutes   2   Probably significant need
... Multiplicative effects   1   Possibly significant need
... Other   0   No grounds for thinking
                                   significant

Comments

2. *Market*

Consider   *Rate*

... Dissemination plan: 4   Very large and/or very
        clarity   important market will be
        feasibility   reached
        ingenuity   3   Large and/or important
        economy   market will be reached
... Size   2   Significant market will be
... Importance   reached
... Other   1   Possible, but not probable,
                                   that a significant market
                                   will be reached
                              0   Inadequate evidence to sug-
                                   gest that a significant
                                   market will be reached

Comments

3. *Performance—True Field Trials* *

Consider

Rate

... Final version?
... Typical user?
... Typical aid?
... Typical setting?
... Typical time-frame?

4 Perfectly typical
3 Minor differences
2 Reasonable bet for general-
   ization
1 Serious weakness
0 Relevance unclear

Comments

(Note: See page 22 for explanation of asterisks).

4. *Performance—True Consumer* *

Consider

Rate

... Congress?
... Federal agency?
... State Department?
... District?
... Principal?
... Teacher?
... Student?
... Taxpayer?
... Other?

4 Full data on all relevant
   "consumers"
3 Fair data on all relevant
   "consumers"
2 Good data on the most
   important "consumers"
1 Weak data on the most
   important "consumers"
0 Only speculation about
   most important "consumers"

Comments

5. *Performance—Critical Comparisons* *

Consider   *Rate*

... No-treatment group   4   Good data on all important
... Existing competitors   competitors
... Projected competitors   3   Good data on the most
... Created competitors   important competitor(s)
... Hypothesized   competitors   2   Fair data on the most
                                             important competitor(s)
                                        1   Lacking data on some of
                                             the more important com-
                                             petitors
                                        0   Little or no useful compara-
                                             tive data

Comments

6. *Performance—Long Term* *

Consider   *Rate*

... Week to month later   4   Good direct evidence about
... Month to year later   the effects at times needed
... Year to few years later   3   Some direct evidence about
... Many years later   the effects at times needed
... On-job or life-space sample   2   Follow-up gives reasonable
                                             support to a conclusion
                                             about effects when needed
                                        1   Follow-up suggests a con-
                                             clusion about effects when
                                             needed
                                        0   Useless or no follow-up

Comments

7. *Performance—Side effects**

Consider

... Comprehensive search?
... Skilled?
... Independent?
... (Goal-free?)
... During/End/Later

Rate

4 Meets all requirements well
3 Generally good
2 Barely acceptable
1 Some study made, but incomplete
0 No worthwhile study

Comments

8. *Performance—Process**

Consider

... Justice and joy?
... Descriptive congruence check?
... Causal clues check?
... Instrument validity?
... Judge/observer reality?

Rate

4 Every point thoroughly checked
3 A good bet on all points
2 Reasonable risk
1 Significant omission(s)
0 Inadequate

Comments

9. *Performance—Causation**

Consider

... Randomized experimental design?
... Quasi-experimental design?
... *Ex post facto*?
... *A priori* interpretation of correlational data?

Rate

4 Impeccable
3 Good bet
2 Plausible bet
1 Weak bet
0 Hopeless bet

Comments

10. *Performance—Statistical Significance* *

Consider	*Rate*
... Appropriate analysis? ... Appropriate significance level?	4 Flawless analysis, astronomical significance 3 High significance, well-tested 2 Reasonably significant 1 Marginal significance 0 Not shown to be significant

Comments

11. *Performance—Educational Significance*

Consider	*Rate*
... Independent judgment? ... Expert judgment? ... Judgment based on item analysis? ... Judgment based on raw scores? ... Teaching to the tests? ... Testing to the teaching? ... Congruence with needs? ... Side effects taken into account? ... Long-term effects taken into account? ... Comparative gains taken into account? ... Multiple consumer groups served? ... Process significance taken into account?	4 Very high significance demonstrated 3 High significance demonstrated 2 Moderate significance demonstrated 1 Slight or rather uncertain significance 0 Negligible or unknown significance

Comments

12. *Cost-Effectiveness*

Consider   *Rate*

... Comprehensive cost analy-   4   A major breakthrough
  sis?   3   Very good
... Expert judgment of costs?   2   Good: competitive
... Independent judgment of   1   Poor or unclear
  costs?   0   Hopeless or not calculable
... Costs for all competitors?

Comments

13. *Extended Support*

Consider   *Rate*

... Post-marketing data collec-   4   Excellent and comprehen-
  tion?   sive
... Post-marketing system for   3   Good and fairly comprehen-
  improvement?   sive
... Inservice training?   2   Minimally acceptable
... Updating of aids?   1   Weak or less than adequate
... New uses and user data?   data
                                                             0   Negligible or no data

Comments

   Notice that the scales are often hybrid crosses of methodological and substantive merit. The top scores require good evidence of good performance; the bottom score implies that *either* good evidence or good performance is lacking. It does not require—for example—that there is good evidence of bad performance, for otherwise programs and products which turned in no data would do better than those that were known to fare badly. It is helpful to circle not only the ratings but the terms, e.g., "No good evidence."

The list of considerations should affect the rater's decision either as to evidential adequacy or merit. By checking or adding salient factors in the judgment, the form can provide an explanation as well an evaluation, and hence be useful for formative as well as summative purposes.

A double check can be used to indicate considerations that were felt to be more important than those receiving a single check.

The scales are often interactive. For example, the need rating is a factor in the market rating, since the greater the need that is met, the more important the market is. But it is diagnostically valuable to have the separate scales at this point. Sometimes this interdependency means that one will want to return to an earlier rating and reassess it after considering a later one.

Some of the scales are simply quality-of-*data* or "methodological" scales (e.g., side effects check). *They are asterisked (*).* They still represent necessities, but a high score on *them* does not show intrinsic merit of the product, only of the data or design. They will be of great importance when the checklist is used to evaluate evaluations or proposals. When evaluating programs or products, the situation is that any score less than 3 on these will weaken the rating on educational significance, and under 2 will destroy it, however high the need/market scores.

Program or Product Evaluation Profile (PEP)

Perspicuous presentation is an essential part of good evaluation, and the profile in Figure 1 does it better than the filled-out checklist (which one can refer back to for amplification of profile features of interest).

One can make use of intermediate scores (3.5, etc.) although it is doubtful whether that degree of refinement (i.e., ±12 percent accuracy) could be validated.

After some practice using the actual verbal equivalents of the numerical scores, the evaluator gets to the point where he or she can score onto the profile form directly—useful when evaluating a large number of products.

There is of course a cumulative dependence of the "pay-off" ratings [Educational Significance and Cost(s) Effectiveness] on the quality-of-data ratings as well as on the Need and Market ratings. Serious flaws in the data automatically drop the later scores as is shown in the profile.

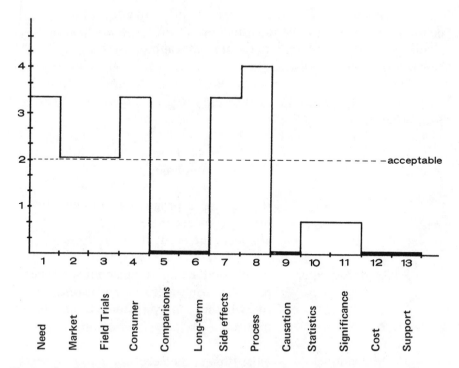

Figure 1. Example of Use of PEP (Product Evaluation Profile) for a Hypothetical CAI Installation.

Comments on Figure 1

5: No data on *the* critical competitors, namely other expensive innovations of same type.

6: No follow-up.

7: Causal side effects study.

8: No observation of student interacting with product at all. Justice not relevant, however.

11: Significance unknown because of #5 above.

12: Cost is so high that there are almost certainly competitors that would outperform for less.

13: Apparently very limited.

I deliberately use the technique of fading to develop short cue-word titles for the various dimensions on the profile form; but it should be understood that these are only abbreviations for the fuller titles on the full checklist.

The sequencing of the 13 scales seems fairly natural, and perhaps they should be segregated by color or lines in a later version of the form, thus:

1. Need	Where it all begins—the justification of product development.
2. Market	If you had a program or product that in principle meets the need, could you *actually* meet the need?
3-10. Performance Data	What you have to know about the program or product in order to draw a conclusion as to whether in principle it meets the needs(s).
11. Educational Significance	Does it meet the need?
12. Cost-Effectiveness	Is it worth it? (Now reconsider Market)
13. Extended Support	If checkpoints 1-12 are passed, here's an important further desideratum, that bears on *continued* production.

The profile form can be prepared on commercially available accounting paper to produce a vertical profile or as in Figure 1 on graph (quadrant or squared) paper to yield the more usual horizontal "block" profile.

Establishing Perspective . . .

PART ONE: ROLES AND CONTEXTS

Part One

INTRODUCTION TO ROLES AND CONTEXTS

Educational evaluation and the cost of living may have one thing in common—their propensity for rapid change. In recent years so many developments have taken place in evaluation that change has become a constant. The fact that the number of new developments in the last 10 years has outstripped those of the past 50 is no longer even startling.

Among these new developments, perhaps one of the most significant has been an awareness of the unavoidably human and personal nature of the evaluator's role. If so, the following chapters reflect important content in that they focus upon the evaluator as a human, interactive person who must deal successfully with many people—developers, sponsors, colleagues, and consumers—in the process of applying his skills and techniques.

It was not long ago that an educational evaluator might approach his task with a handbook of experimental design under one arm and a copy of the *Mental Measurements Yearbook* under the other. This was a time when evaluation was synonomous with measurement and the role of the evaluator often confused with that of the psychometrist or test administrator. The evaluator needed only a catalogue of tests and measures and to know how to apply them successfully in order to complete almost any task. The evaluator's role has changed dramatically from even a short time ago, however; and, as many school personnel can attest, the evaluator's task is now quite distinct from any he has had in the past.

As any new field becomes more sophisticated, clearer distinctions appear between its various roles and functions. Just as evaluation has come into its own, so that the evaluator is no longer confused with the psychometrist, he must now determine the nature of his relationship with a new kind of educationist—the developer. While the task of developing educational programs and products may on the surface appear quite different from that of evaluation, in practice this has not been so. While few deny that the developer should perform a different function from the evaluator, many question the degree of interrelationship that should exist between these two professionals. As the evaluator has chosen a role separate from that of a test administrator, he has almost unavoidably come closer in function to that of the developer. Whether this relationship is for ill or good is in part the focus of the following chapters.

The point at which the functions of the evaluator and developer meet is for the moment clouded. The following chapters attempt to clarify this point and to provide rationale for the interrelationship of development and evaluation. The authors of these chapters, both from an evaluation and a development perspective, have emerged with a picture of the developer and evaluator not as distinct functions but rather as a continuum which has at one pole a pure developer who may not interact with an evaluator and at the other pole a pure evaluator who performs his duties in isolation from a developer. By identifying subsurface tasks and activities which demarcate the space between pure development and evaluation we can begin to link the developer to the evaluator with a logical sequence of real-life responsibilities, perhaps similar to those listed below.

Pure Development						Pure Evaluation
	Planner	Designer	Developer	Formative evaluator	Summative evaluator	Researcher *

*The researcher is also an evaluator of sorts and we must include him in any such continuum. His distinction lies in the fact that he evaluates theory via the formulation of hypotheses whereas the formative and summative evaluators evaluate programs or products that are built upon theories validated by the researcher. Depending upon what is being evaluated—theory upon which a program might be based or theory upon which a program is already based—we may place the researcher at either pole of the continuum. It is important to note that elsewhere in the continuum multiple role functions are often carried out by the same individual as when, for example, a program is planned and designed by the same person.

Planner: organizes and marshals materials and personnel for the development task.

Designer: writes content and performance specifications for the program or product.

Developer: constructs product or program that meets content and performance specifications.

Formative evaluator: assesses product or program components for the purpose of revision and modification.

Summative evaluator: assesses product or program *in toto* for the purpose of adoption or continuation.

Researcher: formulates and tests hypotheses concerning the program or product *vis a vis* theoretical framework.

As we move toward the center of the continuum, we identify those activities for which the evaluator and developer are likely to have the strongest interrelationship. As is noted in subsequent chapters, it is at this point that role functions may change, the developer performing some of the evaluation and the evaluator performing some of the development.

It is at this intersection also that a major question arises and perhaps the most controversy exists: should the evaluator be distinct from the developer or can these roles represent responsibilities of a single individual? For the answer to this question we must look to the contexts in which these two arrangements have been used to determine the extent to which the product or program has profited from each. In doing so, on the one hand, we are warned that when role distinctions become unclear the program may suffer from what has come to be called *co-option*. This refers to the situation in which the evaluator becomes so immersed in the values and feelings of the developer that evaluation is no longer an objective guide to program or product development. And, on the other hand, we are warned that development is so closely tied to formative evaluation that any separation of roles is at best an artificial distinction that may detract from rather than add to the development process. The truth of either claim is not well documented.

While little is usually said about the role functions of planner and summative evaluator, activities of the former lead to, and activities of the latter result from, the kind of interrelationship that takes place between the formative evaluator and developer. It is not uncommon, for example, for a program or product to be planned and designed in such a way as to either encourage or preclude a certain kind of relationship between formative evaluator and developer; or that once this relationship has taken place, the summative evaluator is forced to accept it regardless of its effect upon the quality of the program or product.

One answer to the question of whether an exchange of role functions for formative evaluator and developer results in a poorer program or product may lie with what Scriven (1973) has called goal-free evaluation. The GFE role is one in which an evaluator views program development and evaluation from a perspective more general than any one activity and hopefully from a perspective that includes all activities, so that planning, designing, developing, and formative and summative evaluation may be seen at points in time by a single individual. Co-option may become much more apparent from such a broad perspective than when only the interrelationship between formative evaluator and developer is focused upon. A narrow focus can neither provide data as to why the co-option occurred or what its effects may be at later role functions in the continuum. Therefore, a goal-free evaluator may in some respects perform the role of meta-evaluator inasmuch as he is not tied to a specific role function. Goal-free evaluators operating outside of any one "system" may well encourage any kind of relationship between formative evaluator and developer that seems profitable when no ill effects from it are detected. No one relationship may be appropriate across all development projects and the nature of the relationship between evaluator and developer might better depend upon the nature of the individuals involved and the kind of program or product being produced. Assuming that the goal-free evaluator examines the nature of this relationship to determine any ill effects, one might argue, as do the following chapters, for a *laissez faire* perspective as to the precise role of the evaluator and developer for any given product or program.

Some Attempts to Define Role

Attempts at defining the precise role and qualifications for an evaluator have been no more successful than attempts at defining the role and general qualifications of corporation presidents. The role of the former, like the latter, varies with context, so that it is difficult to apply practical decision rules for deciding what is or is not evaluation or which skills an evaluator needs or does not need. Some attempts to define these skills, however, are noteworthy. Stufflebeam (1973) and Bunda (1973), for example, defined a series of eight evaluator qualifications. These qualifications, which are still undergoing revision, are presented below along with a sample of the skills related to them.

I.   Knowledge of Innovation in Education, e.g.,

         can compare and contrast instructional research and evaluation.

         can present a case for the evaluation of competing instructional strategies and suggest alternative methodologies which might be used.

         can design mechanisms to collect judgmental information concerning the worth of a curriculum package.

         can select, organize, and lead groups of professionals to generate alternative program strategies and project designs.

II.   Public Relations, e.g.,

         can use audio-visual aids appropriately in making oral evaluation reports.

         can design an evaluation report to be presented by video-tape.

         can describe and analyze user attitudes toward evaluation.

III.   Data Processing, e.g.,

         can design and develop a data bank.

         can develop forms and procedures for managing the data processing operations of an evaluation system.

can design an information system according to which data are to be coded, stored, and retrieved.

IV.   Educational Measurement, e.g.,

can list what audio-visual materials are available for the training of evaluators.

can write forced-choice and free-choice test items.

can select a test that has been normed on an appropriate group.

V.   Evaluation Administration; e.g.,

can marshal political support for evaluation activities.

can develop a PERT network.

can delineate evaluation authority and responsibility within the agency's organizational structure.

VI.   Relating Evaluation to Relevant Disciplines, e.g.,

can write an analysis of the relevance of economic theory to educational evaluation.

can relate the major research strategies and theories of sociology, political science, and economics to evaluation problems.

can state the basic principles of value theory and utility theory development in educational evaluation.

VII.   Communications, e.g.,

can prepare a 20-minute slide-tape presentation on problems in evaluation.

can organize and administer an editorial service in relation
to evaluation reports.

can develop and disseminate clear and concise descriptions
of evaluation systems that can be understood by the
public.

VIII.   Research Design Analysis, e.g.,

can design controlled research studies of small units in a
curriculum.

can conduct a literature review, write it up, and present it
to a curriculum development group, irrespective of substantive area.

can defend the choice of an oblique rotation or an
orthogonal rotation in a factor analysis study.

While the list is indeed comprehensive, complete agreement as to
its usefulness and validity may not be possible. A recurrent problem
seems to be that we need not look far to find a particularly competent
evaluator who is not or may not even want to be competent in all of
these areas. Perhaps specific qualifications may be more helpful for
providing training consonant with one's interests than for defining a
comprehensive domain of prerequisite evaluator skills.

The most problematical variable that may upset the usefulness of a
specific set of evaluation qualifications is that of *context*. Depending
upon the context in which the evaluator works, specific qualifications
may or may not be relevant to the role function of that individual.

Some Attempts to Define Context

Context, then, is a second concern taken up in Part One of this
book, a concern that is so closely related to the question of roles that
both issues are treated simultaneously. The following chapters, while
emphasizing either the role of the evaluator or the context in which he
works, deal with both of these issues and the interrelationships among
them. It is important, therefore, that the reader not only look for
emerging roles of the evaluator but also how these roles vary with

context. To make the interaction between roles and contexts even more apparent the following section has been organized so that three types of contexts are treated: educational *programs, products,* and *curricula.* These three areas have been chosen to provide a broad picture of the kinds of contexts in which evaluation is commonly performed and how the role of the evaluator changes with each context.

In the context of program evaluation, the evaluator is customarily seen assessing the effectiveness of large-scale and comprehensive development efforts that are usually less generalizable across time (i.e., of immediate importance) and setting (i.e., specific to a geographic region) than are educational products and curricula. In a second context, the role of the evaluator can be seen in relation to the development of school curricula and instructional materials. Educational curricula are customarily more generalizable across time than either educational programs or products and more generalizable across settings than programs. In a third context, the role of the evaluator is seen in relation to product development. Products are usually most generalizable across settings and intermediate in generality across time relative to programs and curricula. Products can consist of instructional modules, filmstrips, texts, and workbooks, all of which may be important ingredients for educational programs and curricula. These differences in programs, products, and curricula as they are customarily produced are noted below.

Relative Generalizability of Programs, Curricula, and
Products Across Time and Setting

Context	Generalizability Across	
	Time	Setting
Products (To teach skills)	Med	High
Programs (To ameliorate specific needs)	Low	Low
Curricula (To educate)	High	Med

About the Chapters in Part One

Part One of this book begins with two chapters focused upon the role of the developer. In the first of these chapters, Jean W. Butman and Jerry L. Fletcher discuss the role of the evaluator and developer in educational research and development. Their thesis represents the view that the evaluator and developer cannot function without interrelating the needs and requirements of each other's tasks. To do this, the authors suggest an approach in which the developer and evaluator work as team members for a common cause—that of developing the best possible program or product. Their chapter concentrates on two main points: first, the necessity for formative evaluators to be part of the development team and, second, the development and evaluation stages through which products must pass. Their chapter discusses the nature and types of evaluation information which must be gathered in each stage of development to defend the development work and the formal approval mechanism by which a product passes from one stage to another. In addition, the authors suggest that the role of the evaluator must reflect one of three purposes for the evaluation. These are to evaluate the *effect* of a program or product, its *content*, or its *utilization*. These purposes are then used to discuss the role of the evaluator. The authors' discussions are frank and to the point. They identify sources of difficulty for the evaluator-developer team in the context of the research and development process as well as some possible ways in which such an arrangement will yield positive results. Management in organizational matters which must support the activity of a development and evaluator team is outlined. The authors conclude by admitting that co-option can occur with such an arrangement but that the danger of inhibiting the development process is substantially greater when such a team is not employed.

In a following chapter, Eva L. Baker describes the role of the formative evaluator in the development process but this time specifically in the instructional design and development context. Shifting the focus from large-scale research and development projects to specific instructional design and development tasks, the author divides evaluation activity into two types: that which is called internal evaluation and that which is called external evaluation, both occurring in the formative context. Baker contends that internal evaluation can best be accomplished by members of the instructional development staff assigned to collect data related to the adequacy of learning, data related to the level of satisfaction the program produces, and data related to side effects. Afterwards, an external evaluator is employed whose role is to collect data regarding the processes and operations of the project staff, to make judgments regarding the suitability of the criterion measures and the adequacy of program context, and to analyze the side effects recorded by the internal evaluator. Baker goes on to illustrate these activities as they occurred within a recently funded product development project designed to train personnel in skills related to the development process. The project is described in detail and points noted where formative evaluation led to product revision.

The third, fourth, and fifth chapters deal with program, product, and curriculum evaluation, respectively. The first of these concerns evaluation within the context of program development. Barbara J. Brandes discusses the problems and procedures involved in evaluating affective educational programs. Brandes speaks of the kinds of goals and measures that are applicable to affective interventions in order to bring about desired outcomes which may be (a) an attitude or belief, (b) a unique or personalized product, or (c) enhancement of certain attitudes or beliefs. The author draws heavily upon Eisner's (1969) concept of expressive as contrasted to instructional objectives and illustrates their importance for the evaluation of all types of educational programs. Brandes relates the role of the formative evaluator to deriving and verifying a hierarchy of program goals and then illustrates this work in a case study of an affective educational program. Her illustration provides an example of ways in which the formative evaluator can work with profit in close relationship to the program developer. The chapter concludes with questions underlying the formative evaluation process relevant to any type of educational program. These questions are: (1) are the program materials appealing and interesting to students, i.e., do the materials enhance positive attitudes toward the content of the program? (2) are teachers comfortable with the program, i.e., how does the program affect the teacher's relationship to his or her students? (3) is the program compatible with the variety of teaching styles and organizational structures of classrooms? and (4) is the program consistent with educational priorities?

The following chapter shifts to the product development context. Here Marvin C. Alkin and Arlene Fink address the problem of how to evaluate products designed to impart basic skills and knowledge. The focus of their chapter is on the user and how evaluation reports can provide information that is beneficial for making distinctions between educational products. The authors note that individuals who conduct product evaluations have been mainly concerned with presenting their findings to a class of decision makers other than potential users. The authors go on to describe useful techniques for reporting data and how the user-consumer should critically examine evaluation reports to ascertain their usefulness and completeness before using them to make product judgments. The authors utilize the case study format for examining a product report on the evaluation of workshop materials. The authors contend that such a report should contain information to make clear the nature of the product, its purpose, its development and testing, the intended learners, its effectiveness, and its efficiency. The chapter trains the reader to be sensitive to critical components of the product evaluation report and includes a practice exercise which challenges the reader to test his comprehension of key concepts.

In the final chapter in Part One the context shifts to curriculum and instructional materials development. Louise L. Tyler and M. Frances Klein present practical guidelines for the development of curriculum materials which include explicit activities for the formative evaluator. The authors' view of formative evaluation is closely related to curriculum materials development and therefore includes specifications for the evaluation of curricula along with recommendations for its development. The authors' recommendations are divided among their concern for the rationale, specifications, appropriateness, effectiveness, conditions of use, practicality and dissemination of curricula of materials.

References

Bunda, M.A. A partial validation of the new conceptualization of evaluation competencies. Paper presented at the annual meeting of the American Educational Research Association, New Orleans, February 28, 1973.

Eisner, E. Instructional and expressive educational objectives: Their formulation and use in curriculum. AERA Monograph Series on Curriculum Evaluation, 1969, No. 3.

Scriven, M. Goal-free evaluation. In E. House (Ed.), *School evaluation.*
    Berkeley, California: McCutchan, 1973.
Stufflebeam, D.L. A new conceptualization of evaluation competencies.
    Paper presented at the annual meeting of the American Educa-
    tional Research Association, New Orleans, February 28, 1973.

CHAPTER 1

THE ROLE OF THE EVALUATOR AND DEVELOPER IN EDUCATIONAL RESEARCH AND DEVELOPMENT

Jean W. Butman and Jerry L. Fletcher
Northwest Regional Educational Laboratory

Evaluation has often been conceived as a process separate from development. Whether seen as a stepchild—a necessary evil to be tolerated in order to satisfy the requirements of funding agencies; or seen as a super-ego parent—a necessary process for controlling and "socializing" the developer—the effect is similar. Either of these views brings about a "we-they" polarity, distorting both the perceptions of the process in which development and evaluation are embedded and the working relationships necessary to effectively carry out that process.

This chapter will deal with theories that are central organizers of the research and development process. By *theory* is meant not some proven body of established fact, but a set of constructs and basic assumptions, often cast in the form of definitions, about relationships among those constructs, for which there exists or may be developed one or more sets of operational definitions (observable, measurable phenomena). The term *theory* is used in this chapter to refer to *a set of interlocking explanations for some real-world phenomena.* These explanations may be incomplete, inconsistent, and/or have low predictive power. Such defects notwithstanding, it is useful to think of such explanatory conceptions as theories. No theory, however consistent, complete, or powerful, is ever "proven." At best, one can say the evidence at this time indicates that the explanations now available account for everything one can now see about this phenomenon. Theories develop out of and are changed by what is seen and how it is seen; they also guide and direct observers' vision and methods. The scientific process, whether applied by the 10-year-old mending his bike or the laboratory scientist testing a precisely formulated hypothesis about neural transmission, is nothing more or less than the continuous interaction between ideas about why things are as they are seen to be and what it is that is seen. Ideas about how things ought to be, sometimes called beliefs, values, or goals, and how to change from what is seen now to something else, are also theories, and very much in evidence (if not in articulation) in both the 10-year-old's work on his bike and the scientist's work on nerve tissue. In the same sense the R & D process in education is also guided by theory and concerned with the development and testing of theory.

Theory and the Educational R & D Process

Three separate but interconnected theories have evolved from efforts to develop both systematic procedures to guide educational R & D work and to create a conceptual system for understanding those problems (Newton and Butman, 1972). One theory comes from the *content* of the instruction: constructs, relationships among constructs, and operational definitions within the body of knowledge with which the educational product is concerned. The second theory has to do with the *process of teaching* and the conditions for utilization of teaching by a learner or learning system. This theory guides the development and sequencing of the form and style of directions given and the procedures and conditions chosen to ensure acceptability, diffusibility, and maintenance of appropriate use over time. The third theory deals with the *effects* of the use of the instructional system on the user, and on the educational system in which the user is embedded.

Interrelationships Among Theories

Whatever the form of an instructional system, whether a textbook or programmed instruction package for students, a training system for teachers, a course or workshop for administrators, or a publication for school boards, all three theories are operative. Beliefs about the conditions necessary for the growth and development of the learners affect both the choice of specific content and the assumptions underlying the teaching-utilization theory and the range of learners for whom it is appropriate. Selection of a teaching-utilization theory affects both the content which might be appropriately adapted to that theory, and the nature of the learners.

An instructional system can be defined as an operational definition of a finite set of variables drawn from: (1) a body of theory concerning content, and (2) a body of theory concerning teaching and conditions for utilization of teaching—these two held constant at a level predicted to produce a given range of variation in variables drawn from (3) a body of theory concerning development and change in the user.

The R & D process is best seen as a series of successive approximations to build increasing power and validity into the theoretical systems, as well as into the operational definitions of them represented by the product.

Since the product of an educational R & D effort represents one unique interface between these three theories, logical consistency among them is a necessary prerequisite to the development of an effective instructional system. Evaluation must concern itself, therefore, with uncovering and eliminating inconsistencies as critical steps toward improving the product. Adequate testing of the system's validity and reliability is impossible without a logically consistent theoretical structure.

Obviously, the task of both the developer and the evaluator is greatly simplified if more powerful, i.e., reliably predictive, theories are chosen or developed before the specific product on which they are based is developed. However, in educational endeavors the theoretical base is usually weak, if not virtually nonexistent, so few efforts are in the fortunate position of having tasks reduced to straightforward application and verification. Educational R & D work must simultaneously develop the products and build the theoretical bases on which they rest. Those skills, procedures, and technologies subsumed under the label *evaluation* are integral to both of these tasks. Evaluation cannot be separated from development, nor evaluators from developers, without seriously impeding the fundamental scientific process undergirding both.

Explication of Theories and R & D Stages

The *theory of effect* concerns itself with the "so what" questions: What difference does it or should it make in the lives of eight-year-olds if they learn the geography of Latin America? What difference does it or should it make in the lives of teachers to learn to use a token reinforcement system, and secondarily, what difference does it or should it make in the lives of the students that the teacher, having learned it, uses it? If the instructional target is an individual, the focus of the theory of effects is clear. If it is a set of individuals in a role system or structure (a school staff), or an individual providing an educational service (a teacher), then it is as though there were two products under development—the instructional system itself designed to affect the behavior of the teacher, and the changes in teacher behavior designed to affect the behavior of students. In this case the second level of development and testing focusing on the effects the trainee has on the students is required, following verification that the instructional system affects the trainee as predicted.

Theories of effect play a major role at the two ends of the R & D process—initiation and installation. During the planning and feasibility study stage, a theory of effect, however unarticulated, guides the conceptualization of the problem area and the selection of one or more content areas to be developed into an educational product relevant to that problem. It underlies the rhetoric and rationale in proposals for funding and provides the goal statement from which any systems analysis procedure is derived. During the operational testing stage the theory of effect guides the selection and operational definition of variables with which to explain or predict variance in outcome, and the nature of the support systems introduced to maintain or expand the achievement of the learning outcomes over time. And, most importantly, it is in this stage that the theory itself and its operational definitions are tested and revised toward increased power by testing the impact of the instructional system after training. That in many actual R & D efforts these beginning and ending stages of the total process are weak may be attributable to the weakness of the theories used as well as to the tendency to see theory as the obverse of, rather than the necessary base for, effective practice.

Content theories are theories about the content of the system, answering questions such as: "What is this educational product about?," "What is the topic under consideration?," or "What is the subject matter of this instructional system and how is it organized?"

Content theory underlying the curriculum materials of an educational product plays a major role during early developmental work on a system. When the content area selected for development is a subject matter in the traditional academic sense, this body of knowledge is relatively stable. While there may be some choices to be made between competing theories (e.g., standard grammar versus transformational grammar), these are usually fairly clear choices. While consideration of rate of change in the knowledge base of the field and continuing review of new developments for their implications are always indicated, there is likely to be little change in the basic theory during the life of the development program.

When the content area selected is a process (e.g., reading, problem-solving, pupil-teacher interaction), the relevant body of knowledge is likely to draw from several lines of underlying theory, research and practice, and may be less well developed as a coherent, internally consistent unit from which to draw specific curricular materials. It is also likely that differentiation between content theory and teaching-utilization theory may be somewhat blurred when the content theory itself concerns a process, since both deal with "how to" issues. One example that occurs frequently in educational R & D is how to teach someone how to teach; the first "how to" refers to a teaching-utilization theory, the second to a content theory of teaching. In either case, whether the content area is subject matter or process, selection from competing theories is guided by and contributes to the further development of the overarching theory of effects.

The content selected from a body of knowledge can be viewed in at least three ways: as a system of constructs to be learned, as a set of performance skills to be mastered, or as a system of organizers for understanding and recognizing what the "self" is becoming. The curriculum materials of an instructional system develop out of a choice between or combination of these foci. An example may help here. Suppose one wishes to design a program for teaching English grammar. One may choose to focus on grammar as an entity to be learned, e.g., to recognize the labels assigned by historical usage or experts to certain language forms. Another alternative is choosing to focus on grammar as a set of skills, e.g., to write and produce material according to some predetermined grammatical criteria. A third is to focus on the self as a user and interpreter of grammar, e.g., to recognize the effect one's own and other's grammar has on one's thoughts and feelings in the process of using and interpreting language. While these foci are interdependent, there is no simple causal link between them.

This matter of curriculum focus in building materials is seldom clear, nor is it particularly easy to differentiate the relationships of these foci to either a teaching theory or a theory of effects. The key point is that each focus implies a different teaching theory and is inextricably linked to a theory of effects.

If one chooses to focus his curriculum on acquiring the language of a field of knowledge, then selecting dependent variables (or objectives) from a theory of effects dealing with the development of self as user of the knowledge is a logical inconsistency. For example, if the curriculum focus in art history is learning recall and/or recognition of the names and representative examples of periods and styles, a theory of effects involving being able to understand and appreciate new art forms, or experimentation with self-expression using techniques of different styles and periods, is ruled out. Inconsistency between the curriculum focus and theory of effects leads to insurmountable problems in the specification of appropriate dependent variables, and the tracing of specific and predictable cause-effect chains. The theory of effect must be scaled to match the content theory and curriculum focus chosen. It is unfortunate that existing curriculum foci seldom fit hoped for outcomes and the choice is often made to scale down expectations about effects to fit quickly derivable behavioral objectives instead of building the curriculum to meet the needs.

Once a content theory is selected or developed and a curriculum focus chosen, major effort turns to the teaching-utilization theory. The content theory and curriculum focus are returned to in subsequent work primarily to check on the internal consistency of the developing system or when evidence indicates omissions in or inadequate formulations of that theory.

The *teaching-utilization* theory underlies the format and media selected for inputs, the selection of activities in which trainees are to be engaged, or the definition of performance variables; the conditions to be controlled, manipulated, or allowed to vary during training and dissemination; the sequencing, timing, and language of directions to trainee/user; and the derivation of intervening variables to be used in accounting for variance in outcomes. It is to this theory, its internal consistency and its consistency with the content and effects theories, that the analytic interpretation of data gathered during development and testing must return. Only then can decisions be made concerning what in the instructional system, or its underlying theoretical systems, needs to be revised, added, deleted, or experimented with in subsequent testing.

In this process it is necessary to be clear about the distinctions between teaching variables and utilization variables. The evidence from one set does not imply revision or verification of the other. It has been common for data from measurement of utilization variables—like acceptability (Do users report their experience on the system as worthwhile and valuable? Are the filmstrips of adequate technical quality?) or practicality (Is the system easily incorporated into existing structures, functions, forms, and procedures of an educational agency?)—as evidence that the materials or activities do or do not reliably and validly convey the content and therefore are or are not ready for testing of the behavioral objectives. This confusion can lead to revisions of the system on the basis of erroneous inference, and to an almost total lack of attention to intervening variables that would account for performance variation and thus to revisions or statements of qualifications concerning use. From the teaching theory comes the selection of conditions of training or use to be tested for their efficiency in maximizing the chance for all trainees to reach optimum performance levels.

In operating on such a theoretical base one does not *guarantee* acquisition of stated objectives. The personal meaning of any experience to any human organism is not inherent in the experience, but rather a product of that organism's existing conceptual organizers, his momentary state, his needs, expectations, goals, motive patterns, *and* the experience. The best and most one can do is provide a probability statement based on conditions known to account for some portion of the variation.

Role of Constraints and Requirements External to Theories Underlying the R & D Process

While ideally research and development would be governed solely by the requirements and constraints imposed by the theories selected and/or developed, the real world seldom, if ever, approximates this state. The institutions within which R & D takes place, the funding agencies, and the political process within which both are embedded exert a profound effect on what actually happens in and results from any R & D effort. The developer/evaluator is constantly faced with trade-off decisions between reality pressures and logic of development. Timelines, available funds, administrative decisions concerning allocation of resources, perceived institutional reputation, prestige, service and survival needs, all can potentially influence such critical decisions as to whether to make a "best guess" about the effect of a given teaching variable on a set of outcome variables and hold that variable constant at some assumed optimal point, or to test the relationship empirically before making such a choice. Thus, decisions are often made on the basis of external pressures, affecting the internal consistency of the system and the interpretability of effect data. Similarly, such pressures can effect choice of dependent variables. The demand from some quarters that effects be measured in terms of standardized student achievement tests is a prime example. In many R & D efforts the relationship between such measures and the educational product is at best a matter of conditional probabilities involving a chained series of hypothetical cause-effect relationships. To bridge that gap and verify the hypothetical chain requires large-scale longitudinal research that simply has not received the commitment of time, money, and intellectual effort necessary for operational testing.

Since education is one of the major institutions of any social system, that decisions and demands are politically as well as empirically derived is both inevitable and appropriate. Careful distinction between politically derived decisions and those derived from increasingly more powerful scientific explanations, and careful analysis and scaling down of theories concerning effects to bring internal consistency to the instructional system, are necessary to bring the forces of careful, systematic, scientific development to parity.

There is for each individual engaged in educational R & D a point at which external demand reduces the probability of sensible, meaningful effect to insignificance. Only by being clear about one's theories and the effect external constraints have on their operationalization and testing can each individual know where to draw the line and avoid the trap of turning out trash and having, for political reasons, to call it effective.

The Need for a Single Integrated
R, D, & E Process

The fluid movement in development between what we do and see and the conceptual organization of what we do and see demands one integrated R & D process, in which research and evaluation functions are a necessary, integral part. If a development team operates according to the conception of the R & D process suggested above, evaluation functions will be a critical part of the development process and will be carried out to very high quality standards, regardless of whether there is a person labeled evaluator on the team. Various organizational and staffing patterns could be equally effective in carrying out the evaluation functions for the total development process.

In most cases, however, educational R & D does not operate well. There is often little concern with making theory explicit or using the results of actions to reflect on theory. Nearly every instance of R & D work in education should be considered in a transitional state, and efforts to change it should try to move the entire R & D process toward the conceptualization mode in the first part of this chapter. Considered in this light, it is possible to evaluate various organizational policies and staffing patterns and various internal development team decision-making processes according to whether they are likely to move the total process in the desired direction. Most writing about evaluation has missed this point. Many of the particular solutions proposed (separate evaluators to preserve objectivity, give them a separate budget, give them sign-off power) are not only too static, they would undermine any effort to deal with the underlying need for theory-based development.

Sources of Difficulty

If the educational R & D process does not operate well, there are usually two major sources of the difficulty: internal development-team operating procedures and organizational policies. In the former category are examples of development teams that do not have a clear conception of the R & D process. They do not attempt to clarify the theories behind their work, to work on consistency among the theories, to specify intended effects, or to look at intervening variables. Their work is haphazard and unsystematic. In the latter category are policies of the R & D organization that do not reward systematic development work, careful attention to testing products, or the clarifying of the theories underlying those products. Extraneous time demands on the development team and limiting support and money to work that is immediately successful and needs no recycling are examples of poor organizational policies.

These classes of problems are not meant to be mutually exclusive. Any particular situation may be some combination of the two. However, different strategies are necessary for dealing with each cause, and many of the problems in the relationship between evaluation and development stem from an inappropriate strategy for dealing with the problem.

Possible Solutions

Development is best seen as a fluid, rapidly-changing process. It calls for intuition, for a sense of how well something is working and what might make it work better, and for a developing sense of the theoretical basis for the work. One should expect to see a series of attempts to conceptualize the problem, to organize conceptually and operationally the development work, with each new try holding only for a short while until, with further work, a redefined problem and some next steps become clear. All of this happens within a broad political framework, calling for accommodations of various sorts between what would seem to be ideal and what is practical.

Development is and *should be* this way, particularly in the initial stages. It is inevitable that there are more questions than answers, more choices to be made than evidence to indicate which alternative is better. Still, an evaluator can help. Careful review of existing data on practice and theory, careful selection of answerable questions for maximum pay-off, and building ways to get answers into theory development activities are the primary contributions of the evaluation functions of the R & D process.

Evaluators almost routinely claim that their purpose is to provide data to support decision making. To do this well the evaluator must work from the start with the developers to choose the set of theories and values underlying the phenomena to be measured, to devise the measures to be used, and to weigh the data. An important role can be played by a formative evaluator *if* the phenomena he chooses to look at and the methods he chooses to look with represent more adequate operational definitions for the theories being developed, and if he can generate systematically collected information, more logically analyzed, in time for, and addressed to, the questions the developers are facing.

Probably the only way the evaluator can possibly support decision making in an ongoing development process is to be a part of the development team. Only then can he keep in touch with the changes, the concerns, and the problems of the developers. The assumption, in ascribing to a scientific view of the R & D process, is that systematically collected and logically analyzed information produces better decisions than unsystematically collected and illogically analyzed information. But such functions cannot be effectively and constructively performed from a distance.

Transitional Steps

Where the evaluator team member is the one with greater clarity, his work consists of convincing the development team that they should examine the data base for their decisions and, whenever possible, they should try to define, collect, and analyze information related to the decisions they face. This is usually a lengthy process of building a trust relationship with the development team, resting fundamentally on the evaluator becoming identified with and committed to the success of the work of the development team. If he can help the development team think through the theoretical systems on which they are working, broaden and make more incisive the questions to which they seek answers, and improve the products, he will have done the most he can to improve the work of the development team.

Once the team has begun operating according to the general scientific process described initially, the evaluation functions *per se* are often more technical—defining variables, gathering and analyzing information, cautioning against invalid interpretations—than they are during the transitional phases of getting the team to so operate. In either case, but more so initially, the evaluator is not merely a technician—he must be intimately and personally involved as a member of the team attempting to make the best decisions. In the initial stages of transition, many more skills are demanded than are usually included in the skills of an evaluator—interpersonal sensitivity, capacity to work with and synthesize theory, an ability to operate within a variety of sets of value systems, and a capacity to understand the working dynamics of a team to know what kinds of changes might be helpful and constructive.

Once the team has begun operating well, and the evaluator is fully accepted as a member of the team, the range of questions he and the team might agree to address systematically is larger than even evaluators presently realize. Throughout the process, significant questions concerning the teaching-utilization theory and its operational definitions within the context of the one particular content theory and expected long-range effects theory require systematic investigation. Formative evaluation work consists of identifying, describing, and to the extent feasible, establishing the generalizability of and relationships among variables. Issues such as the relationship between the arousal of specific motives through the use of instructions and directions for carrying out activities, and performance in that activity; the relationship between alternative formats or uses of media to present content, and trainee response; and the relationship between individual, triad, or larger group work on a task, and internalization and transfer of learning to another segment of the training/user sequence are as much amenable to systematic investigation during the development process, and as critical to the ultimate effectiveness of the product in reaching its goal, as the more routinely considered questions of generalizability of effects to a population.

Those who see the evaluator's work as exclusively or provisionally providing data indicating that a product has a certain degree of effectiveness under certain kinds of conditions with certain kinds of people misunderstand and unnecessarily constrict their own and others' contribution to the R & D process. Such data *is* important, but not all important data is of this type. It might be necessary initially to accept such limitations to begin work with a wary development team, and it might be reasonable in a final summative evaluation effort to focus on these questions almost exclusively, but formative evaluators ought not to draw back from the full range of development questions because of some sense that they are overstepping bounds.

Probably, too, for summative evaluations the use of people from outside the development team is wise. A new look from a different framework and perspective is helpful. In these cases the development team should contract for such outside people to oversee the testing and the usefulness of their work.

The Need for a Forum
Where the development team has a clear conception of what they are doing and why, and they are saddled with a narrow view of evaluation, they need protection. Where the development team, including evaluators, have a clear conception of the scientific R & D process and they are working within an organization that does not recognize or reward such behavior or adheres to a different set of priorities, they again need protection. The most effective protection, in either case, is to create and live by a set of decision-making processes that support and enhance the scientific R & D process, rather than inhibit it.

Much can be done internally to strengthen the forces supporting the internal logic of the development process. The best approach is for the organization to establish policies calling for periodic, i.e., milestone, reviews of the work of the evaluator/developer R & D teams and demand that the team justify what it has done with logic and evidence. There are two parts to this—milestone points, and review that demands data-based justifications. Most organizations have or will soon establish milestone review points. The data-based review is what is usually lacking.

Many organizations have had for some years a written, many-step development paradigm with milestone decision points. In spite of the paper plan, however, informal, unsystematic, and non-data-based processes are often used for making decisions. Most organizations are not good at insisting on systematic data-based reviews of their work. To be effective, each member of the organization must be convinced that such a process, including the increased time and energy commitment to look at and understand what is going on and why, serves the best interest of the product and the organization.

A team's most important contribution to the quality of the development work, and its greatest protection from misguided impositions, is to seriously set about the task of creating and maintaining a formal review mechanism within the organization. At such periodic reviews the team is required to explain the decisions they have made, justify those decisions on the basis of theory, carefully collect and analyze information supporting those theories, and lay plans for what they intend to do based on the results of previous work.

What sort of forum for the review of work will be powerful enough to prevent end-runs and other ascriptive mechanisms for approval and rewards from operating within the organization? It must be constructive, focusing on improving the product or improving the theory behind the product. It must also be forward looking. Its focus should not be approval of past work to see that what has been done was done right. Only on very rare occasions should it stop development work and demand more data. Rather, it should focus on how to carry out studies during the next phase of work, to clear up doubt raised by alternative or competing interpretations of data, and to assist in the formation of key, maximum pay-off questions, yet unanswered, that can feasibly be addressed in the next development cycle. The R & D team's budget and timeline must also contain sufficient latitude to allow for recycling, for additional data collection, and, frankly, for errors.

The key variable in the acceptability and contribution of such a forum to the process is the experience and capability of the people who review the work of the developer/evaluator team. The review panel should be put together of people mutually acceptable to the team and the administration of the organization, and money should be available to bring in people from outside, if sufficient local expertise is not available.

Many organizations are moving toward placing the power and the budget for all parts of product development in the hands of the R, D, & E team. The team determines with the administrators the members of the review forum, and pays those members outside the organization to come and participate with the administrators in the milestone review. This enhances the learning by the R, D, & E team which comes from personal interaction with people competent to review their work. The product of this review is a formal document that is passed to the administrators. The administrators may, if they wish, contact additional people to review the formal document and take initiative to see that new concerns get incorporated into the next phase of the development work.

The creation of a team-level analogy to the formal organizational review process is an effective transitional step. The formative evaluator will find the establishment of such a review procedure a major source of support in increasing his own effectiveness on the team. If the developers know that they will be expected to defend their decisions with data, they must become part of the inquiry process, and the formative evaluator becomes a significant specialist on the development team, contributing not only technical skill, but also expertise in the process of identifying the underlying theories and of moving logically between data and theory to build increasing strength into the product. The evaluators and developers must, of necessity, reach agreement and clarity about the basic assumptions behind the product, and they must both be concerned with improving the clarity of the theories on which the product is based, the adequacy of the operative definitions of those theories the product represents, and with the effects the product is supposed to produce.

Development teams can set up and operate according to such a review procedure independent of the existence of one within the larger parent organization, if they so desire. Two programs whose ideas are represented in this chapter have such internal processes, and since the organization is supportive of and consistent with such procedures, they function most effectively at that level.

Other Alternatives to Developer/Evaluator Teams

The developer/evaluator team has much more power than the evaluator who is located in a division separate from development.

Evaluators who betray excessive concern about not getting co-opted misunderstand their role, particularly the formative evaluation role, and misunderstand the nature of the development process. When evaluators are separated from the development process, they cannot maintain contact with the shifts and changes so characteristic of development work.

At the very least the data they collect is usually too late, or addressed to the wrong questions. The work of the isolated evaluator is usually ignored in the natural process of development because the developers have not been part of the process of deciding what they needed to know and how to get it.

If the evaluators have power over developers and attempt to impose their data and ideas from outside through that power, the result is usually destructive to development. The developer must take time from his work to counter the data, sometimes redoing the evaluation work himself. Rather than gleaning the most he can from the evaluation data, the developer is inclined to attack the evaluation on design or procedural grounds to discredit its value. And since most formative evaluation has design shortcomings when matched with textbook models, such an attack is easy to make, leaves the parties at a standoff, and simultaneously helps nobody. This defensiveness has effects on the development process also, reducing the likelihood that developers would pay attention to any outside information, regardless of how good. And, evaluation work that relies on a political relationship will inevitably be a specific kind of evaluation, not contributing to our understanding of development or how it should be conducted. Such relationships are indefensible. Evaluation should serve the development process, not constrict it.

Is there not a danger of co-option? Certainly. But the danger of destroying or inhibiting the development process is substantially greater. Procedures can be set up to reduce the likelihood of co-option through strong, data-based reviews of work.

The typical problems of suspicion, competition, and politics find fertile ground where either the developers, the evaluators, or the organization lack a clear understanding of the R & D process.

Suggested Readings

Ben-David, J. Organization of research in the social sciences. *Daedalus,* Spring 1973, 39-52.

While the author uses the term *theory* in its academic sense
to refer to some existing body of generalizable knowledge,
rather than in the broad sense we refer to, his analysis of the
research process as better fitting the clinical, engineering
model than the physics model, and the implications of that
analysis for organization and support of the process provide a
cogent supplement to the basic argument of this chapter.

Berkowitz, N.H. Audiences and their implications for evaluation
research. *Journal of Applied Behavioral Science,* 1969, 5 (3), 411-428.

The author discusses questions to be considered in working
with the theory of effects and relationships between the
teaching theory and theory of effects. By implication, a
cogent case is presented for setting evaluation work clearly
within the process which it serves.

Hunt, D.L. *Matching models in education.* Ontario Institute for Studies
in Education, Monograph Series, 1971, No. 10.

The problem focus here is the development and explication
of a method of interfacing information taken from empirical
and theoretical knowledge of a content, students, and
teaching strategy in order to construct a classroom instructional unit. The parallel to the problems of product development interfacing content, teaching, and effect theories is
obvious.

Rosen, H., and Komorita, S.S. A decision paradigm for action research:
Problems of employing the physically handicapped. *Journal of Applied
Behavioral Science,* 1969, 5 (4), 509-518.

An illustrative study presenting one method of using the
unarticulated theories of effects held by some referent group
(clients, decision makers, experts) in the process of selecting
a curriculum focus (with implication for a teaching theory)
for a developmental effort, either a demonstration project or
a "product."

Scriven, M. Who evaluates the evaluators? Paper prepared for a
conference on the Experimental Schools Program, Berkeley, California,
June 1971 (mimeo).

This paper discusses the issue of different levels of evaluation,
and some of the advantages and disadvantages of inside vs.
outside evaluators. It suggests that different purposes are
better served by one arrangement than another.

Reference

Newton, F., and Butman, J.W. Teaching responsively for individualized meaning: What the training is about. Working paper. Portland, Oregon: Northwest Regional Laboratory, August 1972.

CHAPTER 2

THE ROLE OF THE EVALUATOR IN
INSTRUCTIONAL DEVELOPMENT

Eva L. Baker

University of California at Los Angeles

Formative evaluation has reached the status of a number of other laudable endeavors in the field of education—many people talk about it, but few do it right. It is easy to see how formative evaluation came about, for its common sense quality is overwhelming. When one is trying to develop an instructional innovation or to adapt an existing program, data should be collected, analyzed, and interpreted with the purpose of improving the results of the program. While educators are not captivated by some of the more serious issues in formative evaluation—i.e., Should it be done at all? Are achievement data even partially representative of the effects of instructional programs? Are judgment and empirical results interrelated or even capable of interrelation?—these sorts of metaphysical questions will continue with only partial, if any, answers suggested. Formative evaluation has been seized as one tool to assist this sad state of instructional affairs.

The enterprise of formative evaluation has thus become a bona fide area in education. Individuals proffer models of formative evaluation where decision areas are exhaustively classified (see, for instance, Sanders and Cunningham, 1973). However, as in all things, the actual practice of formative evaluation deviates substantially from the recommendations made or the schemes designed. So, while formative evaluation has become a watchword, a high priority procedure, the activity sometimes does not function as intended. People may have lost sight of the simple dictum: *one must gather information that will assist program improvement.*

As direct as this guideline appears, it is often ignored in the course of a strange and recurring phenomenon: data hypnosis. Those acting in evaluation capacities for instructional development projects have often displayed the symptoms of mesmerization by data. The etiology is, of course, explainable. Collecting data legitimizes the development activity itself, independent from whether the data can actually influence the decision-making processes. Data collection (and analysis) can soothe those individuals who get cramps when too long restrained from the conduct of multiple linear regression analyses. Since many of our present developer-evaluators entered the field by way of statistics and measurement, they may suffer feelings of unworthiness unless they have periodic influxes of data to sort.

Secondly, without regard to the area of training that the instructional product developer experienced, data collection has a resoundingly satisfying characteristic. It is a concrete operation with a beginning, a middle, and an end. One even gets answers and, therefore, data introduce an aspect of veritability into the development act. This anchorage in "fact" is important, since development procedures are often tinged with unreality. Developers are ever placed in situations requiring risk-taking and offering low incidences of success. Because development has very few principles to guide the design of instruction, grasping at data sources is an understandable behavior for workers in the area. Unfortunately, the data-gathering activity may retard the project's success when the following rule is applied: If some data are good, then a mass of data is better (if not merrier). Projects can collect the following sorts of data: pretest scores, response rates within programs, posttest scores, attitude questionnaire responses, transcripts of interviews, observers' reports, instructor plans and records, visual or audio records, and evaluation by judges. There are at least three problems associated with the assemblage of such data. One is logistical: how can a staff feasibly score, record, summarize, and integrate information across a variety of criteria, particularly in the light of the limited resources and rigid scheduling under which most funded instructional development programs operate? Second is the question of the extent to which such scrutiny provides a guinea pig effect (described originally by Hovland, Lumsdaine, and Sheffield, 1949, and unfortunately replicated by Baker, 1973a, and others unnamed). People who have been asked too often and studied too much no longer represent the same sort of individual for which the program is likely to be intended. Reactive data may not be better than no data at all.

Why Collect Data?

The most serious issue in data collection relates to the purpose for which the data are being collected. Beyond ritualized behavior, are the data assembled those pertinent to the class of revisions considered possible for the project? The potential utility of data for decision making has been articulated by Alkin (1969) and Stufflebeam (1968), among others. However, the smoothness of their comments can lull the developer into a "collect now, decide later" mentality. The argument here is that, like instructional programming, data collection ventures should be very *leanly* designed. Counter to data collection mania in formative evaluation, the *least amount of data necessary for a decision* should be collected. And, thus, the range of possible decisions must be explored in advance of the design of the testing plan.

What Types of Data, When?

What kinds of data should be considered essential? Certainly the sort of information that provides indication of *what* problems the program has and *where* the difficulties are likely to be located would be most desirable in terms of the efficiency of revisions. Such data can be assembled usually by focusing not only on the adequacy of criterion performance, but the distribution of errors, comments, and suggestions reflected by responses to practice materials themselves. Certainly data that relate to en route skill performance are critical. Supporting interviews with students, where they are encouraged to respond in a free-association manner regarding their reactions to the entire learning experience, can also provide useful information regarding necessary program revisions. The use of diagnostic sorts of data to pinpoint program deficiencies is most suitable for initial phases of formative evaluation. Questions here are related to the viability of the learning sequence itself.

When the formative evaluation process moves on to test the operational success of a program—how it functions when components are integrated in real (often classroom) settings—the sorts of information that one needs for revision seriously change. The practicality with which the program can be used, rather than solely the learning produced, is of prime concern. Also important is interest in determining the training needs of administering personnel.

Thus, not all available, legitimate sources of formative evaluation data are suitable for use at each formative trial. Certain trials have particular functions in the development process. Each trial should collect data limited to the particular revision considerations possible, at that given stage of development. Such a guideline would reduce the tendency to tally anything that is quantifiable. Data on student characteristics, other than pretests, would therefore probably be excluded. Standardized achievement test scores would not be appropriate in any case. Questions devoted to learning sequence information, such as response rates, would be less important for larger scale field tests for revision purposes. A *lean data approach* should forcibly retard needs to play in mounds of information, information that has been typically used in research but has no residual utility in development enterprises.

Lean formative evaluation permits quick iterations of the tryout revision cycle, particularly in the early stages of development when exploration should be relatively fluid.

Who Does the Evaluating?

Once the amount and source of data have been decided, who should be charged with the responsibility for conducting the data gathering and analysis activity? There are two disparate viewpoints. Recent folklore and some actual practice suggest that a person with a job title of formative evaluator should be employed. Formative evaluators can be members of the project staff or consultants based external to the project organization. The popular view is that external evaluation is important. Scriven (1972) suggests that the formative evaluator come in without knowledge of the program goals and provide his or her assessment of the actual effects of the project. He calls his approach "goal-free evaluation." Scriven's approach is that of an auditor who comes to see what the effects of a program are without influence generated by the rhetoric supplied by program plans, specifications, and the like. Stake (1972) portrays the "responsive evaluator" as one who observes and reacts, with fewer quasi-scientific trappings than typical evaluators carry. The responsive evaluator should, according to Stake, serve to stimulate project staff rather than to provide only the usual sorts of "data for decisions." The responsive evaluator can provide case studies for his clients, and in general, produce a report that is more diversified, less goal-referenced, and probably more interesting than the usual evaluation document. Stake and Scriven both see externally based formative evaluators making serious contributions to program improvement. Scriven sees the evaluator as a dispassionate (for the moment) outsider providing a circumspect preview of summative findings. Stake, while also rejecting the all-constraining influence of program objectives, expects the evaluator to get to know his clients well, to design his reports in attention-arresting ways, to become closely interactive with the project itself. As "external" evaluators, they presumably avoid pitfalls, such as serious financial dependency on the project and inordinate predisposition to see good things emerging in any case. An analog for external evaluators, although tawdry, might be considered. Formative evaluators come on the scene much in the same way that "sparkle girls" in white gloves come to service stations. They want to be sure everything is clean by providing the same sanitizing function. When a project is to be visited by a team of government advisor-evaluators, for instance, the activity stimulated by the impending visit is to "clean up" operations. Probably, more time is spent in preparing for evaluations than in adapting projects to judgments and recommendations made by the visiting panels. Yet, any who have participated in the site-visiting scenario, either as evaluator or evaluatee, can attest to the debilitation, the schedule collapse, and the sense of futility surrounding the entire venture. Outside people, needing orientation, asking questions, can make development itself an overly self-conscious and stilted enterprise.

Internal Formative Evaluation

A cadre of goal-free or responsive evaluators dispersing themselves over the range of projects for suitable recompense giving goal-free or responsive assessments of project success may be Nirvana to some, but for practical reasons, a less exciting approach is suggested. Let us cease to expect incompetence, narrowness, and apple-polishing from instructional development staff in the area of formative evaluation. Consider that formative evaluation should be thought of as a *function* not necessarily limited to a particular, designated set of people named "formative evaluators." We may be able largely to dispense with the universal, external formative evaluator, for a number of reasons. Consider first the thesis that good instructional development or improvement involves evaluation activities. Almost all instructional development models proclaim their dependency on formative evaluation data. Writers such as Baker (1973b), Borg and Hood (1968), and Schutz (1970) have fairly recently described development procedures in which the collection of data is essential. In fact, from the first tentative separations of instructional development from programmed instruction, experts have been describing the essential characteristic of empirical development (Lumsdaine, 1965; Markle, 1967). Thus, formative evaluation is not a concept come-lately to the idea of instructional development. Prior to Scriven's (1967) work, empirical development was a fact. Scriven gave the process a better name and extended it into the area of large-system instructional development where it desperately was needed.

Data gathering is a conscious, planned activity in development. Program failures are attributed to poor instructional design. Formative evaluations are made of objectives, measures, alternative instructional designs, and operational effects. In fact, without a careful integration of formative evaluation activity, instructional development is nothing but an art form, an invention, usually with poor marks in aesthetics.

The previously mentioned lack of research principles for guiding development practice forces developers to rely almost exclusively on their data as the only source of control of their process. Formative evaluators superimposed on a project used to be and, in some cases, still are necessary in instances where program development is instituted by novices. However, the emergence of training programs in instructional development at UCLA, University of Pittsburgh, Florida State University, and elsewhere, suggests that trained professionals are available to whom program development and evaluation roles could be confidently assigned. Further, the growing number of exportable artifacts in development and evaluation training produced at educational research and development centers and laboratories can begin to instruct on an inservice basis the numbers of inadequately trained people who are presently holding instructional development positions. Such programs emphasize skills in field test planning, selection of measures, data analysis and interpretation. Kneller (1972), an educational philosopher, in his response to Scriven's arguments for goal-free evaluation, suggests that evaluators can be trained to attend to concerns broader than project goals, such as side effects or unintended outcomes. If those given the responsibility for design of instruction were well trained in evaluation techniques, the necessity for external evaluators functioning in a formative way would be greatly reduced. Why not assume that developers can be trained to undertake formative evaluation of their own programs? No more can development personnel (particularly those in schools) be envisioned as crazy inventors or typewriting chimpanzees who need to be brought back to earth by roving super-evaluators.

Internal Evaluation: Formative Evaluation
by Instructional Development Staff

1.   *Data related to the adequacy of learning*
2.   *Data related to the satisfaction the program produced*
3.   *Records of side effects*

Because of convenience, intimate knowledge of program capabilities, and location, formative evaluation may often be conducted internally by trained development personnel. These evaluations would attend to the data related to the adequacy of learning. As mentioned earlier, such information is particularly useful during the prototype evaluation stage, where components of larger instructional programs are assessed primarily in terms of the extent to which desired learning occurs. In the light of inadequate performance, the formative evaluation should provide cues regarding program malfunctions, i.e., content segments that are inappropriate sequence problems with subtasks. Internal evaluators are likely to be sensitive to areas of potential weakness in programs. They can integrate the data and alternative revisions in a manner likely to be responsive to cost constraints, scheduling, and real-life development exigencies.

Data gathering related to the satisfaction the program produces also may be assessed formatively and may be a function shared by evaluation staff members and external evaluators. Indices of satisfaction will include interests and attitudes freely expressed in unstructured interview sessions conducted with students, questionnaire responses of students and observational reports of student behavior compiled during exposure to the program. Program satisfaction also may be determined by investigating data sources such as teachers, administrators, and parents. Included in these concerns would be the questions regarding side effects or unexpected interactions of the program's intended goals with some aspect of the context or student population with which the program contended.

One earlier criticism of side effect analysis conducted by program developers is that they will be so blinded by their own maniacal concern with promoting program goals that they will be unable to see unanticipated effects, either good or bad. Kneller (1972) suggests that this tendency, if it exists, might be remedied by training. In the conduct of formative evaluations, unstructured data-gathering interviews with relevant individuals provide one potential source for determining if the program is having strange effects. Another procedure that might be employed involves the inclusion of open-ended questions, such as "The thing I worried about most was . . . " or "I didn't like. . . ."

Often in the quest for finding out if the program operated properly, the formative evaluator can overlook trying to determine if negative outcomes were consequences as well. External formative evaluators might also be concerned with side effects. However, their data should only be corroborating of the internal formative evaluation. Blatant negative effects will be discerned by both internal and external evaluators. Subtle negative effects will rarely be detected in formative evaluation in any case, for one reason: formative trials are usually quick and dirty, with necessity for rapid data analysis and relatively short-term exposure to treatments. Serious but subtle side effects are likely to be a consequence of embedding the developed program into a setting that is not obviously unsuitable to the program. Such effects are likely to come to light after longer trials, and more usually at the point where the program development team is just about to sign off on the program. As an aside, it might be interesting to speculate on the disposition of revision decisions if, at a late date in program development, negative side effects were discovered. External evaluators still have important functions, but the expectations that they will come to a project and right all wrong exceeds the limitations of their functions.

**External Evaluation: Formative Evaluation
by a Qualified Individual Other Than Staff**
1. *Data regarding the processes and operations of the project staff*
2. *Judgments regarding the suitability of criterion measures*
3. *Judgments regarding the adequacy of program content*
4. *Side effect analysis*

External evaluators can obtain data and make judgments about the developmental process itself. Suppose the staff developing reading materials was not insuring that each draft was reviewed by relevant clientele—reading experts, teachers, and parents. The external formative evaluator could suggest that the process be corrected. Such a suggestion has more credibility when made by an outside expert. Obviously, suggestions about project organization and operations are important only when an agency or institution is considered viable for some extended time period. An *ad hoc* group, constituted for a year to develop a given program, probably should not spend too much energy honing its processes to glittering edges. Formative evaluation in this case should be devoted rather to the effects of the program itself.

External evaluation should also be sought for the review of content, format of the instruction, as well as the measures. External review of measures is critical, since subsequent modifications regarding the utility of instructional materials will be based on the adequacy of criterion devices. Better bases for criterion design are emerging, due largely to Hively's work (1968). Accuracy and utility of content suggested is also a task for external evaluators. In both the case of review of measures and programs, however, there is no need for the evaluator to visit the site itself. Review can be accomplished without further depletion of our gasoline or jet fuel reserves, in the privacy of the evaluator's customary cubicle.

An Example of Formative Evaluation

An instance of formative evaluation activity adapted from Baker (1972) will be described. The project considered was funded by the Research Training group, formerly at the National Center for Educational Research and Development. The project was planned to train development personnel in skills related in a set of training materials consisting of text, practice materials, and simulations (Baker and Quellmalz, 1972). The project may serve as an interesting example because of the effort made to "do it right," that is, to use data at relevant points to assist in the development of materials. The degree to which the project was successful will be explored.

An extensive summary of project activity is presented below.

Resume of Activities

Phase One: Formulation, Specification, and Prototyping—(four months). Because the proposal committed the project to a set of gross specifications, the formulation phase of the project was relatively brief. Although the inclusion of five instructional techniques had been stipulated, the project staff needed first to determine which techniques would be selected from the content of the materials.

During this period the following tasks were accomplished:

1. A survey of instructional psychologists was conducted to assess their preference for various instructional techniques.

2. Survey results were tabulated and presented in a paper at the Annual Meeting of the American Educational Research Association.

3. Tentative selection of six instructional techniques was made: practice, prompting, knowledge of results, control of inspection behavior, task description, and advance organizer. Selection was guided by both the results of the survey and the staff's attempt to render the techniques in instructional sequences.

4. Preliminary contacts were made for developmental and field test sites for spring and summer.

5. Examples of short-term instructional sequences in a variety of subject matters were developed. These sequences were to be suitable for different aged learners and to provide a sense of variety with which instruction might be produced. The sequences were planned to be used in discrimination and revision sections of the project.

6. Final specification of the objectives was generated and is presented below:

> Given a set of specifications from which to choose, the trainee would be able to develop an instructional sequence that exhibited the use of the instructional techniques included in the materials.

Subordinate competencies were postulated as follows:

> Ability to discriminate the use of such techniques in sample instructional sequences, both on a single and multiple discrimination basis.
>
> Ability to revise given sequences to improve the use of such techniques.
>
> Ability to correctly select statements relative to the recommended use of techniques.

7. Pretesting of criterion materials was conducted in February on two samples of subjects. One group was comprised of 29 graduate students in curriculum at UCLA; the second consisted of 11 teacher education candidates at a local state college. Students were asked to discriminate the techniques in instructional sequences and also to define the terms presented.

8. The plan for the package of materials was formulated:

> The prototype would consist of text materials, information items, practice exercises for discrimination, revision exercises, writing simulations, and posttest materials. To differentiate materials for graduate students and to lend credence to the notion of research-based

instructional techniques, an extensive annotated bibliography was planned. Materials were intended to be rendered in print because of cost constraints.

9. A literature search was conducted for experiments relevant to instructional techniques selected for the project. Information from these experiments was abstracted and formed the basis for the text section. The notes were also to be refined for inclusion in the annotated bibliography section of the materials.

Phase Two: Prototype Development, Testing, and Draft Writing— (four months).

1. Drafts were produced for advance organizer and control of inspection behavior texts. After editing, criterion items were produced that sampled the information presented in the texts. Practice exercises were either written or adapted to the topics.

2. At the start of this period, a developmental trial was conducted on the two components.

3. A first draft with appropriate test items and practice discrimination exercises was produced for the task description component.

4. An additional trial was conducted that tested advance organizer, task description, and control of inspection behavior texts and discrimination exercises. The materials were collated to form a subsection of the material entitled "Techniques for Directing Attention."

5. Criterion items and practice exercises were written for the second subsection, "Techniques for Response Control." The techniques of prompting, direct practice, and knowledge of results formed the substance of the component.

6. Sets of specifications were produced for the simulation section of the materials. Directions for use of the specifications were also provided.

7. Thirty copies of the materials were produced.

8. Contacts for field test sites were pursued.

Phase Three: Testing and Revision Cycles—(five months).

1. Field test on response control section was conducted in Santa Monica.

2. Directions and items were revised and materials were tested at Arizona State on undergraduates. No staff members were directly involved in the field test.

3. Data from Santa Monica and Arizona were scored. Revisions were made in items, scoring procedures, practice discrimination exercises, and text materials.

4. Field trial was conducted in Torrance. Staff observed, but the training was supervised by local team leaders.

5. Data were compiled and analyzed, and revisions in text, items, and practice discrimination exercises were made.

6. The materials were subjected to external expert review by two educational psychologists. Their responses resulted in the simplification of language employed in materials, as well as modification in the instructional sequence.

7. Revision exercises were produced.

8. Models of instructional sequences were developed and included in materials.

9. The pretest was modified to reflect revision rather than discrimination behaviors.

10. A field test was conducted at Manhattan Beach under optimal conditions. Data were considered to represent the first demonstration trial.

11. Data were analyzed and revisions made.

12. Pretest administered to UCLA teacher education candidates. Field trial not pursued.

13. Individual revision exercises (for each instructional technique) were produced.

14. Directions written for "hands-off" field test at Arizona State.

15. Modifications were made for laboratory field tests.

16. Revisions in directions for Pacific Bell Company field trial.

Phase Four: Final Data Analysis, Revision, and Report Preparation—(four months).

1. Lag in receipt of data delayed production of final version.

2. The bibliography was critiqued and substantially revised.

3. An optional section to organizers was reintroduced.

4. Introduction to materials was written that incorporated the history of development of this project.

5. The research studies generated through the project were compiled. A paper was prepared and presented at the Annual Meeting of the American Educational Research Association.

6. Professional drawings were added to materials.

7. All data from all trials were subjected to reanalysis and graphing.

8. Based on data, minor organizational changes were instituted in materials.

9. Final copies of materials were generated, proofed, and reproduced.

Product Tryout

The purposes of the product tryouts varied with their point of occurrence in the development sequence. Early trials were to verify the suitability of prototype formats and criterion items. Later trials served to identify gaps in the sequence and to provide data for revision of previously developed materials. The trials also were designed so that progressively less staff involvement in the tryout was required, in order to ascertain whether any degree of program replicability had been achieved.

Subjects

Partly by happenstance the subject population varied by trial. The staff believed that the materials should be tested on different kinds of people with various job requirements pertaining to instructional development. Subjects participating in the field trials represented four distinct groups: preservice teacher education candidates, graduate students in instructional development, experienced school personnel, and instructional development staff performing in outside agencies. Universities provided the source of students for the pretest—UCLA (N = 29) and teacher education candidates at San Fernando Valley State College (N = 11). The first prototype trials of the directing attention component was tried on two groups of UCLA teacher education candidates (N = 10; N = 18). The prototype materials on response control were tested on experienced elementary level school teachers (N = 9). The first off-site trial was conducted at the Arizona State University campus on undergraduate education students (N = 18). Curriculum supervisors on the central staff of a medium-sized school district tested revised components of the materials (N = 7). The internal validation trial was conducted in cooperation with the Manhattan Beach School District and California State College, Dominguez Hills, employing interns in teacher education (N = 21). Arizona State University graduate students served as one external validation sample for the almost-final version of the materials (N = 22). The final sets of data were obtained from a trial on staff course-writers employed by the

Pacific Bell Telephone Company, Training Division (N = 14). These individuals deviated markedly from the other groups in terms of educational experience and job requirements.

Testing Schedule

The program was tested in components during the various product tryouts. The following table presents the data, location, number of subjects, and components tested at each tryout.

Revision Activity

The bases for revision were many. They included data from the tryouts of the program on appropriate subjects, reviews by individuals external to the project staff, and judgments made by the staff members. Because 10 separate tryouts had been planned (although only eight materialized) the revision pattern was intended to be controlled by the sequential acquisition of data. Ideally, each version of the program would be revised as a consequence of judgments based on data acquired from the most recent field trial. Thus, data from Trial One should contribute to the development of Version Two, and so on. Unfortunately, procedural problems conspired to upset such progressive application of performance data. Field trials, for instance, needed to be scheduled well in advance, so organizations could commit subjects for the length of time estimated. Therefore, the development team was always working against a schedule: the dates subjects would be ready to begin the program. Second, many of the trials were planned off-site, so that the staff was dependent upon the program administrator to mail the raw data back to them. Often, there were inopportune delays. The multiple responsibilities of the staff members also compounded the problem, for the project could not afford a single person with only a data analysis task. Data analysis responsibilities may have been perceived as interrupting more continuous development activities.

Thus, the inevitable data analysis lag from the previous tryout, when combined with the preordained tryout schedule and the time required to prepare multiple copies of materials resulted in a situation where data from one field trial were being tabulated at the same time the materials for the next field trial were being prepared. Data-based revisions tended to be incorporated in materials at a later time rather than on the next proximate field test. Thus, data from Trial Four had their impact on Trial Six.

Table 1

Testing Schedule
1971

Date	Location	N	Components Tested
February	UCLA	29	Pretest
February	San Fernando Valley State College	11	Pretest
April	UCLA	10	Advance organizer, inspection behavior text, and discrimination exercises
June	UCLA	18	Entire component of directing attention including texts, items, and discrimination exercises
July	Santa Monica	9	Response control text, items, and discrimination exercises with writing simulation prototype
July	Arizona State University	18	Entire package to date: including text items and discrimination exercises for both response control and directing attention, writing simulations
July	Torrance	7	Response control package plus revision exercises
September	Manhattan Beach	21	Entire package, including texts, items, discrimination exercises, models, revision exercises, and writing simulations
November	Arizona State University	22	Entire package
December	Multiple California Locations	14	Entire package

A revision strategy was employed where one could take into account information from the most recent tryouts without unduly deferring material preparation and multiple copy production. Data from the immediately preceding tryout were employed in two ways. First, criterion items were revised. Item editing and revisions in scoring procedures were possible without delaying costly production efforts. Instructions to the user, usually contained in brief letter format, were also revised, as were directions given to the program administrator at the field test site.

The major revision activity occurred in a two-month period. During this period, a rewrite of the entire set of text materials was completed, based in part on the accumulated data from Trials One through Five, and the detailed review submitted by two experts. Subsequent modifications to the project from Trials Six through Eight included variation in sequence and directions to the user, addition of specifications for the simulation tasks, inclusion of the bibliography, and technical modifications in visual design.

Retrospect

The interesting notion in the sequence of activity described is that most of the evaluation was conducted by the development staff. The external review of educational development experts served, first, to verify that the content of the material was accurate and, second, to make suggestions for use of the materials. Administrators of the materials on other sites also provided feedback and suggestions as a consequence of their unfettered observations.

Notice that the project did not have an opportunity to assess the program's effects in the most desirable settings, for instance, regional laboratories or research and development agencies. One would expect that the use of materials in such contexts would have provided fuel for uncovering unanticipated outcomes.

The example is useful because it provides an instance of formative evaluation where field trials were conducted to collect lean data. The interpretation given this procedure is that it is better to have repeated trials on different samples than mining the data from only one or two sets of subjects.

The project demonstrates, if only partially, that designed field tests can be integrated into the development process itself. Thus, the context for formative evaluation is the development activity. It should not be an unfamiliar role for instructional developers. External formative evaluators can provide helpful assistance, but the real impact of formative evaluation will emerge when instructional development projects *as second nature* collect the sorts of information that are really needed to help improve instructional efforts.

Suggested Readings

Baker, E. Technology of instructional development. In R.M. Travers (Ed.), *Second handbook of research on teaching.* Chicago: Rand McNally, 1973, 245-285.
> A chapter describing common precepts of instructional development, including an extensive bibliography of research and examples.

Hively, W., Patterson, H.L., and Page, S.H. A "universe-defined" system of arithmetic achievement tests. *Journal of Educational Measurement,* 1968, *5,* 275-290.
> A description of domain-referenced testing procedures. A critical, conceptual work.

Lumsdaine, A.A. Assessing the effectiveness of instructional programs. In R. Glaser (Ed.), *Teaching machines and programmed learning II.* Washington, D.C.: National Educational Association of the United States, 1965, 267-320.
> Based on the report of the joint committee of AERA-ADA and DAVI on recommendations for standards of empirical testing of programs.

Markle, S.M. Empirical testing of programs. *Programmed instruction.* Chicago: University of Chicago Press, 1967, 104-138.
> A clearly written chapter providing an excellent conceptualization of the place of data in development.

Schutz, R.E. The nature of educational development. *Journal of Research and Development in Education,* 1970, *3* (2), 39-64.
> An excellently prepared paper on the purposes of development. An essential reading.

References

Alkin, M.C. Evaluation theory of development. *Evaluation Comment,* 1969, *2* (1).

Baker, E. *Preparing instructional materials for educational developers.* Washington, D.C.: National Center for Educational Research and Development, 1972.

Baker, E. The practicum: A departure in development training. Paper presented at a symposium for the Annual Meeting of the American Educational Research Association, New Orleans, 1973. (a)

Baker, E. Technology of instructional development. In Travers (Ed.), *Second handbook of research on teaching.* Chicago: Rand McNally, 1973, 245-285. (b)

Baker, E., and Quellmalz, E. *Research-based techniques for instructional design.* Los Angeles: National Center for Educational Research and Development, 1972.

Borg, W.R., and Hood, P. The twenty-seven steps in the development program. Berkeley, California: Far West Laboratory for Educational Research and Development, 1968.

Hively, W., Patterson, H.L., and Page, S.H. A "universe-defined" system of arithmetic achievement tests. *Journal of Educational Measurement,* 1968, *5,* 275-290.

Hovland, C.I., Lumsdaine, A.A., and Sheffield, F.D. *Experiments on mass communication.* Princeton, New Jersey: Princeton University Press, 1949.

Kneller, G.F. Goal-free evaluation. *Evaluation Comment,* 1972, *3* (4), 7-8.

Lumsdaine, A.A. Assessing the effectiveness of instructional programs. In R. Glaser (Ed.), *Teaching machines and programmed learning II.* Washington, D.C.: National Educational Association of the United States, 1965, 267-320.

Markle, S.M. Empirical testing of programs. *Programmed instruction.* Chicago: University of Chicago Press, 1967, 104-138.

Sanders, J.R., and Cunningham, D.J. A structure for formative evaluation in product development. *Review of Educational Research,* 1973, *43* (2), 217-236.

Schutz, R.E. The nature of educational development. *Journal of Research and Development in Education,* 1970, *3* (2), 39-64.

Scriven, M. The methodology of evaluation. AERA Monograph Series on Curriculum Evaluation, 1967, No. 1, 39-83.

Scriven, M. Pros and cons about goal-free evaluation. *Evaluation Comment,* 1972, *3* (4), 1-4.

Stake, R.E. Responsive evaluations. Unpublished, 1972.

Stufflebeam, D.L. Evaluation as enlightenment for decision making. Columbus, Ohio: Evaluation Center, Ohio State University, 1968.

CHAPTER 3

EVALUATION WITHIN THE CONTEXT OF
PROGRAM DEVELOPMENT:
PROBLEMS AND PROCEDURES IN AFFECTIVE EDUCATION

Barbara J. Brandes
State Superintendent's Office, Montana

Despite educators' concern with affective attributes in students, little systematic work on the formative evaluation of exportable affective programs has been undertaken. Most investigations of affective outcomes are lacking both careful conceptualization of the relationship of the intervention to the desired affective outcomes and rigorous assessment of these outcomes. Although the difficulties inherent in designing and evaluating affective programs cannot be entirely overcome, it is possible to obtain much information useful in revising a program when an adequate formative evaluation strategy is employed.

Affective educational programs have in common two characteristics that distinguish them from most programs in the traditional curriculum areas. The first characteristic is that the constructs posited as goals are poorly understood both in terms of the conditions that foster their development and in terms of the particular behaviors that are indicative of the constructs. A second distinguishing characteristic of affective programs concerns the conditions under which outcome behaviors should be elicited. Most instructional programs are designed to teach people *how* to do certain things. The aims of affective education are primarily to increase the likelihood that certain behaviors will be elicited spontaneously, in a free choice, unprompted context.

These characteristics of affective programs pose special problems both for the developer who has few signposts pointing the way toward effecting behavior changes and for the evaluator who must help the developer determine whether a good path has been chosen. This development task calls for an unusual degree of communication between developer and evaluator. They must give early and concentrated attention to the selection and development of appropriate measures of outcomes. In addition, formative evaluation of affective programs calls for greater than usual sensitivity to the usability of the program. Some of the problems to be faced during formative evaluation of affective educational programs as well as some procedures for minimizing these problems will be elaborated in this chapter.

The Components of Affective Educational Programs

Education is future-oriented. Virtually all instructional endeavors are aimed at long-range, diffuse competencies. Since none of these long-range goals can be attained all at once, areas of competency are broken into components and sequenced with the hope that the cumulative effect of the components will result in the desired goal. But until a complete hierarchical analysis of the skills that produce the desired end product has been performed, one cannot know for sure whether the components have been properly sequenced and instruction provided on all essentials. This uncertain relationship between long-range goals and short-term outcomes of instruction is problematic to evaluation in the traditional subject matter areas, but it is a much more serious predicament for evaluators of affective education, where little is known about the skills essential to attainment of long-range goals or whether these goals can even be approached by the teaching of skills.

Because the derivation of program content from long-range goals in affective education necessarily involves educated guesswork, the efficacy of the derived content in enhancing desired affective behaviors must be verified in the evaluation. An exportable affective program must be treated both as an *instructional sequence* designed to teach specific information, concepts, and skills, and as an *affective intervention* intended to modify attitudes, values, or behavior dispositions. Dealing with each of these two components calls for somewhat different formative evaluation strategies.

The Instructional Component

The instructional component of an affective program is that portion of the program presented for learning in a cognitive mode. For example, in a program currently being developed at Research for Better Schools to promote achievement behavior (Hill, Chapman, Campiglia, Beckingham, and Brandes, 1972), the instructional component is the vocabulary, concepts, and operations given to students as tools for enhancing their personal success in goal attainment. The instructional component of an affective program is treated in the same manner as any instructional sequence with criterion-referenced evaluation by behavioral objectives as the most appropriate assessment procedure. Fundamental and axiomatic to instructional design is the requirement that an instructional sequence be objectives-based. This means that the statement of objectives must specify the precise outcome behaviors as well as the conditions under which the behaviors will occur and the content on which the behaviors will be performed. In an affective program, refinement of the instructional component must precede rigorous assessment of the effectiveness of the instruction in promoting affective outcomes. Otherwise one would never be able to determine if the program is not succeeding because of the ineffectiveness of the instructional sequence or the ineffectiveness of the affective intervention.

The Affective Intervention Component

Over and above the content which is taught to students in a cognitive mode is the intervention component of an affective program. The affective intervention is the cumulative effect on students' attitudes, beliefs, values, and behavior dispositions of what they learn, practice, and experience during the program. In one program, in achievement behavior, the affective intervention is the combination of instruction in concepts and skills with the modeling and practice of successful goal attainment. The goal of the intervention is to modify students' achievement behaviors and dispositions.

In most instances evaluation of the intervention component of an affective program cannot be undertaken in the same manner as the criterion-referenced evaluation of the instructional component. Affective goals usually cannot be prespecified as precisely, and a comparison group is usually needed as a standard against which to assess student performance. Some instructional technologists (e.g., Sullivan, 1969) have argued that prespecification of objectives does not limit the kinds of objectives that are set. This assertion may be strictly true, but it is simplistic and misleading because objectives cannot be prespecified unless one knows precisely how the desired outcome, if attained, will manifest itself behaviorally. This degree of precision simply cannot be attained for many affective constructs given our current lack of knowledge without making both the program and the measurement procedures trivial. The criterion-referenced methods of instructional technology can help us to establish sound procedures for measuring students' proficiency in specific skills, but they are ill-equipped to deal with many of the more generally stated goals of education not yet understood in terms of a specifiable hierarchy of skills. The great difficulty in those areas of competency that are not mapped and charted comes in formulating goals which are not only teachable and measurable, but also valid with respect to long-range educational goals.

An Example of an Affective Program

To illustrate some of the conceptual and measurement problems in the formative evaluation of a complex affective program, consider a program designed to enhance students' maturity and self-knowledge. Louise L. Tyler (1969) has discussed how an affective program to enhance these qualities might be developed. The first step is to find out what can be discerned in the behavioral repertoire of mature and self-knowledgeable people which can be taught to students of a given age. Tyler attempts to show how this might be done. Her attempt is quite thoughtful, although it is not very successful from an instructional technology point of view. Since there is very little empirical knowledge or consensus of opinion about how children grow up to be mature and self-knowledgeable, one strategy is to adopt a theoretical position that can fill gaps in our knowledge. Tyler has theoretical leanings toward psychoanalysis, and she moves quickly from the focus on maturity and self-knowledge to psychoanalysis as the basis for deriving instructional objectives. Since it is not clear which of the tenets of psychoanalysis are most germane to maturity and self-knowledge, the prospectus for instruction begins to look more like a course in psychoanalysis than instruction in the components of maturity and self-knowledge *per se*. Tyler is aware of possible flaws in her derivation of program material from her long-range goals and points to the need for verification:

> ... what is needed is some empirical evidence that if these objectives were attained, the aim of maturity or self-knowledge would result (p. 119).

Tyler does not carry her derivation of program objectives to a level of specificity greater than the intermediate goals "to be self-accepting" and "to be optimistic." However, one might extend the derivation to a point where it included some specific instructional content. Formative evaluation of the instructional component could be accomplished easily enough by means of a criterion-referenced mastery test. It is reasonable to conclude that students who do well on the mastery test have learned the instructional content of the program. However, this result cannot be taken as evidence that students have actually become more mature and self-knowledgeable. The effectiveness of the affective intervention must be assessed independent of the instructional component. Instructional product evaluators nurtured on objectives-based systems are not accustomed to dealing with such global issues of validity. It is usually just assumed that students who master the content are progressing toward the more general goals which inspired the program. However, it seems apparent from the above example that such assumptions are unjustified in complex affective programs. The relationship of derived instructional content to affective goals must be verified empirically.

Goals and Measures in the
Affective Intervention Component

It has been argued above that the stringent requirements of objectives-based instruction with the insistence on exact prespecification of outcomes are only partially applicable to the special features of affective programs. In fact the attainment of the true goals of affective programs can be hindered by a restricted focus on rigorous behavioral objectives. Let us then consider in more detail the nature of goals in the affective intervention component. The following are among the distinguishing features of affective goals:

(1)   The desired outcome may be an attitude or belief which could be expressed by any one of a whole range of behaviors.
(2)   The desired outcome may be for students to generate unique or personalized products.
(3)   The desired outcome may be the enhancement of certain attitudes or beliefs to the greatest extent possible. No guidelines may be available for prespecifying a criterion level of performance.

Some curriculum scholars have argued that statements of affective goals must be separated from the statements of measures used to assess attainment of goals (Wight, 1971). Behavioral objectives at the instructional level should include the goal and the measurement device in the same statement (e.g., The student will discriminate fractions from whole numbers on at least 16 items of a 20-item test). But forcing such constraints on statements of affective goals may not only make programs trivial but may also make it impossible to modify programs toward greater congruence with affective goals. Affective programs are often aimed at directional changes in the student which should be recognizable and measurable after the fact but which cannot be precisely specified in advance. Wight argues that a more general statement of affective goals helps both the teacher and the students to keep in mind the true purpose and direction of their endeavors so that they may be alert to alternative means of attaining their goals and always relate specific educational experiences to their more general goals. Measures or indicators of attainment of goals are devised but are not seen as the only possible measures of the goals. Similarly, Eisner (1969) refers to some educational objectives as *expressive* in contrast to *instructional* objectives which are quite specific and invariant across students. Expressive objectives cannot be completely prespecified because they represent the personalization of knowledge rather than the acquisition of knowledge *per se* (e.g., interpreting a poem or producing a work of art). The statement of expressive objectives cannot encompass the range of acceptable outcomes although it should state the procedure by which assessment will take place (e.g., aesthetic judgment by a panel of judges). The formative evaluator of an affective program needs to be able to work with goal statements that are less specific than behavioral objectives.

Although the liberalization of statements of program goals may facilitate the development of affective programs, it can have a regressive effect with respect to quality control if the measurement of outcomes is neglected or devalued. In fact the evaluator must devote a great deal more attention to the development of measures than would be required in a strictly objectives-based system.

There are two major distinguishing features of measurement procedures in the affective intervention component. First, an affective measure must usually be viewed as one indicator of the affective construct sampled from a population of possible indicators. Actually a thorough evaluation will often include more than one indicator of a goal in order to assess generalizability of results (e.g., a pencil and paper questionnaire of attitudes toward school plus number of tardies as two indicators of attitude toward school). A second feature of measurement in affective evaluations is that most indicators will require a comparison group for interpretation of results. The matched comparison group, which should receive an alternate treatment if possible, is really the only standard against which to assess the performance of children in the experimental program.

The selection of indicators for affective goals is the most difficult problem in evaluating affective outcomes. Measurement in the affective domain lags far behind measures of most intellectual competencies. Due to the questionable validity and low reliability of many affective measures, one may not be able to discern whether the failure to show desired results reflects the actual nonattainment of goals or simply the inappropriateness of the measures. This problem stems from the current state of the art in the analysis of affective constructs. It stands in the way of completely informative evaluations. Krathwohl (1972) has commented:

> Perhaps this is the critical point on which accountability stumbles, as does educational research also, for that matter. It has been argued that no science can advance beyond the level that it can reliably measure. Only the simple skills, either with long tests or large groups, can be very reliably measured, although good indications of more complex skills and some affective areas can be attained with careful work.

Evaluators of affective programs must strive for "good indications" of outcomes, recognizing that it will not always be possible and feasible to obtain even that much. Obtaining good indications requires a broadening of standards for what is admissible evidence over those measures usually included in assessment of program impact to include self-reports, situational tests, or perhaps subjective assessment of student products by a panel of judges. There are some procedures to follow during formative evaluation that will increase the likelihood of obtaining good indications of outcomes:

1. Work on the selection and development of affective measures must begin at the earliest possible date, perhaps even before program goals have been finalized. Project-developed measures will often require as much tryout and revision as the actual program materials. If work on measures does not begin early, the evaluation may never include good indicators of impact.

2. A great deal of effort must be channeled into those constructs measured, since affective measures tend to be both cumbersome and unreliable. In complex programs some critical goals of the program must become focal points for

measurement, while less important goals may be neglected. An early decision must be made on these focal points. The global nature of many affective constructs and the unreliability of measures suggests that multiple indicators for critical goals should be used. For example, in the evaluation of the curriculum in achievement behavior (Hill *et al.*, 1972) one critical goal is to enhance realistic goal setting in students. Because the level of risk in goal setting may be specific to a given content area, measures of goal setting have been used which sample from more than one content area. Although situational behavioral measures have the advantage of assessing dispositions in a disguised context, a single situational measure may have very limited generalizability.

3. Measures of affective outcomes should be unobtrusive whenever possible. Since affective goals most often pertain to behaviors or attitudes which are expressed spontaneously, care must be taken to avoid obtaining compliant responses from students. A game context can often be used to disguise the desired response on a measure.

4. Affective constructs should be analyzed as completely as possible with explicit formulation of intermediate or en route goals. Many affective programs are aimed at outcomes too global to be useful. Improvement of the self-concept is often set as a program goal without any further specification of what aspects of the self-concept are to be modified and how program content is expected to achieve an impact on self-concept. Intermediate goals should be measured as well as long-range goals in order to avoid the gamble of putting all of the measurement efforts into those behaviors most difficult to change.

An affective program is both an instructional sequence and an affective intervention. The evaluator must follow different procedures in stating goals and assessing outcomes for these two components. Affective goals must usually be stated more generally than instructional objectives, and multiple indicators of affective outcomes should be used. Moreover, the evaluator must be concerned with verifying the relationship between the instructional and affective components of the program.

**Deriving and Verifying a
Hierarchy of Program Goals**

The derivation of program goals during the earliest stages of program development works backward from the global long-range goal (often not attainable within a semester or a year) to the affective goal or goals desired at the end of the program, and finally to the particular competencies that will be taught in a single unit of instruction. Program developers always operate with at least an implicit derivation of intermediate goals which they see as instrumental in moving toward their long-range goal. However, the derivation needs to be made explicit in order to provide a clear hierarchy of expected outcomes which can be assessed during formative evaluation. If the derivation is not made explicit, it may never be possible to obtain information useful in improving the program. Popham (1969) has presented an example of a teacher who described her course as promoting good citizenship in students. However, the course actually consisted of a set of facts about American history, and the teacher assessed outcomes of her course only by testing student mastery on a true/false test. Thus the teacher never obtained any information useful for revising her course to come closer to attaining her goal of promoting good citizenship. It would appear that the teacher reasoned that teaching facts about American history is a way to promote good citizenship, but her evaluation procedures did not enable her to find out if she reasoned correctly. A complete evaluation of her course would encompass not only students' mastery of course content but also the relationship between content mastery and the true goal of promoting good citizenship.

Once the derivation of goals has been completed, the evaluator can work with a set of testable and hierarchically ordered hypotheses pertaining to outcomes. At the lowest level is an hypothesis about the instructional outcomes that should be attained in a particular lesson or unit of the program. At the next higher level is a statement about the set of behaviors that should indicate content mastery of the entire instructional sequence. These two levels constitute the instructional component of the program. At the third level is a statement about ways in which students completing the program should behave differently from other students. At this level an assertion is made about the relationship of the intervention provided to the affective or other behavior changes being sought in the program. Finally, at the fourth level is a statement asserting the relationship of these behavioral outcomes to the long-range affective goal from which the program was derived.

In Table 1 the four levels of outcomes and the assessment procedures appropriate to each level are presented. The first two levels are those most frequently discussed in prescriptions for evaluation. These levels are the instructional component of the program. Students should be tested following units of instruction and at the end of the entire program to determine their mastery of material presented to them for learning. Test items tend to be a direct extrapolation of the content of the instructional sequence. Students' actual performance can be compared with an *a priori* established level of acceptable performance, and a decision can be made about whether to revise portions of the instructional sequence.

At level 3 an attempt is made to verify the relationship between the instruction provided in the program and the affective goals of the program. Adequate assessment at this level usually requires comparison group testing on measures that are not biased in terms of vocabulary or unique content of the experimental program. In effect there is an explicit attempt to relate the instructional sequence to the affective intervention.

At the fourth and final level the relationship of measured program outcomes to the long-range goal is reassessed. Since longitudinal evaluation studies typically are not feasible and are unlikely to reveal effects of a single program, one must usually rely on informed judgment of the value of program outcomes. However, a thorough evaluation should include some reassessment of program goals based on an updated synthesis of relevant research data.

First Case Study of an Affective Program

The scheme for deriving and verifying the hierarchy of program goals can be illustrated by considering one aspect of the formative evaluation of the Achievement Competence Training (ACT) package (Hill *et al.*, 1972). The long-range goal of this program is to increase students' success in attaining their personal goals.

The first step in developing an instructional product was to derive specific program goals or focal points from this global long-range goal. The procedure was to look at research information about successful achievers and to attempt to select teachable skills from their behavioral repertoire. An attempt was made to describe distinguishing disposi-

Table 1

Assessing Outcomes of Instruction at Multiple Levels

Component	Level	Outcome	Target of Assessment	Method of Assessment
Instruction	1	Students master lesson or unit content.	Lesson or unit instructional content.	Criterion-referenced lesson or unit mastery test.
	2	Students master program content.	Instructional content and sequence for entire program.	Criterion-referenced program mastery test.
Affective Intervention	3	Students display specified behaviors more often than their agemates.	Relationship of instructional content to desired behaviors.	Norm-referenced test with comparison group.
	4	Students display behaviors consistent with long-range goal at adulthood.	Relationship of behaviors displayed by students at end of program to long-range goals.	Longitudinal study or informed judgment based on synthesis of available data.

tional qualities of high achievers and to generate a behavioral sequence that describes the process of goal attainment. This effort culminated in a six-step strategy of goal attainment that became the core of the ACT program. Thus the synthesis of information about the criterion population resulted in two general program goals: (1) to teach and encourage the use of the ACT strategy of goal attainment, and (2) to enhance positive self-evaluation and belief in internal control. Objectives for mastery of program and lesson content were arrived at by conceptual analysis of the goal attainment strategy so as to provide a thorough exposition of each step and repeated practice in the use of the strategy.

One indication of proficiency in the use of the ACT achievement strategy is the level of aspiration or risk reflected in the goals set by students. Students successfully completing the ACT program should set goals for themselves that are challenging for them but not so difficult as to be impossible to attain. The term for this quality of personal goals is "medium risk." Instruction in medium risk-taking was incorporated in the ACT program because of research evidence indicating that high achievers are able to integrate knowledge of their own past performance with their desire for excellence and thereby set goals at a level of difficulty consistent with, or slightly higher than, their past performance. Low achievers, on the other hand, often set goals which are too easy or impossibly difficult.

The process of deriving a hierarchy of objectives pertaining to medium risk-taking from the long-range goal of ACT results in the levels of outcomes depicted in Table 2. Mastery objectives, or the teachable content associated with medium risk-taking, include providing a definition of medium risk, discriminating medium risk goals from low and high risk goals, recognizing medium risk as a quality of goals set by achievers, and so forth. The right-hand column in Table 2 shows the means by which attainment of these objectives is assessed. At the lesson and program mastery levels (levels 1 and 2 in Table 2) assessment procedures directly reflect the objectives as stated and are quite amenable to criterion-referenced testing procedures. At these levels of assessment, the concern is with adequacy of the instruction to teach students information about medium risk-taking. If students fail to grasp and retain this information, the program developers need to revise the sections on medium risk-taking in order to provide clearer explications, more practice, or remedial materials.

Table 2

Assessing Levels of Outcomes for One Act Goal: Medium Risk-Taking

Component	Level	Outcome	Target of Assessment	Method of Assessment
Instruction	1	Students master concept of medium risk-taking.	Instructional content of lesson on medium risk-taking.	Lesson posttest.
	2	Students retain information about medium risk-taking.	Instructional content pertaining to medium risk-taking for whole program.	Program mastery test.
	3	Students take medium risks more often than their agemates.	Relationship of instructional content on medium risk-taking to frequency of taking medium risks.	Situational tests of risk-taking comparing ACT with non-ACT students.
Affective Intervention	4	Students have more success than their agemates in attaining personal goals at adulthood.	Relationship of medium risk-taking to success in attaining personal goals.	Updated synthesis of research data on achievement behaviors.

At level 3, the concern is with the effects of instruction on unprompted behavior. Once students have learned about medium risk goal setting, are they actually more likely to set medium risk goals for themselves when compared with their agemates who have not been similarly instructed? Assessment at this level requires selection of one or more indicators of medium risk goal setting. In the ACT evaluation, ACT and non-ACT students are compared on two situational tests of risk-taking.

Finally, at level 4, it is appropriate to ask whether or not teaching students to set medium risk goals does actually further their success in attaining personal goals. Direct and unequivocal evidence pertinent to this question cannot be obtained, but it is possible to look at several types of evidence to get an idea of whether the program is on the right track. First, one can look at how ACT students perform on other indices of achievement. If the desired effects are found on some of these other indices, this provides reassurance that instruction in medium risk goal setting has some coherence with other achievement behaviors. Second, the growing body of basic research data on achievement behavior can be reexamined to determine whether medium risk-taking still seems to be a significant component of the achiever's repertoire.

Scope of Evaluation Activities Over Successive Tryout Stages

As the developing program progresses through successive stages of tryout and revision, the scope of evaluation activities will change and expand. At each stage the evaluator must seek information regarding those issues necessary in revising the program and moving it to the next stage. There is no invariant scheme for the number of tryout stages in formative evaluation or for the exact types of data to be collected at each stage. Idealized models are rarely appropriate to implement in every situation; so each project will probably evolve its own particular tryout plan. However, there are some general trends in formative evaluation activities which should be part of any evaluation plan.

General Trends for Formative Evaluation

Over successive tryout stages any curriculum should be tried with increasing numbers and types of students. Early tryouts usually begin with only a small group of students, when the developer needs very gross indications regarding the suitability of program content for the target population, the media for presenting the program, or anything else about which the developer does not wish to make an entirely arbitrary decision. By the time the program is approaching large-scale dissemination, it should undergo a field study of sufficient size to use the classroom as the statistical unit of analysis, sampling as widely as possible from the entire population of likely consumers of the program. Optimally, at the field test stage, the experimental program should be compared with an alternative program or at least with some special treatment given to the comparison group in order to avoid the juxtaposition of halo effects with evidence regarding program impact. Comparison with an alternative treatment is of particular importance in evaluating an affective program. Similarly, over successive tryout stages, the conditions of the tryout should move more and more toward the conditions under which the disseminated product will be used. This means that the development team should not be present to support the program when it is being used and that the teacher should be allowed to use the program as she would if she obtained it commercially, incorporating it into the unique circumstances of the classroom.

In any stage of evaluation of any curriculum there are two major categories of data that need to be examined—*usability* and *impact.* Usability refers to all aspects of a program that affect its attractiveness and suitability for consumers—students, teachers, administrators, and parents of students. Usability is a broad category of data obtained primarily through interviews, questionnaires, descriptive observation of lessons, or inventories of program functioning such as the number of classrooms in which the program was successfully completed during a hands-off tryout. The impact or effectiveness of a program refers to the attainment or nonattainment of goals for behavior change. Data relevant to program impact are obtained primarily through the testing of students, although other methods for obtaining impact data are sometimes employed. Over successive tryout stages increasingly reliable data pertaining both to the usability and the impact of a program can be obtained. However, obtaining the best possible data even at early tryout stages is of great importance since program revision depends on this data base.

Additional Procedures for Affective Programs

Beyond these general trends for formative evaluation are some procedures particularly applicable to affective programs. The unique problems encountered in developing and evaluating affective programs call for certain emphases within the general tryout scheme. Empirical data useful for improving the program are obtained less often for affective than for other types of programs. It is a frequent occurrence for participants in a program to be subjectively convinced that the program has had an impact when there are no empirical data to substantiate this feeling. Often there are no data useful either for demonstrating that the program worked or for suggesting how the program might be made to work better.

The formative evaluator should be associated with the project from the very beginning if possible, preferably when the program is still in the planning stage. Dialogue between developer and evaluator can make explicit the derivation of program goals so that there will be testable outcome statements instead of a vague treatment with vague expectations about outcomes. Because an affective program is both an instructional sequence and an affective intervention, the evaluator must play a dual role in devising assessment techniques for both components. To assess instructional outcomes, the evaluator assists in formulating precise behavioral objectives and constructing criterion-referenced tests of content mastery. At the same time, the evaluator must also get started on the arduous task of selecting and developing measures for affective goals, helping the developer make decisions about focal points for measurement, and commencing the necessary psychometric procedures for constructing norm-referenced tests.

Usability data must be given greater than usual attention in evaluating affective programs because affective programs are more apt than traditional curricula to clash with pre-existing attitudes, expectations, and practices. Some otherwise worthwhile programs in affective education may prove to be unsuccessful or never be fully implemented because information about usability was not gathered and used during formative evaluation. Obtaining usability information early in the development process can forestall costly mistakes later. The following are among the questions, of special concern in affective programs, that should be addressed in the assessment of usability:

1. Are the program materials appealing and interesting to students? Do the materials enhance positive attitudes toward the content of the program?
2. Are teachers comfortable with the program? How does the program affect the teacher's relationship to his/her students?

3. Is the program compatible with a variety of teaching styles and organizational structures of classrooms?
4. Is the program consistent with educational priorities in many communities?

Assessment of program impact during early tryout stages must focus primarily on the instructional component. Until the instructional component is refined to an acceptable degree, it is not possible to find out if the program will have the desired effects on students' attitudes, values, and behavior dispositions. Failure to assess the instructional component may lead to the erroneous conclusion that an entirely different approach must be taken to attain affective goals when in fact the program has simply not succeeded instructionally. For example, a course designed to enhance music appreciation might fail to produce the desired affective outcomes, either because what was taught is unrelated to music appreciation or because what was taught was simply not taught well enough.

Typically, during early formative evaluation of a program, significant effects on affective outcomes are not attained. However, information from early tryouts can be quite helpful if it provides some hints of a relationship between content mastery and affective outcomes. Even though it is premature to obtain a direct test of the efficacy of the instructional content in furthering affective goals, some relevant presumptive evidence can be obtained by looking at correlations between student performance at the various levels of outcomes. For example, in the formative evaluation of the ACT program some evidence of relationships between levels of outcomes was found pertaining to the goal of enhancing an internal locus of control. One finding in the tryout was a significant effect showing higher performance of experimental group students on a test designed to measure some of the cognitions involved in self-directed behavior. On the other hand, the effect did not attain significance on the measure of belief in internal control. Although one must conclude that there is no evidence that the ACT program enhances belief in internal control, it was noted that performance on the test of cognitions involved in self-directed behavior correlated significantly with posttest internal control. In a multiple regression analysis with posttest internal control as the dependent variable, the cognitive measure was found to account for the largest portion of variance after pretest internal control was entered. Neither IQ nor academic achievement were significant predictors of internal control. This result suggests that what is taught in the program, as reflected on the measures of cognitions related to self-direction, may have some validity with respect to internal control.

Some additional corroborative evidence comes from an analysis within the sample of children receiving the ACT program. Again using posttest internal control as the dependent variable in a multiple regression analysis, the best predictors in descending order were pretest internal control, the measure of cognitions pertaining to self-direction, and the content mastery test. Students who mastered program content best were, to some extent, the same students who did well on the cognitive measure and on posttest internal control. On the basis of these data it was concluded that some components of self-directed behavior were successfully taught by the ACT program. Of course the final test of the effect of the program on perceived locus of control must be made directly.

Despite the best efforts of a competent evaluation staff, a project may never have good indicators for all affective goals. Valid and reliable measures of affective constructs do not abound, particularly measures usable with young children. Even so, statements of affective goals should be made as precise as possible, and appropriate measures, when they exist or can be invented, should be used. In addition to these measures of impact, procedures for obtaining testimonial or anecdotal evidence regarding program impact should be obtained through interviews, questionnaires, or naturalistic observation. Although testimonial data can never be regarded as objective evidence of program effectiveness, it will in certain instances be the only available data pertaining to some types of outcomes. Moreover, testimonial and anecdotal data can provide insight into the bases on which users judge the value of the program.

Second Case Study of an Affective Program

In Table 3 the formative evaluation activities associated with successive tryouts of the ACT package are outlined for illustrative purposes. The four tryout stages associated with development of the program were:

(1) the lesson pilot in which a single lesson undergoes initial tryout with a few children;

(2) the first package tryout in which the entire sequence of lessons is run with the same group of students although

Table 3

Formative Evaluation Activities in ACT Package as a Function of Tryout Stage

Aspects of Evaluations	Lesson Pilot	Package Tryout 1	Package Tryout 2	Package Tryout 3
Number of experimental classes	Individuals in groups of 3 to 8	1 class group	3 class groups	34 class groups
Tryout conditions	Different groups receive each lesson. At least half the lessons are radically rewritten and re-tried.	Same students receive entire package; uneven pacing of lessons; corrected lessons reintroduced.	Tryout of complete package with time pacing as prescribed by developer.	Tryout largely hands off with teachers agreeing to follow guidelines for pacing and use.
Number and type of comparison classes	None	None	2 classes (uninstructed)	68 classes (34 uninstructed and 34 "Brand X")
Types of data	• Student performance in lessons • Informal observation of lessons • Student critiques of lessons	• Student performance in lessons • Descriptive observation of lessons • Teacher critiques of lessons • Student critiques of lessons	• Student performance in lessons summarized by class • Descriptive observation of lessons • Teacher critiques of lessons • Student performance on mastery test • Structured interviews with teach-ers	• Student performance in lessons summarized by class • Descriptive observation of some lessons • Teacher critiques of lessons • Student performance on mastery test • Structured inter-views with teach-

	...views with students • Pre- and posttests on cognitive and affective goals with comparison groups		...views with students • Pre- and posttests on cognitive and affective goals with comparison groups	Structured interviews with students • Pre- and posttests on cognitive and affective goals with comparison groups • Anecdotal evidence of behavior change • Formal observation of teacher behaviors by lesson
Usability questions	Are materials suitable for age group? Do directions work? Do students make responses in lessons? Are materials appealing and interesting?	Can program function in classroom? Are materials appealing and interesting? Do lessons run well in sequence?	Does program function successfully in different classes? Are materials appealing and interesting? Are teachers comfortable with the program?	Can program function in a variety of class structures with variety of teachers and types of children? Are materials appealing and interesting? Are teachers comfortable with the program?
Impact questions	Do students learn the material?	Do students learn the material?	Do students learn the material? Do students retain lesson material? Are students different from comparison group in competencies, attitudes, etc.?	Do students learn the material? Do students retain lesson material? Are students different from comparison group in competencies, attitudes, etc.?

pacing of the program is uneven, and some modified lessons are reintroduced;

(3) the second package tryout in which the entire sequence of lessons, in fully produced form, is run simultaneously in several classrooms and administered by the regular classroom teacher; data are used to refine the instructional component;

(4) the third package tryout in which the program is tried out in more than 30 classrooms simultaneously and in which tryout conditions approximate those of normal use; success of the affective intervention is assessed.

Table 3 also shows how the types of data collected and the major evaluation questions posed change and increase over stages. During the pilot lesson the developers receive immediate feedback by observing the lesson in use and by discussing lesson material with students. Similarly, during the first package tryout, members of the development team are usually present to observe and to obtain criticisms and suggestions from students. This tryout affords the first opportunity to see whether the lessons have a coherent sequence and can be run successfully as a program. During the second package tryout an initial attempt is made to compare program students with their agemates on cognitive and affective indicators. By this stage the program should be fairly successful in meeting its instructional objectives. In addition, simultaneous use of the program in several classrooms gives some indication of how the program interacts with different types of students and teachers.

During the third package tryout, the final stage of formative evaluation, the program is run in enough classes for the class mean to be used as the statistical unit of analysis. Two comparison groups, each equivalent in size to the experimental group, are included in the design. One comparison group is given no special treatment. The second comparison group receives another affective program that has some overlap with the content of the experimental program. With participating schools randomly sampled from a wide range of income levels and with classes randomly assigned to treatment groups, the design is powerful enough to provide convincing evidence regarding the impact of the experimental program. Data regarding both content mastery and affective outcomes are obtained as well as extensive usability data. Formal observation of teacher behaviors in administering the program makes it possible to relate differences in student outcome behaviors to degree of program implementation.

Although the specific progression described in this case study should not be taken as a model for all affective programs, it does illustrate trends which should be evident in the successive tryouts of any affective program. Formative evaluation during early tryouts is heavily weighted toward effectiveness of the instructional component and user acceptance of the basic content and format of the program. Later formative tryouts should emphasize impact of the program on students' attitudes, beliefs, and behaviors. Adequate assessment at the level of the affective intervention requires that a variety of affective indicators be used. Measurement of affective outcomes may also be supplemented with anecdotal and testimonial evidence. The evaluation design during the final stage of formative evaluation should include a comparison group which receives an alternative (or "Brand X") program.

Concluding Comments

Some procedures have been described that may help developers and evaluators of affective programs obtain information useful for program revision. An affective educational program is something more than an instructional sequence in one of the traditional curriculum areas. An affective program contains both an instructional component and an affective intervention component. The formulation of goals and the design of outcome measures for the affective intervention require different techniques than are appropriate for evaluation by behavioral objectives in the instructional component. Over successive stages of program development, the focus of formative evaluation shifts from the instructional component to the affective intervention.

There is currently much concern among educators about the problems of providing affective education. Too little is known about important affective constructs to enable educators to provide affective education with the same precision as arithmetic and grammar. Some curriculum experts argue that education should not be attempted in areas where analytical understanding is lagging. The argument is straightforward: You cannot teach what you cannot specify. However, if one reviews the lists of important educational goals produced by state departments of education and local districts, it is clear that educational priorities dictate otherwise. Although it may be tempting to argue that there is not an adequate research base for developing sound affective programs, the responsibility of schoolmen for contributing to the total development of children cannot be dismissed so easily. Procedures described in this chapter illustrate how a project developer and evaluator can sequentially test their hypotheses about how to provide affective education.

Suggested Readings

CSE-RBS test evaluations: Tests of higher-order cognitive, affective, and interpersonal skills. Los Angeles: Center for the Study of Evaluation, University of California, 1972.

> Existing tests in the affective and cognitive domains are rated on several dimensions including validity, usability, and normed excellence. The document enables the evaluator to quickly determine whether measures appropriate for his purposes are available.

Hill, R.A. Affective evaluation for the schoolman. Paper presented at the ASCD Annual Meeting, Minneapolis, 1973. Philadelphia: Research for Better Schools.

> This brief summary presents the advantages and disadvantages of various types of measures and experimental paradigms for affective evaluations. It is particularly useful for planning school based evaluations.

Lee, B.N., and Merrill, M.D. *Writing complete affective objectives: A short course.* Belmont, California: Wadsworth, 1972.

> This book is highly recommended for anyone who is trying to formulate affective goals for specific short-term outcomes. Teachers will find it particularly useful and coherent.

Wight, A.R. Affective goals of education. Salt Lake City, Utah: Interstate Educational Resource Service Center, November 1971.

> Affective educational goals are categorized and discussed. The document provides a conceptual frame of reference for anyone formulating affective goals.

Wight, A.R., and Doxsey, J.R. Measurement in support of affective education. Salt Lake City, Utah: Interstate Educational Resource Service Center, January 1972.

> This paper discusses measurement considerations in affective education. It gives a worthwhile orientation for the unsophisticated reader.

References

Eisner, E.W. Instructional and expressive educational objectives: Their formulation and use in curriculum. In W.J. Popham, E.W. Eisner, H.J. Sullivan, and L.L. Tyler, *Instructional objectives.* American Educational Research Association Monograph Series, 1969, No. 3.

Hill, R.A., Chapman, M.L., Campiglia, H., Beckingham, P., and Brandes, B. *Achievement Competence Training.* Philadelphia: Humanizing Learning Program, Research for Better Schools, 1972.

Krathwohl, D. Accountability. Paper presented at the American Educational Research Association Annual Meeting, Chicago, April 1972.

Popham, W.J. Objectives and instruction. In W.J. Popham, E.W. Eisner, H.J. Sullivan, and L.L. Tyler, *Instructional objectives.* American Educational Research Association Monograph Series, 1969, No. 3.

Sullivan, H.J. Objectives, evaluation, and improved learner achievement. In W.J. Popham, E.W. Eisner, H.J. Sullivan, and L.L. Tyler, *Instructional objectives.* American Educational Research Association Monograph Series, 1969, No. 3.

Tyler, L.L. A case history: Formulation of objectives from a psychoanalytic framework. In W.J. Popham, E.W. Eisner, H.J. Sullivan, and L.L. Tyler, *Instructional objectives.* American Educational Research Association Monograph Series, 1969, No. 3.

Wight, A.R. Beyond behavioral objectives. Monograph. Salt Lake City, Utah: Interstate Educational Resource Service Center, 1971.

CHAPTER 4

EVALUATION WITHIN THE CONTEXT OF
PRODUCT DEVELOPMENT:
A USER ORIENTATION

Marvin C. Alkin and Arlene Fink
Center for the Study of Evaluation
University of California at Los Angeles

Educational product development as a technology and commercial enterprise emerged out of the programmed instruction and curriculum development movements of the late 1950's and early 1960's. By the beginning of the present decade the field had achieved a dramatic growth rate. Based on published listings in the Educational Product Information Exchange (EPIE), and including only the more popular products, there has been an estimated 48 percent increase in the number of commercially available products, and an estimated 88 percent increase in the number of commercial procedures, from 1967 to 1970. The growth of the field during this same period is further demonstrated by the evolution of over 20 regional laboratories and R & D centers, and by the many publications in the literature describing various schemes and models of product development processes (Banathy, 1968; Briggs, 1970; Flanagan, 1967; Glaser, 1966a, 1966b; Mager and Beach, 1967; McNeil, 1968; Stowe, 1969). The complexity of these educational research and development models varies considerably from general three- and six-stage schemes (Schutz, 1970) to comprehensive step-by-step procedural checklists (Borg and Hood, 1969).

The primary focus of much of the rapidly increasing activity in this relatively new field has been on refining and improving the technology of product development. This quest for clearly defined and documented development procedures has unquestionably resulted in the more efficient production of reliable educational products. However, the concentration of developers on technology rather than on the commercial marketing and distribution of products has led to the neglect of an important area of the total R & D effort: the preparation of reports oriented to needs, requirements, and instructional contexts of school administrators, curriculum-and-instruction personnel, and teachers—the buyers and ultimate users of most educational products. As a result, substantial amounts of funds are wasted each year on the purchase and installation of educational products that later prove to be inappropriate or ineffective. To prevent the continuation of such economic and educational waste and the negative effect it could have on the future acceptance and use of educational products, developers should provide conveniently assembled and readily interpretable information to potential users before these users are obligated to choose from among competing products.

There are several immediately obvious reasons for the failure to provide user-oriented product reports. In part this is due to the nature of the product development and evaluation process. It is also due somewhat to the perceived roles and interests of the various participants in the process. In order to help clarify the problem of providing adequate user-oriented product reports, this chapter will first define and discuss the roles of evaluation and the evaluator in educational product development and reporting. After this preliminary discussion, six minimum components of a user-oriented report, with examples of the information these components should contain, will be suggested and detailed. The chapter will conclude with a brief practice exercise that requires the reader to determine whether the plans for a product report are adequate in that they include a consideration of each of the six components.

Role of Evaluation and Evaluator in
Product Development and Reporting

Evaluation has been referred to as the process of determining the decision areas of concern and then selecting, collecting, analyzing, and providing significant information to help decision makers choose among alternatives (Alkin, 1971; Klein, Fenstermacher, and Alkin, 1971). In educational product development, the information required by the decision maker is usually related to various strategies to modify or improve a product's content, form, or organization. In many cases the supplier of this information, the evaluator, is also the developer; thus the same individual has a dual role in the product development process. As a result, the evaluator selects and supervises the product's field testing plan, *and* translates the test information into product changes. When the product is ready for dissemination, the evaluator/developer has compiled information into a technical or final report that serves to document the field testing history of the product, to confirm the product's systematic validation on appropriate learners, or to demonstrate the effectiveness of the development procedures. Such information, and the format in which it is presented, is useful for other evaluators/developers, project directors, or funding agencies. However, technical reports are inappropriate for users—the teacher in Philadelphia or the curriculum coordinator in Los Angeles. These people, confronted with an ever-growing array of educational products, cannot be expected to sift through the avalanche of development data contained in technical reports in order to decide which product to buy. In recognition of this consideration, a few development organizations have attempted to provide users with conveniently assembled information about products, while other agencies, such as the Educational Product Information Exchange (EPIE), offer product reports. Nevertheless, educational product developers continue to lag in their obligation to the user, perhaps in deference to their responsibility to refine development procedures and produce products.

Individuals who conduct product evaluations have been concerned mainly with presenting their findings to a class of decision makers other than potential users. Let us examine the nature of evaluation activities and the roles of the evaluator to see why this is so.

Nearly everyone is now familiar with the distinction between formative and summative evaluation. Formative evaluation may be divided into two activities referred to as implementation evaluation and progress evaluation. The purpose of an implementation evaluation is to determine the extent to which an educational program has been put into operation, in the manner in which it was proposed, for the group for whom it was intended. A progress evaluation is conducted to determine the extent to which the program's interim objectives have been obtained.

The purpose of formative evaluation is to provide information to decision makers in order to enable them to modify and improve products. From this definition, it is obvious that much of the activity in product development deals with formative evaluation and that the role of the evaluator in the product development sequence is generally not distinct from product development. Formative evaluation is an inherent part of the product developer's role and, because product development and formative evaluations go hand in hand, they are frequently performed by the same people.

Who are the decision makers and what are their information needs? One decision maker is the project director, another is the director of the development agency, and yet another is the funding agency. What kind of information do these decision makers require? Note that the summative evaluation report, since it serves at least three decision makers or decision audiences simultaneously, must be addressed to those issues that are of interest to all three sources. Thus:

1.   The purpose of the evaluation is to demonstrate that the product developer has been "successful."

2.   The purpose of the evaluation is to demonstrate that the materials developed are in some way better for producing some intended set of objectives than competing materials, or that there are no competing materials available for the stipulated set of objectives.

3.   The purpose of the evaluation is primarily to demonstrate the overall quality of a product *rather than to specifically delineate the conditions under which the product is most useful.*

Let us now consider another class of decision maker, namely the potential user. Suppose a product user were to commission an evaluation report to help him examine the various instructional materials available in order to determine which ones are appropriate for the specific context of a particular school district, school, or classroom. Would the previous evaluation report prepared for project directors or funding agencies achieve the decision purposes just described? Probably *not*. The nature of an evaluation is determined by the decision context and the kinds of decisions that will be made on the basis of that evaluation report. The user simply has a different decision context from the other agencies, and thus most existing formative and summative evaluation reports may be related to it only tangentially.

Product developers have in their possession much of the necessary evaluation information for product users. Continuously collecting formative evaluation information represents an integral aspect of the product development process (Markle, 1967). Unfortunately, the information is simply not summarized and reported to users in an easily interpretable and cohesive form. For example, while many producers of instructional products do provide extensive data on product performance, these typically take the form of technical reports or working papers that describe field test and experimental installation results and procedures. To most teachers and district administrators, this format for presenting data is anything but palatable.

Two partial but notable exceptions to the practice of reporting information are the systems of Quality Assurance and Integrated Instructional Management (Baker, 1972). The former provides en route information on various indicators of student performance and pacing, while the latter is designed to aggregate and synthesize input-output information in a manner that is understandable, comprehensive, and consistent with the informational requirements of students, teachers, principals, parents, curriculum supervisors, district administrators, and development personnel. The distinct advantage of Quality Assurance and Integrated Instructional Management is their tailored comprehensibility for different user interest groups. Their most significant disadvantage, however, is that the information is supplied for purely formative or developmental purposes, so that the instructional product must be purchased and installed without final descriptions or explanations of the information. This means that potential users are placed in the position of providing product test subjects.

If a concerted effort, comparable to that which produced Quality Assurance and Integrated Instructional Management, were made to provide information to users before the purchase of instructional products, much of the problem of providing the user with comprehensible evaluation information could be eliminated. However, the overriding concern is to improve and refine product development as a technology, not to collect and disseminate interpretable information to users. Thus, summative evaluation information relevant to a user's instructional context is neither synthesized nor reported in any single place or in any comprehensible form.

But, is there someone who feels the responsibility for providing a full range of information for these users if not the producers of materials? Certainly not the publishing companies. Supplying such information to users of instructional products represents additional expenditures that are currently considered unnecessary and to some extent undesirable. Why raise a question about the validity of one's product for a variety of instructional contexts if you can get away with not raising the issue at all? It simply is not good business to reduce profit margins by collecting and reporting information that the consumer himself has yet to ask for.

Consumers do not demand contextual summative evaluation

information. Potential users have not become sufficiently sophisticated to call for and expect comprehensive and understandable information before making their decisions. User decisions are most commonly based on the reputation of the commercial publisher or the presumed academic qualifications of the product's author.

Types of User-Oriented Summative Evaluation Information

The problem of establishing standards for product development reports is not new (Lumsdaine, 1965). However, with the passage of time, and the increasing number of available products, the problem has become more obvious, if only because so little has been done to solve it. One document concerned with the user's needs (Tyler, Klein, and Michael, 1971) contains a set of recommendations for curriculum and instructional materials to guide producers, users, and funding agencies. It addresses the full range of curriculum and instructional program decisions, extending from the need to substantiate the initial choice of objectives to the need to utilize appropriate channels of dissemination. In this chapter we are concerned with the problem of what minimum information should be included in an evaluation report to *users* of instructional products.

Common sense and experience suggest that the potential user will be most interested in evaluation information that fits his particular instructional decision context and the instructional product. Clearly, instructional contexts vary, from small rural classrooms to large urban school districts, and from districts without money to spend to individual schools with large bases of financial support. Nevertheless, as a minimum, potential users are necessarily concerned with reports which provide the following information:

1. The product's description
2. The product's purpose
3. The intended learners
4. The product's development and testing
5. The product's effectiveness
6. The product's efficiency

Product Description. A potential user of any new instructional product is necessarily concerned with its name, developer, distributor, and physical attributes. From these descriptive characteristics, the user is provided with indicators of how the product is likely to fit into his instructional context. For example, the title of the product might provide the user with a basis for deciding whether or not the subject matter content is relevant to his needs. The product developer could be known for a particular style of instruction that may or may not be of interest (e.g., self-paced or group instruction). If the user has previous knowledge of the distributor, he might be able to assess the likelihood that the product will be delivered on time and in working condition. Finally, the physical attributes of the product, or its medium of instruction, might help the user determine whether or not the product should be purchased. The medium of instruction refers to the component materials such as printed workbooks, films or computers. It is conceivable that two competing products might appear appropriate. To make a choice between them, the user needs information about the physical attributes of the materials to help him clarify equipment requirements for successful product installation and management. For example, procurement and general maintenance of the audio-visual equipment necessary to sustain a film-based instructional product would be an important financial consideration for a district with very limited resources, especially if the competing product consisted of cheaper, printed workbooks.

An illustration of a product description is provided in the following extract from a product report:

Title:	*Evaluation I: An Orientation*
Developer:	Center for the Study of Evaluation, UCLA
Distributor:	CTB McGraw-Hill, Monterey, California
Materials:	*Leader's Manual*
	Conversations Tape
	Participant's Notebook
	Exercise Materials

From a brief product description, it is possible for the user to make certain inferences about the validity of the product for his instructional content. For instance, the title alone suggests that there are probably a series of workshops, but that this first one is intended primarily to orient or direct the student's attention to the broad subject matter area of evaluation. The implication of the title is that other workshops may be used to supplement this one, if necessary. Further, the list of component materials suggests that the product can be used in many settings since the only relatively "hard" medium of instruction is a tape recorder. Thus, by inspection, the report provides the potential user with the type of fundamental information about the product's scope and nature on which he can base decisions about the product's applicability to his instructional context. Of course, an interested user still needs much more information about the product.

The Product's Purpose. Among the first questions asked by potential users about a product is, "What can my students learn from the materials?" Stated another way, the user wants to know what the product's criterion goals and objectives are so that he can determine whether they are congruent with those previously identified as important in his particular instructional context. Thus a product that contains a set of precisely stated objectives is more valuable to the potential user than one that consists only of broad statements of philosophical or instructional intent.

Precise statements of instructional objectives not only permit users to assess whether a product is appropriate, but also enable them to judge the extent to which it can fulfill the requirements of a given instructional situation. For example, suppose a school district wanted to purchase a product that was designed to instruct students to write simple, compound, and complex English sentences. A careful study of a product's objectives might reveal an emphasis on the structure and form of sentences rather than on punctuation. The school might have to consider the purchase of supplementary resources to ensure that all important objectives would be taken into account. Without the specific statement of objectives, the district could not determine the true purpose and utility of the product.

It is important to the user that the product include descriptions of the types of instruments that are used to assess attainment of the criterion objectives in order to know whether he is expected to buy them separately, or rely upon the developer's measures. In addition, it is important to provide information to the user about whether student assessment involves commercially produced tests that can be hand-scored and locally analyzed, or requires machine-scoring facilities. Should student assessment for a given product demand machine-scored tests, it could present an unexpected strain on a district's product management budget.

An excerpt from the user-oriented product report for *Evaluation Workshop I: An Orientation* specifies that the workshop is directed toward two major goals:

1.   Participant understanding of the kinds of information an evaluation can produce for educational decision making.
2.   Participant understanding of the general procedures and problems involved in selecting, collecting, analyzing, and reporting that information.

The report goes on to note that:

The degree to which workshop participants develop such understanding will be indicated by their attainment of the following objectives:

1.   Name, describe, and properly sequence the major evaluation activities.
2.   Identify appropriate data selection, collection, analysis, and reporting procedures for each major evaluation activity.
3.   Identify proper and improper use of evaluation techniques, methodology, and design.
4.   Identify the kinds of information that should be generated by each evaluation activity.
5.   Identify the kinds of information that are needed before evaluation decisions are made.
6.   Identify the specific functions of the evaluator and those of the project director in each evaluation activity.

The product report specifies that a pretest, posttest, and a questionnaire will be given. The multiple choice pre- and posttests, designed to measure cognitive achievement, lend themselves to either hand or machine scoring and analysis. The questionnaire, designed to appraise affect, should be scored by hand.

Sufficient information is provided in the report for the user to make a decision about the congruence between his objectives and the product's, and to determine whether his resources are likely to enable him to profitably employ the measurements.

At this point in the user's knowledge of the product, he can identify what the product aims to achieve, and the means by which that achievement will be appraised. However, he cannot yet be certain that the product will fit into his instructional context because he does not know for whom the product was developed. Clearly, the user needs information about the intended learners.

Intended Learners. An adequate description of the product's intended learners should specify the background characteristics of learners who might be expected to achieve the goals and objectives of instruction, based on the product's success in field tryouts with similar learners. These specifications should include such factors as age, sex, prerequisite knowledge and skills, and socioeconomic status. For example, in a bilingual school district with a large number of Spanish-speaking students, it would be advantageous to know the linguistic demands of a commercially produced social studies product before it is purchased and installed. Similarly, if ethnicity is a serious district concern, it would also be beneficial to determine in advance the relevance of the objectives of different products to the students' cultural interests.

The product report for *Evaluation Workshop I: An Orientation* states that the "ideal" intended learners are school and state department of education personnel. However, the product was also tested on various other types of learners including research and development personnel in educational laboratories and centers. Thus, the product is known to be applicable for this group as well.

Product Development and Testing. The potential user of an instructional product may be tempted to purchase it because of his reaction to the descriptions of the materials, purposes, and intended learners. In fact, it is still standard practice for school personnel to buy educational products on the basis of such information. However, this information does not provide the user with evidence that the product "works," or that it has been developed and tested in such a way as to guarantee its purposes can be attained, assuming its specified procedures are followed. At least two additional types of information must therefore be provided for the user to help him make a sensible choice:

1. An explanation of the procedures actually employed to develop and test the product to make it "work."
2. A review of the empirical evidence that demonstrates the extent to which the product effectively promotes learning.

Explanations of product development and testing provided for users should be convincingly organized to demonstrate that the product has been systematically designed to achieve its purposes in actual instructional situations. Such explanations should not be made equivalent to technical reports or case studies detailing each of the product's historical problems and successes, since this would probably distract, or even confuse, busy school personnel. Instead, these individuals should be given a brief summary of the techniques employed to prepare the product and to assure consistency among its objectives, instruction, and assessments.

Evaluation Workshop I, for example, underwent three phases of product development and testing. The purpose of the first phase, feasibility testing, was to determine whether it could be used in the way it was planned and/or to what extent the plan might be improved. During the second phase of product development and testing, relatively objective test and questionnaire data were gathered to identify whether the product was meeting its objectives. Operational field tests, the third phase of the development, were conducted by the development staff since the intention in this phase was to determine whether the workshop's objectives could be achieved when no longer conducted under the staff's direction. The report described each phase of development and testing, explained the purpose of each, the type of information gathered, and the uses to which that information was put.

The Product's Effectiveness. Once the user has determined whether the product aims at achieving significant goals for students similar to those for whom he is responsible, he wants to know how effectively the product performs. Basically, he needs data about the success of the product. Such data should be displayed and summarized so that it is readily interpretable. For example, three types of data might be provided:

1. The students' average score for each objective. This will provide the user with relatively precise information about the product's success.
2. The number (or percentage) of students who achieve a given objective. This will provide general information.
3. The number of students who achieved all or a given percentage of objectives. This will provide information about the overall success of the product, including some information about the *rate* at which the objectives were achieved.

Another format for presenting information involves supplying average scores and displaying the data in terms of the difference between how well students did from pre- to posttest within different situations, as well as in terms of the number of students whose performance decreased, increased, and remained the same after instruction within and across situations. An illustration of this procedure for

Table 1

Product Test Results for Evaluation Workshop I: An Orientation

	Portland II Oregon	Newport I Calif.	Newport II Calif.	Newport III Calif.	Helena Montana	Cypress Calif.	Beaverton Oregon	Burlingame Calif.	Lubbock Texas	Dover Delaware	Seattle II Wash.	Honolulu Hawaii	
Mean Pretest	14.31	13.35	14.90	14.40	15.22	14.51	14.15	15.77	13.12	15.22	17.40	15.20	14.69
Mean Posttest	17.44	16.77	17.50	17.10	15.92	17.24	16.92	17.81	15.92	17.04	18.73	18.10	17.15
"t" test results	** 3.84	** 5.71	** 3.0	3.5	1.07	** 7.12	** 3.64	** 3.48	*** 9.49	* 2.08	2.09	*** 6.13	*** 12.67
increase	13	23	12	15	12	33	20	20	20	17	10	29	224 (79%)
same	0	1	0	1	3	3	2	5	1	0	2	1	21 (7%)
decrease	3	2	1	6	8	4	4	1	4	6	3	2	44 (14%)

* significant at .05
** significant at .01
*** significant beyond .01

providing information about a product's effectiveness is given in Table 1.

The user of a product report needs the type of data presented in Table 1 to facilitate decisions about the appropriateness of the product for his own instructional context. However, it is important to remember that the user must not be subject to an overload of data or be forced to consult an expert to interpret the results. The information given to the user should be precise enough so that he has a completely accurate idea of the product's success and general enough so that he does not have to spend more time surveying tables than investigating other portions of the report.

It should also be pointed out that data should be given about the product in *the form in which the product is made available to the user*. It is often tempting for the product's producers to offer developmental data to the user as a way of verifying the product's empirical basis. Although such information may make interesting reading, and should be available if the user wants it, it must be remembered that it was originally collected on forms of the product that may bear only a slight relationship to the current version. Thus, it is of little concern to the user that when the product had three instructional components, students averaged 85 percent criterion performance, if the product now has four components.

The Product's Efficiency. The user's concern for the product's efficiency was previously suggested by his need to consider the costs of assessing student achievement by hand- or machine-scored and analyzed tests. In addition to such concerns, the user is interested in determining how efficiently the product can be delivered to the student.

Efficiency considerations require that a commercially developed product should either demonstrably increase the number of students who are successful with the product within a given time period, or drastically reduce the cost of maintaining the current success rate. For example, if 60 percent of all sixth graders in a given district are successful with the current math curriculum, then the district might insist that a new instructional product in math achieve 85 percent student success. Or, if the current 60 percent success rate costs the district $200 a year for each student, then it might demand that the new product achieve the same 60 percent rate of success, but at an annual expenditure of $100 per student. While it is impossible to provide precise cost data for districts in which a product has never been used, it is often feasible to make accurate cost-estimates based on field test and experimental installation of the product in other comparable districts. As additional districts purchase and install a product, more of this kind of information should be made available for developers to compile and present to other potential users as evidence of the product's proven utility.

An additional consideration related to an instructional product's efficiency is its exportability. Potential users can benefit significantly from information about the product's ability to yield reliable student outcomes given specified instructional procedures, but also assuming some inevitable deviations from these procedures in many school situations. The latter circumstance is particularly important because of the rarity with which instructional programs are implemented exactly as planned. Thus, it would be an advantage for the user to have some idea of the product's flexibility prior to its purchase and district-wide installation.

The product report for *Evaluation Workshop I: An Orientation* describes the cost of the product to each user, but does not yet contain comparative information. Arrangements have been made with the distributor to insert it into the report when it becomes available. However, the product's exportability is detailed:

The *Leader's Manual* describes the step-by-step details for organizing and conducting the workshop. It includes the verbal instructions to the participants, provides the leader with the necessary points to cover in discussion periods, and outlines procedural tasks in handling the workshop materials. The comprehensiveness of the manual allows the workshop to be conducted by an individual who is not an expert educational evaluator. The fact that this workshop is "exportable" is further substantiated by its field testing in which the workshop was led by individuals whose training consisted solely of reading the *Leader's Manual* and the accompanying materials.

Various instructional contingencies which could diminish the workshop's exportability are accounted for by reporting:

The tape included in the workshop package contains a series of conversations which form part of the instructional material presented to the participants. The leader may stop or replay the tape at any time in order to clarify points presented in the conversation.

If a tape recorder is not available or if conditions are poor for hearing the tape, the leader can request participants to read the script of each conversation. This method may also help the leader build a greater feeling of participation, especially in a large group. Copies of each script appear in Appendix I in the *Leader's Manual.*

Summary

The potential user of an instructional product is a decision maker who needs a summative evaluation report that can enable him to determine whether the product "fits" into his instructional context. As a minimum, such reports should provide him with:

(1) the name of the product, its developer, distributor, general goal, and physical attributes and costs;

(2) an operational statement of the product's goals and objectives, and a description of the instruments which will be used to measure student achievement;

(3) a description of the background of the learners who can profit from instruction;

(4) an explanation of the procedures actually employed to develop and test the product to make it "work";

(5) a review of the empirical evidence that demonstrates the extent to which the product effectively promotes learning; and

(6) a summary of the evidence that the product is efficient in that it is exportable and/or can facilitate learning in cost effective terms.

User-oriented evaluation reports are essentially descriptive. They do not necessarily detail the rationale behind the selection of the product's goals, or the procedures that were employed to develop or test it. Such information may, however, be necessary for a decision maker's purposes in some instructional contexts. For instance, before adopting a new product, a school board may want evidence that the product was tested under relatively naturalistic, rather than laboratory, conditions. Such formative information should be available as part of the product's public documentary history. However, to ensure that product reports serve their purpose, their focus should be on providing understandable and readily accessible summative evaluation information which can be used in a wide variety of instructional contexts.

User-Oriented Reports—An Exercise

This chapter has specified six minimum components of user-oriented product reports. It has also provided examples of the summative information these components might contain by drawing upon excerpts from the report prepared for *Evaluation Workshop I: An Orientation*. In the following exercise, you will be given an opportunity to determine whether the plans for a user-oriented product report are adequate in that they include a consideration of each of the components.

Practice Exercise

Directions: The following is a description of a plan for a user-oriented product report which contains *five* errors of omission or commission. Your task is to find the errors. List your answers by line number in the appropriate space on the response sheet provided. An example of one of the errors in the plan is given on the Response Sheet on page 115 as a guide to completing the exercise.

Line No.

1   The Center for the Study of American Institutions has developed an
2   educational product designed to teach college students to understand the
3   evolution of the American public school system and the ideas which have
4   guided it. To enable prospective users like curriculum personnel to
5   decide whether the product fits their needs, the developers plan to pre-
6   pare a detailed product report. The report will begin by describing the
7   product's name, developer, distributor, overall goals, and costs. Three
8   tests of student achievement have been developed to measure attainment of
9   the product's objectives. These will be described in detail in the report
10   because two are essay tests and require special scoring procedures, and
11   the product's developers want users to know about them in advance.
12   The developers tested the product on a variety of students including
13   high school students, adults in an extension class, and college students
14   in seminars, on the history of American education. A complete explanation
15   of the product's applicability to each of these types of students will be
16   given in the user report.
17   The developers are also concerned with presenting an accurate demon-
18   stration of their product's success. They intend to provide users with a
19   comprehensive review of the data collected during each of the product's
20   tryouts, although they are aware of the necessity of restricting the number
21   of statistical tables in the report to a reasonable minimum. Because over
22   300 students were involved in the product's tests, the report will therefore
23   be limited only to tables which depict the number of individuals with differ-
24   ent backgrounds who attained each objective for each of the three different

25 versions of the product.
26   Currently, the developers only have estimates of the product's cost
27 efficiency. This information will be included in the first product report,
28 and will be revised when more reliable data are obtained.

See the following page for the **Response Sheet for the Practice Exercise.**

Response Sheet for the Practice Exercise

Line No.   *Errors of Omission and Commission*

7   A description of the product's component materials has not been included in the report plans.

See the following page for **Feedback to Practice Exercise.**

Feedback to Practice Exercise

Line No.	*Errors of Omission and Commission*
7	A description of the product's component materials has not been included in the report plans.
9	The product's objectives should be specified, preferably in measurable terms.
13-16	The report omits an explanation of the product's development and testing procedures. Therefore, it will not be possible to determine the significance, if any, for testing the product on high school students and adults when it is supposedly designed for college students.
17-25	The developers will be providing information on all versions of the product rather than restricting themselves to student achievement information on the final version.
26-28	No information will be provided about exportability.

Suggested Readings

Alkin, M.C. Evaluation theory development. *Evaluation Comment*, 1969, *2* (1), 2-7.

> A general overview and discussion of the Center for the Study of Evaluation's model of educational evaluation. The potential user of educational products will find the sections on implementation, progress, and outcome evaluations especially important.

Baker, E.L. The technology of instruction. In R. Travers (Ed.), *Second handbook of research on teaching*. New York: Rand McNally, 1973.

> This article contains a comprehensive examination of the current state of the field of instructional technology. Potential users of the products of this technology will find the article a clear and detailed explanation of the development process and a valuable guide to the specific types of information to expect and even demand from producers.

Klein, S., Fenstermacher, G., and Alkin, M.C. The Center's changing evaluation model. *Evaluation Comment*, 1971, *2* (4), 9-12.

> A schematic depiction and brief description of the Center for the Study of Evaluation's model of educational evaluation.

Lumsdaine, A.A. Assessing the effectiveness of instructional programs. In R. Glaser (Ed.), *Teaching machines and programed learning, II*. Department of Audio Visual Instruction, National Education Association of the United States, 1965.

> Professor Lumsdaine is concerned with establishing evaluative criteria for assessing the effectiveness of instructional programs. Although his article is meant for the producers of instructional products and behavioral scientists, he also addresses his attention to the "potential user interested in determining the suitability of a given program for his educational purposes."

Schutz, R.E. The nature of educational development. *Journal of Research and Development in Education*, 1970, *1*, 39-62.

> This article is designed to delineate the boundaries of educational development. By drawing distinctions between science and technology, a framework is provided by the author that can guide users in the anticipation of what might be expected of the products of instructional technology.

Scriven, M. The methodology of evaluation. In *Perspectives of curriculum evaluation*. American Educational Research Association Monograph Series on Curriculum Evaluation. Chicago: Rand McNally, 1967.

> Basic reading for anyone who is interested in understanding the goals and roles of evaluation, and their place in the development of educational programs. Professor Scriven details the differences between formative and summative evaluation.

References

Alkin, M.C. A theory of evaluation. CSE Working Paper No. 18, August 1971, Center for the Study of Evaluation, UCLA Graduate School of Education.

Baker, R.L. Measurement considerations in instructional product development. Unpublished manuscript, Southwest Regional Laboratory for Educational Research and Development, Los Alamitos, California, 1972.

Banathy, B.H. *Instructional systems*. Palo Alto, California: Fearon, 1968.

Borg, W.R., and Hood, P. The twenty-seven steps in the development program. Unpublished manuscript, Far West Laboratory for Educational Research and Development, Berkeley, California, 1969.

Briggs, L. *Handbook of procedures for the design of instruction*. Pittsburgh: American Institutes for Research, 1970.

Flanagan, J.C. Functional education for the seventies. *Phi Delta Kappan*, 1967, *49*, 27-32.

Glaser, R. *Organizations for research and development in education*. Paper presented at the AERA conference, 1966. (a)

Glaser, R. Psychological bases for instructional design. *A V Communication Review*, 1966, *14*, 433-449. (b)

Klein, S., Fenstermacher, G., and Alkin, M.C. The Center's changing model of evaluation. *Evaluation Comment*, 1971, *2* (4), 9-12.

Lumsdaine, A.A. Assessing the effectiveness of instructional programs. In R. Glaser (Ed.), *Teaching machines and programed learning, II*. National Education Association of the U.S., 1965, 267-320.

Mager, R.F., and Beach, K.M. *Developing vocational instruction*. Palo Alto, California: Fearon, 1967.

Markle, S.M. Empirical testing of programs. *Programed instruction*. The Sixth Yearbook of the National Society for the Study of Education, Part II. Chicago: University of Chicago Press, 1967, 104-138.

McNeil, J.D. A perspective of developmental projects. Paper presented to the Developmental Project Guidelines Conference, Minneapolis, June 1968.

Schutz, R.E. The nature of educational development. *Journal of Research and Development in Education*, 1970, *1*, 39-62.

Stowe, R.A. *Case studies in instructional development*. Bloomington, Indiana: Laboratory for Educational Development, Indiana University, 1969.

Tyler, L.L., Klein, M.F., and Michael, W.B. *Recommendations for curriculum and instructional materials*. Los Angeles: Tyl Press, 1971.

CHAPTER 5

EVALUATION WITHIN THE CONTEXT OF CURRICULUM DEVELOPMENT AND INSTRUCTIONAL MATERIALS

Louise L. Tyler
University of California at Los Angeles
and
M. Frances Klein
Research and Development Division, IDEA, Inc.

This chapter will discuss recommendations for the development of curriculum materials. These recommendations reflect to some extent the state of the art in curriculum and instruction at the present time. It is obvious that the state of the art is partially a consequence of forces existing in the world. Some of these forces might be the knowledge explosion, current technology, value structures, and political structure.

The title of this chapter has three significant terms, i.e., "recommendations," "curriculum," and "instructional materials," which need elaboration. The decision was made that recommendations was a more appropriate term than technical standards because of the status of knowledge in the fields of curriculum and evaluation. "Recommendations" are statements which specify ideas about curriculum and instructional materials, about which there is considerable consensus. The term "curriculum" has never been defined; workers have been dealing with questions involving four fundamental questions based upon Tyler (1949).

1. What educational purposes-objectives should the school seek to attain?
2. What learning opportunities should be selected so that the desired behavior will emerge?
3. How can the learning elements be structured?
4. How can the effectiveness of the program be evaluated?

It is with the comprehensive conception of curriculum implied in the above questions that these recommendations deal. "Instructional materials" refers to texts, films, filmstrips, laboratory manuals, chemicals, measuring devices, and other such realia.

An important type of document referred to in these recommendations is a technical manual. Standard practice for educational and psychological tests requires that a manual be supplied by the producer which makes available necessary data about the tests. This notion is also desirable and feasible for presenting relevant information about particular curriculum and instructional materials.

Recommendations as a Guide to Producers, Users, and Funding Agencies

These recommendations are intended to guide producers in the development of curricula and instructional materials; consumers in the selection of curricula and instructional materials; and funding agencies in the evaluation of curriculum and instructional projects.

Technical manuals and informative materials are to be judged not merely by their literal truthfulness, but by the impression left with the reader. If the typical prospective user is likely to obtain an inaccurate impression of the curricula and instructional materials, the technical manual or informative material is not clearly written. The spirit and tone of the informative material is to be straightforward and forthright.

A technical manual will communicate information to many different groups. Many curriculum and instructional materials will be selected by schools with personnel who have very limited training in curriculum and evaluation. These users will not follow much technical discussion or statistical information. Other groups will have evaluators and research specialists who are well trained and who will critically study the information presented. The technical manual must include sufficient information so that all groups can make judgments about the adequacy of the curriculum and instructional materials.

Curricula and Instructional Materials to Which These Recommendations Apply

These recommendations cover all published curricula and instructional materials, as well as any materials which pertain to the curricula and instructional materials. More specifically, these recommendations apply to curriculum and instructional materials produced at a local level as well as at a national level, whether by a group of scholars in the disciplines or by a committee at a state university, whether funded by private foundations or governmental organizations.

Levels of Recommendation

Curriculum and instructional materials producers can probably never acquire and present all the information that might be desirable. The educational program involves factors that are changing rapidly. However, information about certain aspects of the curriculum varies in its cruciality for decisions that must be made. Consequently, some recommendations will be designated *Essential,* some *Very Desirable,* others *Desirable.*

The statements listed as *Essential* are intended to represent the consensus of present-day thinking concerning what is normally required for effective production and operational use of the curriculum and materials. The category, *Very Desirable,* indicates statements which contribute greatly to the production and utilization of the materials. The category, *Desirable,* includes statements which would be helpful but are not normally required.

Cautions

Because of the prevailing status of curriculum and instructional materials, it must be remembered that these are recommendations only; they are not hard and fast rules. As knowledge increases in the field, possibly by verification of these recommendations, more certainty may result and technical standards may be formulated.

Rationale Underlying the Recommendations

The recommendations formulated for evaluating curriculum and instructional materials have been grouped in the following categories:

I.   Rationale
II.   Specifications
III. Appropriateness
IV.   Effectiveness
V.   Conditions
VI.   Practicality
VII. Dissemination

Under *Rationale* will be statements concerning several of the basic commonplaces of curriculum and instruction. *Specifications* includes statements that pertain to objectives. In *Appropriateness* are statements concerning the nature of the learner for whom the material is being developed. *Effectiveness* includes statements pertaining to characteristics and conditions necessary for determining impact of curriculum and instruction. *Conditions* includes statements about characteristics, provisions, and procedures necessary if the curriculum or materials are to be utilized. *Practicality* statements pertain to factors basic to use, e.g., cost of materials, building facilities, etc. And, finally, *Dissemination* relates to effective communication practices.

Underlying the recommendations is a stance concerning education in general as well as curriculum, instruction, and evaluation in particular. This stance may be described by the following nine terms: (1) rationality, (2) values, (3) decisions, (4) accountability, (5) significance, (6) comprehensiveness, (7) causation, (8) behaviorism, and (9) knowledge. Each recommendation will be discussed in relation to these terms. First, however, each of these terms will be discussed briefly.

Rationality. The notion of rationality in curriculum and instruction has two components, which have been elaborated upon mainly by Goodlad and Richter, *et al.* (1966). One has to do with "ends-means" decisions, and the second, the use of reason and data. The "ends-means" notion can be stated rather simply as follows: a means cannot be well selected without concern for ends. If a particular textbook is selected, it is because it makes an essential and unique contribution to the attainment of certain specific ends. That reason and data in curriculum and instruction are desirable is based upon the belief that two kinds of modes of investigation are useful and necessary: the theoretical-deductive and the empirical-inductive. In making decisions about ends and means, there are times when reason is utilized and times when data are available and can be utilized and times when both are utilized (Tyler, 1969).

Values. Values permeate all activity: intellectual, professional, personal. Values are manifest in our statements that smoking is undesirable, in the selection of a particular novel for a certain friend, and in judgments about the use of students for manipulation in studies. Some values frequently encountered in curriculum discussions are the importance of developing potentialities of all individuals, respect for the rights of others, and that all individuals are worthy of respect without regard to race, color, creed. These values are basic to decisions about expanding our facilities, our concern about improving education, and the like.

Values consist of both cognitive and affective facets, and it is important that the separation which has occurred between these two be eliminated. The inseparability of cognition and affect has been dealt with by Tyler (1969).

Decisions. The development of curriculum and instructional materials involves a number of decisions about ends and means. What a curriculum decision *is* is not very clear, but some illustrations might be the selection of a particular curriculum, or the selection of a particular textbook or film. Very little theoretical or empirical work has been done on decision making in curriculum; consequently, there is little understanding of the whole process involved in decision making.

Accountability. Underlying these recommendations is the idea that producers and consumers of curriculum and instructional materials must be answerable for the consequences of their production and/or use. When a producer makes claims for either a particular curriculum or textbook, he should be held responsible for providing certain data about effectiveness, just as the school committee must be held answerable for the selection of curriculum and materials for a particular group. The buyer and the consumer must both beware—they must take heed of their products either produced or selected.

Significance. There are some precursors for the need for standards on the part of the American Educational Research Association's Committee on Curriculum Evaluation. This committee has frequently discussed the need for standards, but concluded that the state of the art was such that guidelines could not be formulated. Other workers in the field, having seen some of the Tyler-Klein recommendations, disagree not only with these recommendations, but with the whole notion of recommendations. Others probably concur with Westbury (1970) that these recommendations are atheoretical. However, the recommendations outlined in this chapter are of varying significance. For example, Recommendation R1—"The value of the objectives must be substantiated"—is of more importance than P3—"The technical manual should indicate the necessary facilities and care required."

Comprehensiveness. Because the effectiveness of a curriculum or set of instructional materials is based upon many factors, recommendations must be formulated so that all pertinent variables can be considered. For example, a text used by one teacher in one kind of community setting with a certain kind of student may have a different effect than the same text used by another teacher in another kind of setting with a different kind of student.

Causation. Implicit in these recommendations is a belief that if certain effects occur they are a consequence of transactions between individuals and environmental conditions. This is, of course, more familiarly thought of as the cause-effect notion. This notion underlies much scholarly investigation.

Behaviorism. Underlying many of these recommendations is a notion simply labeled as behaviorism. It has many meanings, but only two will be commented upon here. The school, as an institution, is partially responsible for the kind of student who emerges, and therefore deals with the behavior of the student involved in the educative process. The term behavioral in this sense means the student's thoughts, feelings, and actions. Unfortunately, many criticisms have been raised about a behavioral orientation in education on the basis that the concern is only about overt behavior and/or that inner meaning (thoughts) are not behavior. This is erroneous. A second meaning of the term behavioral has to do with the study of human behavior and includes the concepts and methods from areas of knowledge which investigate or reflect upon human behavior. Some of these areas are psychology, economics, and sociology. Both meanings of the term are used by the authors of this chapter.

Knowledge. The notion that decisions should be based upon knowledge is implicit in these recommendations. Curriculum and instructional materials must be based upon the most accurate knowledge we have at the present time of all the factors involved. A few examples may suffice. When the knowledge in the field of physics changes, the instructional materials must reflect these changes. As the school's clientele changes in the sense of the knowledge and attitudes that are brought to the school, these characteristics must be known and considered by the producers and consumers of curriculum and instructional materials.

Recommendations and Their Justification

Rationale

R1. The value of the objectives must be substantiated.

Essential

(Comment: The producer should present documentation about the value of the objectives formulated. For example, what is the basis for thinking that objectives having to do with understanding the structure of the disciplines are important? However, even though the producer may present documentation for the importance of the objectives, it does not necessarily follow that the consumer will arrive at the same judgment.)

There are several reasons for this recommendation. First, if the producer is required to substantiate the value of the objectives, it is more likely that this will result in the development of curricula and materials which are concerned with *significant* objectives. The consumer will profit from this substantiation because it will facilitate the selection of curriculum and instructional materials which are consistent with the values held by the consumer and incidentally may be persuasive enough so that the consumer changes his objectives. Lastly, if a wise selection is to be made, the consumer must know the reasoning behind the selection of particular objectives. For example, what is the reasoning behind the formulation of objectives having to do with understanding the structure of the disciplines? This objective may be based upon a lack of data. Recommendation R1 is predicated upon the notions of rationality, values, decisions, accountability, significance, and knowledge.

R2. The source from which the objectives are derived must be indicated. *Very Desirable*

(Comment: This recommendation emerges from Tyler's rationale [1949] of curriculum development. In that rationale, Tyler indicates objectives can be obtained from studies of the learner, society, and subject matter. Furthermore, they must be screened by philosophy and psychology. Tyler also indicates the inadequacies of each source, or of using only one source.)

This recommendation requires that the source of the objectives must be given, that is, whether the objectives were derived from the learner, society, subject matter, all three sources, or combinations of two. The consumer must have this information so that he can select materials which are appropriate to his group of learners. This recommendation is based upon rationality, values, accountability, and significance.

R3. The basis for the selection of the content of the curriculum and instructional materials must be described. *Essential*

(Comment: The developer or producer should explain on what basis content was selected. For example, on what grounds were topics of time, space, matter, light, and motion, selected as basic components of a textbook?)

The basis for this recommendation is similar to that of R1, that is, if the producer must substantiate the basis upon which content is selected, more significant content will be selected. A producer having to think through the basis for selection of content will select better content. Similarly, a description of the basis upon which content was selected makes it possible for the consumer to more wisely select materials appropriate for a particular group of learners. Values, rationality, accountability, decisions, and significance are involved here.

R4. The selection of organizing elements must be described.

Essential

(Comment: In some instructional materials, statements are made that they are organized around unifying themes or skills. For example, the B.S.C.S. material is built around themes such as change in living things, the genetic continuity of life; *Science—A Process Approach* is built around skills of observation, classification, etc. In any case, the selection of these elements must be explicated. Why are the particular themes and skills chosen, and how do these themes or skills appear over the span of the program?)

This recommendation requires that the producer make apparent the basis upon which organizing elements have been selected. Have the organizing elements been selected on the basis of behavior alone, or content alone? Making clear the basis of selection will facilitate the selection of significant elements by the producer. Furthermore, this information is necessary so that a consumer can select materials wisely. Rationality, values, accountability, and significance underlie this recommendation.

R5. Learning opportunities should be directly related to the behavior and content of the specified objectives.

Essential

(Comment: Inspection of learning opportunities, e.g., films, texts, activities, can be done in order to make some judgments about appropriateness. For example, if the objective were to develop the ability to formulate problems in biology, and the laboratory manual was so written that the problems always are given to the student some questions could be raised as to whether the learning opportunities are appropriate for the objective. If experts have been used to judge whether the learning opportunities are appropriate, the bases on which their judgments were made should be described. For example, it is possible that the objectives of a program could be classified according to the taxonomies of Bloom [1956], Krathwohl, Bloom, and Masia [1964], and Simpson [1966-67]. Then, the learning opportunities could be analyzed and related back to the objectives.)

This is a recommendation based upon logical considerations that the means should be related directly to the ends. For example, if a programmed instruction sequence has been developed, it would seem to be essential that the frames be related to the objectives. More specifically, if the objectives involve application of principles, the frames in a program should stimulate the application of principles. In addition, the relationship of learning opportunities to each other must be considered; for example, the relationship of a programmed instruction sequence to a textbook or film. Primarily, this recommendation is based upon rationality, decisions, comprehensiveness, and knowledge.

R6. Learning opportunities must be arranged so that the
behavior of the student is developed.   *Essential*

(Comment: The belief is held that for the development of behaviors, opportunity to interact with learning opportunities at appropriate levels of complexity is required. This may be particularly true for the higher level objectives in the taxonomy [Bloom, 1956]. Analysis of the learning opportunities in this manner would be useful.)

This recommendation is based upon the common sense notion that most significant changes in behavior do not occur as a consequence of a few encounters. Rather, there need to be frequent exposures to appropriate learning opportunities. This recommendation relates to reason, causation, and some knowledge from the field of learning.

R7. The kind of evaluation strategy used in developing the
instructional materials must be reported.   *Essential*

(Comment: Evaluation has an impact on what students learn. Consequently, if evaluation has been used as a systematic aspect of the instructional development process, this must be reported. Sufficient information is appearing about the influence of evaluation on instruction that its use must be made clear.)

This recommendation is based upon knowledge and causation.

This knowledge suggests that evaluation used throughout a curriculum project influences the outcome. Therefore, the nature of the evaluation used must be described so that the outcomes are understood. Furthermore, the consumer would need to utilize evaluation in a similar fashion. Another way of stating this is that evaluation is an intervention strategy and influences student outcomes as well as teacher behavior.

R8. An evaluation package should be built in.   *Essential*
(Comment: This evaluation kit would make explicit the objectives and present evaluation devices appropriate to the curriculum and materials.)

These authors believe that evaluation is an integral part of the curriculum and instructional process. It is unlikely that the average teacher has skills adequate for developing valid and reliable tests for particular curricula or materials; therefore, evaluation kits are an essential part of a curriculum-materials package. This recommendation is based upon notions of rationality, accountability, and knowledge.

Specifications

S1. The technical manual should state in detail the objec-
     tives.   *Essential*
(Comment: The objectives are so basic to adequate selection and use of the materials that they must be stated explicitly and in detail.) This recommendation is based upon experience of product researchers along with our strong convictions that the stating of objectives in detail facilitates the development of curriculum and materials. Also, specification of objectives is necessary so that the consumer can select curriculum and materials which are appropriate for particular situations with certain clientele. Recommendation S1 is based primarily upon knowledge, rationality, accountability, and comprehensiveness.

S2. Objectives should be specified operationally, i.e., behav-
     ioral responses of students.   *Essential*
(Comment: Behavior is broadly defined as thoughts, feelings, and/or actions of the student. The objectives can be exemplified by describing the evaluation devices which are regarded as appropriate.)

This recommendation is based upon the argument that schools are for the purpose of educating students and that it is their behavior (thought, feeling, and action) which is to be the focus of concern. Only as a clear conception of learner's behavior can be formulated can it become possible to effectively develop curriculum and instructional materials which can then be empirically evaluated. These authors believe that objectives must be stated differently for various curricular purposes. To develop programmed instruction it may be useful to state objectives as Mager (1962) suggests. However, to be stating objectives in this form for writing a book might be of little value, and stating objectives for classroom interaction in this manner is undoubtedly impossible. This recommendation is based upon rationality, account-ability, behaviorism, and knowledge.

S3.   Objectives should be consistent with each other.

Desirable

(Comment: It would appear that objectives should be consistent with each other if the curriculum and materials are to have a maximum effect. Also, there should be consistency from one content area to another, if appropriate. The difficulty lies in determining what is meant by consistency. If at one time one topic of the curriculum or materials is emphasizing the value of cultural norms, it may be inconsistent to later emphasize the value of diversity.)

Underlying this recommendation is the belief that consistency is necessary if learners are going to consolidate gains in behavior over a period of time. Objectives that are contradictory would logically result in conflicting behavior. If a student is to develop critical thinking skills in science, it seems necessary that critical thinking skills also be an essential part of curriculum in other curriculum areas, such as social studies and humanities. On a smaller scale, if a curriculum is developing inquiry skills in social studies, all content areas of the course must be viewed this way—our government is not exempt. This recommendation is based upon rationality, decisions, knowledge, and behaviorism.

Appropriateness

A1.   The kind of student for whom the curriculum and instructional materials are designed should be specified.

Essential

(Comment: Characteristics such as age, sex, prerequisite skills, and socioeconomic class are to be reported.)

Curricula and materials are most effectively designed if characteristics of the learner are specified. Information should include age, cultural background, prerequisite skills, etc. This information is also necessary so that the consumer can select materials appropriate for his particular learner. This recommendation draws upon notions of rationality, behaviorism, accountability, and knowledge.

A2. The curriculum and instructional materials should be
     revised at appropriate intervals.   *Essential*
(Comment: Changes can occur in subject matter and in the nature of students' abilities and interests which make revision of curriculum and instructional materials essential. For example, in some subject areas such as biology, the knowledge and methodology are changing rapidly, therefore, curriculum and instructional materials must reflect these changes.)

This recommendation is based primarily upon two notions. First, the knowledge explosion requires that materials be revised so that new knowledge is immediately available. Second, students are changing too; culture influences the attitudes and skill which students bring to school. These must be determined and materials revised so that they are appropriate to the changing student populations. Notions of knowledge and behaviorism are basic to this recommendation. Rationality, decisions, and comprehensiveness also apply.

Effectiveness

E1. Technical manuals should cite sources of available
     evidence to document any claims made about effective-
     ness and efficiency.   *Essential*
(Comment: These sources should include not only the projects' studies, but evidence from other carefully documented studies. Studies done to evaluate the programs should be described in a straightforward manner.)

Underlying this recommendation exists the belief that evidence is necessary so that consumers can make wise choices, and, of course, producers' efficiency will be improved. This recommendation is based upon notions of rationality, values, behaviorism, accountability, and comprehensiveness.

E2. Technical manuals should clearly distinguish between kinds of evidence presented about effectiveness: (a) internal evidence, (b) external evidence.   *Essential*

(Comment: Internal refers to features that can be revealed through visual inspection and study of the materials. External refers to tryouts, revisions, etc.)

This recommendation is based upon rationality, behaviorism, accountability, comprehensiveness, and knowledge. The point of view that is taken is that there are various types of evidence which are necessary. For example, content analysis of a curriculum's objectives according to the taxonomies would be useful. Also, a content analysis of instructional materials according to the taxonomies could be done. In addition, however, such things as author's qualifications, the data of their tryouts and revisions, should be reported. Both internal and external evidence is essential.

E3. Evaluation should be utilized when appropriate in the process of instructional development. Also, evaluation should be used when materials are in final form.

                                                        Essential

(Comment: This relates to the notion of formative and summative evaluation. Both are important and if formative evaluation has been utilized in the process of curriculum development, it also must be reported as a part of the curriculum development.)

The notion that has long existed that evaluation is an integral part of curriculum and material development is basic to this recommendation. It has been discussed by Scriven (1967) in terms of formative and summative evaluation. It is particularly important that if evaluation has been utilized in the development of materials, this be described— because of the fact that this factor has probably influenced the results in the tryout situations. The same conditions should exist when the materials are being utilized. Rationality, behaviorism, accountability, and comprehensiveness underlie this recommendation.

E4. Effectiveness of programs should be reported in terms of program objectives as well as unintended outcomes.

                                                        Essential

(Comment: Curriculum developers are expected to report studies which are related directly to stated program objectives. In addition, however, there are other important objectives, possibly not stated, about which the consumer would be interested and information should be reported on such objectives. For example, projects may report on acquisition of knowledge and application of principles, but neglect data regarding interest. Also, the kinds of attitudes which exist in students who decide to participate in particular curricular projects may be significant. Or, in some cases, projects may be concerned about understanding the nature and structure of the discipline, but what about a consumer's interest in acquisition of information? Various kinds of evidence and how it was obtained should be reported.)

That there are unintended outcomes of instruction has long been known in education, but that they need to be reported so that a consumer may make decisions of selection in light of unintended as well as intended outcomes has not been so well articulated. There probably should be data about a minimum set of outcomes that should be reported regardless of stated program objectives. Some such might be knowledge, interests, attitudes, and critical skills. Underlying this recommendation are the notions of rationality, values, behaviorism, comprehensiveness, accountability, and knowledge.

E5. Curriculum and instructional materials should be evaluated in relation to different types of students, e.g. intellectual level, sex, age, and socioeconomic level.

Essential

(Comment: Producers of curriculum and instructional materials have an obligation to describe the nature of the students upon whom the materials were developed and tested. It cannot be assumed that curriculum and instructional materials adequately developed for upper-middle-class children will be effective with lower-class children. A caution is needed here. It is possible that curriculum or materials may be developed just for a particular group, e.g., mentally retarded; however, in this case comparisons need not be made to a "normal" population. Even in this instance, though, important characteristics of the group should be investigated and reported.) Rationality, behaviorism, and accountability are basic to this recommendation.

E6. Curriculum and instructional materials should be evaluated in relation to the context in which they are being
utilized.   *Desirable*

(Comment: The outcomes of an instructional program are
partially dependent upon such factors as teacher attitudes, parental
support, and climate. These factors must be considered in evaluating
curriculum and materials in their development and selection.)

Effectiveness of materials is based upon factors other than the
materials themselves. For example, teacher attitudes toward the
material, the objectives, etc., will influence the attainment of the
objectives of the program. Materials tried out in situations with teachers
who are knowledgeable, skillful, and accepting of inquiry objectives
may be less successful when used in situations with teachers who are
less knowledgeable and skillful and who disapprove of inquiry
objectives. Rationality, behaviorism, and comprehensiveness are germane to this recommendation.

Conditions

C1. The technical manual must indicate the qualifications of
the teacher which are required for using the materials
effectively.   *Essential*

(Comment: Many of the newer curriculum and instructional
materials require student investigation. Teachers accustomed to didactic
approaches may not have the necessary skills. Many teachers are
accustomed to telling, not to encouraging students to explore and
investigate.)

As indicated in E5 and E6, many factors determine the effectiveness of materials, e.g., students' abilities, parental support,
climate, but the teachers' attitudes and skills are of great significance. A school district may decide not to use a particular curriculum or set of instructional materials because the teachers do
not possess the required skills, or the district may plan an in-
service program for the faculty so that the materials can be used.
Basic to this recommendation are accountability, comprehensiveness, behaviorism, and knowledge.

C2. If the teaching personnel do not possess the behaviors required for using the materials, some provision must be made. This may take the form of a teacher training package. *Desirable*

This recommendation is based upon the belief that teachers are members of a professional staff and that they are continuous learners, which will make it possible to acquire skills and understandings. Rationality, accountability, behaviorism, and knowledge are notions underlying this recommendation.

C3. The technical manual must describe in detail the kinds of behavior which the teacher is to utilize.

Desirable

(Comment: Materials may require behaviors of teachers quite different from those which they now possess—these must be described so that the curriculum and materials can be effectively utilized.)

If a curriculum or set of materials is based upon the student developing inquiry skills, and the teacher's behavior is essential, this behavior must be described so that the teacher can adequately utilize the materials with the proper verbal interaction. This recommendation is based upon rationality, accountability, behaviorism, and comprehensiveness.

C4. Procedures and arrangements of utilizing the materials for defined samples of students—including procedures for administering the evaluation devices— must be specified. *Essential*

(Comment: The condition necessary for implementing the curriculum must be specified. If the stated objectives of the curriculum involve the process of inquiry, this undoubtedly requires a longer block of time than 30 minutes per week.)

Basic to this recommendation is the knowledge that the effectiveness of curriculum and instructional materials is dependent upon a number of factors—not just the materials. Rationality, comprehensiveness, accountability, also underlie this recommendation.

Practicality

P1. The technical manual should indicate which instructional materials are required and whether any of
the instructional materials can be reused.   *Essential*

(Comment: It is important that consumers be able to determine readily what a particular package is going to cost. If supplementary materials are to be used, these also should be described,
along with statements of initial maintenance cost.)

This recommendation is based upon the belief that it must
be clear what the cost of the curriculum and materials will be to
the district and to the student. Accountability and comprehensiveness are the two notions underlying this recommendation.

P2. The technical manual should indicate what may be
involved in teacher training.   *Desirable*

(Comment: If teacher education is required, the kind of
training necessary as well as estimated costs should be indicated.)

It is necessary to provide this information so that a school
district can decide whether to utilize the curriculum or materials
and what might be required for the teachers. Rationality, accountability, comprehensiveness, and knowledge are relevant to
this recommendation.

P3. The technical manual should indicate the necessary
facilities and care required.   *Desirable*

(Comment: If special facilities are required, such as care of
animals, these must be indicated.)

Schools must know what will be involved in the upkeep of
the materials or facilities. For example, a particular school might
not be able to care for laboratory animals over weekends. Knowledge, accountability, and rationality are relevant to this recommendation.

Dissemination

D1. Provisions should be made for continued dissemination of new materials, new approaches, and new
studies.   *Very Desirable*

(Comment: As supplementary texts are developed and/or new evaluation studies done, this information must be published.)

While materials may have been adequately tried out with particular groups and found satisfactory, the clientele changes and the materials may no longer be adequate. For example, eight-year-olds know more now about missiles than such pupils did 10 years ago. Rationality, accountability, and knowledge are basic to this recommendation.

D2. Appropriate channels and means to reach concerned audiences, e.g., researchers, school personnel, lay public, should be utilized.   *Desirable*

(Comment: Technical reports could appear in professional journals for researchers and school personnel. Less technical reports might be prepared for popular consumption. This information could be made available in book or television format.

This recommendation is based upon notions of accountability, values, and knowledge. All groups concerned with education must be adequately informed.

Conclusions

It is doubtful that any curriculum or set of instructional materials will meet all recommendations. However, every educator must be aware of these recommendations and what is involved in making judgments if this material is not made available. Development of curriculum and instructional materials as well as selection of them must be done on some rational basis.

As is abundantly clear, most of the recommendations are not based upon empirical grounds in a narrow sense. Rather, what seems to be involved is a combination of reason and data interwoven with value judgments about various aspects of the topic. The lack of thorough scholarly work suggests many areas for further investigation.

Suggested Readings

American Educational Research Association. AERA Monograph Series on Curriculum Evaluation, 1967, 1-7.

    A series of monographs written to facilitate the development of a methodology for the evaluation of educational programs. Issues are devoted to such topics as perspectives on evaluation, evaluation activities of curriculum projects, and classroom observations.

American Educational Research Association. *Review of Educational Research*, Educational evaluation, April 1970, *40* (2).

    An issue which offers some critical reviews of some of the important work done in evaluation. Includes chapters on politics and research and public policy which are infrequently encountered.

American Psychological Association, Joint Committee on Test Standards, APA, AERA-NCME. *Standards for educational and psychological tests and manuals*. Washington, D.C.: APA, 1966.

    A series of recommendations to assist producers and users of tests to make wise decisions about test development and reporting.

Goodlad, J.I., Von Stoephasius, R., and Klein, M.F. *The changing school curriculum*. New York: Fund for the Advancement of Education, 1966.

    A report of the analysis of some recently developed curriculum materials. Includes a description of projects and a discussion of problems and issues pertaining to aims and objectives, organization, evaluation, and instruction.

Travers, R.M. (Ed.) *Second handbook of research on teaching*. Chicago: Rand McNally, 1973.

    A handbook of ideas on topics and issues related to teaching. Chapters on social and political forces, technology of instructional development, and educational technology are of particular value for those interested in the development of instructional materials. Chapters 5-17 are particularly pertinent.

References

Bloom, B.S. (Ed.) *Taxonomy of educational objectives, Handbook I: Cognitive domain*. New York: Longmans Green, 1956.

Goodlad, J.I., with Richter, M.N., Jr. *The development of a conceptual system for dealing with problems of curriculum and instruction.* Report of an inquiry. U.S.O.E., U.S. Department of HEW. Contract No. SAE-8024, Project No. 454, 1966.

Krathwohl, D., Bloom, B.S., and Masia, B. *Taxonomy of educational objectives, Handbook II: Affective domain.* New York: David McKay, 1964.

Mager, R.P. *Preparing instructional objectives.* Palo Alto: Fearon, 1962.

Scriven, M. The methodology of evaluation. In R. Tyler, R. Gagne, and M. Scriven, *Perspectives of curriculum evaluation.* AERA Monograph Series on Curriculum Evaluation, 1967, No. 1.

Simpson, E.J. The classification of educational objectives, psychomotor domain. *Illinois Teacher of Home Economics*, Winter 1966-67, *10*, 110-44.

Tyler, L.L. A case history: Formulation of objectives from a psycho-analytic framework. In W.J. Popham, E. Eisner, H.J. Sullivan, and L.L. Tyler, *Instructional objectives.* AERA Monograph Series on Curriculum Evaluation, 1969, No. 3.

Tyler, L.L. Inner meaning and outer behavior. *Curriculum Theory Network,* Monograph Supplement. Toronto, Canada. O.I.S.E., 1971, 53-59.

Tyler, R.W. Basic principles of curriculum and instruction. Chicago: The University of Chicago Press, 1949.

Westbury, Ian. Curriculum evaluation. *Review of Educational Research, Educational Evaluation.* Washington, D.C.: AERA, April 1970.

Choosing a Plan . . .

PART TWO: MODELS AND STRATEGIES

Part Two

INTRODUCTION TO MODELS AND STRATEGIES

A model is a methodological tool used to guide and focus inquiry. Many different types of models exist and the uses to which they are put vary. For the mathematician, chemist, or physicist, for example, a model is a precise tool often technical in nature used to study a well-defined and often minuscule event, as in analyzing the results of an experiment. For the evaluator it is often a general plan or guide used to study a not so well-defined and often large and complex event, as in evaluating educational programs and products. The following chapters introduce specific models for evaluating educational programs and products. Before turning to these chapters, it is important to consider the nature of models in general as they are used to observe and seek knowledge about a variety of events.

Models, particularly those used in the sciences, have at least three identifiable characteristics. They are *precise*, which means that elaborate forms of measurement are usually devised to describe the phenomena of interest and that the model is basically quantitative in nature. Second, they are *specific*, which means that the model deals with only a select number of phenomena, purposefully avoiding complex summary or aggregate characteristics of an event. Third, they are *verifiable*, which means that hypotheses are posed to check the precision of the model, i.e., empirical evidence is accumulated that eventually determines the model's accuracy and usefulness. Scientists and evaluators have over the years constructed many different models, all of which have these characteristics to varying degrees.

Three different types of models can be constructed. The first of these is an iconic model, which may take the form of either a large- or small-scale representation of the "real thing." Iconic models look like what they represent and take the form of small-scale replicas, for example, of a new downtown office building. A second type of model that can be constructed is the analog model, which uses one property to represent another. A thermometer is one such example in that temperature (one property) is measured indirectly by the height of mercury (another property). The height of mercury, therefore, is used as a model—or analog—of temperature. A third type of model is a symbolic model, which describes properties in coded—usually mathematical—terms. The psychologist Kurt Lewin, for example, used a symbolic model for describing behavior so that observations such as "the child chose the toy he liked best" could be expressed with such symbolic formulae as $F_pG_1 > F_pG_2$, meaning the child liked goal 1 (G_1) better ($>$) than goal 2 (G_2) and that personality characteristics (p) of the child could account for his behavior. This symbolic process uses a type of mathematics called typology that Lewin felt could accurately model human behavior.

Common sense will tell us, however, that we often use less sophisticated models in everyday life. For example, when traveling about the country, we employ a road map that is, in effect, a model of the geographic region in which we are traveling. The road map is of most help when it is (a) *precise* (i.e., drawn in equal units, e.g., miles); (b) *specific* (i.e., deals with detailed portions of the environment); and (c) *verified* (i.e., authorized or constructed by sources with proper credentials in map making). To the extent that it is not precise, specific, or verified, the map is of less use as a model. With a map, we are usually less concerned with whether it is iconic, analog, or symbolic than we are with whether or not it will get us from point of departure to point of destination. Nevertheless, a common sense model such as this often employs many iconic, analog, and symbolic characteristics.

Models for educational evaluation are neither strictly iconic, analog, or symbolic, but rather are often a combination of all three and map-like in purpose. While evaluators strive to construct models that are precise, specific, and verifiable, the end result often falls short of that which can be expected in the sciences. Much of the discrepancy between a model in evaluation and a model in science, however, is by design and not chance. Because of the complexity of events the evaluator must describe, he is usually cautious about using a model that is too specific to a particular set of phenomena. Even though the evaluator attempts to be precise, there are often so many inputs at work in a given program or product that it is difficult to describe all of them with a great deal of precision. Also, in contrast to the scientist, the evaluator usually spends much less time verifying his model than he spends using it. Much like the traveler who finds that a soiled and outdated map has gotten him successfully to his destination, the evaluator sees his model as a means to an end; if it works reasonably well in achieving that end, the evaluator rarely takes the time to document the effectiveness of the tool that got him there.

The following chapters are presented in the spirit that the effectiveness of some models can and should be documented. If models are carefully developed and illustrated, evaluators can choose to stay true to a particular model to test its effectiveness and to record discrepancies between the model and events as they occur in the real world. So few models for evaluators have ever appeared publicly that it has been difficult for others to judge their adequacy or suggest revisions even when they were thought necessary. One purpose of the following chapters is to expose selected models to diverse applications in the hope that further cycles of improvement and refinement can be undertaken. To the extent that they become more *precise, specific,* and *verifiable,* evaluation models will more closely approximate the utility and accuracy of scientific models.

It is important to draw several distinctions between *general* and *specific* evaluation models. While both general and specific models are important to evaluation, specific models have proliferated for the purpose of circumventing several disadvantages of using more general models such as those posed by Provus (1971), Stake (1967), and Stufflebeam *et al.* (1971). Such general models, while helpful to an evaluator in establishing a general perspective toward his task, often yield special problems in later stages of evaluation by:

(1) not covering in sufficient detail specific dimensions relevant to a particular context. (Because these models must be

applicable to a variety of settings, they do not focus on the unique characteristics of any one setting.)

(2) lacking specification of strategies, i.e., how to describe, monitor, examine, and analyze when these activities are suggested by the general model. (While such terms are commonplace in descriptions of general models, it is the overall perspective that is important rather than the methodology of specific activities posed by the models. Therefore, one is left to find other guides for methods of implementing the general model.)

(3) being applicable to so many different contexts that claims for its success usually vary considerably. (Because such models are purported to be as applicable to a health education product as to a physics curriculum, for example, the contexts in which these models are applied are often not considered as integral components to their success or failure.)

On the other hand, general models generate important and universal evaluation concepts (e.g., Stufflebeam's "context," Stake's "transaction," Provus' "discrepancy"), are usually applicable to many contexts, and use language sufficiently general so that they may be employed by a diversity of users.

Several general models have received a great deal of use and popularity. These models and the purposes for which they were constructed should not be confused with the models that appear in the following chapters. The models that follow have been constructed specifically to avoid problems inherent in more general models, particularly their lack of specificity for a particular context.

It has become increasingly important, due to the construction and utilization of many different kinds of evaluation models, to attempt to interrelate concepts either specific or general that run across different models. The field of educational evaluation has been increasingly complicated in past years by the growth and development of many evaluation models. Some of these models may only confuse evaluators by suggesting different approaches and by using diverse terminologies purported to be applicable to the same kinds of problems. While the evaluator can, of course, choose only one model or a combination of models, it is important to the development of evaluation that concepts in one model be related to concepts in others. The reader's primary aim in studying the following chapters should be to interrelate evaluation concepts and to note when discrepancies between the same concept appear for different models. These, then, are important intersections where models must be expanded and clarified in order to be of greatest use, i.e., precise, specific, and verifiable. Interrelationships across models presented in the following section appear in a table at the conclusion of this introduction. The reader is challenged to extend the entries in the table and to clarify any ambiguities that may exist within it.

About the Chapters

The authors contributing to this section are evaluators who deal on a day-to-day basis with practical problems in program and product evaluation. These chapters differ somewhat from others in this volume in that they are meant to be specific guides to be implemented, not propositions or general concepts. In this spirit, the authors present their models as directly as possible. In some cases, chapters take the form of extended outlines from which the reader can, in a step-by-step fashion, follow the implementation of a model. In other cases, case study material is included to illustrate application of the model in the setting for which it was designed. Tabular headings, sequenced steps, charts, and graphs are the major vehicles which these authors employ for explaining practical concepts in such a manner that their models can, by reference to these chapters, be implemented true to form without ambiguity of process or procedure.

In the first chapter in this section, William J. Wright and Robert J. Hess present a criteria acquisition model for educational product advancement. Their model addresses a recurrent problem in educational development, that of balancing potential information available against the information needs of the decision maker. The model takes into account a number of variables that can offset this balance as the product moves through stages of the development cycle. The authors contend that, because different information about a product is needed at each stage of development, different sets of performance criteria are required; their model indicates what these criteria should be. Wright and Hess provide a detailed explanation of five stages of product evaluation, five classes of criteria that need to be considered at each stage, and five different audiences that must be considered in developing and evaluating an educational product. Their chapter ends with an extensive summary table illustrating the complexity of the evaluation effort as it is depicted by the model.

Charles L. Bertram and Robert D. Childers, in the next chapter, illustrate a seven-step process for planning, developing, and diffusing educational products. Their model focuses on three stages of a product development strategy. These stages are:

(1) *product design and engineering*, in which evaluation activities detail a plan for the evaluation of a product, specify a set of measurement procedures and instruments to determine the product's effectiveness, and determine the criteria used for assessing the effectiveness of the product in meeting performance objectives;

(2) *field testing*, in which measurement procedures are revised and validated, the product is tested in a large-scale educational setting, and formal evaluation reports document the result; and

(3) *operational testing*, in which the product is diffused and monitored during its use in selected demonstration sites.

During implementation of the model, major evaluation activities include *goal refinement and formulation, organization of measurement procedures, data collection*, and *analysis and reporting*, each of which is described and illustrated by the authors. Of particular note are discussions of how an evaluation unit functions within an educational development organization. Administrative and organizational concerns are discussed alongside specific evaluative procedures and the interrelationship between these two functions is focused upon when these functions can enhance or jeopardize the evaluation effort.

In the following chapter in this section, Chapter 8, Douglas S. Katz and Robert L. Morgan present a systems approach to the formative evaluation of educational programs which they call their *holistic* model. The chapter examines the interrelationship between the organizational system which might give birth to an educational program and the policy makers and program administrators that guide an agency's mission to produce desired products and processes. The chapter clarifies such often used words as *mandate, policy*, and *mission*, and places them within a strategy that clarifies their distinctions and commonalities. The authors conclude the chapter by applying their model in case study fashion to indicate how human and material resources can be used to guide the modification of educational programs in their formative state. Readers who are in need of placing formative evaluation activities within the context of state and local agencies will find the authors' systems approach valuable.

Chapters 9 and 10 should be read consecutively, as both deal with the concept of quality assurance. Chapter 9 applies the concept to large-scale research and development, and Chapter 10 applies the concept to the formative evaluation process. Quality assurance for both of these chapters refers to the process by which the quality of a program or product is certified before it is summatively evaluated.

Jerry P. Walker, in Chapter 9, presents a quality assurance model devoted to assessing internal decision events in a research and development setting. Walker's chapter sets out specific criteria for the acceptability of a successful quality assurance model and relates these criteria to individuals within the R & D setting who may be responsible for them. Walker's chapter, while setting forth a sequence of events that can be used as a model, focuses upon the criteria on which all quality assurance models must be based. Readers who are interested in generating new process strategies and activities need to consult Walker's criteria for an effective quality assurance model. Walker, as do all the authors in this section, discusses the interrelationship between specific criteria for program and product advancement and the individuals in a development setting who must be responsible for these criteria.

In a related chapter (Chapter 10), Max Luft, Janice Lujan, and Katherine A. Bemis present a quality assurance model for process evaluation that may be considered a substage to any of our more general evaluation models. In step-by-step fashion, the authors delineate 11 activities that comprise a process evaluation sequence that begins with determining pretest behavior and ends with constructing graphs for reporting the relationship between process and performance outcomes. Readers will find of particular interest their examples of observation schedules for process evaluation.

References

Provus, M. *Discrepancy evaluation for educational program improvement and assessment*. Berkeley, California: McCutchan, 1971.

Stake, R.E. The countenance of educational evaluation. *Teacher's College Record*, 1967, *68*, 523-540.

Stufflebeam, D.L., Foley, W.J., Gephart, W.J., Guba, E.G., Hammond, R.I., Merriman, H.O., and Provus, M.M. *Educational evaluation and decision making*. Itasca, Illinois: F.E. Peacock, 1971.

Summary of Evaluation Models Presented in Part Three

	Wright and Hess	Bertram and Childers	Katz and Morgan	Walker	Luft, Lujan and Bemis
Model Characteristics	Criteria Acquisition and Product Advancement Model	Multistage Model for Evaluating Educational Products	Holistic Model for Formative Evaluation	Quality Assurance Model for Educational Research and Development	Quality Assurance Model for Process Evaluation
Purpose	To provide a strategy for deciding when a product is ready to move to the next stage of the development process	To delineate activities for the evaluator and developer during product planning, development, and diffusion	To provide a framework for the formative evaluation of educational programs taking into account systems and subsystems affecting the development process	To provide a procedure for making explicit information-based decisions as to the validity of the developer's claims, i.e., to reduce uncertainty about the program or product	To maximize terminal behaviors posited for an educational program by assuring full implementation of planned processes
Procedure	Assessing the degree to which the product attains prespecified criteria for each of five stages in the development process	Obtaining and providing evaluative data for judging decision alternatives concerning revision and adoption of products	Determining congruencies, e.g., between mission and desired outcomes, and between desired outcomes and actual processes	Testing intentions (claims) against reality (evidence) as a means of achieving incremental trial and revision	Utilizing a project management system to monitor program implementation
Stages	1. Initiation 2. Hot house 3. Pilot test 4. Field test 5. Public diffusion	1. Needs assessment 2. Feasibility analysis 3. Program planning 4. Product design and engineering 5. Field testing 6. Operational testing 7. Dissemination and implementa-	Determining: 1. congruency within processes and products 2. congruency between processes and products 3. discrepancies between desired and actual processes and prod-	1. Identification and selection of decision events 2. Monitoring program/product development 3. Conducting decision event review 4. Deciding upon alternatives	1. Identify teacher and student entry and terminal behavior 2. Construct observation schedules 3. Conduct observations 4. Relate teacher behavior to student per-

Unique Contribution	Stages of evaluation by audiences (professionals, consumers, developers, managers, sponsors) and domains of criteria (desirability, feasibility, effectiveness, usability, generalizability)	Sequence of activities delineating evaluator-developer responsibilities in product design and testing	Role of external systems and pre-developmental activities in program development	Qualitative as opposed to quantitative process for reviewing program and product development	Procedure for interrelating teacher and student behavior
Evaluator's Decision-making Responsibility	Deciding whether the product stands up to claims made for it, that there are no adverse consequences from it, and that sufficient data exist to allow consumers to make informed adoption decisions	Deciding the degree to which the product meets intermediate and long-range performance objectives and whether or not consumers can effectively implement the product	Deciding upon program modification when incongruities exist	Deciding with program personnel and project director which decision alternatives to pursue	Deciding whether the program is fully implemented, i.e., teacher behavior is goal directed, not random
Evaluator's Role	To assist in establishing criteria, to construct evaluation designs, to establish a working relationship with developer	To provide product development teams and sponsor with information concerning product effectiveness and usability	To recommend program modifications and interventions and to conduct evaluations to assess their effectiveness	To act upon reports and recommendations of the decision event review team	To administer pre- and postassessments, construct and implement teacher observation schedules
Advantages and Limitations	Comprehensive delineation of evaluator's responsibilities during product development but time consuming if the model is fully implemented	Specific delineation of evaluator's role during product development (stages 4-6) but very broad focus on evaluator's role in planning and diffusion (stages 1-3, 7)	Comprehensive as a guide for planning formative evaluations but general in regard to methods and techniques	A quick and economical means of reviewing product and program development but depends upon the knowledge and objectivity of a small number of decision event reviewers	Relates program implementation to student performance but utilizes classroom observation and coding systems that could be costly to validate and implement

CHAPTER 6

A CRITERIA ACQUISITION MODEL FOR EDUCATIONAL PRODUCT EVALUATION

William J. Wright and Robert J. Hess
CEMREL, Inc.

Within the recent past the evaluation of curriculum innovation has become a matter of ever-increasing importance. The advent of large curriculum development projects, such as the Physical Science Study Committee, the School Mathematics Study Group, and others, as well as the establishment of federally funded centers for educational research and development and national education laboratories, has served to focus considerable attention on the need for systematic and comprehensive evaluation. The evaluation of educational products is still a new field, however, and definitive guidelines and standards for its conduct have yet to emerge.

In this chapter, one model for the evaluation of educational products is presented. The central notion of the model is that there are discernible evaluation stages in the life of educational products, and that it is possible to specify criteria that ought to be met before the product is advanced to the next stage of development. Product is an ambiguous term in the sense that it might refer to a curriculum package intended to serve as the basis for 10 or 15 hours of instruction concerned with a concept in aesthetics or it might refer to a set of materials, workbooks, and teacher guides intended to serve as the basis for a third-grade mathematics program. Clearly there is no single evaluation system equally applicable to such diverse entities. In many instances we are guilty no doubt of oversimplifying the complex realities involved in pragmatic decision-making situations. In the interest of providing a model with wide applicability, however, an idealized case has been assumed. This model may require adaptation to be of value in the context of a specific product.

One can treat the model as a three-dimensional configuration in which the dimensions are stages of evaluation, audiences for the evaluation, and domains of evaluative criteria. We will first define and discuss the meaning of these dimensions; then illustrate how the model might be employed; and, finally, examine the implications of this approach with respect to the practice of evaluation and its potential utility.

Stages of Development and Evaluation

There are many ways one can section the process of developing an educational product from the time one determines in some way that a need exists to the time something is made available to the public. The stages to be delineated are points at which evaluation occurs. There are, in this conception, five such stages.

Initiation stage. A general specification of what the curriculum project intends to do, how it is to be done, and for whom it is to be done.

Hot house. The initial tryout of a prototype product, typically in one or two classrooms with teachers who have a continuing relationship with the program.

Pilot test. A systematic, small-scale trial of the revised product, generally in proximate school systems. The teachers of these classrooms have access to staff and resources not expected to be available to eventual users.

Field test. An extended use of the ultimate or penultimate product in sites removed from the development institution; the program development staff serves no mediating role; the product is "on its own."

Public diffusion. The life of a product within the host institution has ended, the product is commercially published in large quantity and is made available to interested consumers.

In dealing with any real product, development must be a more flexible process. Certain material may require recycling through parts of the process; other material may need only a truncated portion of the sequence due to the limited goals held for the product. It is useful, however, to identify a delimited set of stages.

Each stage in the development/evaluation sequence represents a relatively easily identified milestone in the life of a curriculum product. Moreover, the entry of a product into a given stage can be viewed as a decision point. If a product lacks certain characteristics or has failed to meet certain criteria required for entry into the next stage, one can terminate or recycle the product.

The Audiences of Evaluation

In addition to identifying the stages of product development, it is necessary to characterize the various audiences for the information acquired by evaluative activities. The audiences we have identified fall into five general categories.

The sponsor. Within this category are the public and private support organizations who provide the financial resources necessary for development: the National Institute of Education, state departments of education, foundations, and the like. The major interests of these parties are perceived to be the identification of educational needs and the monitoring of development activities to insure that the products will have substantial impact in the natural setting of the schools within an established time limitation. The major decision made by the sponsor is whether or not to fund or continue funding a development effort.

Institutional management. The organization allocating resources to the development program is represented by its officers and officials. The major concern of these individuals is insuring that the management and direction of the project are fundamentally sound, and that the work undertaken is in accord with the established contracts and mission of the institution. This group also has a vested interest in the quality control of products developed under its auspices. The central administration of educational laboratories and research and development centers and their boards of directors would fall into this classification.

The developer. The developer, usually the project staff director, is the person with the greatest variety and breadth of decision-making accountability. It is his duty to make the fundamental decisions concerning project goals, means of achieving them, allocation of resources within the project, product sequencing, etc. In a single mission or a small organization the developer and the institution might be equivalent.

Consumer representatives. This group is made up of those who will eventually use the products or be immediately affected by their use—superintendents, principals, teachers, students, parents, and the community to which the schools are responsible. The preeminent concerns within this category are cost issues, pupil outcomes, and teacher usability.

Representatives of the professions. Many product development institutions make use of advisory groups comprised of prominent individuals within the discipline or domain with which that program's products are concerned. They serve to aid the developer in the specification of goals and means, and to periodically review the work in progress, using intrinsic evaluative criteria. Some institutions have, in addition, an advisory group concerned with evaluation. These groups are typically comprised of prominent methodologists and researchers who review the procedures used to evaluate products and suggest alternative approaches. Their major interest is the assurance that adequate precautions have been taken to promote quality products through the collection of valid, reliable information about their use and effects.

The Criteria Domains

There are a great many questions one can ask about any new educational product in order to reach some decision about its worth. Imposing structure on this array of questions requires a procrustean approach, yet it does seem that these questions fall within five general domains, and that a comprehensive evaluation must attend to each of these domains. Within each domain is a set of questions one can ask about a new educational product. One can then think of the criteria that must be met before a product advances to the next stage as answers to these questions. These domains are:

Desirability. Issues of interest within this domain are concerned with the establishment of a sound rationale for the commitment of the resources necessary to fulfill a consumer need of recognizable import. In many respects this is simply the first step one takes in responsible product development.

Feasibility. Issues of interest in this domain are related to questions of management, cost, and alternative development possibilities. Typically, the concerns are administrative efficiency and resource allocation.

Product effectiveness. The criteria within this domain are related to the specification of the nature of the product and assessments of the effects of product use.

Usability. Within this domain one is typically concerned about the use made of the product by different samples of the target population so as to identify and characterize implementation strategies of known worth.

Generalizability. In this domain, one is asking questions about the quality of the evidence presented concerning the product's value and possible new applications for the product.

Matrix Representation

One can represent the model as a three-dimensional matrix with stages of development and evaluation, audiences of evaluation, and criteria domains as the dimensions, as shown in Figure 1. One of the benefits of this representation is that it clearly shows that it is the interface between product stages that constitute the major milestones or decision points in the life of a product.

In Figure 1, for example, we have emphasized the line between the initiation and the hot house stages. Before a product could advance to the hot house stage it would have to satisfy the appropriate criteria at the initiation stage.

Illustrative Criteria

Although the range of questions that one might ask about a product is almost limitless, it is possible to identify a series of questions for each of the criteria domains that illustrate how one might use the model to design an evaluation. Tables 1 to 5 (in the Appendix to this chapter), contain questions that fall within each of the domains of criteria juxtaposed to the development and evaluation stages. Within each cell of these two-dimensional matrices, criteria have been specified to show how the nature of the evidence required for a satisfactory answer to a given question changes during development of the product. The audience to whom that evidence is most appropriate is also noted.

As noted above, it is the stages of development and evaluation that constitute the major milestones or decision points in the life of a product. According to the extent to which a product meets the criteria established for it at a given stage, it would be advanced, revised,

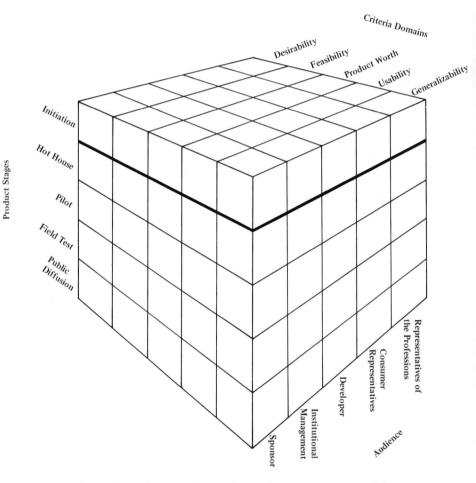

*Figure 1. A Three Dimensional Representation of the
Evaluation System Elements.*

recycled, or terminated. Deciding how much weight is to be applied to any criterion is, of course, a product-specific decision.

To illustrate the way in which this manner of thinking about evaluation might be of use, let us consider one criterion domain, product effectiveness, and examine the evidence that would be required at each of the first three stages of development and evaluation according to the illustrative criteria shown in Table 3 in the Appendix to this chapter. In actual practice one should attend to the criteria within all domains before reaching a product advancement decision.

Initiation stage. Before product development begins, two criteria ought to be met: (1) the goals that the product is intended to meet should be known; and (2) if there are anticipated longitudinal effects, these should be identified. The argument for the inclusion of the first criterion is obvious. One ought not to begin development without some idea of what he hopes to accomplish and he certainly should not be funded to develop a product without goals. The argument for the second criterion relates to cost factors. It usually entails more money to develop and evaluate products presumed to have cumulative or longitudinal effects, as opposed to immediate effects, because one is required to follow the subjects over some period of years. Therefore, this information should be known prior to initiation so that potential sponsors can examine the costs in terms of their own priorities.

Note that the issue of whether the goals are worth attaining or intrinsically valuable is not dealt with in the product effectiveness domain. The reader is referred to Table 1 in the Appendix, the Desirability Domain, for several illustrative questions concerned with this issue.

The hot house stage. After development of the product has begun, and before its first trial use, there are several illustrative criteria specified:

The first criterion is that the objectives be stated in terms that permit observation of their accomplishment. It is not necessary to specify in detail the expected outcomes of product use, at least not at this stage. Nonetheless, the evaluator must have an idea of what the foci of his observation should be so that the development of appropriate data collection instruments and techniques can be initiated.

The second criterion is that there should be evidence of the content validity of the measures to be used in the hot house trials. Before the hot house trial begins, one should make an effort to insure that the observation, recording, and/or measurement procedures to be used are indeed related to the goals of the product developer. This process usually involves three activities—discussions with the developer, review of the literature, and review by specialists in the discipline of the product.

The third criterion is approval by advisors of the general evaluation strategy. Some time prior to the hot house stage, an advisory group ought to review and approve the intended evaluation. This procedure is a check and balance to insure that, insofar as possible, the evaluator is attending to the proper concerns and is using the available resources efficiently.

The fourth criterion is the establishment of some methodology for identifying deviations from instructional procedures specified by the developer. The implementation of a new product varies greatly from class to class. Some teachers install it in rigid adherence to the suggestions of the developer. Other teachers merely use the new material, and continue to instruct in the same way that they always have. For this reason, one must collect data, in a systematic fashion, about the manner in which the product is implemented in the classroom. The first step in the evolution of a recording system for alternative procedural options is establishing the methodology to be used in the hot house trial to discover deviations from intended practice, e.g., classroom observation, student or teacher logs, questionnaires.

The fifth criterion is the specification of the prerequisite variables of interest and the selection of instruments with appropriate properties to measure these variables. In this first product trial it is usually good practice to acquire information about the participants with respect to their status on variables that might be related to the efficacy of the treatment. One should learn of the possibility that the product is differentially effective with different classes of subjects as early as possible. In later studies it may then be possible to limit the premeasures used to those which are of known value in predicting pupil achievement.

The sixth criterion is the inclusion of some means for the discovery of unanticipated consequences. If an observation system is used to attend to the implementation issue, one might use the same approach here, i.e., the observer is not limited to one function. It is important that a wide angle view of product effects is adopted. It is entirely too easy to develop a product that accomplishes its primary goal well but has unfortunate side effects, e.g., the children learn to dislike school or the subject being taught.

The reader will note that no criterion is included for the illustrative question, "Are there important longitudinal effects?" at this stage. The hot house (and the pilot) schools usually have a close relationship to the developer, and it is unwise to begin a longitudinal study in an atypical site. Moreover, one should defer longitudinal studies until the product is in a more final form.

Assuming that the six criteria have been met, as well as the criteria within other domains, then the hot house trial should take place. In practice, of course, one cannot afford to delay a trial because of what is viewed as a less than critical criterion. The advantage of identifying the criteria which ought to apply beforehand rests in the fact that one can then make deliberate judgments about the relative importance of the criteria.

The Pilot Stage. After the hot house trial, several events presumably take place. The product is revised in light of the information gained in the hot house trial or it is abandoned. More precise research tools are developed for use in later trials. Assuming that a pilot trial is planned, more polished prototypes of the intended product are prepared for use in that trial. What criteria might be applied before one decides to proceed with a pilot test?

The first criterion is that the objectives are stated in more precise terms and related to observable phenomena. After the experience of the hot house trial, one should be able to identify the outcomes the product is expected to promote in terms of observable events such that an independent witness could determine whether or not they had occurred. There is no need for restrictive statements that fit neatly into known methodologies of measurement. Emphasis should be upon measurement, however crude, of one's real goals. The improvement of measurement practices is as likely to flow from this emphasis as is an increase in the meaningfulness of research and evaluation studies.

The second criterion is that the data collection instruments and techniques are revised based on the experiences of the hot house trial. As the product matures, so should the procedures and material used to evaluate it. It is perhaps unfair to insist that the means of data collection used in the hot house trial be demonstrably objective and reliable, but certainly as a consequence of that use, and other subsidiary efforts, the instruments and procedures to be used should acquire these characteristics by the time of the pilot study.

The third set of illustrative criteria relates to whether or not the objectives of the product are being met. First, there should be some indication that the postulated outcomes were achieved during the hot house trials. This evidence may be somewhat indefinite, in that the assessment techniques are usually being used for the first time, the product is new, and the situation is atypical. Nonetheless, there ought to be some indication that the product holds promise before one commits resources for a pilot trial. Otherwise the product should either be abandoned or revised for a second hot house trial.

The nature of the evidence about product effectiveness should become more precise and definite over time. For this reason the second criterion related to the illustrative question is that an experimental, or quasi-experimental, design is established for the pilot trial (Campbell and Stanley, 1963; Stufflebeam, 1971). At the conclusion of the pilot test, one should be able to attend to the question of whether the objectives are being met, at least in part, by means of hypothesis tests.

The next illustrative question—are there different effects from alternative procedural options?—also results in two criteria at this stage of the development and evaluation cycle. The first criterion is that deviations from the recommended procedures that took place in the hot house trial are appropriately identified and classified. By keeping careful track of the ways in which the product is used, one can begin to identify alternative recommendations and to specify the means of recording and appraising degree of implementation. This specification constitutes the second criterion. The argument, once again, is that the tools of evaluation must mature with the product.

If the hot house trials indicate that there are differences in the achievement of individual students seemingly related to their status on some pre-experiment measure, then two events should occur: the important variables should be identified and used as premeasures in future trials, and the experimental design should feature the investigation of the importance of the premeasures. These conditions constitute criteria for the pilot stage.

Again, there are no criteria associated with the question of longitudinal effects at this stage of the development and evaluation cycle. The site is atypical, and the product is usually not yet close enough to its final form.

The last illustrative criterion for this stage of the model is that of unanticipated consequences. Paralleling the criteria for degree of implementation and alternative procedural options, one wants to insure that findings are built from earlier investigations into future research, and that the development of the evaluation procedures proceeds along with product development.

Hopefully, illustrative criteria in the product effectiveness domain depict that it is possible to identify criteria that (1) pertain to specific questions within one of the domains, (2) evolve over the developmental life of the product, and (3) permit one to make decisions about the progress of a product through the development cycle by considering whether or not criteria for a given stage have been met.

Role of the Project Evaluator

Usually when a product is being developed there is an individual, or a group of individuals, designated as the project evaluator, or evaluation staff. These individuals normally have extensive interactions with the development staff. Over a long period of time they work together with the developers to obtain information about the product and its effects.

There are those on the development staff who view evaluation as a meaningless exercise. They hold that the purchasers of educational products usually do not consider any evidence other than their own perceptions of the product and perhaps the opinions of a select group of colleagues. Why, then, expend resources that could be spent on product development for evaluation? For this group, evaluation is the price you pay in order to obtain a sponsor for the product.

For some others, evaluation is useful only insofar as it focuses on the presentation of evidence which will help to convince others that the development effort has succeeded. These individuals usually do not admit that the product in question may be flawed and, therefore, view as a betrayal any attempt to seriously examine its worth from a more independent stance.

Still others want the evaluator to focus on obtaining specific evidence that would be of great help to the developers, but may be of little value to any potential consumer. The variety of expectations about the evaluator's function can range all the way to those who view him as a fifth column for the consumer. For this last group, the evaluator is someone who is able to adopt an independent and "objective" stance while working on a day-to-day basis with those whose work he evaluates.

Even with the professional evaluation community there is ongoing debate as to whether the function of evaluation is principally utilitarian or judgmental. Some argue that the evaluator merely collects information upon which others may, or may not, base a decision (Astin and Panos, 1971; Guba and Stufflebeam, 1968). Others hold that it is the job of the evaluator to render a judgment about the worth of something in comparison to its potential competitors (Glass, 1970).

It is doubtful that any system or approach to evaluation can entirely eliminate the conflict that may, in fact, be an integral part of the role of the project evaluator. Yet, that conflict can be minimized. If the criteria on which decisions about the continuance of the product are stated in unambiguous terms prior to the collection of evidence, then several events can occur to reduce conflict. First, arguments about the criteria relevant for a given product can take place among several different parties, including notably the sponsor, and not just between developer and evaluator. Second, an evaluation plan that is incomplete because it does not attend to significant aspects of a product can be expanded or modified before major evaluations take place. And, finally, the developer and the evaluator can establish a more harmonious relationship based on the fact that the evaluation represents protection for the project. The developer knows from which quarter attacks are likely to come and, therefore, supports the efforts of the evaluator to discover a product's weaknesses so that it can be revised.

It is, of course, impossible to completely specify all of the criteria for every development stage at the beginning of a project. It should, however, be possible to identify in detail the criteria that will be used during the next stage. As the project proceeds, it should be possible to flesh out the criteria so as to inform relevant audiences of one's intentions well in advance of a given trial.

Summative Evaluation as Consumer Protection
Typically, evaluation ceases when the product enters the diffusion stage. At this point the product is presumably finished and, while revision in the form of a second edition is possible or even probable, the product as it stands is available to the public. It is undoubtedly

considered by those responsible for its development as something distinct and meritorious, and is promoted as such by them. Indeed, they may have firm grounds for so doing, assuming that evaluations up to this point have been well conducted.

Yet, regardless of how thoroughly accomplished it might be, evaluation done in-house, while the product is still in development, is somewhat suspect. The dangers of co-option and vested interests on the part of a project evaluator are very real. For that reason, at some point in time evaluation must be externally conducted.

The salient characteristic of summative evaluation at the end of product development might be conceived of as consumer protection. Drug companies, for example, tout the virtues of their patent medicines on the basis of their own research, some of which is unquestionably sound. Yet the intelligent consumer relies on other sources for his information. The reports of the Food and Drug Administration, for example, inform him that the product has met certain standards. Reports of the Consumer's Union and other similar groups provide him with comparison data on certain frequently used classes of drugs. For more precise information, he may rely on a physician who has access to specialized data sources and is presumed competent to interpret them.

The formal mechanisms for consumer protection that exist for educational products are inadequate. The work of Oscar K. Buros (1965) in the testing field is a notable exception, and the work of the Educational Products Information Exchange (E.P.I.E.) is a step in the right direction. Nonetheless, a far more comprehensive process is needed—the benefits from which will be worth the admittedly high cost.

A three-tiered process may be needed wherein:

1. the product developer establishes the criteria in conjunction with the funding agency and other interested parties and formatively evaluates his product in those terms;
2. some private agency or center, or less desirably, one established by the federal government, examines the product to insure that:
   a. it does indeed stand up to the claims made for it (the truth in advertising issue);
   b. there are no aversive consequences from use (for example, the thalidomide or withdrawal effects discussed by Weiss [1971]); and

    c.   that a conscientious, external evaluation is conducted and reported so that the intelligent consumer can make informed adoption decisions; and

3.   local education agencies should establish regional institutions whose function it would be to determine the worth of given products for their own population of students. (By combining resources in this way, the necessary technical expertise and capability could be acquired at a minimal cost to individual school systems.)

The Issue of Pluralism

One argument that has been made against this system, and others like it, is that it smacks of an industrial approach to education. One perceived danger is that the application of such a system would result in a less pluralistic society. Such would not be the case. Pluralism does not result from the random interaction of haphazard forces; but from deliberate decision. The alternatives that exist in education came about because various individuals and groups felt the need for something qualitatively different from that which was available and set out to create something to meet their own criteria.

Indeed, by using a system requiring the *a priori* specification of criteria, one promotes pluralism. Hopefully, funding agencies would not find themselves sponsoring more of the same development programs, but rather would focus on fundamentally different alternatives. Two of the critical questions one can ask of a new product are "To what extent is it distinctive?" and "Is that which is distinctive, meritorious?" A criterion acquisition before advancement approach would seem to facilitate the search for answers to these questions.

It must, on the other hand, be acknowledged that pluralism is best promoted when those who desire alternatives have access to resources at least proportional to their number. How best to bring about such a situation is an extremely complex political and economic question beyond the scope of this chapter.

Utility of the Procedure

The specification of criteria in the manner proposed is an involved and time-consuming task. Is it worth the effort? Do the anticipated beneficial consequences warrant the expenditures? In order to experimentally investigate the question, one would need to compare the results of two attempts to generate similar products, one of which used this approach and the other of which did not, while controlling other variables such as the quality of the personnel, the facilities, etc. Such a study would cost an enormous amount of money. It is also perhaps impossible to carry out. Yet, it may be worth the gamble if at its conclusion there is a chance that one would have evidence with respect to the worth of evaluation, or at least, of evaluation as described here. It may well be time to determine empirically whether or not evaluation itself is worth its costs, both in terms of dollars and the effort it requires.

In the absence of such an investigation, however, a case can be made for the use of this or a similar procedure on pragmatic grounds. Perhaps the most frequent complaint of product developers is that in order to continue their work, they are subject to frequent reviews, site visitations, annual reports, and the like. These events are disruptive in the sense that the principal mission of the program must be abandoned momentarily while preparations are made to meet the needs of the sponsoring agency. As someone has put it, in order to see if the rose is growing, you pull it from the soil and examine its roots at least once a week. We doubt that many would argue seriously that the sponsor is not entitled to investigate the progress of funded projects. What is needed, however, is a mechanism for insuring that the investigation attends to the right issues and does not serve merely to generate anxiety.

If we can view the developmental and evaluation stages as milestones in the life of a product, then it is possible to specify a procedure for reviews that might be minimally disruptive. Given the product specifications of the developer, the expected milestones within a calendar period (e.g., one hot house and one pilot trial in a calendar year), and the criteria for advancement for the given product stages, it should be possible for the sponsor to examine merely the discrepancies between anticipated and actual milestone accomplishment in order to determine whether the developer's efforts are worthy of continued support.

One could, moreover, use the criteria postulated to determine whether the "fit" between the plans of the developer and the perceived needs of the sponsor was sufficient to warrant funding in the first place. The general goals might be similar, but if, for example, the developer would weight very highly criteria related to student affective consequences and he plans to develop a product which requires teacher reeducation, whereas the sponsor perceives the need, in this discipline, for a product that is low cost, can be used by teachers without special training, and emphasizes cognitive outcomes, then a lack of fit exists and negotiation must lead to resolution or to the rejection of the proposal. The advantage is that once criteria are specified and agreed to, the efforts of the developer must be judged on those terms, not on some arbitrary fluctuating grounds.

In terms of the operation of a project, the specifications of the criteria should promote more appropriate research and evaluation. There is no justification for collecting information irrelevant to the decision-making process. Unless one is aware of the criteria for decision making, however, the collection of the relevant information is at best haphazard. Evaluating the evaluator is possible only if one knows what the evaluator's responsibilities really are (Scriven, 1971).

In the final analysis, one might state that the purpose of this approach to evaluation is improved communication, and that its utility rests in the necessity for this communication. If evaluation at all levels is to become more precise and valuable, as it must, then all those who are involved in or affected by educational evaluation need to better understand each other's information requirements. The value of this approach to evaluation can be determined, then, by whether or not its use facilitates that understanding.

Suggested Readings

Cronbach, L.J. Course improvement through evaluation. *Teachers College Record*, 1963, *64*, 672-683.
Scriven, M. The methodology for evaluation. *Perspectives of curriculum evaluation: AERA monograph series on curriculum evaluation.* Chicago: Rand McNally, 1967, 39-83.

> Of all attempts of the last decade to define what evaluation is and how it is accomplished, these two papers stand alone in terms of the influence they have had on evaluation practice. They are important reading for anyone who wants to understand the foundations on which current evaluation concepts have been built.

Glass, G.V. The growth of evaluation methodology. Research Paper No.

27. Boulder, Colorado: Laboratory of Educational Research, University of Colorado, 1970.

This paper contains a cogent and comprehensive discussion of what is labeled here the judgmental conception of evaluation.

Smith, L.M. The microethnography of the classroom. Occasional Paper No. 1, St. Louis: CEMREL, Inc., 1966.

Smith, L.M., and Geoffrey, W. *The complexities of an urban classroom: An analysis toward a general theory of teaching.* New York: Holt, Rinehart and Winston, 1968.

Although not written from the standpoint of curriculum evaluation, the above readings are important for those concerned with the use of classroom observation techniques as an aid in the evaluation of innovative curricula.

Taylor, P.A., and Cowley, D.M. *Readings in curriculum evaluation.* Dubuque, Iowa: William C. Brown, 1972.

This book includes the articles by Cronbach and Scriven recommended above, as well as an impressive array of other important documents on evaluation. It presents as complete a review of the field as could be contained in a single volume.

References

Astin, A.W., and Panos, R.J. The evaluation of educational programs. In R.L. Thorndike (Ed.), *Educational measurement.* Washington, D.C.: American Council on Education, 1971.

Buros, O.K. *The sixth mental measurements yearbook.* Highland Park, New Jersey: Gryphon, 1965.

Campbell, D.T., and Stanley, J.C. Experimental and quasi-experimental designs for research on teaching. In N.L. Gage (Ed.), *Handbook of research on teaching.* Chicago: Rand McNally, 1963.

Glass, G.V. The growth of evaluation methodology. Research Paper No. 27. Boulder, Colorado: Laboratory of Educational Research, University of Colorado, 1970.

Guba, E.G., and Stufflebeam, D.L. Evaluation: The process of stimulating, aiding, and abetting insightful action. An address delivered at the Second National Symposium for Professors of Educational Research, Boulder, Colorado, November 21, 1968.

Scriven, M. Who evaluates the evaluators. 1971.

Stufflebeam, D.L. The use of experimental design in educational evaluation. *Journal of Educational Measurement,* 1971, *8* (4), 267-274.

Weiss, J. Formative curriculum evaluation: In need of methodology. Paper presented at the AERA Annual Conference, New York City, February 1971.

Appendix
to Chapter 6

Table 1

Desirability Domain

ILLUSTRATIVE QUESTIONS	CRITERIA:	Initiation CRITERIA:
A. What are the unmet needs of the schools?	Specification via a literature review—consultation with subject matter specialists AUDIENCE: Institution, Sponsor	
B. Is this problem a high priority issue?	1. Commonly identified problem in the literature 2. Identified as such by public representatives (e.g., congressional committee) AUDIENCE: Institution, Sponsor	
C. Are there products available or in development which might be adapted to this purpose?	Substantive specialists serving as advisors state that new development is needed AUDIENCE: Institution, Sponsor, Developer	
D. What type of product is necessary to fill the need?	Acceptance by substantive advisors of developer's proposed products AUDIENCE: Institution, Sponsor	Products monitored by substantive advisors AUDIENCE: Institution, Sponsor
E. Identification of target population	Target population identified by developer and accepted by sponsor AUDIENCE: Substantive Advisors	Selection of target population sample by evaluator AUDIENCE: Developer, Institution

Table 1

Desirability Domain
(continued)

Pilot	Field Test	Public Diffusion
CRITERIA:	CRITERIA:	CRITERIA:
Products monitored by substantive advisors AUDIENCE: Institution, Sponsor	Products monitored by substantive advisors AUDIENCE: Institution, Sponsor	
1. Evidence that Hot House population could use product AUDIENCE: Institution, Developer 2. Adequacy of sampling procedures for pilot stage established AUDIENCE: Evaluation Advisors, Institution, Developer	1. Evidence that pilot target population could use product AUDIENCE: Institution, Developer 2. Adequacy of sampling procedures for field test established AUDIENCE: Evaluation Advisors, Institution, Developer	

Table 2

Feasibility Domain

ILLUSTRATIVE QUESTIONS	CRITERIA: (Initiation)	CRITERIA: (Hot House)
A. Has a schedule been established/is it being met?	Approval of schedule established by developer AUDIENCE: Sponsor, Institution	Milestone review (projected vs. actual accomplishments) AUDIENCE: Sponsor, Institution
B. Are there sufficient resources?	1. Approval of developer's budget request by sponsor AUDIENCE: Sponsor, Institution 2. Availability of necessary personnel AUDIENCE: Substantive Advisors	1. Actual costs are in line with projected budget (milestone review) AUDIENCE: Sponsor, Institution 2. Staff is adequate for the task AUDIENCE: Substantive Advisors
C. Are potential consumer costs reasonable? (Within this category one must consider such costs as: installation, training, replacement, maintenance, etc., as well as the cost of first product purchase.)	Evidence from developer that projected product costs can be met by those serving target population AUDIENCE: Sponsor, Institution	Product unit costs for first version are within specified range AUDIENCE: Institution, Sponsor
D. Are alternative, less costly, versions of the product possible?	Identification of options that are sufficiently reduced in cost to be worth testing AUDIENCE: Developer, Sponsor, Institution	Reduced cost options characterized as usable in intended population AUDIENCE: Developer, Institution, Substantive Advisors
E. Are there opportunity costs?		

Table 2

Feasibility Domain
(continued)

	Pilot	Field Test	Public Diffusion
	CRITERIA:	**CRITERIA:**	**CRITERIA:**
	Milestone review (projected vs. actual accomplishments) AUDIENCE: Sponsor, Institution	Milestone review (projected vs. actual accomplishments) AUDIENCE: Sponsor, Institution	Milestone review (projected vs. actual accomplishments AUDIENCE: Sponsor, Institution
	1. Actual costs are in line with projected budget (milestone review) AUDIENCE: Sponsor, Institution 2. Staff is adequate for the task AUDIENCE: Substantive Advisors	1. Actual costs are in line with projected budget (milestone review) AUDIENCE: Sponsor, Institution 2. Staff is adequate for the task AUDIENCE: Substantive Advisors	Contract with publisher to produce in quantity AUDIENCE: Sponsor, Consumer, Representatives
	Product unit costs for Pilot version are within specified range AUDIENCE: Institution, Sponsor, Consumer, Representatives	Purchase of product by Field Test sites in sufficient quantity to insure "large-scale" test AUDIENCE: Institution, Sponsor, Consumer Representatives	1. Marketability established by experience of diffusion staff in locating Field Test sites 2. "Critical Comparison" of product with alternative approaches to same ends designed and ready for implementation by external summative evaluator AUDIENCE: Institution, Sponsor, Consumer, Representatives
	Selection of the cost option(s) most worthy of development by comparison of alternatives in Hot House AUDIENCE: Developer, Institution, Sponsor, Substantive Advisors	Specification of product to be used in Field Trials based on comparison of any remaining cost alternatives in Pilot AUDIENCE: Developer, Institution, Sponsor, Substantive Advisors	
		If the use of the new product requires the elimination of some other discipline or activity from the curriculum, identification of elements omitted and of possible consequences AUDIENCE: Sponsor, Consumer Representatives	Identification of what is eliminated in the field. Evidence of the consequences of eliminating elements predicated on the basis of pilot tests AUDIENCE: Sponsor, Consumer Representatives

Table 3

Product Effectiveness Domain

ILLUSTRATIVE QUESTIONS	Initiation — CRITERIA:	Hot House — CRITERIA:
A. Are the objectives clearly stated?	Specification of the goals which the product is intended to accomplish	Objectives stated in terms which permit observation of accomplishment
	AUDIENCE: Substantive Advisors, Sponsor, Institution	AUDIENCE: Evaluation and Substantive Advisors
B. Is there a sound rationale for the measures used?		Evidence of content validity of evaluation procedures to be used in the hot house trial
		AUDIENCE: Substantive and Evaluation Advisors, Developer
C. Are the objectives being met?		Approval by evaluation advisors of general assessment strategy
		AUDIENCE: Evaluation Advisors, Sponsor, Institution, Developer
D. Are there different effects from alternative procedural options (e.g., degree of implementation effects)?		Establishment of some methodology for identifying deviations from instructional procedures specified by the developer (e.g., observation schedules, questionnaires, etc.)
		AUDIENCE: Developer, Substantive and Evaluation Advisors

Table 3

Product Effectiveness Domain
(continued)

	Pilot	Field Test	Public Diffusion
	CRITERIA:	CRITERIA:	CRITERIA:
Objectives: stated in more precise terms, related to observable phenomena AUDIENCE: Evaluation and Substantive Advisors			
Revision of data collection instruments or techniques AUDIENCE: Developer, Institution, Evaluation and Substantive Advisors	Evidence that measurement techniques have desired psychometric properties AUDIENCE: Developer, Institution, Substantive and Evaluation Advisors	Data collection and measurement procedures established that can be appropriately used by qualified individuals in the educational research community AUDIENCE: Evaluation Advisors, Consumer Representatives
1. Evidence that postulated outcomes were achieved in Hot House 2. Experimental Design established AUDIENCE: All Audiences	1. Verification of experimental hypothesis in pilot 2. Means established to acquire date in disparate sites AUDIENCE: All Audiences	Evidence that experimental effects generalized across sites AUDIENCE: All Audiences
1. Identification/classification of deviations from procedural specifications as outlined by developer 2. Some systematic means of recording and appraising degree of classroom implementation ready for use AUDIENCE: Developer, Institution, Evaluation and Substantive Advisors	Methodology for relating degree of implementation effect (if any) to dependent variables established AUDIENCE: Evaluation Advisors, Developer	Information available to prospective users concerning differential implementation effects AUDIENCE: Consumer Representatives, Sponsor

Table 3

Product Effectiveness Domain
(continued)

ILLUSTRATIVE QUESTIONS	CRITERIA:	Initiation CRITERIA:
E. Are there important differences in the accomplishments of individual students that warrant the investigation of output to prerequisite variable relationships?		1. Specification of prerequisite v. ables of interest 2. Evidence of the integrity of measures to be used for assessment of prerequisite v. ables AUDIENCE: Substantive and Eval tion Advisors, Developer
F. Are there important longitudinal effects?	Any hypothesized longitudinal effects identified AUDIENCE: Sponsor, Substantive Advisors	
G. Are there any unanticipated consequences (e.g., cross-curricular)?		Inclusion of some means for the d covery of unanticipated consequenc in assessment strategy AUDIENCE: Developer, Evaluati Advisors

Table 3

Product Effectiveness Domain
(continued)

Pilot	Field Test	Public Diffusion
CRITERIA:	**CRITERIA:**	**CRITERIA:**
Selection of prerequisite variables to be used in future studies based on evidence collected in Hot House Experimental design which appropriately handles prerequisite variables established	If evidence of crucial individual differences exists, experimental design which relates prerequisite and dependent variables established	Recommendations for appropriate use patterns (to capitalize on prerequisite and dependent variable relationships) based on field test evidence available to public
AUDIENCE: Substantive and Evaluation Advisors, Developer	**AUDIENCE:** Evaluation and Substantive Advisors, Developer	**AUDIENCE:** Sponsor, Consumer Representatives
	1. Experimental design established for the investigation of longitudinal effects in the population which has used the most advanced developmental version of the product 2. Data collection instruments and procedures established	Recommendations for longitudinal studies available to educational research community
	AUDIENCE: Developer, Substantive and Evaluation Advisors	**AUDIENCE:** Consumer, Representatives, Sponsor, Substantive and Evaluation Advisors
Unanticipated consequences identified are built into future research designs for more controlled investigation Procedure for continuing attempts to identify unanticipated consequences established	1. Product revised to eliminate negative and emphasize positive unanticipated consequences 2. Additional unanticipated consequences identified in Pilot built into field test research design	1. Final version takes into account identified consequences 2. Consequences discovered in earlier trials as well as efforts to deal with them reported to educational research community
AUDIENCE: Developer, Substantive and Evaluation Advisors, Institution	**AUDIENCE:** Developer, Substantive and Evaluation Advisors, Institution	**AUDIENCE:** All Audiences

Table 4

Usability Domain

ILLUSTRATIVE QUESTIONS	CRITERIA:	Initiation CRITERIA:
A. Can teachers use the product in the intended manner?		Procedures for acquiring feedback from classroom use (Re: Teacher's acceptance of product, materials, activities, guide, etc.) formalized
		AUDIENCE: Developer, Institution, Sponsor, Substantive and Evaluation Advisors
B. Is teacher training necessary/ adequate?	Substantive advisors state that goal achievement will or will not require specialized classroom practices and/or training for the intended teacher population	See 4, A
	AUDIENCE: Sponsor, Institution, Developer	

Table 4

Usability Domain
(continued)

	Pilot	Field Test	Public Diffusion
	CRITERIA:	**CRITERIA:**	**CRITERIA:**
	1. Evidence that product A. Is generally usable from hot house classrooms and teachers B. Has been revised to attend to discovered logistical difficulties 2. Some systematic means of recording and appraising degree of classroom implementation ready for use (See 3, D)	1. Procedures established for the collection of data from the field, re: teacher use patterns	
	AUDIENCE: Developer, Substantive and Evaluation Advisors	AUDIENCE: Developer, Evaluation Advisors	Evidence that the product and the training that accompanies it (if any) can be used by the targeted teacher population AUDIENCE: All Audiences (especially Consumer Representatives)
	1. Classroom practices which are critical for implementation identified 2. See 4, A	1. Evidence that teachers who deviate from intended practices do so knowingly implies that teacher training is probably unnecessary 2. If teacher training is necessary, it is a separate product—criteria need to be established for its developmental/evaluation stages (recycling of product)	
	AUDIENCE: Developer, Substantive and Evaluation Advisors	AUDIENCE: Sponsor, Institution, Developer, Substantive and Evaluation Advisors	

Table 4

Usability Domain
(continued)

		Initiation	Hot House
ILLUSTRATIVE QUESTIONS	CRITERIA:	CRITERIA:	
C. Is community acceptance a problem?	Evidence that values underlying product goals are acceptable to a substantial portion of target population. Perhaps acquired from public representatives (e.g., community action groups)	Procedures established to collect affective/value data from communities served (parents, school personnel, students, etc.)	
	AUDIENCE: Sponsor, Institution	AUDIENCE: Sponsor, Developer, Institution, Evaluation Advisors	
D. What strategies for diffusion/ dissemination are most successful?			

Table 4

Usability Domain
(continued)

	Pilot	Field Test	Public Diffusion
CRITERIA:	**CRITERIA:**		**CRITERIA:**
Review by appropriate audiences of the implications for product of any substantial negative community response	Continue Process		Clear statement of values underlying product goals (especially those which seem controversial) such that informed community acceptance can occur
AUDIENCE: Sponsor, Developer, Institution, Substantive Advisors	AUDIENCE: Sponsor, Developer, Institution, Substantive Advisors		AUDIENCE: Consumer Representatives
	Variety of approaches for the acquisition of field test sites put into practice		Analysis of the suitability of approaches used to identify those that were most efficacious
	AUDIENCE: Developer, Institution		AUDIENCE: Developer, Institution

Table 5

Generalizability Domain

ILLUSTRATIVE QUESTIONS	CRITERIA:	Initiation CRITERIA:
A. Is the evaluation of the program adequate?	Sufficient resources allocated to carry out necessary evaluation activities	Information to be collected in Ho House enables responsible decisio making in terms of identified cr teria
	AUDIENCE: Sponsor, Institution, Developer, Evaluation Advisors	AUDIENCE: Sponsor, Institution Developer, Evaluation Ad visors
B. Can the materials be used to accomplish other than stated goals or be used with other than targeted population?		

Table 5

Generalizability Domain
(continued)

	Pilot	Field Test	Public Diffusion
CRITERIA:	**CRITERIA:**	**CRITERIA:**	
1. Information and data collection activities match criteria 2. Design, sampling, instrumentation, and intended analyses certified as appropriate and adequate (If applicable)	1. Information and data collection activities match criteria 2. Design, sampling, instrumentation, and intended analysis certified as appropriate and adequate (If applicable)	Evaluation Report available to the public identifying characteristics, virtues, flaws, etc., of product and specifying the data and analyses on which conclusions were based	
AUDIENCE: Sponsor, Institution, Developer, Evaluation Advisors	**AUDIENCE: Sponsor, Institution, Developer, Evaluation Advisors**	**AUDIENCE: All Audiences**	
	1. If pilot test results indicate positive unanticipated consequences (see 3, G), a designed study to empirically test findings is planned 2. Preliminary attempt in field study to investigate use with other populations (If perceived as important and desirable by developer)	1. Guidelines for use details experience with other populations as well as consequences of use to attain other than stated goals 2. Efforts and findings reported to the educational research community	
	AUDIENCE: Developer, Substantive and Evaluation Advisors, Institution	**AUDIENCE: All Audiences (especially Consumer Representatives)**	

CHAPTER 7

A MULTISTAGE MODEL FOR
EVALUATING EDUCATIONAL PRODUCTS

Charles L. Bertram and Robert D. Childers
Appalachia Educational Laboratory, Inc.

A statement must be made concerning the environment in which evaluation activities are conducted before evaluation can be discussed or even defined. The setting may range from a Title III (ESEA, 1965) program conducted by a local education agency and monitored by a state department of education to a children's commercial television series or a set of instructional materials for occupational training. However, the environment into which the model for the evaluation of educational products fits is educational development. The elements of that environment are planning, product development, and diffusion, as well as evaluation.

Educational Development

Educational development is the systematic process of creating and diffusing alternative products that will contribute to the improvement of educational practices (USOE, 1971). Educational products are exportable methods and materials which will produce specified outcomes with designated target populations. Diffusion is the process of exporting educational products, both during and following design and construction of the products.

A Model for Educational Development

Most organizations engaging in educational development pay allegiance to a model (Curtis, 1968; Edmonston, 1972; Hess and Wright, 1972; Klein, Fenstermacher, and Alkin, 1971; Research for Better Schools, Inc., 1970; Sanders *et al.*, 1972; Sanders and Worthen, 1972; Scriven, Glass, Hiveley, and Stake, 1971), and a seven-stage model is presented in Figure 1 (AEL, 1971). The model indicates interrelationships between product development and product diffusion

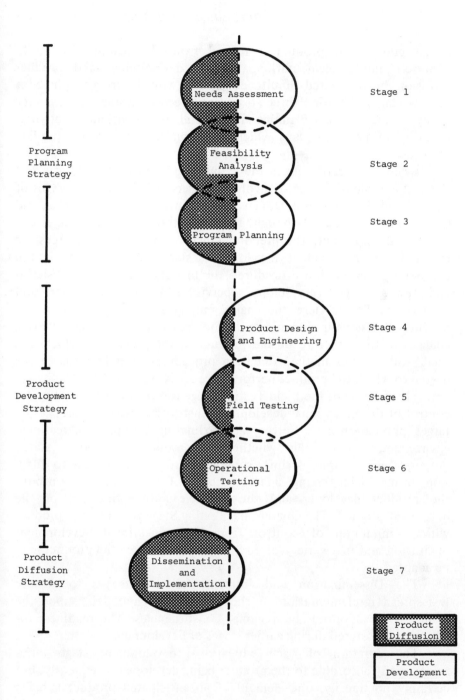

Figure 1. Model for Educational Development.

as an educational product is moved from the planning phase to adoption and implementation. Product development and product diffusion are conducted simultaneously but with differing emphases at various stages. The first three stages are Needs Assessment, Feasibility Analysis, and Program Planning. These tend to be continuous activities resulting in program plans which are submitted to various funding agencies.

Evaluators participate in the activities of the first three stages, but the major evaluation thrust involves the second of the three stages of educational development: Design and Engineering, Field Testing, and Operational Testing. Although the first three planning stages are considered important, the preponderance of evaluation resources are required for the product development stages. As described in the discussion of evaluation procedures, the prototype product is designed and tested under very close supervision during the Design and Engineering Stage. Here the major emphasis is on revision of the product. Revisions in design may include restatement of original goals, changes in the structure of the product or the process by which it is used, and changes in the evaluation procedures used to measure the degree to which the product performance goals are met.

The purpose of the Field Testing Stage is to test the product under control of the educational development institution, with a subset of the target population in a setting approximating a typical educational environment, to ascertain whether the product can produce stated outcomes. The emphasis shifts somewhat from development to diffusion during Field Testing, and the results of evaluation concern both the product developer and the clientele anticipating use of the developed product. The Operational Testing Stage is to test the product with a minimum of control from the educational development institution and in a variety of circumstances to which the product may be adapted.

The Dissemination and Implementation Stage is to achieve widespread implementation of the product by capitalizing upon the readiness for adoption by regional constituencies. The readiness for adoption is fostered during earlier stages of development.

The duration of each educational development stage varies substantially according to the product being developed. Frequently, but certainly not ideally, one element of an anticipated product is being field tested while another is yet to be designed. The size of the sample during the Design and Engineering State is generally small. The sample size increases as the product moves into Field Testing and Operational Testing.

Products Under Development

The evaluation model described in a following section is based on the experience of four product development efforts. The four products with which evaluation procedures will be illustrated are Home-Oriented Preschool Education (HOPE), Career Decision-Making (CD-M), Experience-Based Career Education (EBCE), and the Educational Cooperative (Ed. Coop.).

Home-Oriented Preschool Education. HOPE was designed for rural three-, four-, and five-year-old children and utilizes an integrated delivery system which includes daily TV lessons, weekly visits to the children's homes by paraprofessionals, and group instruction in a mobile classroom.

Career Decision-Making. The Career Decision-Making product consists of instructional materials for grades K-12. These materials are designed to assist students in developing an understanding of themselves and of the world of work and in developing the capability to make knowledgeable career choices.

Experience-Based Career Education. The EBCE model is one of four career education models being developed by the Career Education Program of the National Institute of Education. An emphasis of this model is on using employer sites to give high school students career-related orientation and experience. A consortium of local employers will assume administrative responsibility for this alternative to public schooling once materials and procedures are produced by the EBCE product development team.

Educational Cooperative. An Educational Cooperative is a voluntary confederation of local school agencies, colleges and universities, and a state department of education, all cooperating to increase local ability to improve the quality of and access to education. The objective of the Educational Cooperative is to create and field test a new educational structure that will enable Appalachian school superintendents to increase their administrative and leadership capabilities.

Rationale and Organization for Product Evaluation

Rationale

Product evaluation is the process of obtaining and providing useful information for judging decision alternatives concerning revision, disposition, and adoption of products (Stufflebeam, 1971). It is based on three assumptions: (1) that product development deals with (a) changes in product design as the product is being developed, (b) decisions made by institutional management or funding agencies regarding the disposition of the total product development effort, and (c) decisions concerning adoption and implementation of the total product after it is developed; (2) that a program plan should contain information about the desired output and outcomes of product development and that changes in both product description and anticipated effects of using the product may (and should) occur during development (Hemphill, 1969; Scriven, 1972); and (3) that methods at the disposal of the evaluator include such diverse tools as automatic data processing, cost analysis, opinion sampling, research design, strategies, and testing.

Given these three assumptions, the functions of product evaluation are to:

1. Provide product development teams with information concerning the degree to which product elements are reaching performance objectives as the product is developed.

2. Provide institutional management (and/or funding agencies) with information concerning the degree to which product components are reaching intermediate performance objectives and information concerning the ultimate effectiveness of the total product.

3. Provide information about the performance characteristics of the developed product for product users to support implementation decisions.

An ordering of activities is implied by the evaluation functions, and these activities will be further described as the various activities of the evaluation model are noted. In general, evaluation activities occur in the following order, and recur in cycles as the product is moved through Design and Engineering, Field Testing, and Operational Testing:

1. Assist in formulation and/or revision of product goals and objectives.

2. Select and/or revise the categories of information needed to support most critical decisions (criterion variables).
3. Select specific indicators of the performance levels associated with each criterion variable (performance indicators).
4. Describe the process by which specific data will be obtained (measurement procedures).
5. Obtain data, preferably before and after the product (or elements of the product) has been used.
6. Analyze data and document other information obtained through the use of prototype product.
7. Organize results into the most understandable form to provide information about product effectiveness.
8. Report progress as product development is recycled or proceeds through stages of educational development.

Proposed Staff Organization

The director of evaluation has rank and responsibility equal to that of the product development directors, as well as the directors of diffusion or planning. These directors make up a management team which gives direction to all programs of the educational development organization. At least one member of the evaluation staff is primarily responsible for the evaluation of each product and is assisted by other evaluation staff when additional competencies or services are required. Other than product evaluation, specialties of an evaluation staff include school administration, educational psychology, clinical psychology, research design, curriculum and instruction, and systems analysis.

This particular staff organization has several advantages: (1) product developers and evaluators are able to interact daily; (2) total evaluation talent can be pooled to provide a variation in competencies available to any one product or to meet peak work periods; and (3) evaluation reports tend to be more objective, since the evaluators are not under the direction of product development directors.

Two disadvantages of a separate evaluation unit versus evaluator(s) being attached to each product development staff are that lines of communication are more difficult to establish and maintain, and a greater potential for role conflict is induced.

Fitting Product Evaluation to the Product

Although it may sound rudimentary, the reader is cautioned that not all suggested evaluation procedures will be appropriate for all product development efforts. A suggested maxim is that "the evaluation must be tailored to the product."

The model presented in the following discussion is based on experience with the four previously described product development efforts, which vary from an in-school type curricular offering to a product with school administrators for a target population. In the latter case, an Educational Cooperative is composed of several local education agencies and current funding levels permit a field test sample size of only two Cooperatives. With the Cooperative, pre- and posttesting in the conventional sense are entirely inappropriate, and the "control" groups of conventional experimental design are impossible. Alternative evaluation designs must either be discovered through literature search (Glass, undated) or invented (Stepp, 1972).

Description of a Model for Evaluating Educational Products

The Model for Evaluating Educational Products, as depicted in Figure 2, is a series of activities designed to produce information useful for making decisions concerning the disposition of the product. Many of the activities have been found to occur simultaneously and some activities, e.g., designing measurement procedures, are often only partially completed during one cycle and frequently revised during the next.

The educational development activities of the Needs Assessment, Feasibility Analysis, and Program Planning Stages result in a program plan which should include fairly well-defined product goals, a description of the structure of the product and its use, required funding, development time lines, plans for evaluation, and ideally, a set of behavioral objectives based on identified educational needs. The evaluation staff assists in the formulation of the program plan. This program plan, if funded, is a source document for the product evaluation staff.

The three stages of development of primary concern here are Design and Engineering, Field Testing, and Operational Testing. The development activities may recycle one or more times through a given stage before product performance will permit movement to the next stage.

Evaluation of Products During the
Design and Engineering Stage

The important outputs of evaluation activities during the Design and Engineering Stage are a detailed plan for evaluation of the product, a set of measurement procedures including necessary instrumentation to determine the product's effectiveness, and information concerning the success of the prototype product in meeting performance objectives in a simulated environment.

Product goals. Evaluators have found that considerable refinement of product goals is required before adequate procedures for measuring product effectiveness can be selected or designed. Goal refinement is usually achieved through face-to-face interaction of the evaluator(s) and product development staff, and often occurs at both the total product level and the subproduct level. For example, two of the goals against which the effectiveness of the total Home-Oriented Preschool Education product is measured are (1) that the cost of operating HOPE be no more than $250 per child, and (2) that children achieve cognitive objectives at a satisfactory level as evidenced by scores on a curriculum-specific test. Satisfaction may be defined later in the development sequence and certainly after the test is constructed.

A second level of goal (or objective) formulation is at the unit, lesson, or subproduct level. Again, using the HOPE example, one goal of a particular television lesson may be to teach the child recognition of the numeral 7 or to react overtly to rhythmic sounds.

An indication of the relative importance of the product goals is helpful in communicating product effectiveness. Klein (1972) has suggested several procedures for comparing the relative importance of product objectives.

Product description. The product description is prepared by the product development staff and serves as a guide to the evaluation staff in designing measurement procedures. Ideally, product goals would give sufficient guidance, but a description of the product—usually a revised and enlarged program plan—has been found most helpful in determining whether the product is being developed and used in accordance with the original design. For example, the Experience-Based Career Education Program requires a product development team to produce procedures for the preparation of materials and a field team to implement the procedures with students. The evaluator(s) will determine whether the procedures for the preparation of materials were

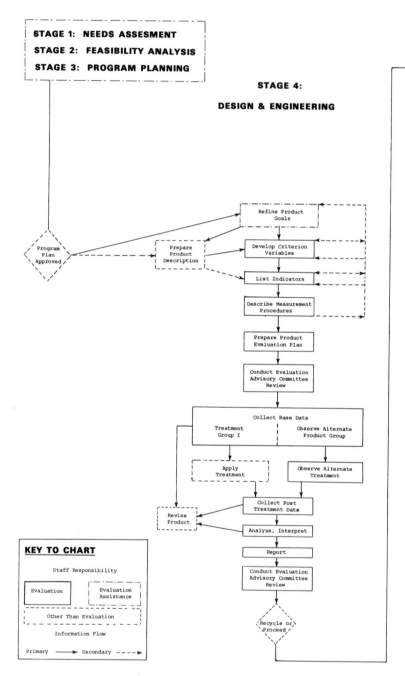

Figure 2. Model for Evaluation of Educational Products.

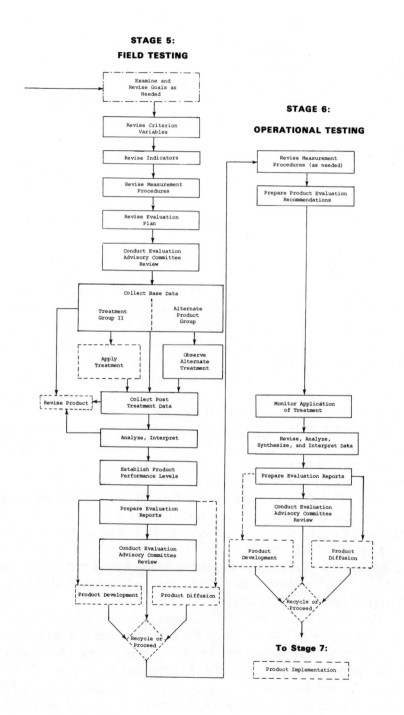

STAGE 5:
FIELD TESTING

STAGE 6:
OPERATIONAL TESTING

Examine and
Revise Goals as
Needed

Revise Criterion
Variables

Revise Indicators

Revise Measurement
Procedures

Revise Evaluation
Plan

Conduct Evaluation
Advisory Committee
Review

Collect Base Data

Treatment
Group II

Alternate
Product
Group

Apply
Treatment

Observe
Alternate
Treatment

Revise Product

Collect Post
Treatment Data

Analyze, Interpret

Establish Product
Performance Levels

Prepare Evaluation
Reports

Conduct Evaluation
Advisory Committee
Review

Product Development

Product Diffusion

Recycle or
Proceed

Revise Measurement
Procedures (as needed)

Prepare Product Evaluation
Recommendations

Monitor Application
of Treatment

Revise, Analyze,
Synthesize, and Interpret Data

Prepare Evaluation Reports

Conduct Evaluation
Advisory Committee
Review

Product
Development

Product
Diffusion

Recycle or
Proceed

To Stage 7:

Product Implementation

designed by the product development team and whether the procedures were used successfully by the field team.

Criterion variables. Decision makers usually prefer to base their decisions on a few categories of highly pertinent information. Individuals can quickly become lost in a maze of tests, subtests, treatment groups, levels, and measures occurring over several time intervals. Although the evaluation may of necessity be based on a complex design, the results are more efficiently conveyed by a few broad categories of information which are called criterion variables. A criterion variable may be supported by several indicators.

An example criterion variable from the Educational Cooperative is the problem-solving ability of school superintendents. One from the Career Decision-Making product is vocational maturity. Cost of operation or required resources is a criterion variable for all products.

The criterion variables are derived through consultation with the product development staff, by review of literature to determine what areas others have measured, and by a survey of potential consumers to determine the types of product information they desire. To be of maximum use, the survey of potential consumers must be completed near the beginning of the Design and Engineering Stage. The criterion variables often become section headings in summary evaluation reports and the substance of more detailed technical reports.

Indicators. Indicators are primary units of observation which reveal the degree to which a product has reached an acceptable level of performance. For example, an indicator of "knowledge of career opportunities" for CD-M students is Part 2 of the *Career Maturity Inventory* (Crites, 1973). An indicator of social skills development by three-, four-, and five-year-old HOPE children is the coded interactive behavior of children as they participate in a small group task (Pena, 1971). Another indicator is cost in dollars per child, and indicators are often based on instruments and other management procedures developed by the organization conducting educational development (Bertram, Hines, and MacDonald, 1971).

Measurement procedures. The real purpose of the preceding evaluation activities is to produce efficient measurement procedures or sets of activities to obtain data for product indicators. The procedures usually support a broad range of indicators and are limited only by the evaluator's (and his consultant's) imagination. Examples are an EBCE Employer Interview Schedule and curriculum specific measures. A procedure used in the HOPE program for measuring the curiosity level of small children is to code their behavior as they manipulate (or fail to manipulate) an unfamiliar but unusually interesting toy.

Product evaluation plan. The product evaluation plan is a statement of the results of the preceding activities, plus a schedule for completing the evaluation, and an indication of specific staff assignments and responsibilities. The purposes of the plan are (1) to document the evaluation intent, (2) to promote a consensus among developers, diffusers, evaluators, and administrators, (3) to provide a guide for completing the evaluation, and (4) to give an advisory committee a statement on which to base its reaction.

The product description, including goals and objectives, is given in enough detail so that the plan can stand alone. Criterion variables, indicators, and measurement procedures are also listed. The plan, as prepared during the Design and Engineering Stage, is revised at least annually as product revisions occur.

Advisory committee review. An advisory committee may be formed for each product being developed and may meet once or twice a year. The committee members should have competencies in evaluation, research design, measurement, statistics, or the content area. Members may also represent product users, such as school superintendents, state department of education officials, and employers.

The purpose of the committee is to (1) give advice concerning more appropriate evaluation procedures, (2) serve as a stimulus to the evaluation staff, and (3) add credibility to the entire product development effort. The evaluation plan is revised, if needed, to reflect the input of the advisory committee following a thorough review.

Base data. Base data are the facts and figures which indicate the initial level of performance of the target population as measured by the product indicators. Data are obtained from a sample of the target population which will use the prototype product *and* from samples who are to use alternate products, including those who will use no identifiable product at all.

Collection of base data for the Educational Cooperative involves conducting structured interviews with school superintendents to determine, for example, the procedures by which resources are allocated, the nature of planning activities, or the types of evaluation conducted by the local education agency. Alternate products on which similar data are collected may include the Board of Cooperative Educational

Services, Intermediate Units, or other products which encourage regional cooperation.

Certain products, such as CD-M, may require controlled pre- and posttesting; however, all products require collection of data such as resource requirements which are not treated according to classical research design. As indicated in Figure 2, the base data are also used to give an early indication of needed revisions in the product, e.g., to raise the language level of HOPE television lessons.

The application of the product and alternate treatments are monitored by the evaluation staff. Arranging for testing sites is a diffusion responsibility, and product development teams introduce the product to the target samples.

Collect posttreatment data. Many products move through annual cycles. Therefore pretreatment data can be collected in the fall and posttreatment data in the spring. Some products, such as the Educational Cooperative, may require a systematic collection of data throughout the year, e.g., local board of education minutes. Another nontypical example is that each of the 16 CD-M instructional units requires approximately one week to introduce to high school students, and requires pre- and posttesting before revisions can be made.

As indicated in an introductory section, the evaluation staff is involved closely in the product development cycle. For example, "usability" data derived during preliminary testing of the CD-M units are relayed to the CD-M development team so that immediate adjustments can be made.

Analyze, synthesize, and interpret data. Following the treatment, the data are analyzed as directed by the evaluation plan. The analysis may be a simple percentage tabulation, a structuring of certain facts about the product development effort, or a rather complex analysis completed through the use of a large computer system. The results of the various analyses are organized in the most meaningful way, and the interpretation is an effort of the total evaluation team.

Problems with the treatment of data cause failure to meet production schedules more often than any other evaluation activity. The information resulting from the interpretation of the analyses is always needed soon after the data are collected, or the evaluation results cannot be used to suggest changes in product designs or as a basis for decisions regarding implementation of the product. The evaluator should be especially careful to insure proper screening of data, selection of appropriate "canned" computer programs, program labeling of subtests, and accurate recording of the age of children (such as at time of pretest rather than at different times). More problems are usually encountered in the Field Testing Stage (in which larger samples are required) than during the Design and Engineering Stage.

Prepare initial evaluation report. The primary recipients of the first evaluation are the product development staff and the administration of the educational development organization. One purpose of the report is to document a comparison of the product as originally designed with the product as used in preliminary testing. Deviations from the original design may be necessary, but they should be noted. The comparison is of both the product structure (what it is) and the process (how it is used). Questions of product comparison, with EBCE as an example, included "Were materials developed to orient the high school pupils to the world of work?" and "Did the pupils have a positive interaction with the employers during the orientation activities?"

A second purpose of the initial evaluation report is to document the performance of the product as it was used during the Design and Engineering Stage. The changes (or lack of changes) in behavior of the target samples are recorded and comparisons with groups using alternate products are usually made. An estimate of the resources required to use the product is included, as well as the results of a study of product receptivity among potential users.

Conduct advisory committee review. If an advisory committee is used it is invited to review the evaluation report in draft form to make suggestions concerning additional data analyses, different interpretations, and changes in reporting style to more efficiently communicate evaluation results. The committee members usually require one day for review of materials before interacting with evaluation and development staff. The interaction requires approximately two days. From this interaction a written report is prepared and submitted to the organization's administration, product development team, and possibly to funding agencies. The report may be included as an appendix to the evaluation report. Suggestions usually range from a general statement about the readability of the evaluation report to suggestions for a different post analysis of variance test.

With proper planning the committee will review the evaluation plans for the next cycle of product development in addition to the consideration of the evaluation report, thereby decreasing the time and cost required for a second review.

Recycle or proceed. The decision to either proceed or return to a previous stage of the development sequence is based on several considerations, of which evaluation results may be only one factor. Recently acquired diffusion information, such as a change in potential marketability, is another factor. A third is the ability of the product development staff (as judged by the educational development organization's administration) to proceed with the development activities. A fourth factor is the availability of sufficient funds or the degree to which the product conforms with priorities established by various funding agencies.

According to the Model For Educational Development (Figure 1), the criteria for advancement from the Design and Engineering Stage to the Field Testing Stage are documented high efficiency of the product in producing specified outcomes in a limited, simulated environment and evidence that the product is consistent with the potential users' needs and capabilities.

Evaluation of Educational Products
During the Field Testing Stage

As indicated in Figure 2, evaluation activities encountered in the Field Testing Stage are similar to those in the Design and Engineering Stage. Therefore, the activities will not be described in detail as in the previous section. As for evaluation, the major differences between the Design and Engineering and the Field Testing Stages are that revised and validated measurement procedures are used, the product is introduced to larger samples, and formal evaluation reports document the results of the latter stage.

The goals are examined by both the evaluation and product development teams to determine if changes, deletions, or additions are appropriate. The reasons for changes may be that unanticipated uses are found for the product, an unexpected market potential is found, certain former goals were not easily achieved in a cost effective manner, or the funding agency requires changes in the product. The criterion variables, indicators, and measurement procedures also need revision, since revised goals imply different areas of measurement, and one purpose of the preceding stage was to produce effective measures of product performance.

The evaluation plan for field testing is a revision of the previous one and also includes a brief sketch of the evaluation results from the previous cycle. The previous cycle may have been the Design and Engineering Stage or a previous cycle of the Field Testing Stage.

The revised plan serves as a statement to which the advisory committee reacts, and additional revisions are based on its recommendations. The committee should be composed of the same personnel during the different reviews if possible.

The base data are collected on larger samples than during the previous stage, and more demands are placed on organization and data storage capabilities. For some products, major testing programs must be organized, testers trained, and provisions made for scoring tests, coding scores, and keypunching data cards. Caution should be used to insure the compatibility for data card formats for pre- and posttesting.

One purpose of collecting and analyzing data during field testing is to establish product performance levels. By the termination of the final cycle of field testing, the potential user should be informed that the product will perform at a specified level on the various indicators if the product is used as specified, and a specified amount of resources will be required to adopt and use the product. For example, with HOPE, the five-year-old children will average achieving 80 percent on a curriculum-specific test of cognitive objectives, and the cost of operation will be one-half that of a kindergarten program which requires approximately $500 per year for each child (and in which the children achieve 75 percent of the items on the test of cognitive objectives achievement). These performance levels are based on the actual performance of the product while the product is under the supervision of the product development staff.

The evaluation reports during field testing fulfill a dual purpose: (1) they indicate needed changes in the product and (2) they provide users with an indication of product performance as noted above. The reports have more variability than in the previous stage and may include technical reports, summary evaluation reports, brief descriptions of findings, and verbal presentations. The intended audience for the technical reports is research and evaluation persons in public schools, state departments of education, and institutions of higher education. The summary is intended for curriculum supervisors, teachers, and others who may not require the technical backup. A brief synopsis of evaluation results is of most use to those who need only an introduction to the results, those who have very busy schedules, and, perhaps, those who make the final decisions about using products.

The advisory committee review may be conducted as previously described. A workable format is for an administrator of the educational development organization to describe briefly the organization's mission and model for educational development (if one is available), for a representative of the development staff to describe the product or program events since the most recent review, and for the evaluation team to discuss the pertinent reports.

The decision to proceed from the Field Testing to the Operational Testing Stage is an administrative one and is again based on diffusion and evaluation considerations. The advancement criteria are evidence that the product meets specifications and a high probability that it will produce specified outcomes in an Operational Test, and evidence of interest in the product on the part of regional constituencies.

Evaluation of Educational Products
During the Operational Testing Stage

Only minimal revisions in the product are expected during the Operational Testing Stage, and the emphasis is shifted to diffusion of the product. Supervision of product use is the responsibility of the user, and the educational development organization is responsible only for monitoring product use and determining its effectiveness at selected demonstration sites. The evaluation responsibility is for suggesting measures of product effectiveness, receiving and analyzing data, and reporting product effectiveness.

The first evaluation activities of the Operational Testing Stage are making any needed revisions in measurement procedures and preparing product evaluation recommendations. An example of revising measurement procedures is the reorganization of the items on a curriculum specific test so that subtest scores could be obtained. Care must be taken to retain the original items so that comparisons can be made with achievement measured in previous years.

The purposes of preparing recommendations for the product evaluation to be conducted by the user are: (1) to permit the educational development organization to monitor without close supervision, (2) to give the user an opportunity to evaluate the product and thereby gain confidence in the evaluation results, and (3) to permit the educational development organization staff to determine if product performance standards continue to be met with a minimum of control.

The recommendations are usually organized so that the user can either conduct a minimum or maximum evaluation effort, i.e., ranging from the use of one or two instruments to a full battery of instruments and other measurement procedures, including forms for obtaining cost data. The evaluations conducted by the demonstration sites are usually much less sophisticated than those conducted during field testing. Recommendations for these evaluations might include sources for standardized and "home grown" instruments and instructions for scoring instruments, collecting other data, data coding, and data processing. One suggested alternative is for the user to contract with the educational development organization to complete at least certain parts of the evaluation.

The base data may need to be updated to reestablish a base against which to continue measuring growth resulting from product use. The application of the treatment is monitored through visits to demonstration sites by the evaluators. Deviations from intended product use are recorded for inclusion in the final evaluation report. For the HOPE product, the educational development organization agreed to receive pre- and posttest data, analyze them, and provide the demonstration site with a report including the results of all participating HOPE demonstrations. This arrangement proved advantageous to both the demonstration sites and the parent organization, and similar arrangements with other products are anticipated as the products reach the Operational Testing Stage.

The evaluation reporting style shifts from the formal technical reporting of Field Testing to less formal interpretive evaluation summaries. The reports must remain credible, but the audience shifts from technically-oriented to consumer-oriented groups as the diffusion function of educational development becomes more prominent. Reporting methods may include evaluation summaries, publications in journals, and oral presentations.

An advisory committee review may be conducted following the completion of the final evaluation report. If the educational development process is successful, the product is implemented by the target population following the Operational Testing Stage.

Product Evaluation During
and After Implementation

Unfortunately, the evaluation activities usually must terminate when the other product development activities have been completed, because the funding agency chooses to support another product development effort. Therefore, funding is usually not available for follow-up studies or continued monitoring of product effectiveness. One possible solution is for the educational development organization to contract to perform the evaluation of the product at the various implementation sites. Advantages are that (1) effective procedures for implementing the product can be noted and communicated among users, (2) the educational development organization may be made aware that needed revisions in a product require a new development effort, and (3) the evaluation talent assembled and trained for evaluation of a particular product can be used for the benefit of both the developer and the consumer. One major disadvantage of the developer performing the evaluation is that attention is diverted from product development to what is essentially a service function to a broad clientele.

Criteria for Effective Evaluation

A discussion of an evaluation model should include some hints for evaluating it, and true to the previously described model, the suggestions are listed according to procedures for assessing the effectiveness of the evaluation as it is performed (process evaluation), and procedures for determinging how effective the evaluation was (outcome evaluation).

Process Evaluation of Evaluation Activities

Indicators of the effectiveness of the evaluation on which measures may be obtained *during the evaluation* are (1) reports of consultants who assist with the evaluation; (2) reports of the advisory committee; (3) the attitude of the educational development organization's administration and governing bodies; (4) the use of information by the product development team and organizational administration; and (5) acceptance of colleagues.

The reports of consultants and advisory committees may be used to revise specific evaluation procedures, or perhaps even to redesign the evaluation strategy for the entire development organization. The attitude of the administration and board of directors is probably the most obvious indicator but also the most difficult to measure. These attitudes may cause the evaluation to change as it is being conducted. A less subtle indicator is the funding allocated for evaluation by various funding agencies.

Another possibility for assessing the progress of evaluation is a systematic documentation of the frequency of usage of evaluative information as a basis for decision making, either by the product development staff, administrative staff of the development organization, diffusion staff, or clients who consider adoption of the product. One difficulty with this indicator is that the information is often used unconsciously, and fellow staff are sometimes reluctant to admit that the information was of *that* much value. Acceptance of colleagues is a fifth possible indicator of the effectiveness of the evaluation. Other than the obvious problem of quantification, one difficulty is determining from which colleagues to accept advice concerning the acceptability of evaluation procedures.

Evaluation of the Outcomes
of Product Evaluation

Three indicators by which one may determine how effective the evaluation *was* are: (1) the degree to which evaluation was used in decision making; (2) the degree to which the product in use meets the performance standards; and (3) the proportion of products that passed the field testing stage and were later successfully implemented.

As discussed earlier, product evaluation is defined as a process of obtaining and providing useful information for judging decision alternatives. The degree to which the information was used in decision making is a measure of the effectiveness of the evaluation. Measurement procedures are not presently refined enough to permit precise quantification of the use of evaluation in decision making, but a simple log may be used to gather frequency data on the number of evaluation recommendations that were implemented.

A second indicator of how effective the evaluation was is the degree to which the implemented product meets performance standards established during the Field Testing Stage. With the CD-M product, for example, the performance standards may be based on students' decision-making ability and knowledge of career opportunities. If further testing indicates that these standards are maintained at Field

Test levels after the product is in the Operational Test Stage, the assumption that the evaluation effectively forecast performance levels seems warranted. If the performance levels are not met through use of the product, either the evaluation was inadequate or the product is not used as intended.

A third indicator of how effective the evaluation was is the number of products which received a positive evaluation during the Field Testing Stage and were later successfully implemented. Positive results from this indicator imply that the product did reach adequate performance levels during implementation and that the marketing forecasts of the Field Testing Stage were accurate.

Summary

An outline of selected strategies and procedures used to evaluate educational products has been presented. The outline has indicated how an evaluation unit functions within an educational development organization, and has described a sequence of evaluation procedures referred to as an evaluation model.

The activities of the model are cyclical in nature. Major categories of activities include goal refinement, formulation and organization of measurement procedures, data collection, analysis, and reporting. One additional feature is that for each product, an advisory committee may examine an evaluation plan before measurements are taken, and then react to the evaluation reports as they are completed. Suggestions are provided for assessing the effectiveness of the evaluation in order to improve the techniques while the product is being evaluated, and for determining the effectiveness of the evaluation after the product is developed.

Suggested Readings

Cook, D.L. Management control theory as the context for educational evaluation. *Journal of Research and Development in Education*, Summer 1970, *3*, 13-16.

> Cook proposes that "the concept of management control theory can serve as an effective context for educational evaluation and that the more foundational concepts and principles of control theory, information theory, and cyber-

netics provide both a sufficient model and theoretical base for educational evaluation."

Sanders, J.R., and Worthen, B.R. A descriptive summary of frameworks for planning evaluation studies. *SRIS Quarterly*. Bloomington, Indiana: Phi Delta Kappa, Spring 1972, 10-14.

> The authors present a two-page chart which compares eight systems of evaluation on the basis of 12 aspects. The evaluation systems include those by Stake, Scriven, Provus, etc., as well as school accreditation evaluation, and the aspects are categories such as purpose, key emphasis, and role of the evaluator. The chart is an excellent guide to further study.

Scriven, M., Glass, G.V., Hively, W., and Stake, R.E. *An evaluation system for regional labs and R & D centers*. Washington: U.S.O.E., August 31, 1971. ERIC ED 061 299.

> The system proposed by the authors was selected to evaluate the development and research programs conducted by labs and centers, and is one of the few systems known in education by which large programs with diverse objectives can be compared and selected for funding. One other system is the Design for Evaluating R & D Institutions and Programs by Daniel Stufflebeam, *et al.* (1971, unpublished).

Stufflebeam, D.L. *Educational evaluation and decision making*. Itasca, Illinois: F.E. Peacock, 1971.

> A product of a Phi Delta Kappa study committee, this book presents a detailed conceptual design that is especially useful as a guide to evaluation as done by school systems and other agencies with ongoing educational programs.

Tyler, R.W. (Ed.) *Educational evaluation: New roles, new means*. The Sixty-Eighth Yearbook of the National Society for the Study of Education. Chicago: University of Chicago Press, 1969.

> Nineteen authors discuss the use of evaluation in various settings including evaluation of ongoing programs in the public schools.

References

Appalachia Educational Laboratory, Inc. Abstract of AEL model for educational development. Unpublished manuscript. The Laboratory, Charleston, West Virginia, 1971.

Bertram, C.L., Hines, B.W., and MacDonald, R.R. *Summative evaluation report: Appalachia Preschool Education Program.* Charleston, West Virginia: Appalachia Educational Laboratory, 1971. ERIC ED 052 837.

Crites, J.O. *Theory and research handbook, career maturity inventory.* Monterey, California: CTB/McGraw-Hill, 1973.

Curtis, W.H. *Educational resources management system.* Chicago: Research Corporation of the Association of School Business Officials, 1968.

Edmonston, L.P. A review of attempts to arrive at more suitable evaluation models: An introspective look. Austin, Texas: Southwest Educational Development Laboratory, April 1972.

Glass, G.V. *The growth of evaluation methodology.* Boulder, Colorado: Laboratory of Educational Research, University of Colorado, undated (mimeo).

Hemphill, J.K. The relationship between research and evaluation studies. In R.W. Tyler (Ed.), *Educational evaluation: New roles, new means.* The Sixty-Eighth Yearbook of the National Society for the Study of Education. Chicago: University of Chicago Press, 1969.

Hess, R.J., and Wright, W.J. Evaluation strategies as a function of product development stages. St. Ann, Missouri: CEMREL, April 1972.

Klein, S. Procedures for comparing instructional objectives. Report Number 76. Los Angeles: Center for the Study of Evaluation, UCLA Graduate School of Education, 1972.

Klein, S., Fenstermacher, G., and Alkin, M.C. The center's changing evaluation model. *Evaluation Comment.* Los Angeles: Center for the Study of Evaluation, UCLA Graduate School of Education, January 1971.

Pena, D. Analysis of social skills development in the Appalachia Preschool Education Program. Technical Report No. 18. Charleston, West Virginia: Appalachia Educational Laboratory, 1971.

Research for Better Schools, Inc. Educational development processes. Philadelphia: Research for Better Schools, Inc., December 8, 1970.

Sanders, J., *et al. Instructional development at the Ohio State University Evaluation Center.* Columbus: The Ohio State University Evaluation Center, August 1972 (draft).

Sanders, J.R., and Worthen, B.R. A descriptive summary of frameworks for planning evaluation studies. *SRIS Quarterly*. Bloomington, Indiana: Phi Delta Kappa, Spring 1972, 10-14.

Scriven, M. Pros and cons about goal-free evaluation. *Evaluation Comment*. Center for the Study of Evaluation, UCLA Graduate School of Education, December 1972, 1-4.

Scriven, M., Glass, G.V., Hiveley, W., and Stake, R.E. *An evaluation system for regional labs and R & D centers*. Washington: U.S.O.E., August 31, 1971. ERIC ED 061 299.

Stepp, E., Jr. *General evaluation design for the Educational Cooperative*. Charleston, West Virginia: Appalachia Educational Laboratory, 1972 (mimeo).

Stufflebeam, D.L. *Educational evaluation and decision making*. Itasca, Illinois: F.E. Peacock, 1971.

U.S. Office of Education, National Center for Research and Development. *Information and instructions for submittal of the Basic Program Plan for educational laboratories and research and development centers*. Washington: U.S.O.E., June 3, 1971 (mimeo).

CHAPTER 8

A HOLISTIC STRATEGY FOR
THE FORMATIVE EVALUATION OF
EDUCATIONAL PROGRAMS

Douglas S. Katz and Robert L. Morgan
Center for Occupational Education
North Carolina State University at Raleigh

The development of any new approach in education usually engenders speculation about the probable results of that approach. Light and Smith (1970) have credited current evaluation methods with possessing far greater power in detecting failure than inspiring success. It is our contention that while many programs may have failed in some absolute sense, current evaluation models have also failed, since only a few cases have been cited which indicate that programs have been changed for the better as a result of the evaluation process. The current view of evaluation assumes a static model in which some external source monitors a system at discrete time periods (usually after the program is completed) and imposes arbitrary criteria in order to determine if a program is successful, based on mean scores of the various functional subsystems. Such approaches to evaluation, usually termed summative, may be described as being product-oriented, stressing what is produced rather than how it is produced. This approach is less suited for program development and improvement than approaches that study a program in its formative state.

Formative evaluation, on the other hand, refers to " . . . the use of systematic evaluation in the process of curriculum construction, teaching, and learning for the purpose of improving any of these three processes" (Bloom, Hastings, and Madaus, 1971). Formative evaluations are designed specifically to serve as a source of information for decision makers during the development of their programs. It is our contention that a program that includes a formative evaluation has a higher probability of achieving its desired outcomes because of the increased amount of useful information available to decision makers. It is quite possible, indeed probable, that many programs that have failed summatively could have succeeded had information from formative evaluations been available during program development. For example, if the implementors are not carrying out the desired processes, it is unlikely that the desired outcomes will be achieved. The implementors might be unaware of the discrepancy between their actual behavior and the behavior necessary to the success of the program. This discrepancy will continue unless they are informed of it. A formative evaluation could correct this situation, while a summative evaluation would only include this discrepancy as part of the cause of the program's failure to achieve its desired objectives.

The purpose of this chapter is to present a general model for formative evaluations of educational programs. The distribution of decision-making duties contained in this model may need to be modified when applying it to a particular educational program. However, the relationships between products and processes should prove beneficial in conceptualizing most educational programs. The model is applicable to the summative evaluation upon completion of the formative stage. Modified versions of this model are currently being used in the evaluations of four federally funded programs in vocational education.

The initial implementation of an educational program is facilitated if a descriptive model is first developed to represent the components of the program. Figure 1 depicts a general model of this type containing eight different classes of components:

1. *Mission*: The ultimate purpose of the program.
2. *Desired products*: Descriptions of the throughput entities that must be produced to achieve the mission of the program.
3. *Desired processes*: Descriptions of the observable processes necessary in order to produce the desired products.
4. *Observed processes*: The observed processes described in terms of their approximation to the desired processes.
5. *Observed products*: The observed throughput entities of the system described relative to the desired products. Products may include entities that are still involved in the program as well as those that have left the program.
6. *Throughput entities*: Entities that are acted upon by the implementors in carrying out the processes of the program.
7. *Environment*: The forces external to the program that may affect the attainment of the desired processes and products.
8. *Decision makers*: The people responsible for the specification and implementation of the desired products and processes.

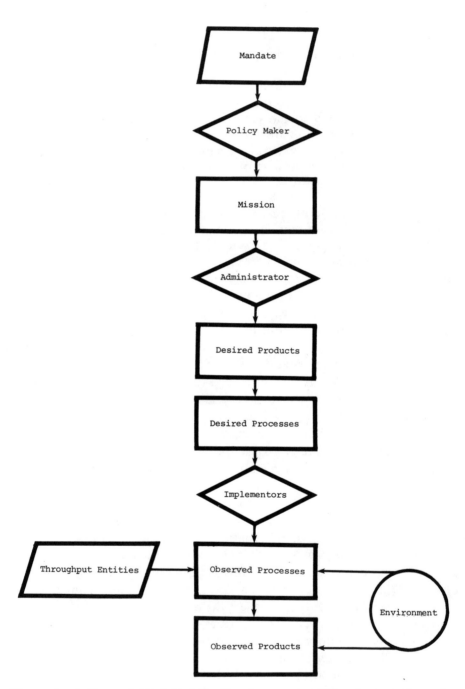

Figure 1. *A General Model of the Development and Implementation of an Educational Program.*

Mandates and Missions

The mission is the foundation of the program, and in the conceptualization of the current model it is considered to be the only component that must remain constant for the duration of the program. Identifying the mission of an educational program is likely to be a rather frustrating process. Does one look at the community, state, or national level of the ultimate foundation of the program? One should not look exclusively within the educational system itself, for educational systems are created by, supported by, and serve a larger system (e.g., the community, state, and nation). The mission, in turn, reflects the needs and values of this larger system. In some cases the mission of an educational program is partially imposed upon the educational system in the form of a mandate, which is a formal statement of the suprasystem's expectations of the educational process. A mandate is always imposed upon the educational system by legislation, regulation, charter, or other means, whereas a mission can be generated by a much less formal process.

While the mission of a program must contain the intent of any mandate imposed on it from higher levels of authority, it may also encompass the local needs and values. If the program is to be supported by funds appropriated from national legislation intended to attain national priorities, neither state nor local priorities can be substituted for the national priorities; although they may be added to the national mandate. Thus the program may include not only that which is defined in terms of the mandate but also additional components that relate to state or local concerns.

The mission of an educational program is thus likely to reflect a combined mix of the value structures of the community, state, and nation. For example, the mission of one exemplary program in occupational education presently receiving financial support in accordance with the 1968 Vocational Education Amendments, Part D, is stated as follows:

> The primary objective of this project is to plan and implement a developmental program of occupational education in a cluster of schools . . . to enable the system to achieve its objective of education to *all* its students in developing work skills that are suited to an area of rapid growth in population, industry, and technology.

The above mission incorporates the national mandate as presented in the Vocational Education Amendments of 1968, Part D—Exemplary Programs and Projects:

> The Congress finds that it is necessary to reduce the continuing seriously high level of youth unemployment by developing means for giving the same kind of attention as is now given to the college preparation needs of those young persons who go on to college, to the job preparation needs of the two out of three young persons who end their education at or before completion of the secondary level, too many of whom face long and bitter months of job hunting or marginal work after leaving school. The purpose of this part, therefore, is to stimulate, through Federal financial support, new ways to create a bridge between school and earning a living for young people, who are still in school, who have left school either by graduation or by dropping out, or who are in postsecondary programs of vocational preparation, and to promote cooperation between public education and manpower agencies. (Vocational Education Amendments of 1968, Public Law 90-576, Part D. Section 141.)

If one compares the national mandate with the program's mission, it will become apparent that the mission contains provisions that are not made explicit in the national mandate: (1) the mission is directed at a developmental program, and (2) particular types of skills are being focused on to best meet the rapidly changing needs of a growing community. It should be noted that neither of these provisions is in conflict with the national mandate.

Desired Products

Once the mission has been identified, it becomes necessary to define the desired products of the program. The desired products can be defined at various levels of specificity, ranging from desired outcomes to behavioral objectives. The desired outcomes (or goals) represent the desired interactions between the output of the program and the environment. They are derived from the mission, but are more content specific than the mission and stated in terms of the expected time of their occurrence. Hilton and Gyuro (1970) emphasize that the goals of education programs should:

a.   relate to the ultimate objective or mission of education;

b.   point the direction for future program development;
c.   indicate the trend of education in the State;
d.   be based upon the need for educational programs;
e.   be broad in scope; and
f.   be ranked on the basis of priorities (a result of balancing needs and constraints).

The number of desired outcomes to be derived from a mission is likely to exceed the resource capabilities of the system. Thus, it becomes necessary to rank the goals in terms of their priorities. An estimate of each goal's priority can be derived from (1) the probability of achieving the goal, (2) the expected utility of goal achievement, and (3) the expected cost of goal achievement. The probability of goal achievement is at least partially dependent upon the money expended on the goal, with some upper limit of the probability usually being less than one (i.e., there is a probability level for any given goal that is not increased by additional expenditures). For a detailed description of goal selection, the reader is referred to Vivekananthan (1971), and Coster and Morgan (1969).

Once the desired outcomes (goals) of the program have been defined, the desired outputs of the program must be established. The distinction between desired outputs and desired outcomes is frequently overlooked in educational planning, and the results of such oversights are likely to be costly. The desired outcomes represent interactions between the outputs of the school system and the environment (e.g., the community). The desired outputs, on the other hand, represent the desired conditions of the throughput entities upon completion of the program but prior to any interaction with the environment. If program planning stops at the desired output level, the environmental needs and constraints are not being given adequate attention. The outputs of a program should be chosen in such a way as to cause their interaction with the environment to result in the desired outcome.

Desired outcomes and desired outputs both refer to desired products that are measurable only after a throughput entity, e.g., student, has left the program. Prior to that time, the implementors should be concentrating their efforts on attaining behavioral objectives, which are sequential or parallel objectives necessary for the attainment of the desired outputs. They represent the specific behaviors that are the components of the desired outputs, and should always be stated in measurable, objective terms. Unlike the desired outputs, behavioral objectives can be measured while the throughput entities are still within the program.

Behavioral objectives are the most basic level of desired products used to evaluate a program. Every program is intended to modify specific attributes of its throughput entities, and unless a change in these attributes is measurable it is pointless to define such a change as a behavioral objective.

Another constraint in the selection of behavioral objectives is the cost of measuring their attainment. This cost must be viewed in relation to the value of the information it will provide. It is not uncommon for a behavioral objective to be rejected as unfeasible due to the cost of its measurement; unfortunately, this sometimes occurs when it is unnecessary. Some objectives can be measured in a variety of ways (e.g., academic achievement), and costs can usually be drastically reduced if random samples are used rather than exhaustive samples. Webb, *et al.* (1966) offers a variety of methods for collecting information through unobtrusive measures; many of these methods require negligible expenditures.

The most common rationale for the selection or rejection of particular behavioral objectives is their ease of measurement. This frequently results in sets of behavioral objectives that are only vaguely related to the desired outcomes. Flanagan and Jung (1970) point out that " . . . this tendency to emphasize the easily measured is a human failure and not a deficiency inherent in evaluation procedures" (p. 132). Information useful to decision makers requires the selection of relevant behavioral objectives. "It is important that measures be selected or developed on the basis of their relationship to the goals of the system rather than solely on the basis of convenience or availability" (p. 138).

Desired Processes

The desired processes are the strategies and tactics believed to be necessary to achieve the desired products. They describe the procedures to be activated by the implementors in their interactions with the throughput entities. As such they may consist of both recommended and required activities. It is the authors' opinion that each desired process should be functionally related to at least one of the desired products; however, frequently the implementors consider some processes to be valuable independent of any particular desired product. In the aforementioned case, any process that cannot be related to a desired product should be carefully examined for its utility.

Desired processes can usually be divided into two general categories based on their level of specificity; process goals and process objectives. Process goals are the more general descriptions of desired processes. They frequently apply to a large number of implementors, and are typically difficult to observe directly. An example of a process goal presently existing in a federally funded vocational education program is: "This program will develop and implement vocational clusters within the senior high school around which academic subject matter will be centered." Notice that this statement is so general that it can be interpreted in numerous ways; therefore, it would be difficult to evaluate its attainment. Nevertheless, process goals serve a valuable function in serving as the conceptual basis for formulating more specific process objectives and in assuring that the linkage between the desired products is clear.

Process objectives convert the more general process goals into both implementable and observable objectives. The process objectives represent the specific processes in which the implementors will be engaged. An example of a process objective derived from the previously mentioned process goal is:

> Each teacher in grades 10 through 12 will provide one learning activity with supporting lesson plans per month designed to help students see the relationship between her subject matter and a cross-section of occupations, with occupations at each level in the *Dictionary of Occupational Titles (D.O.T.)* being given major focus at least one time.

It should be evident that the increased specificity of the process objective, when compared to the process goal, facilitates both its implementation and evaluation.

Observed Processes

The observed processes are the actual activities engaged in by the implementors and/or throughput entities. It is perhaps misleading to refer to these processes as observed, for some of them can be measured without directly observing them. On the other hand, the observed processes do not include all of the activities engaged in by the implementors and/or throughout entities, but only those activities that are delineated by the process goals and objectives or felt to be facilitative or inhibitive to product achievement.

Let us first clarify what we mean when we say that the observed processes need not always be directly observed. Suppose that one of the process objectives was, "Each teacher will take her class on at least one field trip (per grading period) to an on-job site." A fairly accurate estimate of the attainment of this objective could be gained from the school records on buses utilized for field trips.

Much of the information related to the observed processes can be gathered by means of interviews and questionnaires administered to the implementors and/or throughput entities. For example, the process objective "Each teacher will have at least two community resource persons per grading period into her classroom to discuss their work roles with students" could be measured through questionnaires administered to the teachers and/or students. The works of Barker (1963, 1969), Fitzpatrick (1970), Griffiths (1969), Medley and Mitzel (1963), and Webb (1966) offer a variety of approaches for the measurement of behavioral processes.

Observed Products

An educational program is intended to modify specific attributes of its throughput entities. The products of the program can be conceptualized in several ways depending upon how and where the attributes of the throughput entities are examined.

Object attributes refer to the most basic level of observed products. They are the specific attributes that are defined by the behavioral objectives, and thus can be measured while the throughput entity is still within the program. Since the object attributes being measured reflect the behavioral objectives, they are program specific: the behavioral objectives for a program in business and distribution are likely to be quite different from those for a program in industrial arts. While the former program might focus on the number of words per minute the student can type and on his ability to operate various calculating machines, the latter program is likely to measure the students' skill with various types of industrial machinery. The behavioral objectives delineate the desired behaviors in objective, measurable terms of the throughput entities in a particular program; the object attributes represent the actual behaviors of the throughput entities at various points in time.

The observed output of a program can be thought of as the second level of products. Observed outputs refer to the attributes of the throughputs leaving the program either by dropping out or completing it. This is the cumulative effect of behavioral objective attainment and is measured relative to the desired outputs. The evaluator must now determine whether the throughput entities leaving the program possess the attributes described by the desired outputs, and if not, where the deficiencies are and how the program can be modified to prevent the reoccurrence of the discrepancy.

The third and final level of products is the observed outcome, which represents the interaction between the output of the program and the environment. The environment has been defined to include the factors external to the program that may affect the attainment of the desired products. In the case of the observed outcomes, the environment plays a crucial role in determining whether or not they are congruent with the desired outcomes. Decision makers responsible for the development of the program must realize that the ultimate success or failure of the program will depend on the conditions within the environment when the outputs leave the program. If the outputs of the program are not able to meet the needs and demands of the environment there is little chance for the attainment of the desired outcomes.

It should be emphasized that a program can achieve its desired output but not achieve its desired outcome. For example, one of the desired outcomes of a program in industrial arts might be to increase the number of graduates employed within a year after graduation. To achieve this outcome, the program administrator might decide that an appropriate output, considering the industrial needs of the area, would be to increase the number of students with job entry level skills in the aerospace industry. Two years after the beginning of the program the desired output may be achieved, but due to a reduction in government funds the aerospace industry may not be hiring any new employees: the desired output would have been achieved while the desired outcome had not been accomplished. Hypothetical examples are not needed to illustrate the difference between the achievement of desired outputs and outcomes; one need only look at the large number of qualified teachers who are unable to find employment in the field of education.

Throughput Entities

Educational programs can be thought of as throughput systems: an entity (e.g., a student) enters the system, is processed, and is eventually released into the external environment. Modification of the entity takes place while it is within the system's boundaries, i.e., while it is a throughput. The entities that are acted upon by the implementors in an educational program are therefore referred to as throughput entities.

The throughput entities in an educational program will frequently include people who are not students. Take for example the following process goal: "The job placement coordinator will establish channels of communication between the school and the community world of work utilizing resources of business placement offices, the local labor department, the Chamber of Commerce, and any other manpower agency in the area." None of these entities are students, but nevertheless their activities must be modified if the program is to function as planned.

At any point in time the entities acceptable as inputs into a given program should be capable of being defined. The types of entities that the program accepts as inputs can significantly affect the program's operations; therefore, as the types of inputs change the program should also be expected to change. A program that is not cognizant of changes in its inputs is not a viable program. Likewise, a program that is able to predict future changes in its inputs is likely to be able to adapt.

Environment

The environment of a program consists of the resources and forces external to the program that may effect the selection and attainment of the desired processes and products. Churchman (1968) points out that

... when we say that something lies "outside" the system, we mean that the system can do relatively little about its characteristics or its behavior. Environment, in effect, makes up the things and people that are "fixed" or "given" from the system's point of view (p. 35).

The environment may include other programs and components within the school system, the needs and resources of the community and state, parental attitudes, and the preexisting roles of the implementors and throughput entities.

It is quite possible for some of the desired processes to take place in the environment outside of the school system. Take, for example, the following two process objectives: "The student will be exposed to the actual work settings of all levels within job clusters," and "The student will interview workers in order that he may know how various workers view their jobs." The attainment of these processes is now dependent upon the conditions that exist in the environment. If the decision makers who select the desired processes do not attend to the environmental constraints there is a possibility that the process goals and objectives cannot be attained. The process objective "The student will be provided opportunities for on-the-job work experience in the community" is feasible only to the extent that the community is receptive to such a plan.

Decision Makers and Decision Making

The development and implementation of an educational program requires the selection of specific courses of action from a variety of alternatives. Two concepts are paramount in the decision-making process: the utility of the desired products and the probability of achieving the desired products. The decision-making process seeks to maximize both entities, that is, to maximize the utility and the probability. The utility of the desired products reflects their contribution to the mission of the program if they are attained; i.e., if they are isomorphic to the desired products. The probability of achieving the desired products is largely a function of the amount of resources expended on the related desired processes. However, it is assumed that there exists some probability ceiling for each desired product which cannot be exceeded by expending additional resources. The relationship between the probability of achieving a desired product and the amount of money expended on it is likely to be a unique function for each particular product. The probability of achieving some products cannot be substantially altered by reallocating resources, while others are extremely sensitive to changes in the level of resource allocation. The slope of the function indicates how sensitive the probability of achieving the desired products is to resource allocations; the steeper the slope the more sensitive the probability. Vivekananthan (1971) gives a complete description of the mathematical calculations involved in goal selection as well as a computerized presentation of the algorithm.

If the decision maker wishes to play it safe, he can allocate his resources to ongoing programs that have fully demonstrated their success. The probability that these ongoing programs will attain the outcomes set for them is relatively high, approaching the upper end of the continuum. New programs are more risky. First, they involve a risk because the actual outcomes are unknown, possibly due to a lack of specificity as to the operational procedures and resources needed to attain them. Second, there is a risk in disturbing the status quo of the entire system. Existing programs may be firmly entrenched in the system, and reallocation of resources may represent a threat to the operation of existing programs. Political pressure to continue operation in the ongoing pattern may also be great. Thus the decision maker may be unwilling to substitute a high-risk program for a low-risk program when the probability for success may be lower and the pressures to maintain the status quo may be high.

Concomitant with the probability of success for attaining a desired outcome is the utility factor of the attainment of the outcome. Utility is related to the goals of the program. As goals shift, so do the utility loadings for the specific objectives. Probability of success and utility are not necessarily related and they may be diametrically opposed. New programs may initially have a relatively low probability of success but a relatively high utility loading. Programs that have outlived their usefulness may have a high probability of success but a relatively low utility rate. Here is where the decision maker demonstrates his mettle, especially if he is faced with the allocation of scarce resources. He can play it safe, maintain the status quo, maximize the probability of success, and largely ignore the utility loading in relation to changing needs. Such an alternative maximizes the stability and political security, at least for those within the system who are likely to be affected by a shift in goals and reallocation of resources. Progress, however, is not made by playing it safe. Utility rates higher, in the long run, than probability of success.

We can apply the probability of the success-utility model for decision making to research projects. A research project may have a high probability of success from the standpoint of adequacy of design and execution, and a relatively low utility factor, where the information produced may add very little to improving or changing educational programs. Or, a research project may have a low probability of success due to inadequacy of design or execution, and a high utility rating due to its potential contribution to producing knowledge useful in inventing new solutions to long-range operational problems of education.

Obviously, both probability of success and utility must be maximized if research is to be of value. Basic research initially may have a low probability of success and a low immediate utility, but through replication the probability of success may be increased and ultimately the utility may be extremely high. *Safe* projects generally rank high in probability of success and low in utility, whereas *risk* projects may rank low in probability of success initially but may have high utility value. In research, as in program planning and evaluation, high risk often leads to progress.

Application of the Model: Evaluation Procedures

During the development of the program, some modifications in the desired products are likely to occur. The desired products (i.e., desired outcomes, desired outputs, and behavioral objectives) can be viewed as a series of subsets contained within the mission. Each set of objectives is derived from the set of objectives immediately preceding it and, therefore, any change made in one of the product objectives will cause some change in the sets of objectives derived from it. If a change is made in the desired output to closer approximate the desired outcomes, it is imperative that the behavioral objectives be modified to accommodate this change. It is important, therefore, that the procedures outlined in this section be viewed as an iterative process.

A teacher and her class are a subsystem within the school. Changes that are forced upon this system from outside are likely to be resisted. Pellegrin (1966) believes that forced change from outside the system is likely to result in overt compliance but covert resistance. The teacher might readily verbalize the process objectives while in fact she pays no attention to them when in the classroom. Change is more likely to be accepted when the teacher is given the role of a professional who is responsible for the planning of instruction rather than a mere manager of recitations or a monitor of self-instructional processes (Brickell, 1969).

Goodwin Watson (1967) suggests that resistance to change can be reduced if:

1. The people involved in the project feel the project is their own—not one devised and operated by outsiders.
2. The project clearly has the wholehearted support from top officials of the system.

3. The change is seen as reducing rather than increasing present burdens.
4. The change is in accord with long-standing values and ideals.
5. The change offers a new kind of experience that interests the participants.
6. Participants feel their autonomy and security are not threatened by the change.
7. Participants have joined in diagnostic efforts leading to agreement on basic problems and feel its importance.
8. The project is adopted by consensual group decision.
9. Provision is made for feedback of perceptions of the project and future clarification as needed, realizing innovations are likely to be misunderstood and misinterpreted.
10. The project is kept open to revision and reconsideration.

For effective implementation of congruent behavioral and process objectives the values of the implementor must be given serious consideration:

There is no doubt that the task of determining the objectives of instruction must rest largely with the teacher. We believe that at the beginning of the year the teacher should make explicit to himself as well as to the students the changes that are expected to take place in them as a result of the course. With these goals in mind, he will consciously make his selection of materials, teaching procedures, and instructional strategies (Bloom, Hastings, and Madaus, 1971, p. 9).

A formative evaluation of desired products would serve to refine them so that all levels would be consistent with the mission. Each subset must be congruent with the set from which it was derived; inconsistencies are a partial cause of program failure.

Many of the subsets of possible desired products are nonexhaustive, thus part of the evaluation of them should deal with their utility. The best choice of desired products at a particular level would have greater utility than any other subset of desired products. For example, if the desired output of an industrial arts training program was for each student to have skills that would enable him to perform adequately in the job area he was trained in, the utility of the particular areas chosen for instruction would be partially determined by the salability of those particular skills upon graduation and by the applicability of those skills to other occupations.

The formative evaluation of the desired processes (i.e., process goals and process objectives) would assist the program administrators and implementors in choosing the most expedient method for achieving the desired products. Feedback from the actual implementation of the processes is a valuable source of information for all decision makers. As Brickell (1969) states:

It may be that the roles they [the implementors] are called upon to perform are so different from those that are customary, and from those that they will continue to perform in other parts of the school system, that they cannot or will not undertake the drastic role shifts necessary. Moreover, if local role norms are supported by similar norms held throughout the profession, the role-changing innovation will have extremely difficult going (p. 294).

A formative evaluation allows for the ongoing program to be perfected rather than adhering to an initial best-guess strategy.

The formative evaluation consists of a series of analyses of (1) the congruency of desired products across levels of specificity, (2) the expediency of the processes to be used to achieve the products, and (3) the actual effects of the processes on achieving the desired products.

The first stage involves analyzing the congruency between each set of desired products. Beginning at the mission level this would entail (1) mission vs. desired outcomes, (2) desired outcomes vs. desired outputs, and (3) desired outputs vs. behavioral objectives.

The second stage consists of the analysis of (1) desired outputs vs. process goals, (2) process goals vs. process objectives, and (3) behavioral objectives vs. process objectives. It should be noted that the first and second stages can and should be carried out prior to as well as during the actual implementation of the project: these phases deal with *desired* products and processes rather than the actual products and processes.

All phases of the third stage of analysis deal with the discrepancies between the desired and actual processes and products, thus they require intervention and/or measurement after the project has been put into operation. Stage three of the evaluation involves comparisons between (1) process objectives vs. the observed processes during implementation, (2) behavioral objectives vs. object attributes, (3) desired output vs. observed output, and (4) desired outcomes vs. observed outcomes.

Table 1 presents the sequences of steps involved in the total

Table 1

Evaluative Comparisons Listed in
Their Order of Occurrence

Step	Comparison	Recommended Modification If Incongruent
1	Mission vs. desired outcomes	Desired outcomes
2	Desired outcomes vs. desired outputs	Desired outputs
3	Desired outputs vs. behavioral objectives	Behavioral objectives
4	Desired outputs vs. process goals	Process goals
5	Process goals vs. process objectives	Process objectives
6	Behavioral objectives vs. process objectives	Process objectives
7	Process objectives vs. observed processes	Observed processes
8	Behavioral objectives vs. object attributes	Process objectives
9	Desired outputs vs. observed outputs	Behavioral objectives
10	Desired outcomes vs. observed outcomes	Desired outputs

program evaluation. The first six steps are of primary importance during the early development of the program. These comparisons should be made in the sequence in which they are presented, for each comparison assumes that the preceding comparisons are congruent. It would be futile to modify the desired outputs so that they were consistent with the desired outcomes unless one could assume that the latter were consistent with the mission. The interrelationship among these steps is shown in Figure 2.

Evaluation of the first six steps is similar to a process in test construction called content validation. Content validation relies primarily on judgment. Each set of desired products must be viewed in relation to its representativeness of the set from which it was derived. Likewise, each process objective and goal must be functionally related to one or more desired products. The judgmental nature of this part of the evaluation strongly recommends that several competent people take part in this series of comparisons.

The seventh step of evaluation compares the process objectives with the observed processes. This will sometimes involve observing the interaction between the implementor and throughput entities. While there is no completely reliable and unobtrusive method for collecting such information, the methods described by Medley and Mitzel (1963) offer the evaluator a variety of approaches for measuring classroom behavior. As the authors point out, "To know how teachers and pupils behave while they are under observation seems better than to know nothing at all about how teachers and pupils behave" (p. 248).

Steps (8), (9), and (10) are likely to require statistical analysis. These levels of evaluation require measurement of student behavior and/or attributes; the desired information will come from both direct and indirect sources (e.g., observed behaviors, test scores, school records, and follow-up data). It should be noted that, as one attempts to measure these last three levels, an increasing amount of time will have to elapse since the initial implementation of the program. If a program deals with students in grades 10 through 12, it will take at least three years to gain accurate measures of steps (9) and (10), while step (8) can be measured after a much shorter period of time. Likewise, step (7) can be done sooner than step (8), since the actual process will always precede a change in object attributes.

Steps (9) and (10) are comparisons between the actual products of the system and the desired products. Statistical tests should be

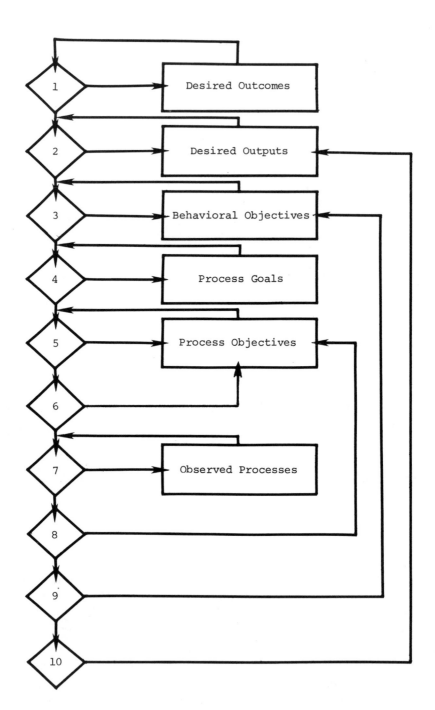

Figure 2. Schematic Representation of the 10 Steps Presented in Table 1.

employed to determine if there are significant differences between the observed and desired products. The individuals responsible for choosing the desired products are likely to find that the level of achievement for which they are striving is based on a combination of experience with the student population, educational research, and program zealotry; the desired levels might not be realistic. If there is considerable doubt about the appropriateness of the desired levels of achievement, a relative evaluation might prove useful.

A relative evaluation of the last two steps would involve a comparison of the observed products of the program with the observed products of a similar program. The outputs of the two systems may be compared in order to ascertain the possible effects of the processes on the products; however, in most cases the linkages between product and process are clouded by many confounding variables.

Formative evaluations of education programs are intended to provide decision makers with relevant information that can assist them in monitoring and modifying their programs. Just as education is a process of changing the learners, the products of the educational system must be modified to meet the needs of a changing society. Unless the educational system continues to modify its desired outputs the best it can possibly do is eventually turn out a product that is no longer needed.

The present model of the relationships between products and processes is intended to clarify the conceptualization of educational programs; hopefully it will assist decision makers in the development of innovative programs.

Suggested Readings

Armstrong, R.J., Cornell, R.D., Kraner, R.E., and Roberson, E.W. (Eds.) *A systematic approach to developing and writing behavioral objectives.* Tucson, Arizona: Educational Innovators Press, 1968.

> This handbook for educators presents in simple terms the mechanics of developing behavioral objectives which can be evaluated. Nine tests are included for the reader to review and evaluate his own progress in understanding the content of the book.

Bloom, S. (Ed.) *Taxonomy of educational objectives: The classification of educational goals.* Handbook I. *Cognitive domain.* New York: David McKay, 1956.

Teachers, curriculum builders, educational evaluators, and test constructors should familiarize themselves with Bloom's taxonomy. This comprehensive handbook makes extensive use of examples to clarify the wealth of information it contains.

Glass, G.V. (Ed.) *Educational evaluation. AERA Review of Educational Research,* 1970, *40*(2).

This issue provides the reader with critical reviews of the major issues in educational evaluation. Each of the six articles contains an extensive list of references.

Medley, D.M., and Mitzel, H.E. Measuring classroom behavior by systematic observation. In N.L. Gage (Ed.), *Handbook of research on teaching.* Chicago: Rand McNally, 1963.

The authors present a variety of methods for collecting and analyzing data on classroom behavior. The reader without some exposure to analysis of variance and covariance will find this chapter quite difficult.

Tyler, R.W. (Ed.) *Educational evaluation: New roles, new means.* The Sixty-Eighth Yearbook of the National Society for the Study of Education. Chicago: University of Chicago Press, 1969.

This NSSE yearbook contains 17 chapters on various aspects of educational evaluation. It is informative without being overly complex.

References

Barker, R.G. (Ed.) *The stream of behavior.* New York: Appleton-Century-Crofts, 1963.

Barker, R.G. *Ecological psychology: Concepts and methods for studying the environment of human behavior.* Stanford, California: Stanford University Press, 1969.

Bloom, B.S., Hastings, J.T., and Madaus, G. *Handbook on formative and summative evaluation of student learning.* New York: McGraw-Hill, 1971.

Brickell, H.M. Appraising the effects of innovations in local schools. In R.W. Tyler (Ed.), *Educational evaluation: New roles, new means.*

The Sixty-Eighth Yearbook of the National Society for the Study of Education. Chicago: University of Chicago Press, 1969.

Churchman, C.W. *The systems approach.* New York: Dell, 1968.

Coster, J.K., and Morgan, R.L. The role of evaluation in the decision making process. Raleigh, North Carolina: Center for Occupational Education, North Carolina State University, 1969.

Fitzpatrick, R. The selection of measures for evaluating programs. In *Evaluative research: Strategies and methods.* Pittsburgh, Pennsylvania: American Institutes for Research, 1970.

Flanagan, J.C., and Jung, S.M. An illustration: Evaluating a comprehensive educational system. In *Evaluative research: Strategies and methods.* Pittsburgh, Pennsylvania: American Institutes for Research, 1970.

Griffiths, D.E. (Ed.) *Developing taxonomies of organizational behavior in education administration.* Chicago: Rand McNally, 1969.

Hilton, E.P., and Gyuro, S.J. *A systems approach: 1970 vocational education handbook for state plan development and preparation.* Frankfort, Kentucky: State Department of Education, 1970.

Light, R.J., and Smith, P.V. Choosing a future: Strategies for designing and evaluating new programs. *Harvard Educational Review,* 1970, *40*(1).

Medley, D.M., and Mitzel, H.H. Measuring classroom behavior by systematic observation. In N.L. Gage (Ed.), *Handbook of research on teaching.* Chicago: Rand McNally, 1963.

Pellegrin, R.J. An analysis of sources and processes of innovation in education. Paper presented at Conference on Educational Change, Allerton Park, Illinois, February 28, 1966.

Vivekananthan, P.S. Development of a planning system for educational research and development centers. Raleigh, North Carolina: Center for Occupational Education, North Carolina State University, 1971.

Watson, G. Resistance to change. In *Concepts for social change.* Washington, D.C.: National Training Laboratories, National Education Association, 1967.

Webb, E.J., Campbell, D.T., Schwartz, R.D., and Sechrest, L. *Unobtrusive measures: Nonreactive research in the social sciences.* Chicago: Rand McNally, 1966.

CHAPTER 9

A QUALITY ASSURANCE MODEL FOR EDUCATIONAL
RESEARCH AND DEVELOPMENT

Jerry P. Walker
The Center for Vocational and Technical Education
The Ohio State University

One must remember that amid the collage of educational research and development models, systems, paradigms, and schemata—each replete with its particular set of assumptions, logic, boxes, charts, arrows, and triangles—there are many people every day who are actually conducting and evaluating educational R & D efforts. Despite the diversity of organizational structures, institutional settings, management styles, and political atmospheres under which this group conducts its work, there is a common and ever-present need to assure that certain qualitative standards are met. It is the purpose of this chapter to describe an evaluation strategy designed to help assure that quality is maintained throughout the complex research and development process.

Rationale

The fundamental rationale for this strategy is based on the nature of the R & D process itself. The fact that educational R & D is best characterized by and defined as a systematic process of uncertainty reduction is sufficient to set the stage for logically extracting other R & D characteristics that combine to form a rationale for a quality assurance strategy. One of these characteristics is the incremental and iterative nature of R & D, and the other is the necessity of making explicit, information-based decisions throughout the R & D process.

R & D as an uncertainty reduction process is one which begins with some type of plan. A plan is a set of intentions (ends, goals, objectives) and prospective means (strategies, designs, methods) for realizing the intentions. Uncertainty is highest at the beginning of a plan and becomes successively reduced as plans interact with reality. This interaction is at the heart of the R & D process and is called testing. The consequences of testing can include revisions in the

232

planned intentions, in the means for their attainment, or in portions of the environment in which the plans were tested. Thus, the R & D process is incremental and iterative, since plans are continuously tested and revisions made. As the incremental trial and revision process is carried out, uncertainty is progressively reduced. Uncertainty is reduced, from the point of view of the quality assurance strategy to be described, by having the R & D process interspersed with key decision events. The decision events must be planned systematically and incrementally; they must be explicit and information-based; and they must precipitate and ensure necessary changes.

In brief review: educational R & D continues to be depicted by myriad models and characteristics; at its core is the need to reduce uncertainty and maintain quality; this R & D process is necessarily incremental and iterative; the means by which the process progresses is one of assuring that key decisions are anticipated, prepared for, and made; the strategy includes the principles and procedures necessary to carry out an incremental, decision-oriented, quality assurance function in an educational R & D setting.

The Setting

A quality assurance strategy would have applicability in a variety of settings. It is particularly suited to an educational R & D agency but is suited as well to other contexts. A brief description of one R & D setting will help point out the contexts in which the strategy may or may not apply.

The R & D setting to be described is supported primarily through the National Institute of Education. The setting contains several divisions, including a Field Services and Special Projects Division and an Information Services Division. The division in which the quality assurance strategy is being implemented is the Research and Development Division. The five basic programs to which the strategy applies comprise the division. Each program is headed by a program director who is responsible to the Associate Director for R & D. Each program is broken down into work units; work units are further divided into milestone tasks. The programs vary widely in scope and purpose but all have as a principal responsibility the need to develop outputs tested and proven to improve a specified state of affairs. Program outputs range from developing competency-based curricular modules for teacher educators to the development of a technology for identifying and selecting curricular content. Each program is in effect a contract to develop time and performance defined outputs. Thus, the need to maintain and assure quality is evident throughout the R & D (uncertainty reduction) process. These milestones represent points at which important decisions must be made. Generally the decision alternatives at these points are to continue as planned, to discontinue the R & D efforts in that work unit, or to revise or redirect the effort. Interspersed throughout the activities of all programs are decision events; they may represent questions to be answered at any combination of program, work unit, or milestone levels of activity.

The purpose of this brief description of a particular setting is to provide a basis for better understanding the conditions to which the strategy applies. To summarize the organizational setting, it may prove helpful to highlight those conditions *not* characteristic of an R & D agency:

1.   The R & D agency is *not* charged with providing a direct, day-to-day service to clients. Unlike a public school system, it does not have to meet the daily needs of students; but like any school system, it shares a responsibility to improve educational opportunities. The differences are those of strategy—the R & D agency pursues a strategy of longer term payoff justified by the leverage potential of tested and generalizable products.

2.   R & D specialists are *not* basic researchers. The knowledge they seek must be justified by the ends of the R & D programs.

3.   Funding continuity is *not* assured. Support is contingent on evidence of progress. Therefore, the need for an increment quality assurance is necessary for both the R & D agency and its sponsors.

Conditions

If any strategy or system is to be operative and functional, one must clearly set forth the sets of conditions under which the strategy will operate and the criteria or standards that set forth the purposes it must meet. The 10 following statements represent the most important of these conditions and criteria.

Credibility—independence of evaluation from development. A necessary condition for the successful operation of a quality assurance strategy is the set of organizational arrangements that maximize the independence of evaluative responsibilities from those of development. This condition can easily be debated; it can also be easily misunderstood. Independence does *not* mean that evaluators work in isolation from developers; it *does* mean that the evaluative information serving internal and external decision processes must be credible. Evaluative information will have virtually no utility for decisions if it is not credible. Note also that credibility is an attribute of information that is independent of intrinsic qualities such as validity and reliability. Consistent with this condition, the strategy is administered through the evaluation division. The evaluation division is organizationally independent of the R & D division.

Compatibility. It is essential for a quality assurance strategy to be compatible with the set of rules, roles, and relationships that make up any organization. For example, a strategy would be unnecessary in an organizational setting developing products under a *caveat emptor* philosophy; nor would it fit within an organization not having some division of labor and specialization of roles. The strategy must not duplicate ongoing organizational processes. It must operate within the real time, money, and people constraints of the organization. It must also be consistent with the expectations and monitoring styles of sponsors.

Acceptance. At the very least, acceptance requires that the strategy's purposes and procedures are shared and clearly understood among those to be affected by it. While acceptance does not necessitate that all hold totally positive attitudes toward the strategy, it is evident that a quality assurance strategy cannot be viewed by all as a necessary evil simply to be tolerated. Each member of the R & D agency should view quality assurance as serving the best interests of the educational system, the R & D agency, and the individual. Acceptance is, of course, increased to the extent that those to be affected by the strategy are involved in its design and implementation. The strategy was designed by two "advocate teams" comprised of members of both the evaluation division and the R & D division. This early participation in the key design decisions has helped assure acceptance in both divisions.

Flexibility. A quality assurance strategy must be firmly rooted in basic purpose and strategy, but the operational tactics and procedures must be sufficiently flexible to adapt to the real-world conditions of conducting R & D. The R & D process is one that is punctuated with myriad contingencies: field sites must submit timely data; response rates to instruments must be sufficient; staffing expectations must materialize; collaborative efforts must mesh; and many other conditions and events are requisite for the R & D process to continue successfully. A quality assurance function must, therefore, adapt to these contingencies. Dates for reviews must remain flexible; specifications of the evidence to be reviewed may change; and times, places, and key actors for decision events may have to adapt to shifting circumstances. What cannot change, however, are the qualitative criteria around which a decision event review is organized. It is equally important that sponsor expectations recognize the need for reasonable flexibility in the tactics and strategies used to pursue R & D program objectives.

Openness. Similar to acceptance, it is necessary that the true purposes of a quality assurance strategy be openly communicated and understood. R & D specialists should understand fully that the consequences of any given decision event review might, from their perspective, negatively affect their day-to-day work. Similarly, evaluators must recognize that their role is inevitably potentially threatening to R & D program personnel. The responsibilities attached to each set of roles—evaluation or R & D—are such that only the naive would expect tensions of whatever sort to be totally absent. It is important to anticipate and to communicate the full range of possible consequences accruing from a quality assurance capacity in an R & D setting. The working relationships should be harmonious and productive, but they must also be devoid of hidden agendas and oblique purposes. The strategy must be seen for what it is; it is not a means of malevolent inspection and intervention, nor is it an innocuous ritual.

Resource effectiveness. One of the more difficult issues for the strategy to answer, and yet one of the most important, is the straightforward question: "Is it worth it?" The absence of a criterion by which this question can be unequivocally answered increases the difficulty of adequately responding to it. Pragmatic proxies for such a criterion include sponsor willingness to fund the strategy, policy support of it within the agency, and an assumption that its existence in actual operation is some evidence that it is not antithetical to the needs of the R & D agency or to the individuals in that agency. It may well be that the final answer must await the judgments of historians of educational R & D in the 1970s. In the meantime, one must accept with some degree of faith that an earnest effort to maintain and assure quality in an R & D setting is a worthwhile undertaking. The resource effectiveness question should, however, be ever present among the criteria by which policy sources within and outside the R & D agency determine allocation decisions. It is clear that too much effort and resources could be allocated to quality assurance; it is also clear that too little could be allocated and that the goals of government, the agency, the R & D specialists, and the evaluators could be thwarted by either extreme.

Focus on programs. Although programs are structurally subdivided into work units and milestone tasks, only the purposes of the total R & D programs can legitimize a decision event review. The condition (and caution) here is that often a quality assurance strategy must simultaneously maintain both a micro and macro focus. At a micro level the decision event may center on a question such as instrument reliability, but at the macro level the "instrumentation for what?" question must also be addressed. It is important that the strategy not be so narrowly focused that one discovers (probably too late) that one has been doing the wrong things well or that the program's elements are individually sound but not interpretable into a total R & D program designed and funded to reduce specified problems.

Internally initiated. If a quality assurance process is to have any real meaning or utility, its existence within the R & D agency should come from decisions *within* that agency to have such a system. The alternative is simply to react to and comply with sponsor demands for such a capacity. In such cases, a "reluctant compliance" syndrome would defeat the true purposes of a quality assurance strategy. A workable quality assurance process must be one which would exist independent of sponsor expectations.

Decision-oriented. While it should be apparent that a quality assurance strategy would in fact be decision-oriented, it is worth pointing out what this means and why this criterion is of critical importance to the strategy. In the first place, it is apparent to anyone involved with traditional evaluations that evaluation reports are notorious for being independent from the decisions to which they supposedly relate. Often, no necessary relationship exists between the evaluation report and subsequent decisions. On occasion, the evaluation report even follows the decision; at its worst it is a *pro forma* legitimizer of previous decisions.

Many steps in a quality assurance strategy are taken to safeguard against such conditions. Among them are the requirements that:

1. each decision event plan include a set of feasible decision alternatives;
2. candidates for decision events be developed by those who will make and/or be affected by the decisions; and
3. each step in the strategy be recorded and retrievable for in-house or external review.

Incremental decisions. If decision events are to be realistic and have potential for improving R & D programs, they must be identified and selected incrementally. If one cannot realistically identify as a key decision an event that is to occur a year or so in the future, then the identification should be delayed until it becomes clear that the decision event will in fact be important and realistic. At its simplest, this condition supports the adage that one should "cross the bridge when he comes to it"; from other perspectives, it means that the "fallacy of the synoptic idea" must be avoided. Incremental decision events do not obviate the need for sound and farsighted planning. In fact, they increase the need for planning in that the consequences from decision events update and bolster the continual planning process. Plans are essential to set forth the directions to be sought, incremental decisions are essential in determining the progress toward and necessary adjustments in seeking those directions.

Because the decision events must be incremental, they by definition also become aperiodic. Thus, one does not have monthly or quarterly decision event reviews. They occur when and as necessary to make decisions about R & D activities.

Characteristics of the Strategy Related to Criteria and Conditions

In summary it has been noted that among the conditions and criteria for a quality assurance strategy to operate effectively, it must be:

1. Credible
2. Compatible
3. Accepted
4. Flexible
5. Open
6. Effective

7. Focused on programs
8. Internally initiated
9. Decision-oriented
10. Incremental

Each of these has been briefly explained as either a condition necessary to the strategy's effectiveness or as a standard with which the strategy can be judged. Characteristics of a quality assurance strategy that address the foregoing 10 criteria and conditions are depicted in Table 1.

Strategy Functions and Procedures

There are four principal functions of a quality assurance strategy: (1) identification and selection of decision events; (2) monitoring progress toward the preparation for their review; (3) actual conduct of the decision event review; and (4) provision of information for decision making. Within each function there are numerous steps and procedures. A synthesis of the procedures for each function is depicted in Table 2.

Identification and Selection

Which decision events should be formally reviewed is perhaps the single most important set of decisions within the strategy. The source of information for these identification and selection decisions must come from the R & D programs. The identification and selection function begins with a request for candidate decision events made of the program directors and initiated jointly by the associate directors for R & D and evaluation. An evaluation resource person is deployed to individual programs at this time. The principal purpose of a resource evaluator is to provide technical and logistical assistance to program personnel as they identify and delineate decision events. Another continuing purpose of the resource evaluator is to maintain a log of occurrences relative to preparing for and conducting procedures for purposes of: (1) providing a procedural "audit" for sponsors and other interested audiences; (2) providing realistic information to program personnel and management to improve subsequent program planning, conduct, and evaluation; and (3) to help assure that program evaluation is conducted conscientiously and rigorously.

After an iterative process of identifying, reviewing, revising, and delineating decision event candidates, a final selection is made by associate directors for R & D and evaluation. The identification and selection function is one characterized by checks and balances in which

Table 1

Strategy Characteristics Related to Necessary Conditions and Criteria

Strategy Characteristics	Credible	Compatible	Accepted	Flexible	Open	Effectiveness	Focused on programs	Internally initiated	Decision oriented	Incremental
Administered by an organizationally separate evaluation division	R	R				R		R		
Use of decision event reviewers who are external to the program under review	R					R			R	
Provision for annual audit by the R & D division		R	R	R						
Review of procedures after each decision event review		R		R	R					
Designed by inter-divisional teams		R	R		R					
Decision event candidate recommended by program personnel		R						R		R
Decision event plans require a set of decision alternatives									R	
Separate fiscal control within evaluation division	R									
Resource evaluators assigned to evaluation; deployed to programs and specific decision events	R						R			R
Decision event plans require rationale demonstrating relevance to program goals							R			
Director for R & D receives all decision event review reports									R	R
Resource evaluators update decision event status after each review									R	R

Table 2

A Synthesis of a Quality Assurance Strategy

Function	Procedures		
	Input	Process	Output
I. Identification and selection	Request of program directors for decision event candidates made by associate directors for R & D and evaluation.	Program directors respond through an iterative process of designing, nominating, and refining decision event candidates.	R & D and evaluation associate directors select the decision events to be reviewed. With each is a complete and detailed evaluation design.
II. Monitoring and preparation	Program directors begin collection of decision event evidence.	Evaluation and program personnel maintain, update, and monitor progress toward decision events.	After decision event evidence is collected, the final selection of the decision event review process is made by the associate director for evaluation.
III. Decision event review	Performance objectives, evidence of attainment, and decision alternatives are arrayed for review team by evaluation personnel.	Review team examines evidence and objectives and judges extent of discrepancies.	Review team prepares substantiated recommendations for subsequent decisions.
IV. Decision making	Program directors review output from team and submit reactions and recommendations.	R & D associate director studies all reactions and recommendations and makes decisions.	Decisions are implemented by program directors.

different organizational units and roles select the final decision events for review.

The decision events selected for review are in the form of fully described plans containing four elements: (1) the exact nature of the decision event and decision alternatives; (2) a set of performance objectives derived from the decision event with each performance objective describing the output, relevant conditions under which the output was developed and is to be reviewed, and criteria or standards that each output must meet; (3) an evaluation design for each of the performance objectives that spells out in detail the sources of information, various means of obtaining, analyzing, and interpreting information, and the overall timetable; and (4) a description of the process by which the decision events will be reviewed.

Plans accompanying the selected decision events become the blueprints for each of the remaining functions of monitoring and preparation, conducting the review, and decision making.

Monitoring and Preparation

This function involves the continual adaptation and matching of plans and actualities in the day-to-day conduct of an R & D program. Throughout the monitoring and preparation period, the program personnel remain responsible for collecting, analyzing, and providing evidence called for by the evaluation plan. The resource evaluator remains available to the program for the same purposes as the preceding function of identification and selection.

The actual selection of an external team to review the decision event is not made until the latest possible moment. Once the selection and the review dates are agreed upon, the resource evaluator and program personnel begin final preparations for the review. The evaluation division has the responsibility for selecting and orienting the review teams. Program personnel nominate potential team members while the actual screening and selection is a joint decision of the associate directors for evaluation and R & D. The review teams are selected on the basis of expertise and independence. Each team member must be substantively expert in the area to be reviewed and have a minimum of vested interests in the possible outcomes from a review.

In general, the function of monitoring and preparation is relatively straightforward. The program director is responsible for following and updating his evaluation plan as he obtains and analyzes the decision event evidence. The resource evaluator continues to maintain the audit-planning log and provide technical and logistical assistance to the program. The evaluation and R & D divisions agree upon the specific reviewers and review process and the evaluation division assures that each team member selected is provided sufficient orientation to the task ahead—conducting the decision event review.

Conducting the Decision Event Review

There are a variety of options for conducting the decision event reviews. Materials can be sent to reviewers either simultaneously or in some order of sequence; reviewers can be brought to materials under the same conditions. Regardless of the specific review procedure which will vary from decision event to decision event, the conditions described below must characterize each review.

First, the evaluation division, through its resource evaluators, must obtain and array certain information for the review team. This is the same information called for in the plans that accompanied the selected decision events. The review team must know the decision alternatives characterizing the decision event, the specific performance objectives, the evaluation designs, and the complete set of evidence obtained by program personnel that demonstrates the extent to which the performance objectives have been attained. The review team will then make judgments as to the extent of, and likely consequences from, discrepancies between the evidence collected and the standards to be met by the performance objectives. This discrepancy is the principal focus of the team's review. The team is not to be concerned with such things as the philosophical directions taken by the programs, staffing patterns, or organizational arrangements. Team members apply their judgment to the discrepancies between evidence and standards in the form of substantiated recommendations for pursuing subsequent decision alternatives. Both individual and team reports are required. This task is completed when team members have provided these reports to program personnel for review prior to the last and most important function of the strategy—decision making.

Decision Making

While it is recognized that the decision making is not a simple or isolated event, it is described here as a separate function of the strategy because it is the culmination of all preceding functions, and it is the operationalization of the fundamental premise that R & D quality, responsibility, and accountability are enhanced to the extent that decisions are explicit and information-based.

The review team reports are sent first to the program director. Under his direction, program personnel review the reports and prepare recommendations for future actions. These recommendations may coincide with those of the review team or they may differ. If they differ, they must be accompanied by a rationale that explains why the review team's recommendation should be altered. These reports and reactions from program personnel are then forwarded to the associate director for R & D who has the responsibility for acting upon the reports and recommendation by stating and conveying clearly which decision alternatives will be pursued. He will most probably seek the advice and counsel of others from the R & D program, the director's office, and the evaluation division.

The associate director for research and development then conveys his decision to the program director who is responsible for its implementation. Throughout this process, the resource evaluator maintains and updates the log. Concurrent with the decision notification, the associate directors again submit their request for decision event candidates and the cycle is repeated.

The quality assurance strategy is continually evaluated, revised, and adapted to meet the continuing changes in the R & D process. Just as educational R & D as a macro strategy for planned change and improvement in American education is an experiment, so is any strategy designed to help maintain and increase the quality of R & D outputs.

Some Final Comments
The Assessment of Internal Decision Events strategy as it has been presented might be perceived by some as either an unrealistically "tidy" process ill-suited to the vagaries of the real world, or as a bureaucratic labyrinth of rules, roles, and procedures. To dispel either perception, it is important to point out that the strategy is a structure in which people, with all the idiosyncracies that people tend to have, interact daily. The strategy provides a sense of purpose and reciprocal responsibility to the interaction. The fact that the purposes of the strategy are public and understood by all actors in the system actually facilitates the R & D process. It is a legitimizing system in which

reviews of progress toward R & D goals become expected, normal, and legitimate activities. Thus, a decision to change the course of events need not be precipitated by some kind of crisis, by a wasteful accumulation of consequences from default decisions, nor by external or internal interventions that appear as authoritative disruptions. Rather, such decisions become normal and routine events viewed as necessary to the successful conduct of educational R & D.

Suggested Readings

Braybrooke, D., and Lindblom, C.E. *A strategy of decision.* New York: The Free Press, 1967.
> This is an elaborate, philosophical, occasionally rambling, but very convincing argument for an incremental approach to program planning, design, and evaluation. The authors thoroughly refute the "synoptic ideal" decision model which they argue is one that permeates our rhetoric but is virtually non-existent in practice. They offer instead an approach termed "disjointed incrementalism" which is better suited for planned social change.

Cronbach, L.J., and Suppes, P. (Eds.) *Research for tomorrow's schools: Disciplined inquiry for education.* New York: Macmillan, 1969.
> Research ("disciplined inquiry") is viewed as either conclusion-oriented or decision-oriented. The authors indicate that assumptions and techniques must differ accordingly and that it is a mistake to expect decision-oriented research to produce sound generalizations or for conclusion-oriented research to serve the immediate needs of decision makers.

Pratzner, F.C., and Walker, J.P. (Eds.) *Programmatic research and development in education: Positions, problems, propositions.* Columbus, Ohio: The Center for Vocational and Technical Education, The Ohio State University, 1972.
> This monograph, to which nine authors from diverse research, development, evaluation, and management roles contributed, represents the many perspectives held toward programmatic research and development. It portrays a field bound together by a shared purpose of "educational improvement" and pursued through a variety of approaches. Perhaps

the most important conclusion is that while there is not a *single* technology for educational R & D, each approach adheres to the principle of R & D as a process of systematically obtaining feedback and making key adaptation decisions.

Stufflebeam, D.E. *et al. Educational evaluation and decision making.* Itasca, Illinois: F.E. Peacock, 1971.

This is a state of the art treatment on educational evaluation which, appropriately, centers on the macro problems faced by educational evaluation. The authors offer their views on the processes and techniques needed to realize the (normative) definition of evaluation as a "process of . . . providing useful information for judging decision alternatives."

Walker, J.P. Installing an evaluation capability in an educational setting: Barriers and caveats. Paper presented at the American Educational Research Association Annual Meeting, Chicago, 1972. ERIC ED 063 339.

This paper provides a set of experientially-derived propositions necessary for successfully installing an evaluation capability in an educational R & D setting. These propositions and the explanations for their implementation are based on the premise that evaluation must be a process which is legitimate, systematic, and *decision-oriented*.

CHAPTER 10

A QUALITY ASSURANCE MODEL FOR PROCESS EVALUATION

Max Luft, Janice Lujan, and Katherine A. Bemis
Southwest Research Associates

During the last 100 years, the role of the educational administrator has changed from facilitator of education to financial accountant of education. The principal, formerly the master teacher, has become a "paper tiger" of the local education agency. With increased federal funding, his role has become oriented toward accounting rather than accountability. It is interesting to note how little of a current administrator's time is actually spent improving the role of the teacher as a facilitator of education. Principals, coordinators, and superintendents are engaged in a fight to keep records flowing to the governmental agencies, assuring money for their programs. These programs are often ineffectively evaluated, and their success is determined basically by their ability to be re-funded.

To facilitate the role of the educational administrator as an evaluator, the Quality Assurance Model for Process Evaluation has been developed. The purpose of this model is to provide administrators with an opportunity to maximize the identified terminal behaviors of educational programs. Highlighting this technique is an evaluation scheme that provides constant feedback regarding success of program objectives. This is accomplished by isolating instances of program failure and providing prescriptive feedback for these cases. Successful educational techniques and activities are also identified, and these activities generated from specific teachers to the entire participating population. The model permits varying degrees of time and financial commitment by utilizing an approach that allows the administrator to select the phases of the evaluation model that he feels he can adequately implement within given constraints of program, time, and money.

It is usually possible to increase the effectiveness of the evaluation's output by increasing the inputs into the evaluation. Inputs are basically a function of time and money. If a project is spending X percent of its funds on evaluation, and spending Y man-hours in completing the evaluation, the results should be more precise and more prescriptive, covering a wider area than a similarly-funded project that spends X%/2 of its allocation and Y/2 man-hours on the evaluation.

There is, however, a tradeoff of resources spent on the evaluation and the quality of the evaluation. While increasing evaluation cost allows for fewer expenditures on program supplies, equipment, and personnel, it should compensate by providing a more *productive use* of supplies, equipment, and personnel. Decreasing evaluation cost has the opposite effect of allowing more initial program expenses, which will probably be used less effectively.

Project management must then decide what allocation is available to be used for educational evaluation purposes. This specific model allows for two levels of involvement. Phase I has a lower level of financial and time commitments—with the restriction that there is a loss of output. Phase I, however, is basic to the model and must be completed alone or in addition to Phase II. The second phase requires more time and finances to complete. However, it generates additional prescriptive data valuable for program modification.

This chapter deals with the practical implementation of the Quality Assurance Model, Phase I and Phase II. Figure 1 indicates a sequence of events for implementing the Model. Steps 1 through 7 are basic to Phase I, while steps 8 through 11 are basic to Phase II. The steps are sequential with allowance for an interim process for correcting existing mistakes and updating existing data.

Phase I

If the Quality Assurance Model for Process Evaluation is to be implemented in a program, Phase I must be used. It is the goal of the first phase to determine if the project is being implemented on time, to identify behaviors that are relevant to the success of the program and generalize them, to identify behaviors or techniques that are negatively related to the program and remove them, and to produce a project management system that is aware of what is going on in the program and is capable of producing data that will validate the program's implementation. There are many unanticipated or side outcomes that usually result from implementation of this phase. They include greater

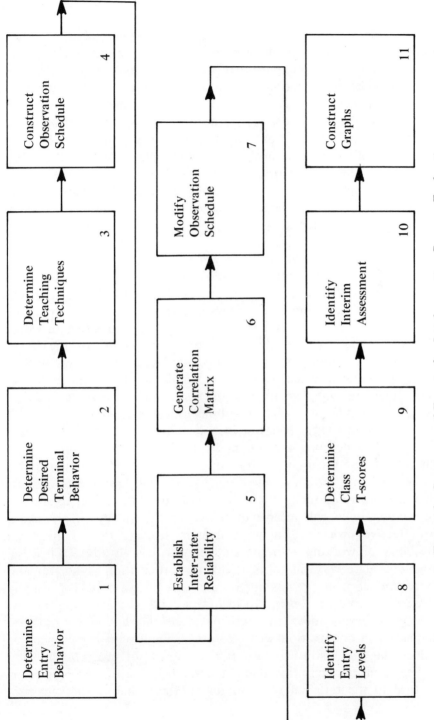

Figure 1. Sequence of Events for Implementing Process Evaluation.

teacher awareness of the program, improved rapport between project administrator and program implementors, and a general research attitude about the program that usually produces enthusiasm for program modification, rather than modification for modification's sake.

Implementation of Phase I cannot take less time than six months and can be effectively completed during a one-year program. It is, however, through repeated use year after year that the program benefits from the quality assurance notion. It is the general scheme of Phase I to identify the entry behaviors, identify the desired terminal behaviors, and then implement a system which provides feedback on the techniques and activities being employed in order to move from entry behaviors to desired terminal behaviors.

Step One: Determine the Entry Behavior

The first step in implementing Phase I is to assess the participant's entry behavior. This is accomplished by gathering baseline data. Many see this as an extension of the needs assessment, and this step can be included in the needs assessment model. Here the aim is to gather data relevant to the program that will provide a picture of the initial behaviors of program participants. Baseline data at the entry point are scores on a standardized instrument. Standardized assessment instruments may be supplemented with unobtrusive measures such as checklists, attendance rosters, and observational instruments.

Determining entry behavior includes not only identifying baseline data but also defining the program's maximum and minimum entry behaviors. Some programs are intended for a specific population, and it is theorized that certain types of participants will have greater benefit from the programs than others. It is important, therefore, to sift out the students who will receive the most for the money to produce a cost-effective program. Entry parameters attempt to minimize the possibility of working with the student who has already reached the program goal or who will not benefit from participation in the program. For example, if a process is being applied to a remedial reading program, it would be unwise to include a child who is reading two or three grade levels above the anticipated reading level. This must be established in conjunction with those who implement the program as well as the administrative staff. If a succession of programs is being implemented, one may find that the entry behavior for one program is identical to the terminal behavior for another. That is, the behaviors that one desires to achieve in a seventh-grade science class may be the entry behaviors required for an eighth-grade science class.

Step Two: Determine Desired Terminal Behaviors

The second step is to identify the program's desired terminal behaviors. Once the participant's entry behavior is known, we must identify the program's goals. (Such goals may have been established already and at this point may need only minor modification.) Once global goals have been identified, terminal behavior or performance objectives must be stated. These statements should include specific desired levels of the terminal behavior. Rather than saying the students will increase in reading achievement, a better statement would be "every student will increase .75 months in reading achievement for each month in the program, and 25 percent of the students will increase 1.5 months in reading achievement for every month in the program."

It is expedient at this point to identify the assessment instrument to be used with the objective. Criterion-referenced instruments are most appropriate for determining terminal behavior. One hundred percent attainment of terminal behavior is often possible if, in fact, the behavior is stated in criterion-referenced terms. Often, behavioral objectives or performance objectives may be stated for certain milestones within the program as well as for terminal goals. For example, after implementation of a program for eight to 10 weeks one may expect a 30 percent improvement over the child's entry behavior. This does not indicate, however, specific behaviors anticipated at project completion.

Step Three: Determine Teaching Techniques

After identifying entry and desired terminal behaviors, techniques and activities are identified that will most effectively move the student from the entry behavior to the terminal behavior. These are called *goal-directed behaviors* and are generated by the teachers or project staff in conjunction with the program directors. They may also be taken from previous lists as generated by other research studies.

All teacher behaviors can be identified as either *goal-directed* or *random*. Random behaviors are not necessarily "bad" behaviors; rather, they are behaviors that have not been identified as having a maximum probability of increasing students' success for reaching terminal behaviors. At this time, eight to 10 teacher behaviors or activities should be isolated which, it is hypothesized, will relate positively to student attainment of desired behaviors. These should be observable, specific actions, by which the teacher or student can be objectively measured. They are elicited from the teacher by the project director or other staff, usually in answer to the question: "What do you do that helps you reach these goals?" (The goals here identified are the terminal behaviors.) First answers by teachers usually are global and nonspecific in nature, such as "I help them enjoy class," "I let the students think that they are always right," "I try to increase their self-concept," but later teachers can be encouraged to reveal such statements as "I touch the student in a positive manner," "I verbally praise the student," "I let the student discuss with me things that are not related to class work," or "I reinforce the students for what they say." Emphasis must be on what does happen, not on what does not happen; e.g., "I don't hit the child," "I don't scold the child when he is late." These specific behaviors then form the parameters for teacher behavior. The parameters may be activities that occur as well as specific behaviors. An example of the activity might be: teaches three lessons in five days. This information can only be gathered by asking the teacher. It is not feasible to observe the teacher every day to find out whether or not she is teaching toward the terminal goal three out of five days. This is, however, a measurable objective. These parameters form a framework for teacher behavior. It is theorized that the more time the teacher spends in these goal-directed activities, the greater the chance for the students to reach the terminal behavior. Figure 2 summarizes the

Figure 2. Relationship Between Assessment of Student Entry Behavior and Identification of Terminal Behavior.

relationship between assessment of the student entry behavior and identification of the terminal behaviors. By periodically monitoring the behavioral parameters, one can find whether or not the teachers are, in fact, doing the things they have identified.

*Step Four: Construct
Observation Schedule*

The goal-directed behaviors are placed on an observation schedule or checklist that can be used to ascertain whether these behaviors are occurring. When using the observation schedule, observers must establish some degree of validity and inter-rater reliability. Validity is gained by identifying the specific behaviors leading to the affirmation of goal-directed behavior. This is accomplished by writing exactly what the behavior is. Thus, if "teacher touches student" has been identified as a desirable behavior, then this behavior needs to be more precisely defined as "teacher makes any physical contact with student, whether or not it is accidental."

There are three general techniques in constructing an observation schedule. If an item is a categorical situation that either occurs or does not occur during the observation period, then the statement may be checked either *yes* or *no*. Here, a genuine dichotomy is formed if all students are expected to respond. If all of the students respond during the lesson, it is checked *yes*. If all but one respond, it is checked *no*. A tally mark occurs each time a specific behavior occurs. Thus, each time the observer notes a specific behavior occurring, he tallies it during that observation. There is generally little need for making more than nine tallies of any behavior during a specific period. A third method of recording observational data is the slash-cross technique (/, X). Here when an opportunity exists for one of the teacher behaviors to be performed, it is recorded as a slash (/) and if the teacher takes advantage of the opportunity, the slash is crossed (X).

To be more precise, suppose that the desired behavior is "teacher positively reinforces the pupil's correct response." If Mrs. Brown asks Johnny what 2 x 2 is, and Johnny replies "four," the observer records a slash. If the teacher does not reinforce Johnny, a slash remains on the schedule. If, however, the teacher does reward Johnny, the slash is crossed. This marking system not only identifies which behaviors are completed, but provides a recording of teacher goal-directed behavior as well as opportunities for such behavior that the teacher missed. The following observation schedules are models and should not necessarily be implemented in any specific program. Each project staff should design an observation schedule or checklist that meets its own needs and reflects the activities and behaviors that are hypothesized as leading to the desired terminal behaviors. (See Samples A, B, and C.)

Interaction Observation Schedule: Sample A

	Tallies	Total
pupils fighting in seats		
pupils leaving seats (without permission)		
pupils speaking inappropriately		
pupils looking at objects at rear of room		
pupils interrupting others (talking, poking, etc.)		
pupils dropping objects		
pupils refusing teacher's request		
pupils ignoring teacher's request		
pupils not working on assigned task		
pupils making inappropriate, disruptive response (unsolicited communication)		
pupils shy, fearful (head down, etc.)		
pupils daydreaming (gazing out window)		
pupils copying from others		
pupils raising hand before speaking		
pupils asking questions about subject content		
pupils asking teacher for help		
pupils asking teacher for approval		
pupils volunteering information		
pupils offering assistance or cooperation to fellow pupil		
majority of class makes solicited responses		

Sample A continued

teacher allows pupils to leave seat without permission		
teacher praises pupils		
teacher calls pupils honey, dear, etc.		
teacher touches pupils		
teacher asks or allows pupils to help each other		
pupils ask for help and teacher helps immediately		
teacher uses encouraging remarks, praise, reward verbal		
teacher gives or promises reward		
teacher apologizes		
teacher allows pupils to speak without permission		

teacher warns pupils (or threatens)		
teacher frowns, glares at pupils		
teacher punishes pupils		
teacher calls on non-volunteers		
teacher uses sarcasm		
teacher criticizes or corrects pupils		
teacher speaks over pupil noise		
teacher ignores, interrupts, rejects pupil answer or question		

Teacher: ....
School: ....
Observer: ....
Date: ....
Time: ....
Boys: .... Girls: ....

visual aids neat and organized ....
classroom is neat ....
classroom is cheerful and stimulating ....

Observation Schedule: Sample B

Tally below each time the following teacher behaviors occur.

Check at right if behaviors below occur:	Verbal Behavior				Non-verbal Behavior		
	Encouraging remark	Praising	Warning	Speaking over pupil noise	Smiling	Touching	Frowning
1. *Establish criteria*							
T. stands by clock and mouse							
T. shows pupils how high mouse will go if they get all correct							
T. moves mouse down to zero							
2. T. states purpose for child							
3. Suggested T. Activity (only when it occurs in lesson)							
4. *Presentation*							
T. holds up stimulus card							
5. *Re-presentation*							
T. says, "Watch again."							
6. *Example card*							
T. says, "Watch me mark the ...."							

7A. *Distribution*					
P. have appropriate worksheets					
P. have names on worksheets					
7B. *Distribution time*					
0-3 minutes					
3-5 minutes					
More than 5 minutes					
8. *Administration*					
T. tells pupils to move cover sheet down					
9. *Grade and collect papers*					
0-3 minutes					
3-6 minutes					
More than 6 minutes					
10. *Confirm*					
T. tells pupils if criterion was reached					
T. moves mouse up clock					
11. *Rewards*					
T. gives out toys					
T. gives out tokens					
T. gives social praise					
None of the above occurs					

Quality Assurance Tally Sheet: Sample C

			4. Evokes Questions		Activity	
Teacher: .... Observer: .... School: .... Date: .... No. of Boys: .... No. of Girls: .... Lesson No.: .... Time Began:			*Gives Cue* (To asking of questions; "ask...")			
Mark every opportunity as it arises. (/ when arises; X when occurs)			*Teaches Cue* (To asking of questions)			

1. Reinforcement	Activity	5. Correcting Errors		Activity	
Waits (For child to respond)		*Central* (Corrects errors central to lesson objective one at a time)			
Prompts (With first word if he continues to have difficulty)					
Immediately (Lets child know right away that he made good response)		*Immediately* (Corrects errors immediately, uses response block, if pupil is secure)			
Group (Reinforces group verbally, nonverbally)		*Reinforces Correct Response* (Not the error)			
2. Modeling	**Activity**	*Re-evoke* (Have pupil say correct response again to practice)			

2. Modeling	Activity	6. Summary Data		Yes	No
Signal (Precedes modeling with signal, waits for attention)		1. Every pupil had chance to talk.			
Clearly (Modeling loudly, close to children)		2. Teacher followed lesson plan.			
Consistency (Repeats the same model the same way each time)		3. Teacher used test results for recycling and revision.			
Backward Buildup (Proceeds from last part of sentence to first)		4. Teacher taught three lessons in last five days.			

3. Conventions	Activity				
Listen (Uses verbal and hand signal)		5. Teacher used content tests.			
Repeat Individual (Repeat after me; "Johnny, say...")		6. Teacher does *not* proceed without pupils' attention.			
Repeat Group (Group repeat after me)		7. Teacher does *not* discourage vocal responses.			
Chain Dialogue (A to B, B to C, C to A)		Time lesson ended: .... Length of post-observation conference:			
Comments:					

Step Five: Establish
Inter-Rater Reliability

Once an observation schedule has been designed, those using the schedule must establish its reliability. This can be done by having observers who will use the schedule observe the same classroom at the same time to see where they agree and where they differ. After the observation session, the observers compare recorded schedules and note differences. Differences are discussed, and agreements are reached as to whether the specific behaviors should have been marked. Observers then reenter the classroom and observe again.

Reliability can be established through correlational techniques. One must, however, be aware that more than a "high" correlation is needed. If on three successive behaviors, A, B, and C, Observer One has observed three, five, and one instances of these behaviors, while Observer Two has observed six, 10, and two instances of these same behaviors, there would be perfect correlation. In addition to computing relationships between observers, it is necessary to note the number of instances. A rule of thumb is that the observers should be in perfect agreement on 80 percent of the responses and, therefore, when looking at 10 different items on the observation schedule, one would anticipate perfect agreement between Observer One and Observer Two on eight of them.

If a single observer is to be used in the evaluation, he may establish reliability by using a video-tape recorder. By recording a classroom situation and viewing the tape on separate instances, he may then roughly establish test-retest reliability. The observer should review the tape periodically to make certain that recorded scores on several observations agree. In a recent study reliability was established between two observers in each of four cities who never met. It was not possible for the observers to travel to a common point, so a video-tape was made of a classroom scene and taken to each city. The two observers viewed the tape and by comparing scores on video-tapes in each of the four cities, inter-rater reliability was established.

Step Six: Generate Correlation Matrix

Process evaluation permits ongoing changes in the program. If a program is modified, the evaluation techniques also require modification. The observation schedule will show many items that possibly have a low relationship to student gain. One purpose of the Quality

Assurance Model is to improve the predictability of the observation schedule. This is done by regressing observed behaviors and activities with student gain measured as the difference between pre- and posttest scores. A method that can be used is to generate T-scores for the pretest and for posttest data. Gain is then the difference between the posttest and pretest T-score. If several measures of gain are used and several entry behaviors are identified, it is possible to arrive at several different measures of gain.

Multiple regressions are computed to find the percent of variance in student gain that is accounted for by variables on the observation checklist. By squaring the multiple regression coefficient, the percentage of total variance that is accounted for by these behaviors on the observation schedule can be noted. Should more than one measure be used, various measures can be combined to construct a single measure of gain.

Step Seven: Modify Observation Schedule

Toward the end of the first phase, one must evaluate how effective the use of the observation schedule has been. The observation schedule should be utilized six to 15 times during the monitoring period and a copy should be given to the observed teacher so that she knows what has been recorded. One outcome is that teachers are constantly made aware of the behaviors they have identified as leading to desired student behaviors. Teachers then have the opportunity to modify their behavior by finding out which of the behaviors identified as goal-directed are not being performed. They are also simultaneously reinforced by knowing which of the goal-directed behaviors they have performed. Judgment as to the effectiveness of the observation schedule must be used wisely in formulation of a revised observation schedule. If every teacher is performing a specific behavior, there is no need, in fact, to include it in future observation schedules. From data being fed back by the teachers as to use of the observation schedule, and from the results of the multiple regression analysis, the observation schedule is modified. Modification is made by including new goal-directed behaviors chosen from the previous random behaviors and replacing those previously identified goal-directed behaviors having low correlation with student success. It is hypothesized that the revised observation schedule should predict student gain better than the original. As much as 80 percent of student growth can be accounted for by observation schedules.

However, it takes several revisions and many observational variables to reach such a level.

The observation schedule is only a means to an end, and not an end in itself. The end is being able to increase student behavior by identifying those activities relating to it, and guiding more staff to successfully use goal-directed behaviors. It is complemented by being able to remove those behaviors identified as having a negative relationship with student gain. The entire model is dynamic, constantly providing for modification and change as goals are changed, as entering behaviors change, and as different behaviors are changed from random to goal-directed.

Phase II

The goal of Phase II is to provide accountability through assessing student behavior. Where Phase I examined teacher behaviors, Phase II addresses student behavior and relates this to teacher behavior to provide program accountability. The rationale for Phase II is that students with the highest entry level will also have terminal behavior at the highest level. Students with low entry level behavior will have the lowest terminal behavior, providing that all of the students receive the same treatment. If the treatment varies from teacher to teacher, then those treatments that are successful (i.e., generate increased student gain) must be generalized to all teachers, and those treatments that are ineffective must be removed.

Step Eight: Identify Entry Levels

The first task of Phase II is to identify entry levels of the students. If Phase I and Phase II are implemented together, this should occur at the same time as step 1. Through the use of an assessment device, the relative standing of several classes participating in the same program is sought. The assessment measure may be either standardized achievement tests or criterion-referenced tests. Many programs have incorporated performance objectives in which measures are actual skill attainments as opposed to paper and pencil drills. Class averages are obtained for each teacher's group participating in the project.

Step Nine: Determine Class T-Scores

After calculating class averages for each teacher, the averages are changed to standardized T-scores. The purpose of modifying scores to the standardized T-score is to allow different assessment devices to be used throughout the evaluation. This also normalizes the distribution. A T-score has a mean of 50 and a standard deviation of 10. Normally, two-thirds of the class averages will fall between 40 and 60; 95 percent of the teacher's class averages will fall between 30 and 70. Table 1 gives an example of several teachers' class averages with raw and converted (T) scores. If teachers used exactly the same teaching techniques, if all students always responded perfectly to all instruments, and if all instruments were completely valid and reliable, one would expect teachers to obtain the same scores on subsequent assessments.

Table 1

Teacher	Class Average of Raw Score	Converted T-Score
A	22.3	66.3
B	19.1	56.5
C	15.3	44.8
D	14.8	43.2
E	13.5	39.2

Step Ten: Identify Interim Assessment

The next step is to identify an assessment device that may be used repeatedly during the project. If the project evaluation is to be for one school year, then assessment devices may be used at different intervals (i.e., each month, every two months, or every three months). The more frequent the student assessments, the better the evaluation; however, consideration must also be given to the time spent in test administration. No more than six student assessments should be made during the year, although different techniques may be used; multiple forms of the same test, or different tests, are among the possibilities.

Step Eleven: Construct Graphs

After administration of the first process evaluation, the scores are then changed to standardized T-scores. T-scores are now plotted on a special graph as shown in Figure 3. Change scores—that is, the relative change in class performance from entry assessment to the first process evaluation–are noted. The teachers who show an increase in their T-scores are theoretically using behaviors that allow students to learn at a greater rate than anticipated. Chance variation has been computed, and for four or five teachers participating in the program a fluctuation of 11 points will not occur more than five times out of every 100. The declining graph line would indicate a teacher whose students are not performing at their expected level of performance. Thus, in Phase II process evaluation, one can begin to get an assessment of the teacher's behavior by looking at the students.

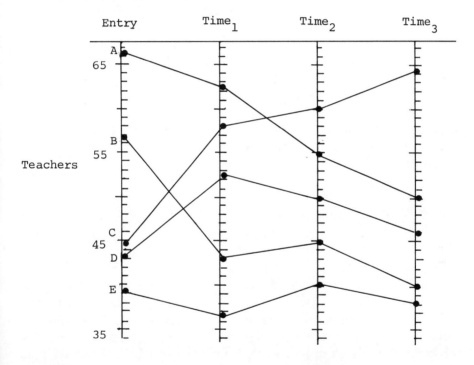

Figure 3. Profile of Standardized T-Scores for Teachers Across Three Observations.

If change in standardized T-scores exceeds the chance level, teacher behaviors causing the change should be identified. Two important conditions occur when the graph shows more than an 11-point change. If there is an increase greater than 11 points (note

Teacher C in Figure 3), the teacher is doing something to motivate the students. It is the evaluator's responsibility to identify teacher behaviors that are exciting the students to learn more than anticipated. When these behaviors are identified, they can be generalized to all program teachers, so all have an opportunity to benefit. The second condition (shown by Teacher B) occurs when the decline in student achievement is greater than would be anticipated. The project evaluator identifies how the teacher might want to change her behavior, and tries to replace random teacher behaviors with goal-directed behaviors. This may be theoretically sound but is often difficult to accomplish. However, by using video-tapes, repeated classroom observations, and consultation from other staff members, these behaviors can usually be identified.

Subsequent evaluations are made throughout the project with each successive standardized T-score being compared with entry behavior. Graphs of teacher performance on the basis of student assessments are then plotted at several intervals. It can then be determined what behaviors are and are not being performed. At this stage, it is most legitimate to modify program objectives as well as desired teaching behaviors.

Summary

Phase I includes identification of student entry behaviors, desired student terminal behaviors, and parameters of teacher behaviors having a predictive relationship to desired student terminal behavior. During this phase of evaluation, teachers are monitored with an instrument that identifies behaviors as either within the given parameters (goal-directed) or outside given parameters (random). Through Phase I evaluation, an attempt is made to replace the teachers' random behaviors with goal-directed behaviors. The monitoring instrument is periodically updated in two ways. Parameters of teacher behavior that have shown only slight statistical correlation with student behavior are removed, while different parameters that might be predictive of student gain are added. Seven to 10 observations are generally needed to generate enough data to complete an observational revision cycle.

Phase II concentrates on student performance. A number of student assessment devices are created or identified using either criterion-referenced measures or item sampling from standardized instruments; these are then administered to participating students.

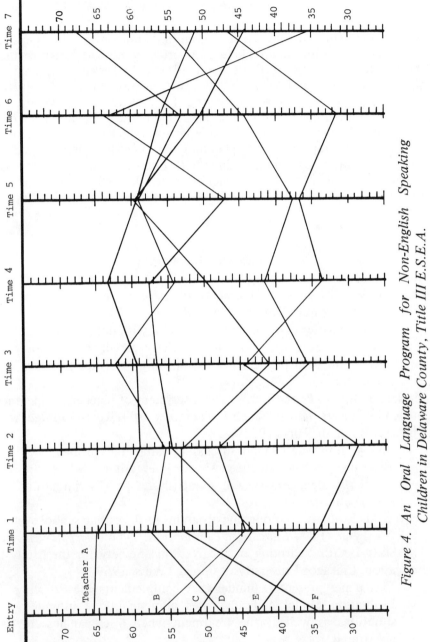

Figure 4. An Oral Language Program for Non-English Speaking Children in Delaware County, Title III E.S.E.A.

Averages are formed for each classroom unit and converted to T-scores. Teachers' classes are then ranked in the order of students' performance. After administration of the second assessment instrument, analyses similar to those performed in the first assessment are completed. Teachers with significantly increasing T-scores are then classified as using the program at above-average competence. In the case of a decreasing T-score, behaviors hampering the effect of the program are identified and replaced with goal-directed behaviors. Where teachers have high rates of increase in their T-scores, their goal-directed behaviors are identified and generalized to all participating teachers. Figure 4 shows an actual situation where this assessment was applied throughout the school year.

Suggested Readings

Glass, G.V. *The growth of evaluation methodology*. Laboratory of Educational Research, University of Colorado, 1969.

> Glass identifies two problems associated with data collection: (1) determining the level of specificity at which the most meaningful data lie; and (2) establishing priorities for their collection.

McNeil, J.D., and Popham, J.W. The assessment of teacher competence. In R.W. Travers (Ed.), *Second handbook of research on teaching*. Chicago: Rand McNally, 1973.

> The authors survey and discuss research and problems of assessing teacher effectiveness, critique criteria which are popularly used, and suggest six attributes for discriminating among criterion measures.

Provus, M. Evaluation of ongoing programs in the public school system. In R.W. Tyler (Ed.), *Educational evaluation: New roles, new means*. The Sixty-Eighth Yearbook of the National Society for the Study of Education. Chicago: University of Chicago Press, 1969.

> This paper presents a model that complements the Process Evaluation Model and advocates adjustments of intended situations as well as the treatment when discrepancies are discovered.

Simon, A., and Boyer, E.G. (Eds.), *Mirrors for behavior: An anthology of observation instruments*. Philadelphia: Research for Better Schools, Inc., 1967.

This two-volume anthology of observation instruments synthesizes and summarizes 92 observation systems. Included are comparison charts between each of the systems and detailed explanations of how systems are coded. Specification and monitoring of teacher behaviors can be facilitated by reviewing some of the instruments discussed in the anthologies.

Stake, R.E. Objectives, priorities and other judgment data. In G.V. Glass (Ed.), Educational evaluation. *AERA Review of Educational Research*, 1970, *40* (2).

Stake reviews evaluation methods, discusses judgment data, methods of obtaining such data and cites pertinent articles emphasizing what educators should be doing and not necessarily what educators have done.

Examining the Data . . .

PART THREE: METHODS AND TECHNIQUES

Part Three

INTRODUCTION TO METHODS AND TECHNIQUES

The following chapters present methodological considerations for the formative and summative evaluation of educational programs and products. The chapters are divided into formative and summative considerations, but these divisions need not be considered mutually exclusive. It is the spirit of this section that distinctions between formative and summative techniques not be made on the nature of the technique itself but rather on the *purpose* for which it is used. The following chapters on summative techniques, therefore, while of high interest to the summative evaluator, may also be useful during formative evaluation and vice versa.

Questions that have searched for commonalities between research and evaluation have precipitated distinctions between formative and summative concepts. Some of these questions have asked whether the methods of the evaluator are different from or the same as those of the researcher and whether new methodologies need to be developed for evaluation, or whether evaluation might profit more from using methodologies that already exist. Arguments on both sides have divided evaluation methodology into what is now called formative and summative, the former providing an arena for developing new techniques and the latter for employing old techniques in a new setting.

The concepts of formative and summative, however, may not represent different techniques as much as different ways in which techniques are used. For formative evaluation, techniques are used in ways that provide information for program or product revision. For summative evaluation, techniques are used in ways that provide information for program or product adoption. In the formative mode, information takes the form of changes in a program or product recorded over time. In the summative mode, the focus is upon overall differences between the program or product in competition with another, usually at one point in time. Information for program revision is perhaps the single most important characteristic of formative evaluation, while information for program adoption is the single most important characteristic of summative evaluation.

Just as it is difficult to distinguish formative from summative evaluation solely on the basis of statistical techniques, it is equally difficult to distinguish between formative and summative evaluation solely on the basis of time. Formative evaluation is not solely the process of assessing the effectiveness of a program or product during development, and summative evaluation is not solely the process of assessing the effectiveness of a program or product after it has been developed. These are often important distinctions, but they must not preclude the possibility of insights for program revision derived from a summative test or repeated formative assessments of a program long after it has been implemented. Therefore, just as formative and summative should not be separated by distinct techniques, they also should not be distinguished as predevelopment and postdevelopment activities. How then do we distinguish formative from summative evaluation?

While indeed some techniques appear more appropriate for summative evaluation, and in the main most summative evaluation occurs after a program or product has been developed, these need not become criterial dimensions for defining the concepts of formative and summative. More important than either of these distinctions is the *kind of information* that a particular technique can provide to the developer and whether this information has direct implications for revising the program or product. In formative evaluation, the developer is looking for what the researcher often takes great pains to avoid, i.e., he is hoping that as a function of his activity a program or product changes both as he is developing it and as it might be implemented across pilot or field tests. The summative evaluator, on the other hand, as does the researcher, goes to great lengths to hold the program or product constant. Interestingly enough, at this point the formative evaluator's interests are diametrically opposed to those of the summative evaluator. While the formative evaluator hopes for change, the summative evaluator guards against it; yet the key to both modes of evaluation is the type of information about program differences that they can yield.

Formative and summative might best be expressed as states of mind, viewpoints, or perspectives rather than techniques or points in time. The formative state of mind not only tolerates but hopes for changes in the program or product. From these changes, trends are recorded that validate some parts of program or product while suggesting the revision of others. The formative evaluator, while wishing for the best of all worlds, expects some failure and uses it to the best advantage for revising the program or product.

Information that can depict trends or profiles in the development of specific parts of a program or product are of primary concern to the formative evaluator. Even when such activities are carried out at the completion of a program or product and with techniques that may be used for summative testing, the activity may very well be formative in nature, and neither the technique nor the time at which it was applied makes it otherwise. When there are options to revise a program or product, then developers need the kind of information that will help them make program or product modifications. This information is cyclical in nature, documenting the program's or product's progress over time.

When options to revise a program or product are few and developers to carry out the task nonexistent, then the viewpoint, state of mind, or perspective of the evaluator reflects the summative concept. Profiles or trends are of less importance than tests of statistical significance. While the techniques may not change from those of formative evaluation, the kind of information that is produced must change significantly from documenting trends of component parts of the program to documenting the effect of the whole program as compared to a realistic alternative program. At this point the reporting of information takes the form of program or product comparisons. While the formative evaluator writes many reports, the summative evaluator may write only one report, in which he provides data that unambiguously state the effect of his program or product in competition with another. Results of the summative test, while of interest to the developer, are of primary concern to those who will decide whether or not the program is to be continued or adopted. Summative tests, therefore, provide the basis for policy decisions that do not necessarily concern revision of the program or product.

There have been important developments recently in both formative and summative evaluation. Three of these developments in formative evaluation which have been instrumental in shaping recent perspectives are reflected in the chapters that follow.

The first of these is the development of models and frameworks specifically designed to aid in the formative process. These models and frameworks serve as heuristics which the evaluator uses to provide more immediate kinds of information to the developer. Just as this book has illustrated elsewhere general models and frameworks for the overall evaluation process, several of the following chapters present specific models for the formative evaluation of programs or products. These models help demarcate important variables in the formative process— variables which may, by the way, be uninteresting to the summative evaluator. One such model is proposed in a chapter by Sanders and Cunningham, while the implication for other models is apparent in other chapters as well.

A second development in formative evaluation has been the introduction of experimental and quasi-experimental concepts to the formative evaluation context. Old arguments that have separated evaluation from research are falling by the wayside as formative evaluations become more sophisticated, utilizing concepts that have long been a part of educational research. Two such concepts are sampling and the use of statistical inference. Both concepts are increasingly used in formative evaluation. While formative evaluation may first have been conceived as descriptive in nature, increasing possibilities for sampling subjects and increasing evidence as to the robustness of traditional experimental techniques have led to the use of sampling and statistical inference in the formative mode. Many other techniques frequently used in experimental designs have been employed in formative evaluation when their repeated use produces profiles of the effective- ness of component parts of a program or product. Some of these techniques, particularly those discussed in the chapter by Porter and Chibucos, have become important for documenting the effectiveness of a program or product or its component parts during both formative and summative evaluation.

A third development in formative evaluation has been the application of correlational techniques to the problem of revising an educational program or product. Typically, correlations have been used to provide descriptive information of the barest sort, but new uses and extensions of the concept have led to sophisticated strategies for formative evaluation. Uses of correlational techniques for formative evaluation are emphasized in the chapters by Borich and Drezek and by Eichelberger. These authors show that correlational techniques can provide important information for program and product development.

Several equally important developments have related to summative evaluation. These developments include use of the general linear model and reporting of the "percent of variance accounted for" by the program or product. This approach, as Edwards' chapter suggests, is particularly suited to evaluative types of questions in that an integral part of this model is the reporting of variance accounted for as well as whether or not a particular program or product is significantly different from another.

There also has been a tendency in summative evaluation to break down distinctions between research and summative evaluation methods, with an increasing awareness that both employ hypothesis testing techniques and are conclusion-oriented. Previous distinctions between summative evaluation and research seem to have brought forth no new methodologies or revealed any real methodological differences between these two types of inquiry.

Lastly, there has been a trend in summative evaluation to choose designs that "fit the data" rather than to choose that part of a data base that seems to fit a particular analysis strategy. Such designs have included pretests, covariables, and potentially confounding variables as viable forms of information in the evaluation design, thereby using all of the data available to the evaluator. In this regard, as Poynor's chapter will point out, it is important for the evaluator to choose the proper unit of analysis, e.g., individual pupil's scores or the classroom average, in order to provide the most sensitive and appropriate test of a program or product.

The following section of this book is devoted to the evaluation methodologist. Hopefully, this section will encourage evaluators to develop new frameworks for both summative and formative evaluation that will be useful for the construction of new measurement instruments and in new applications of current statistical techniques. The evaluation methodologist is an important breed of evaluator. All other evaluators, no matter what their task, lean upon his methodology for appropriate tools and techniques to evaluate their programs and products. While every evaluator is a methodologist of sorts, those who have authored the following chapters devote a significant amount of their time to developing new frameworks and models, constructing and validating instruments, applying statistical techniques, and even at times fitting new statistical analyses to special contexts. It is hoped that the following chapters will both report new and useful methodologies for educational evaluation and to encourage their use in both formative and summative evaluations.

About the Chapters

In the first chapter of this section, James R. Sanders and Donald J. Cunningham identify four stages of the formative process. The first of these they call the *predevelopmental stage*, which precedes empirical data collection and seeks to identify needs through logical and empirical analyses. The second stage is called *evaluation of objectives*, in which both logical and empirical analyses are brought to bear to develop, revise, and clarify objectives. The third stage is called *interim evaluation*, and seeks to evaluate pieces of the product as they are developed. The final stage is called *product evaluation*, in which the program or product as a whole is evaluated, after which it may be recycled for further development. Of central focus is the specificity of techniques and instruments which Sanders and Cunningham relate to their framework. Their chapter, in effect, provides a catalog from which formative evaluators can choose instruments and techniques across four stages of the formative evaluation process.

In the next chapter, Gary D. Borich and Stan F. Drezek present a formative evaluation model for assessing instructional transactions for which they posit the need to collect three types of measures: implementation variables, outcome variables, and concomitant variables. Concomitant variables are defined as those variables that can alter the relationship between program implementation and criterion performance and therefore lead to "spurious" conclusions as to the effectiveness of any given transaction. The authors posit nine causal models that can be constructed from the interrelationships of these variables and suggest a procedure that discriminates among the models to determine which is the most tenable, e.g., does implementation cause learning, the concomitant variable cause learning, or is some other model more tenable? A step-by-step approach illustrates the procedure sufficiently to enable evaluators to implement the procedure in a variety of settings. The presentation concludes with an example of the procedure, showing how it is employed in an ongoing setting to provide feedback to the developer.

In a related chapter, R. Tony Eichelberger uses similar techniques in the context of evaluating ongoing instructional programs. Eichelberger provides a rationale for using correlational techniques in evaluation and, as do Borich and Drezek, cites correlational methodology as a viable tool for educational evaluators. Eichelberger's chapter relies heavily upon evaluation methodology that can compile evidence relating to particular questions. These questions, the author indicates, relate to documenting the strengths and weaknesses of a program or product, identifying implementation variables and their effects, identifying variables necessary for the program to operate effectively, and comparing the program or product with those having similar objectives. Only the last question falls clearly in the realm of summative evaluation. Both in the Eichelberger chapter and the chapter which precedes it, the authors identify the degree to which parts of a program are implemented as an important variable which, in the formative realm, must be used to ascertain the effectiveness of an ongoing program. Eichelberger concludes his chapter with a case study to illustrate the evaluation of an ongoing program during the course of five years. The author indicates what variables are important to study, how they are measured and collected, and what statistical analyses are appropriate. Of particular note is an illustration of a technique which provides a diversity of information to developers as to the nature and effectiveness of program inputs, processes, and outcomes.

In the fourth chapter in this section, Keith J. Edwards interrelates concepts of research and evaluation by illustrating methods of sampling and statistical analysis that are common to each. Edwards clearly dispels the belief that research and evaluation have nothing in common and illustrates some important conceptual points which bind them together. He contends that experimental design in statistics should be viewed as a neutral field to either research or evaluation, and then he goes on to illustrate how some important research concepts can be employed with ease and effectiveness in a diversity of evaluation settings. At one point the author illustrates a technique for using the classes of teachers with parallel schedules to form equivalent evaluative groups. This technique forms a basis for establishing a random sample, where before it might have been difficult to do so. Randomization then leads Edwards to employ quasi-experimental techniques to an evaluation problem and to illustrate these techniques sufficiently so that the reader who is unsophisticated in quantitative techniques may, if he wishes, employ them to his own evaluation problems. Edwards' discussion rests heavily upon the usefulness of the regression approach over traditional analysis of variance. Evaluators who wish to employ sophisticated techniques to their evaluation designs with understanding will appreciate Edwards' clear and straightforward presentation of an alternative to analysis of variance designs.

In the fifth chapter in this section, Hugh Poynor considers the important problem of selecting the appropriate unit of analysis for an evaluation study. The author points out that the evaluator has two options. One is to use individual pupil scores as data for a study, and the second is to use class means as the evaluative unit. The author's straightforward presentation of the pros and cons of each unit of analysis deals simply and directly with the question of making an appropriate choice. The author goes further, however, and presents the results from simulated experiments that make clear the effects of each unit of analysis upon the statistical test. Poynor provides a good case for choosing the class mean as the unit of analysis in some circumstances, particularly when the evaluator cannot control all of the confounding influences upon the study. As with the previous chapter, practical implications result for the design and conduct of an evaluation study.

In the final chapter in this section, Andrew C. Porter and Thomas R. Chibucos provide a rationale for selecting different analysis strategies to evaluate educational programs and products. While an increasing trend has been to favor one particular form of analysis over another, Porter and Chibucos make a strong case for the interrelationship that exists between strategies. They show how an understanding of this interrelationship can lead evaluators to choose the most appropriate design. The authors examine different variations of analysis of covariance and analysis of variance in an attempt to point out the advantages and disadvantages of each variation to problems in educational evaluation. Extending concepts presented by Edwards, Porter and Chibucos go on to provide a guide for educational evaluators in choosing the analysis strategy best suited to their particular problem. Of special interest is their comprehensive treatment of key issues which should be taken into consideration before choosing an analysis strategy.

CHAPTER 11

FORMATIVE EVALUATION: SELECTING
TECHNIQUES AND PROCEDURES

James R. Sanders and Donald J. Cunningham
Indiana University

Sanders and Cunningham (1973) recently extended the writing of Scriven (1967) on the nature of formative evaluation. Formative evaluation was defined as the process of judging an entity, or its components, that could be revised in form, for the expressed purpose of providing feedback to persons directly involved in the formation of the entity. The authors defined a two-dimensional framework comprising formative evaluation activity as one dimension and source of information as the other. Four types of formative evaluation activity were identified and defined as follows:

1. *Predevelopmental Activities*—formative evaluation work that occurs before formal product development has started. Formative evaluation tasks related to the evaluation of needs, tasks, or other planning activities fall into this category.

2. *Evaluation of Objectives Activities*—formative evaluation work directed at judging objectives in product development. The emphasis of work in this category is on the provision of reliable information about the worth of goal statements produced by the product developer. Both logical and empirical evaluation strategies are included.

3. *Formative Interim Evaluation Activities*—formative work dealing with the appraisal of early product development efforts. Formal evaluation activities in this category are interim payoff evaluation work, interim intrinsic evaluation work, and the evaluation of program or project operations. Informal evaluation activities, often unobtrusive, are also included.

4. *Formative Product Evaluation Activities*—formative evaluation work that focuses on the appraisal of a finished draft of

the proposed product. Strategies such as validation studies, cost analyses, descriptive analyses, and goal-free evaluation directed toward a product draft comprise this category.

Three primary sources of information are identified for consideration as the evaluator engages in the four types of formative evaluation activity listed above. These sources are labeled and defined as follows:

1. *Internal Information*—information that could be generated by inspecting the entity itself. Included in this category are descriptive information about and critical appraisals of the entity.

2. *External Information*—information concerning the effects of an entity on the behaviors of relevant groups. Student achievement after using a product or parental attitudes toward the objectives of a product are examples of information placed in this category.

3. *Contextual Information*—information concerning the conditions under which an entity is expected to function. Classroom environment, pupil characteristics, and time of year are three examples of information that fall into this category.

The two dimensions are crossed in a summary table including evaluation techniques and procedures as cell entries (see Table 1).

**Techniques and Procedures for
Predevelopmental Formative Evaluation**

Procedures and techniques for predevelopmental formative evaluation are often nonexistent in typical evaluation systems, or at best they are very informal. Given the immediate need for production in most developmental projects, this situation is often explained away, but it can never be reconciled when expensive errors are made during later stages of development. For this reason, we recommend the fullest amount of predevelopmental formative evaluation possible (within the constraints of scheduling, costs, and politics) using inexpensive approximations whenever formal, complete techniques and procedures are ruled unrealistic. In the following paragraphs are a few of the methods that the formative evaluator may want to draw on before development actually begins.

It is instructive in this regard to consider carefully procedures used by the National Assessment of Educational Progress (NAEP) project

(1970) and the Institute for Social Research (ISR) (1969) at the University of Michigan to identify refined techniques for accomplishing necessary predevelopmental activities. The techniques described here are ideals that can be quite expensive, but there is nothing to prevent the formative evaluator from adapting them to meet his needs. One technical problem area that has emerged recently is that of choosing an appropriate sample.

Sampling techniques. The NAEP sampling plans have been developed to meet two criteria: high accuracy in parameter estimation and low cost. The nationwide probability sampling plan comprises a stratified multistage design. The parameter of interest, P_1, is the proportion of the total number of persons in a certain subpopulation of the United States that answers an exercise in a certain way (e.g., P_1 = proportion answering "yes;" P_2 = proportion answering "no"; P_3 = proportion answering "I don't know" to a three-option exercise). Each parameter is estimated by first estimating the total number of persons in the subpopulation, then estimating the number who would select each option on an exercise, and then expressing the estimate, P, as a ratio of the latter to the former. This becomes a combined ratio estimate when applied to a stratified sample. The sampling plan includes *listing units* (small geographic areas, often counties, with a minimum size of 16,000 persons and easily identified boundaries) as the major unit, *primary sampling units* (PSU) within each listing unit determined by size of community according to census populations, income, and geographic location, and *secondary sampling units* (SSU) into which PSU's are divided consisting of clusters of 35-40 housing units. Ten SSU's are randomly drawn from each PSU and are expected to yield 12.5 adult respondents on the average.

The Institute for Social Research also uses a multistage sampling plan for most of its large studies. The steps of the sampling procedure progress through various stages of selection going from larger to smaller areas. These steps parallel closely those used by NAEP. Briefly, the ISR sampling plan leads to the identification of *primary sampling units* (PSU), usually counties or metropolitan areas, first. The PSU's are then stratified by relevant dimensions, such as urban versus rural areas, income of areas, and so on. PSU's are then randomly drawn from the strata, proportionate to the total number of PSU's in each stratum. PSU's are then subdivided into smaller areas called *sample places* and each sample place is subdivided into *chunks* which are areas within a

Table 1

Summary of Techniques and Procedures
Appropriate for Formative Evaluation

		Formative Evaluation Activity			
		Predevelopmental	Evaluation of Objectives	Interim	Product
Source of Information	Internal	Logical analyses of needs: 1. Cogency 2. Consequences 3. Higher order values Empirical analyses of needs: 1. Group data: Surveys Scaling Q-technique Semantic differential Delphi technique Sentence completion 2. Observation and expert opinion Unobtrusive measures Accreditation processes Category systems Rating systems 3. Analysis of documents Unobtrusive measures Content analysis	Logical analyses: 1. Cogency 2. Consequences 3. Higher order values Empirical analyses: 1. Group data: Surveys Scaling Q-technique Semantic differential Delphi technique Sentence completion 2. Observation and expert opinion Unobtrusive measures Accreditation processes Category systems Rating systems 3. Analysis of documents Unobtrusive measures Content analysis	Materials analysis guidelines Content analysis Analysis of learning structures Group data (critical appraisal) Expert opinion (including author) Unobtrusive measures PERT PPBS System analysis	Cost analyses Materials analysis guidelines Content analysis Group data (critical appraisal) Expert opinion Unobtrusive measures

Table 1 continued

			Operationalization of objectives Experimental tryout of goals statements	Experimental and quasi-experimental design Clinical methods Quantitative naturalistic observation techniques Unobtrusive measures	Experimental and quasi-experimental design; hypothesis testing Cost analyses GFE Correlational analyses Quantitative naturalistic observation techniques Unobtrusive measures Group data perceived (on effectiveness of product) Observation techniques
External					
Contextual	Needs assessment	Context assessment (if no needs assessment results available)	Literature reviews Informal observation	ATI procedures Context assessment (focus on external validity)	

sample place which have identifiable boundaries (e.g., township, city block, an area bounded by identifiable roads, streams, etc.). Several chunks are then selected randomly from each sample place for the sample and *dwelling units* are then identified within the selected chunks. A final step in the ISR sampling procedure is the random selection of 3-4 dwelling units within a chunk, called a *segment*, and these dwelling units are used in the study.

Reporting procedures for survey data used by NAEP provide a useful model for reporting predevelopmental formative evaluation activities. It is most informative to the reader to provide the complete item along with estimates of the proportion of persons in each subpopulation who would choose each item. It is also important to provide normative data for the subpopulation that can be used to interpret the reported parameter estimates. For example, data reported by geographical region on an overlap item given to respondents aged 13, 17, and adult, should include response estimates for the entire population (over all geographical regions) as well as data by age reported side by side for comparison purposes. It is recommended that all planning data (on needs, objectives, etc.) be reported alongside data on relevant referent groups (norms). Descriptive statistics and parameter estimates are the most useful data reduction procedures at this stage of the development of large-scale assessment procedures.

The value of using multistage scientific sampling procedures for collecting survey data should not be underestimated. Obtaining precise estimates of relevant human parameters is an essential part of precise product development. While the above discussion has not been prescriptive by any means (considering the almost infinite number of variations of basic multistage sampling plans, context-free recommendations are virtually impossible), it supports the adaptation of sampling plans already in use for predevelopmental formative evaluation.

Q-sort. One technique for evaluating needs and objectives frequently mentioned in many recent papers on formative evaluation is the *Q-sort.* Methods for collecting appraisal or judgmental data from relevant groups of persons on simply and tersely stated needs or objectives is essential in predevelopmental and objectives formative evaluation. Fortunately, the procedures developed by Stephenson (1953) and labeled Q-methodology are most appropriate. The Q-technique is the logical operationalization of Stephenson's theoretical Q-methodology. Briefly, a list of need statements or goal (objective) statements may be assigned numerals, placed on cards, and given to persons to rank order according to some predetermined rules. The ordinal data that result from the sorts may then be analyzed to yield a number of useful statistics such as:

1. consistency or homogeneity of ranking within a group of persons (answering the question of how much do people agree on their perceptions of the needs or objectives);

2. overall (and subgrouped) rankings (or sets of priorities) on the list of needs or objectives (and also the variance for each need or objective statement);

3. differences in ranking profiles among groups of persons (e.g., a summary of differences among a school board, the school teachers, the school administrators, and parents on the priorities or values assigned to a list of needs or objectives);

4. clusters of needs or objectives as ranked by a given group of persons;

5. clusters of persons as they rank needs or objectives (e.g., Do Republicans versus Democrats cluster respectively on their priorities?); and

6. similarity of the distribution of rankings by a group of persons to an ideal or criterion distribution.

There are two basic types of Q-sort, each with a particular use: *structured* and *unstructured*. Structured Q-sorts include a set of rules whereby a certain number of cards (needs or objectives) must be placed in each of a certain number of piles (e.g., left-hand piles for most valuable and right-hand piles for least valuable needs or objectives). Cards are forced into a predetermined distribution according to some theory. Unstructured Q-sorts are those used where there is no underlying theory and cards are placed into a predetermined number of piles according to the sorter's own perceptions of where they should be placed. In essence, this says, "Let the cards fall where they may."

The procedures used to collect Q-sort data generally follow these steps:

1. Place unambiguous needs or objectives statements on cards, one to a card. Theoretically, at least 75 but no more than 140 items should be sorted.

2. Shuffle or randomly order the cards and give them to a person to sort. The same random order should be given to each person.

3.   Sort the cards into some predetermined distribution. Usually 7-13 piles of cards are used, but this can be modified, depending on the needs of the investigator. For example, if 80 items were to be sorted into a quasi-normal distribution, the following rules might be set: Sort the cards into 9 piles with the number in each pile set as follows:

4   6   10   12   16   12   10   6   4

The left-most pile represents most valuable needs or objectives and the right-most pile represents least valuable needs or objectives.

4.   Collect the cards as sorted by the person and assign ranks to the cards in each pile (e.g., 1 to cards in left-most pile and 10 to cards in right-most pile).

5.   Calculate desired statistics on resultant data.

Task analysis. A set of procedures which are not often used, but which should be essential to systematic product development are those that fall under the rubric of task analysis. This activity is described by Davies (1973) and Thiagarajan, Semmel, and Semmel (1973). Early work by developers of programmed instruction has also contributed greatly to the refinement of task analysis techniques. This activity is not clearly evaluative, since the judging process is not involved, but task analysis (like objectives writing) is often a function assigned to the evaluator by his clients.

There is some uncertainty about whether this activity is appropriate to the predevelopmental stage of product development. At a point when global needs and goals are the only existing descriptions of the final product, it is worth partitioning these global outcomes into component parts. This activity could then lead directly into the preparation of interim and terminal objectives that have cogent bases for their existence. Because of the uncertainty associated with the appropriateness of task analysis activities at this point, the technique is discussed both here and in the formative interim evaluation section of this chapter. Task analysis techniques are involved primarily with the prescription of the prerequisites and conditions under which behaviors may be developed and a description of the behaviors which comprise a given performance. Thiagarajan, Semmel, and Semmel (1973) list the following steps for performing a task analysis:

1. Specify the main task (or performance). This statement should indicate how the subject is to use a given product and the situation in which he is to perform.
2. Identify subtasks. These statements should include the skills that the subject must possess in order to demonstrate the criterion performance.
3. For each subtask, identify sub-subtasks which contribute to that subtask.
4. Terminate reduction of tasks into subtasks when the subtasks are equivalent to the subject's entry behavior.

An example of such a task analysis is found in Figure 1.

Davies suggested that task analysis approaches such as the one described above are but one of six different approaches. His six categories of task analysis are:

1. Task analysis based upon objectives. This method includes the specification of instructional objectives and the specification, for each objective, of the type of behavior (e.g., knowledge, comprehension, receiving, responding, etc.) required for each.
2. Task analysis based upon behavioral analysis (above).
3. Task analysis based on information processing. This method includes a prescription of information to be processed for the performance to be mastered. Considerations of cues, manipulations to be made, feedback, etc., are central to this method.
4. Task analysis based on a decision paradigm. Underlying decisons which must be made to perform a given task are analyzed and decision chains and procedures are provided.
5. Task analysis based on content structure. This method includes the identification of rules and examples of value to the task, the presentation of these rules and examples and the discussion of relationships between them.
6. Task analysis based on vocational schemes. This method involves the reduction of a performance into jobs, duties, tasks, and task elements.

Davies noted that these six categories are not mutually exclusive, but do suggest central elements of different approaches to the problem of task analysis. The state of the art in this area is such that a considerable amount of research is still needed to expose the utility of each task analysis approach for use in quality product development. While the

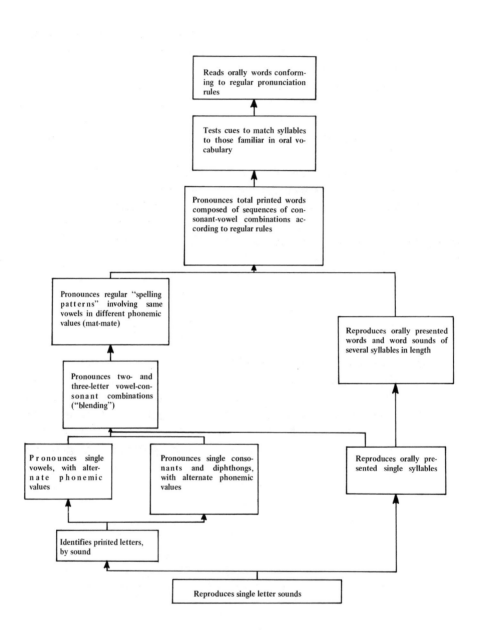

Figure 1. A Learning Hierarchy for a Basic Reading Skill (Gagné, 1970).

approaches are quite promising, the methods of task analysis are still evolving. They should be refined by formative evaluators, and data should be presented on the relative payoff of each.

Task analysis and learner analysis are not clearly evaluative functions, but they are essential evaluation-related functions of the development process. Often formative evaluators are called upon to perform such functions, and, as such, they should be techniques and procedures which the formative evaluator has in his repertoire. The techniques and procedures used to evaluate needs or objectives are appropriate for the evaluation of task analysis and learner analysis results.

Additional references. Surveys (Herriott, 1969; Oppenheim, 1966), scaling (Torgerson, 1958), Q-technique (Stephenson, 1953), semantic differential (Osgood, Suci, and Tannenbaum, 1957), delphi technique (Helmer, 1967), accreditation procedures (NSSE, 1969, 1970), observation techniques and category systems (Burnett, 1968, 1969; Simon and Boyer, 1970; Wolcott, 1970), rating systems (Lawson, 1973), content analysis (Berelson, 1952; Guttentag, 1971).

Techniques and Procedures for the Formative Evaluation of Objectives

Stake (1970) suggested three categories of judgmental data that might be collected in evaluating objectives: group data, expert opinion and observation data, and document analysis data. Two essential strategies for collecting group data include the use of survey questionnaires and the delphi technique.

Questionnaires. The development of questionnaires is the most critical and possibly the most underemphasized part of survey inquiry. A common attitude among many evaluators and researchers is the predisposition to write quickly a list of questions to be answered, put them on a form, and call the resulting instrument a developed questionnaire. In reality, if the questionnaire has not undergone critical appraisal before being sent to potential respondents, little usable information will be yielded.

The early stages of survey design comprise decision making about the aims of the study and identification of hypotheses to be tested or questions to be answered. Talking to experts and reviewing literature related to the evaluation focus should enable the evaluator to get a feel for the problem. After deciding on the questions to be answered, it is important to consider the analyses, results, etc., needed to answer the questions. At that point, the evaluator should be able to infer the questions that are to be asked and how they should be quantified. Criteria that could be used to evaluate draft versions of the questionnaire include:

I.   *Question Sequence*
    A.   Are later responses biased by early questions?
    B.   Is the questionnaire attractive and interesting? Does it start off with easy, impersonal questions?
    C.   Are leading questions asked? Is there a logical, efficient sequencing of questions (e.g., from general to specific questions; use of filter questions when appropriate)?
    D.   Are open/closed-ended questions appropriate? If closed, are the categories exhaustive, mutually exclusive? (Could ordinal or nominal data be collected as interval data?)
    E.   Are the major issues covered thoroughly while minor issues are passed over quickly?
    F.   Are questions with similar content grouped logically?

II. *Question Wording*
    A.   Are questions stated precisely? (Who, what, when, where, why, how?)
    B.   Does the questionnaire assume too much knowledge on the part of the respondent?
    C.   Are double questions asked?
    D.   Is the respondent in a position to answer the question, or must he make guesses?
    E.   Are definitions clear?
    F.   Are emotionally tinged words used?
    G.   Are technical terms, jargon, slang, words with double meanings avoided?
    H.   Are the methods for responding consistent?
    I.   Are the questions impersonal?
    J.   Are the questions short?

III. *Establishing and Keeping Rapport*
    A.   Is the questionnaire easy to answer?

  B. Is little respondent time involved?
  C. Does the questionnaire look attractive (e.g., layout, quality of paper, etc.)?
  D. Is there a "respondent orientation?"
  E. Is the questionnaire introduced with an explanation of purpose, sponsorship, method of respondent selection, anonymity?

IV. *Instructions*
  A. Is the respondent clearly told how to record his responses?
  B. Are instructions for return due date and procedures included?

V. *Technical Quality*
  A. Validity
    1. Are second information sources used as cross-checks (interviewer ratings, other findings, etc.)?
    2. Are responses of like respondents (e.g., husband/wife) checked?
    3. Have content experts read pilot versions of the questionnaires?
  B. Reliability
    1. Are factual questions reasked?
    2. Are phony items used?
    3. Are respondents reinterviewed?
    4. Have responses been checked for logical consistency?
  C. External Validity
    1. Are nonresponse bias checks planned?

An excellent annotated bibliography on the design, construction, and use of questionnaires for inquiry is provided by Potter, Sharpe, Hendee, and Clark (1972).

  Delphi technique. A variant of survey procedures for collecting judgmental data is the delphi technique. This technique makes use of a panel of experts who are mailed a set of questions to which they respond independently. A follow-up questionnaire reports a summary of the original responses using the median and interquartile range as descriptive statistics for the responses to each original question. Each panel member is then asked to reconsider his first responses and revise them if he so desires. If his second response is outside the interquartile range, he is asked to justify his deviation from the majority judgment.

In the third round, the second round responses are summarized and a summary of the reasons provided for deviant positions is also included. Each panel member is asked to reconsider his second round responses, given the results and reasons yielded from that round. A respondent who desires to remain outside the interquartile range on the third round is asked to present his reasons. This iterative procedure can continue for several more rounds after the third, but the payoff begins to diminish quickly. On the final round, panel members are asked to revise their responses one last time, given the results and arguments yielded by the previous round. This procedure has been used in management to attain consensus judgments from a panel of experts. Often the results have been less than spectacular due to weaknesses inherent in the process, but on many occasions useful results have been obtained. This is a procedure that the formative evaluator may find useful in the early stages of product development when commitments on selected developmental goals must be made.

Members of the target population are experts who are often overlooked in formative evaluation. Abedor (1972) suggested procedures for collecting judgmental data about objectives from this expert resource. His procedures could be adapted so that subjects are given an objective or a list of objectives and are asked to react to them as behaviors that the subjects could be asked to demonstrate after using the product. Subjects are one of the most critical and insightful audiences available to the evaluator. Since they will be suffering the consequences of bad development in the long run, they have something to lose by not providing feedback to the evaluator.

Content analysis. For the analysis of documents for collecting judgmental data about objectives, content analysis procedures have much to offer. Content analysis aims primarily at the objective quantification of content classified using a system of categories and explicitly formulated rules. The categories should be developed to fit the questions to be answered by the data and they should be mutually exclusive and exhaustive. Coding units (e.g., words, themes, paragraphs, etc.) are actually counted and placed within the categories. A sample set of categories (Berelson, 1954) into which themes contained in newspaper articles dealing with sex education could be tabulated are shown in Figure 2.

The uses of this technique for collecting judgmental data on objectives are many. Thematic analysis of board meetings or editorials in professional journals or word counts on federal policy statements can identify and clarify value data that are unavailable from any other source.

Techniques and Procedures for
Formative Interim Evaluation

At this point in the product development process, pieces of the intended final product are beginning to emerge. A film maker, for instance, often begins by constructing a series of verbal descriptions of the visual stimuli that he intends to film, coordinating that description with a preliminary version of the stimuli to be presented on the sound track (if any). A frequent next step is the construction of a story board, or simulation of the visual and oral stimuli, with hand-drawn pictures or photographs serving for the visual stimuli. Some film producers use the relatively less expensive video-tape medium to "film" initial versions of their film for debugging purposes. Film is a particularly difficult medium to revise once it has reached the finished product stage in that changes are likely to cost as much as the product itself. So it is extremely important to locate points in the interim stages in development of filmed materials where evaluative information can be provided concerning potentially useful revisions.

But, the fact that revisions of a finished product are less costly in some other medium should not obscure the usefulness of seeking evaluation at the interim stage of product development. Most textbook authors begin by constructing some sort of topical outline, chapter summary, etc. Rough drafts of chapters often undergo several revisions based upon feedback and small-scale tryouts of each chapter. The point is, of course, that in the development of nearly any product many opportunities exist prior to the completion of the initially satisfying version of the complete product for evaluative information to be collected. The particular techniques useful for formative interim evaluation of various media will differ somewhat from medium to medium, but many general principles can be noted.

Formative interim evaluation information can involve collecting internal information such as descriptive information and processing

Newspaper:　　　　　　　　　Date:　　　Story Source:

Expressions of opposition to sex education		Expressions favoring sex education	
Actions in opposition to sex education		Actions in support of sex education	
Statements supporting opponents of sex education		Statements attacking opponents of sex education	
Statements attacking proponents of sex education		Statements supporting proponents of sex education	
Statements listing opponents of sex education		Statements listing proponents of sex education	
Provisions of alternate plans		Statements opposing alternate plans	
Some other plan satisfactory		Authorities insist on current objectives	
Miscellaneous-		Miscellaneous+	
0		Other themes	
School board to discuss issue			
School board vote to be close			
Possible areas of compromise			
Miscellaneous			

Content totals	Headlines	Headline content
+ .... - 0	Head size .... Location on page .... Length .... Total score and direction	(+1, -1, or 0)

Figure 2. Sample Set of Categories for Content Analysis.

critical appraisals. Descriptive information refers to the objective information that can be generated by inspecting the pieces or preliminary versions of the product. Critical appraisals are judgments made concerning the pieces by representatives of concerned populations (e.g., experts, parents, students, etc.). Each of these will be discussed in turn.

Descriptive information. The intent of collecting descriptive information is to describe fully and completely what *is*, not what should be. A comprehensive characterization of what *is* will aid greatly in making judgments and in determining where to revise once some deficit is identified.

One type of descriptive information, physical specifications, is simply a description of the tangible characteristics of the product consisting in large part of media characteristics. This type of information is best collected by means of a checklist that includes the majority of the characteristics upon which products can vary. These characteristics are usually media specific in that any general purpose checklist would be impossible to construct. Some sample characteristics are listed in Table 2, using programmed instruction as an illustrative medium.

Some points in the sample checklist note whether certain features are present or absent in this product (points 1 and 2). Other points identify the type of procedure that is employed for features present invariably (or nearly so) for every product of this type. That is, nearly every program requires some type of response from the student and nearly every one provides knowledge of results in some form. But different programs require different types of responses and use different methods of providing knowledge of results (points 3 and 4).

Similar checklists could be developed for any medium or combination of media. Checklists have, of course, been developed and used for many years (e.g., Edmonson *et al.*, 1931; Hoban, 1942) but these checklists require rather global judgments by the user and are likely to be of more use to the summative evaluator. One would expect that a number of generally accepted checklists of potentially useful descriptive information for formative evaluations would be available for instructional products of many types, but this is not the case. The disadvantage of such a state of affairs is that the developer may not be aware of potentially useful types of descriptive information.

Content analysis. One method offering promise for describing product content is content analysis. The content analysis procedures

Table 2

Sample Items from a Checklist for Evaluating
Descriptive Characteristics of a Programmed Textbook

1. Pretest provided? . . . . . Yes . . . . . No

2. Objectives listed? . . . . . Yes . . . . . No

3. Confirmation procedure. Check one.

   . . . . . Knowledge of results provided on same page, students asked to shield answer.

   . . . . . Knowledge of results on another page of text.

   . . . . . Knowledge of results provided in separate booklet.

   . . . . . Knowledge of results not provided.

   . . . . . Other (please specify).

4. Response requirement (intended):

   . . . . . Overt constructed.

   . . . . . Covert constructed.

   . . . . . Overt selection.

   . . . . . Covert selection.

   . . . . . Other (please specify).

5. Can student alter response requirement? . . . . . Yes . . . . . No

6. Blackout ratio.

   . . . . . Percent of material could be blacked out.

discussed earlier in this chapter are also appropriate for formative interim evaluation. Berelson (1954) defined the technique as a "research technique for the objective systematic and quantitative descriptions of the manifest content of communication." In addition to the content analysis techniques described earlier, an introduction to content analysis may be found in Kerlinger (1973), while more advanced treatments of the topic may be found in Budd, Thorp, and Donohew (1967) and Holsti (1969). Grobman (1972) has provided a useful discussion of the uses of content analysis in formative and summative evaluation although her discussion is more oriented toward summative evaluation.

Content analysis, however, does not lend itself easily to a consideration of the relationship among concepts in the subject matter. The learning structure analysis of Gagné (1970) is very useful in this regard. This technique, described earlier under task analysis procedures, is relevant for the formative evaluation of interim products. Gagné (1970) presents examples of learning hierarchies, and the technique seems to offer many advantages.

The construction of learning hierarchies is quite time consuming, however, and the construction of a learning structure is no guarantee that it is correct. In essence, the learning structure is a logical analysis of the objective, but, as is well known, logic does not always simulate reality. Skills which are presumed to be subordinate to a particular objective may turn out not to be, or the sequence of subconcepts may prove to be wrong. Learning hierarchies are, in essence, hypotheses concerning the content—hypotheses that can only be confirmed empirically. The usefulness of a particular learning hierarchy will depend upon how well it fits the reality of the situation. Many subject matters do not lend themselves to hierarchical analysis. In other words, this, and systems similar to it, do not possess unlimited applicability, but they should prove useful in many situations.

The reader may wonder whether the collection of descriptive information is really necessary. Many would argue that all that really counts is how well the product works, not what it consists of. However, not all products work, especially in first draft form. When a product fails to perform as expected, explanations must be found. An adequate inventory of descriptive information will assist greatly in locating the points at which the product needs revisions. The particular information collected will depend on many complex factors: cost, utility, past experience, etc. As such information is collected more often, the collection should become easier. Instruments such as a checklist will already be constructed, past content analysis systems already debugged, etc. The reader is also referred to procedures provided by the Educational Products Information Exchange (EPIE) (1972).

Critical appraisal. Critical appraisal is not the appraisal of the effects of a product upon people who are using the product but upon people other than those directly involved in its use. Often the distinction between people using the material and those appraising the material is difficult to maintain for some techniques (e.g., individual student tryouts), but the distinction has nevertheless proved useful.

The techniques for collecting critical appraisals overlap to a great extent with the methods of evaluating objectives described earlier. Collections of opinions from experts of all sorts, teachers, parents, students, administrators, authors, etc., can be accomplished by means of questionnaires, checklists, interviews, panels, diaries, Q-sorts, the delphi technique, etc. The criteria against which each of these populations can appraise the materials will vary. Teachers will undoubtedly be concerned with such factors as congruence of content with their own biases or capabilities, practicality of the format, mode, and/or requirements of the instruction, degree of integration with existing curricula, extent of teacher input, flexibility, and so on. Parents may be very concerned with the type of value system implied in the material, currency of content, orientation (i.e., to college-bound or vocationally-oriented students), sex or racial bias portrayed, and so on. Any or all of this information can bear upon the subsequent revision of instructional materials, especially when external information supports the critical appraisal.

One judgmental data source which has not been tapped thus far and which deserves attention is the author. The definition of the term "author" differs somewhat from medium to medium. In the case of the print media, text, or audio-tapes, the definition is fairly easy. But with film or video-tape the term "author" is probably closest in meaning to director. The author is often not recognized as a source of revision information but he is in fact a major, if not the major one, especially at the early stages of the product. The author makes literally thousands of decisions when he embodies the content he intends to teach in a suitable form—decisions concerning sequence, phrasing, orientation, value, difficulty level, and so on.

When textbook authors write their prose, they are writing with a particular audience in mind, with a particular standard of difficulty and clarity. As the sentence is written, judgments are being made as to its adequacy in conveying intended meanings, the sophistication of the audience, the contribution of the sentence to the orderly development of the intent of the paragraphs, etc. If the sentence fails to meet these criteria, it will be rewritten until the author is satisfied. It should be obvious that estimating the number of these decisions that the author makes as in the thousands is probably quite conservative.

Authors, however, are often only dimly aware of the decision process. Explicit standards are rare and, probably as a consequence, consistency in decision making is less frequent than would be desirable. Some profit might accrue, therefore, by increasing author awareness of his decisions. Lawson (1973) has constructed questionnaires and checklists that should prove useful in this regard. In one of his questionnaires, authors are queried on whether specific learner objectives are provided, whether entry behaviors are specified, whether provision is made for learners to enter the product at points other than the beginning, whether the format and display are appropriate for the intended population, whether examples and illustrations used are likely to be of interest to the intended population, etc. The effects of such procedures upon authors is unknown at this time and should be the object of future study. The willingness of authors (or more accurately what type of authors would be willing or unwilling) to explicate their decision processes would be very interesting to examine.

It should be noted that the descriptive and critical appraisal techniques described thus far on formative interim evaluation can be used at the formative product stage as well. The difference is primarily one of the closeness of an interim format that is being evaluated to the final product, but the principles involved are generally comparable from stage to stage.

Much useful external information at the interim stage can be gathered by using the same criterion measures which will be used at the formative product stage. If an achievement test is carefully constructed to measure the complete set of objectives of the instruction, there is no reason why, if the test has been carefully criterion-referenced, appropriate items from that test could not be used to evaluate pieces of the instruction designed to teach certain of the objectives. If, however, the criterion test does not measure every objective, but merely samples from among many, then it would not be appropriate to use that test as an interim evaluative device. Although very desirable at the formative product stage, it is mandatory at the interim stage that some evaluative information be provided on every objective of the instructional product.

The principles of construction and the theoretical bases for external evaluation devices of many types should be familiar to readers of this chapter. That the evaluation of instructional products should emphasize the attainment of the particular objectives of the product (be criterion-referenced) rather than individual differences among students (be norm-referenced) is almost at the status of a truism. Likewise, it is widely acknowledged that evaluation should be as direct and performance based as possible; for example, if students are supposed to be able to correctly assemble an automobile distributor after instruction, they should be tested by giving them a disassembled automobile distributor, not a paper and pencil test of their knowledge of the functions of the distributor. Discussion of these issues can be found in the *Handbook on Formative and Summative Evaluation* (Bloom, Hastings, and Madaus, 1971).

Student tryout. At the interim stage of product development, one should not limit his information-gathering activity to highly structured procedures. Much useful information can be gathered in informal types of operations. One that has received increasing attention during recent years is variously called developmental testing (Markle, 1967), individual student tryout (Scott and Yelon, 1969), and oral problem solving (Cunningham, in press). Essentially this technique consists of placing the author (or his agent) with one or more students as they use the materials. Ideally the student(s) will, by means of oral or written comments, help the author locate ambiguities, errors of sequence, and the like, and allow the author to test his assumptions concerning the mental operations that will be employed by students using the material. The students are generally told to think aloud as they work through the materials, a procedure that should give the author insights into the students' thinking processes and into how well his materials have coordinated with those processes.

Unfortunately, very little empirical knowledge exists concerning individual student tryouts. Beyond an unpublished master's thesis by Robeck (1965) and the recent work by Abedor (1972), little research on this technique has been completed. The present state of the art is crude, consisting of a number of unsubstantiated tips as to how to carry off the procedures. And any inspection of the literature relevant to this topic quickly reveals the inconsistency and lack of agreement among those tips. Some recommend that high ability students be used, others recommend low ability students. Some sources argue that students can only clean up semantic and syntactic errors while others insist that the student can make more substantive suggestions concerning sequence, intended prerequisites, etc. Recommendations vary with respect to preferred level of student incentive, author behavior in the tryout situation, number of cycles of tryout and revision, etc. At present few standard procedures can be recommended with confidence. Even the simplest of experiments comparing the quality of instructional products that have and have not used individual student tryouts as part of the development has yet to be completed. A more detailed discussion of the issues and considerations of individual student tryouts can be found in Markle (1967) and Scott and Yelon (1969).

Systematic assessment of context at the interim stage is likely to be wasteful, since only pieces of the product are available. The impact of small pieces of a product on a particular context is likely to be unrepresentative of the impact when the product as a whole is integrated into a particular situation.

The evaluator must be aware of intended contexts, however, to guide his choice of students for individual student tryouts or small-scale field tests or to guide in the choice of people to conduct critical appraisals. The systematic testing of context and the search for relationship between context and other information about the product is best delayed, however, until the formative product stage.

Additional references. Materials analysis guidelines (EPIE, 1972), PERT (Cook, 1966), PPBS (McCullough, 1966), systems analysis (Cleland and King, 1968; Kershaw and McKean, 1959).

Techniques and Procedures for Formative Product Evaluation

At this point in the product development sequence, a version of the complete product is produced. Rather than being discrete, this stage is continuous with evaluation of interim stages of the product. Most often the first evaluative information collected concerning the product as a whole is the same information collected at the interim stage and many of the same techniques are applicable. However, the major thrust of the formative product evaluation effort should be toward the eventual establishment of the relationship between contextual and other product characteristics. External validity becomes crucial for formative product evaluation activities.

The major techniques for collecting internal information (check-lists for descriptive information, questionnaires, interviews, etc., for critical appraisals) have already been discussed and are essentially the same for this stage.

It is also possible when collecting external information to use many of the same methods and procedures as were used in the interim stage, including individual student tryouts with the complete product. The emphasis now shifts to large-scale tryout, where the complete product is tested under the circumstances in which it is supposed to operate. Although having an author hovering over a student is acceptable during developmental testing of an instructional program, it would not be acceptable in a field test of the product.

An inventory of the possible measures that could be collected would be very large indeed, but Metfessel and Michael (1967) have made a useful beginning. They list five major categories here called external information:

1. indicators of status or change in cognitive and affective behaviors of students in terms of standardized measures and scales;
2. indicators of status or change in cognitive and affective behaviors of students by informal or some formal teacher-made instruments or devices;
3. indicators of status or change in student behaviors other than those measured by tests, inventories, and observation scales in relation to the task of evaluating objectives of school programs;
4. indicators of status or change in cognitive and affective behaviors of teachers and other school personnel in relation to the evaluation of school programs; and
5. indicators of community behaviors in relation to the evaluation of school programs.

Under these five headings are listed many particular information sources including unobtrusive sources. The strategy to emphasize is the use of multiple criterion measures in which all criterion measures are recognized as fallible and in need of collaboration by other methods whose fallibilities are likely to be different from the first measure. An attitude scale that purports to measure attitude toward a subject would be more credible if it could be shown to correlate highly with some unobtrusive measure like the proportion of books checked out of the library on that subject or with a classroom observation schedule that demonstrates a high proportion of activities related to the subject during free periods.

Due to space limitation, the following discussion is limited to problems of obtaining external information found to be particularly apparent in several product development efforts. At the end of this section are listed references for other major methods of gathering external information.

Problem 1: higher-order inference. By far the most frequently sought after outcomes from instruction are student cognitive outcomes, especially higher order cognitive outcomes such as concept learning or problem solving. Yet it often is the case that the criterion measures of these objectives do not allow the inference that higher order outcomes have occurred. Consider the following paragraph which might be taken from an introductory measurement text and some potential test items.

> The mean is the average score of a set of scores and is computed by dividing the sum of all the scores obtained on the test by the number of the scores. If 10 students score 1, 3, 4, 4, 5, 5, 6, 7, 7, and 7, respectively, then the mean would be 49 ÷ 10 or 4.9. The mean is the most frequently used measure of central tendency.

1. The . . . . . is the most frequently used measure of central tendency.
2. Define mean.
3. What is the mean of the following set of scores?
   1, 3, 4, 4, 5, 5, 6, 7, 7, 7
   a. 4
   b. 4.9
   c. 5.1
4. The measure that is most often used to describe the average score of a distribution is the . . . . .
5. In your own words, define the mean.
6. Compute the mean of this set of scores.
   12, 19, 15, 30, 57
   a. 26.6
   b. 19
   c. 21.5

Note that items 1-3 demand nothing more than verbatim recall or recognition on the part of the student. The student need only remember the form of the information as it was stated in instruction, since the wording of examples used in the test items does not differ substantially from the wording and examples used in instruction. Students answering questions 1-3 correctly could have an understanding of the concept of mean as expressed in the brief passage, but the items used to test the concept do not unambiguously allow that inference. Items 4-6 adequately test the higher order objectives in that students probably could not answer those items on the basis of verbatim recall or recognition alone. Key sentences from instruction have been paraphrased, examples have been changed.

As obvious as this point may seem to some, it is apparently not obvious to many of the formative and summative evaluators. Perhaps under the influence of the performance contracting fad, all too often a very trivial sort of "teaching for the test" can be seen in many product evaluations. Such information can be grossly misleading concerning the actual level of attainment of particular outcomes. Particularly lucid discussions of these issues can be found in Bormuth (1970) and Anderson (1972).

Problem 2: product effects. A second problem area is in the procedures for collecting information about effects of the product. Data concerning the effects of a product are not collected at random but, rather, according to some plan that will allow an assessment of the effects of the product in relation to some other state of affairs. It is at this stage of product development that experimental and quasi-experimental designs are useful. The standard reference on this topic continues to be Campbell and Stanley (1963), a summary of the relevant considerations in experimental designs.

The choice of design for a formative product evaluation is a complicated decision depending upon a number of considerations: cost, utility, practicality, tolerance for certain forms of invalidity, extent of generalizability desired, and so forth. Campbell and Stanley (1963) have discussed the major considerations in the choice of a design: internal and external validity, or, alternately replicability and generalizability. The evaluator needs to be concerned with replicability in that if the effect of his product cannot be reliably established, decisions about how to make the product better are meaningless. The formative evaluator must also be sensitive to the extent and type of generalizability of his product. He may not be interested in making generalizations from his evaluation to other products or other contexts than the intended one but within the intended contexts he has to take steps to ensure generalizability. Campbell and Stanley (1963) list eight potential sources of internal invalidity and four potential sources of external invalidity. Each design discussed in their chapter is evaluated against these threats to validity and the consumer is able therefore to choose those designs that minimize threats of most concern.

Without doubt, the most frequently used design in product evaluations is the single group pretest-posttest design. In this quasi-experimental design a single group of students is first tested to determine how much of the terminal behavior they possess, then are administered the product, then tested again, often with the same test. If learning gains are demonstrated, the product developer will conclude he has a successful product. The problem with such a design is that it allows so many other plausible rival explanations for the observed result: other events occurring between the first and second testing may have caused the results, the pretest alone may have influenced the posttest, shifts in standards and scoring pretest and posttest could occur. Markle (1967) has pointed out that improvements in posttest performance can often be shown to be due to an increased familiarity with terminology used in the product rather than any new learning. In sum, this design does not have a great deal to offer except that it is probably better than nothing. As the only type of evaluation for the product it is inadequate, but as a first step in a more elaborate set of procedures, it can serve a useful function. When it is the only possible design, care should be taken to investigate as many as possible of the potential sources of invalidity specified by Campbell and Stanley (1963). More fruitful designs have been discussed by Glass in Worthen and Sanders (1973).

Problem 3: contextual information. With regard to contextual information, developers typically have an average student, a particular average classroom setting in mind when they construct a product. It is the function of the formative evaluator to identify and make explicit those assumptions and to provide a context (if one exists) for the field test. This description implies a two-stage process: the identification of intended contexts and then the testing of products within specified contexts. Testing may force modification of the intended context or of the product so that it better fits a more realistic set of context variables. The collection of contextual information involves the use of instruments already discussed in this chapter. Questionnaires or interviews with the author could be used to identify intended contexts on such variables as entering behaviors, student attitudes, socioeconomic status, student interest, teacher experience, teaching style or personality, etc. The intended curricular context for the product including the type(s) of concurrent course work, availability of instructional aids, and the like should also be assessed.

The identification of actual contexts will center upon the intended contextual variables but the evaluator should be aware of and sensitive to other context variables that might conceivably influence the outcome of the field test. Systematic observation and survey instruments similar to those used for needs assessment could be used to collect this information.

It was stated earlier that the proper focus of formative product evaluation is on the establishment of relationships between context. The purpose of formative evaluation is to provide information of use to the developer of the product concerning potential revisions. These revisions will be most efficiently and effectively made if all information discussed in this chapter is available to the evaluator. If, for instance, it is demonstrated that students have failed to master a particular objective, the formative evaluator must find out why and determine what to do about it. He should at that point begin to hypothesize various patterns of relationship among all of the information already collected. Were student entry behaviors overestimated (context)? Was the readability level of the text at that point too low (descriptive)? Did subject matter experts predict difficulty with those concepts and, if so, why (critical appraisal)? Any one or combination of these considerations could conceivably shed light upon the particular deficiency identified and perhaps imply the steps which should be taken to remedy the situation. In the course of this procedure, relationships are identified that might have some degree of generalizability to other problems within the same product or perhaps even with other products as well.

The potential usefulness of such a focus has been discussed already by Sanders and Cunningham (1973) with respect to a field test conducted by Anderson (1969) in which he found that a discrepancy between an intended context factor and an actual one could account for some disturbing external information. One developer, for example, was at a loss to explain why students did not seem to profit from being provided knowledge of results from a self-instructional program. A cursory glance at the internal characteristics revealed a great proportion of formal prompts, so many in fact that the program was too easy. Knowledge of results after each frame was simply not needed since more than sufficient information about the correct answer was contained in the frame itself.

We might reiterate that both the collection of multiple measures of many types of information and the search for relationships among these data should be of primary importance to the evaluator. One should not be so naive, however, as to expect that formative evaluators have unlimited time and resources available to them to pursue all of the recommendations which have been set forth. What is proposed is an ideal, a goal to strive for, rather than a firm set of prescriptions.

Additional references. Cost analysis (Fisher, 1971; Prest and Turvey, 1965; Tanner, 1971), GFE (Scriven, 1972), ATI (Cronbach and Snow, 1969).

Suggested Readings

Bloom, B.S., Hastings, J.T., and Madaus, G.F. *Handbook on formative and summative evaluation of learning.* New York: McGraw-Hill, 1971.
> This work remains one of the best collections of papers on basic measurement procedures. This is a reference work that evaluators in many subject areas will find useful.

Campbell, D.T., and Stanley, J.C. Experimental and quasi-experimental designs for research in teaching. In N.L. Gage (Ed.), *Handbook of research on teaching.* Chicago: Rand McNally, 1963. Also in monograph form, 1966.
> This work is a classic reference on experimental logic and methods. The procedures and techniques found in this monograph are fundamental for formative and summative evaluation.

Travers, R.M.W. (Ed.) *Second handbook of research on teaching.* Chicago: Rand McNally, 1973.
> This volume contains excellent reviews and insightful suggestions for inquiry in many areas of education. At a time when evaluators should be refining their methods, this work provides a wealth of ideas.

Webb, E.J., Campbell, D.T., Schwartz, R.D., and Sechust, L. *Unobtrusive measures: Nonreactive research in the social sciences.* Chicago: Rand McNally, 1966.

Assuming that educational evaluation can and should be as noninterventional as possible, this work should be required reading for all formative and summative evaluators. Methods for unobtrusive data gathering found in this text are valuable for educational evaluation.

Worthen, B.R., and Sanders, J.R. *Educational evaluation: Theory and practice*. Worthington, Ohio: Charles A. Jones, 1973.

This text provides excellent coverage of recent work on general evaluation methods. This treatment of evaluation as a field of study is basic reading for all practicing educational evaluators.

References

Abedor, A. Second draft technology. *Bulletin of the School of Education, Indiana University*, 1972, *48*, 9-43.

Anderson, R.C. The comparative field experiment: An illustration from high school biology. *Proceedings of the 1968 Invitational Conference of Testing Problems*. Princeton, New Jersey: Educational Testing Service, 1969, 3-30.

Anderson, R.C. How to construct achievement tests to assess comprehension. *Review of Educational Research*, 1972, *42*, 145-170.

Berelson, B. *Content analysis in communication research*. New York: The Free Press of Glencoe, 1952.

Berelson, B. Content analysis. In *Handbook of social psychology*. Cambridge, Massachusetts: Addison-Wesley, 1954, 458-518.

Bloom, B.S., Hastings, J.T., and Madaus, G.F. *Handbook on formative and summative evaluation of learning*. New York: McGraw-Hill, 1971.

Bormuth, J.R. *On the theory of achievement test items*. Chicago: University of Chicago Press, 1970.

Budd, R.W., Thorp, R.K., and Donohew, Lewis. *Content analysis of communication*. New York: Macmillan, 1967.

Burnett, J. Ceremonies, rites, and economy in the student system of an American high school. *Human Organizations*, 1968, *28*, 1-10.

Burnett, J. Event description and analysis in the microethnography of urban classrooms. Urbana, Illinois: University of Illinois, 1969.

Campbell, D.T., and Stanley, J.E. Experimental and quasi-experimental designs for research in teaching. In N.L. Gage (Ed.), *Handbook of research on teaching*. Chicago: Rand McNally, 1963.

Cleland, D., and King, W. *Systems analysis and project management*. New York: McGraw-Hill, 1968.

Cook, D. *Program evaluation and review techniques, applications in education*. U.S. Office of Education Cooperative Research Monograph, Number 17, OE-12024. Washington, D.C.: U.S.O.E., 1966.

Cronbach, L., and Snow, R. Final report: Individual differences in learning ability as a function of instructional variables. Palo Alto, California: Stanford University, 1969.

Cunningham, D.J. Evaluation of replicable forms of instruction. *AV Communication Review*, in press.

Davies, I. Task analysis: Some process and content concerns. *AV Communication Review*, 1973, *21*, 73-85.

Edmonson, J.B. *et al. The textbook in American education*. Thirtieth Yearbook of the National Society for the Study of Education. Part II. Bloomington, Illinois: Public School Company, 1931.

Educational Products Information Exchange (EPIE). Early childhood education, how to select and evaluate materials. *EPIE Report Number 42*, 1972.

Fisher, G.H. *Cost considerations in systems analysis*. New York: American Elsevier, 1971.

Gagné, R.M. *The conditions of learning* (2nd ed.). New York: Holt, Rinehart and Winston, 1970.

Grobman, H. Content analysis as a tool in formative and summative evaluation. Paper presented at the Annual Meeting of the American Educational Research Association, Chicago, April 1972.

Guttentag, M. Social change in a school: A computer content analysis of administrative notices. *Journal of School Psychology*, 1971, *9*, 191-199.

Helmer, O. Analysis of the future: The delphi method. Santa Monica, California: Rand Corporation, 1967.

Herriott, R. Survey research method. In R.E. Ebel (Ed.), *Encyclopedia of Educational Research*. New York: Macmillan, 1969.

Hoban, C.F. *Focus on learning*. Washington, D.C.: American Council on Education, 1942.

Holsti, O. *Content analysis for the social sciences and humanities*. Reading, Mass.: Addison-Wesley, 1969.

Institute for Social Research. *Interviewer's Manual*. Ann Arbor,

Michigan: Institute for Social Research, University of Michigan, 1969.

Kerlinger, F. *Foundations of behavioral research* (2nd ed.). New York: Holt, Rinehart and Winston, 1973.

Kershaw, J., and McKean, R. *Systems analysis and education.* Memorandum RM-2473-FF. Santa Monica, California: Rand Corporation, 1959.

Lawson, T.E. *Formative instructional product evaluation instruments.* Urbana, Illinois: Center for Instructional Research and Curriculum Evaluation, 1972. Also in *Educational Technology*, 1973, *5*, 42-44.

Markle, S.M. Empirical testing of programs. In P.C. Lange (Ed.), *Programmed instruction.* Sixty-Sixth Yearbook of the National Society for the Study of Education. Part II. Chicago: University of Chicago Press, 1967.

McCullough, J. Cost analysis for planning-programming-budgeting cost-benefit studies. Santa Monica, California: Rand Corporation, 1966.

Metfessel, N.S., and Michael, W.B. A paradigm involving multiple criterion measures for the evaluation of the effectiveness of school programs. *Educational and Psychological Measurement*, 1967, *27*, 931-943.

National Assessment of Educational Progress. National Results, Science. Denver, Colorado: Education Commission of the States, 1970.

National Study of School Evaluation. *Evaluative criteria, secondary school.* Arlington, Virginia: National Study of School Evaluation, 1969.

National Study of School Evaluation. *Evaluative criteria, junior high school/middle school.* Arlington, Virginia: National Study of School Evaluation, 1970.

Oppenheim, A. *Questionnaire design and attitude measurement.* New York: Basic Books, 1966.

Osgood, C., Suci, G., and Tannenbaum, P. *The measurement of meaning.* Urbana, Illinois: University of Illinois Press, 1957.

Potter, D., Sharpe, K., Hendee, J., and Clark, R. Questionnaires for research: An annotated bibliography on design, construction, and use. Portland, Oregon: Pacific Northwest Forest and Range Experiment Station, 1972.

Prest, A., and Turvey, R. Cost-benefit analysis. A survey. *The Economic Journal*, 1965, *75*, 683-735.

Robeck, M. A study of the revision process in programmed instruction. Unpublished master's thesis. University of California, Los Angeles, 1965.

Sanders, J., and Cunningham, D. A structure for formative evaluation in product development. *Review of Educational Research*, 1973, *43*, 217-236.

Scott, R.O., and Yelon, S.L. The student as co-author—The first step in formative evaluation. *Educational Technology*, 1969, *9* (10), 76-78.

Scriven, M. The methodology of evaluation. In R.E. Stake (Ed.), *AERA monograph series of curriculum evaluation*. Number 1. Chicago: Rand McNally, 1967. Also in B.R. Worthen and J.R. Sanders. *Educational evaluation: Theory and practice*. Worthington, Ohio: Charles A. Jones, 1973.

Scriven, M. Pros and cons about goal-free evaluation. *Evaluation Comment*, 1972, *3*, 1-4.

Simon, A., and Boyer, E. (Eds.) *Mirrors for behavior: An anthology of classroom observation instruments*. Philadelphia: Research for Better Schools, 1970.

Stake, R. Objectives priorities, and other judgment data. *Review of Educational Research*, 1970, *40*, 181-212.

Stephenson, W. *The study of behavior: Q-technique and its methodology*. Chicago: University of Chicago Press, 1953.

Tanner, K. A heuristic approach to program cost/effectiveness analysis. Paper presented at the Annual Meeting of the American Educational Research Association, New York, 1971.

Thiagarajan, S., Semmel, M., and Semmel, D. *Sourcebook on instructional development for training teachers of exceptional children*. Bloomington, Indiana: Center for Innovation in Teaching the Handicapped, Indiana University, 1973.

Torgerson, W. *Theory and methods of scaling*. New York: Wiley and Sons, 1958.

Wolcott, H. An ethnographic approach to the study of school administrators. *Human Organization*, 1970, *29*, 115-122.

Worthen, B.R., and Sanders, J.R. *Educational evaluation: Theory and practice*. Worthington, Ohio: Charles A. Jones, 1973.

CHAPTER 12

EVALUATING INSTRUCTIONAL TRANSACTIONS

Gary D. Borich and Stan F. Drezek
The Research and Development Center for Teacher Education

The number of innovative educational programs developed during the past decade surpasses that of the preceding five decades. Yet few of these programs are likely to endure long enough to engender a lasting impact upon American education. While some programs of the past decade have produced valuable outcomes, the fact remains that the effects of surprisingly few of the new programs are apparent today.

The reason for this situation is both interesting and complex. A political scientist might point to the leanings of two administrators to account for it; a sociologist, the social and political milieu of an expanding and progressive nation; and an economist, the Gross National Product. However, these factors, by themselves, neither explain why American education has produced so many innovations in so short a time nor why so few of these innovations continue to play an integral role in American education. For the answer to these questions we must turn to the educator, who, knowingly or unknowingly, determines whether an innovative program appears briefly or becomes a lasting contribution to American education. This chapter suggests that only the latter is a viable alternative and that the success of directing innovative programs over pitfalls and hurdles, whether political, philosophic, or economic, depends upon a process of continuous program growth and development called formative evaluation.

Formative evaluation is a process by which program practices and procedures are refined in systematic cycles of trial and revision. Formative evaluation differs from what is called summative evaluation in that the former assesses the effectiveness of specific program practices and procedures for the purpose of revising them while the latter tests the efficacy of a program, *in toto,* for the purpose of recommending its continuation or adoption. Summative strategies are applicable to testing the efficacy of a total program after it has been developed, while formative strategies are best suited to refining specific instructional components during their development.

It is important to distinguish formative from summative evaluation in order to identify the appropriate methodology for each. To help relate formative and summative to specific strategies, three types of evaluative questions may be posed. These questions and the decisions an evaluator makes regarding them are:

1. *What program is best?*

   Evaluator decides whether a favored program is better than an alternative, the alternative better than the favorite, or if there is no difference between programs for the purpose of recommending program adoption or continuation (summative).

2. *How is the program working?*

   Evaluator decides whether program practices and procedures are implemented according to specifications for the purpose of bringing actual implementation into parity with program specifications (formative, how).

3. *Why does the program work?*

   Evaluator decides upon the effectiveness of each program part in bringing about desired outcomes for the purpose of modifying, deleting, or creating new instructional components (formative, why).

Evaluations that compare one program with another often make two assumptions: instructional components of the experimental program are able to elicit at some minimal level the behaviors specified for them, and the structure and organization of the comparison program is similar to that of the experimental program. When these assumptions are true, summative tests can determine the overall merit of a program as well as point to ways of improving it. To the extent that they are not true, statistical comparisons between programs need to be subsequent to posing the formative *why* and *how* questions. *What, how,* and *why* questions represent distinctly different but complementary strategies that, when applied to educational programs, guide and direct their outcomes. These strategies are briefly explored, after which a model for the formative evaluation of an educational program is proposed.

What Program is Best?

Evaluator determines the best program among alternatives. Statistical analyses determine differences between pretest and posttest and between experimental and control groups in order to decide whether to adopt the program.

Comparative tests are most useful when differences between experimental and comparison programs are small and systematic so that significant differences between programs can be unequivocally attributed to the dimension on which the programs differ. Rarely, however, are differences between experimental and comparison programs small and systematic. Comparison programs used as "controls" customarily vary widely from the experimental version and more often than not represent only the most accessible alternative at the time of the summative test.

When a test is used for program revision as well as for deciding upon program adoption, the test is called a critical comparison. Such comparisons manipulate critical components of a program for the purpose of identifying the exact cause of a significant difference. While many such critical comparisons are possible, two might be represented in the following manner:

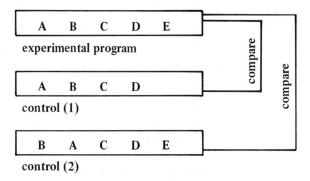

Here A-E are major program components constructed to produce specific behavioral outcomes. Component E in the first comparison and the order of A and B in the second constitute critical components. Should differences between experimental and control groups be significant in either comparison, we would have answered both *what* program is best (summative) and *why* it is best (formative).

Unfortunately, such examples are for all practical purposes in the realm of fiction. Hardly an evaluation study on record could boast of both the simplicity and precision of either of the above examples. Real-world contingencies make the search for such ideal conditions almost futile and point to the need to evaluate complex programs with separate formative and summative strategies.

If we were to contend with evaluation practice, we would more likely face either of the following conditions:

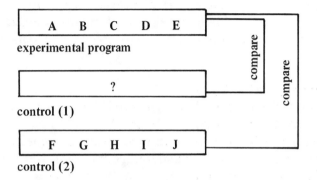

Here either a comparison program is left unexplicated so that we do not know what its component parts actually are, or upon examination they are found to be considerably different from our own. A summative test for either example, while able to determine the efficacy of adopting or not adopting the experimental program, could not provide empirical data for determining why one program is better than another. Neither could it reveal directions for improving the program should the summative test show either no differences or that the control program is significantly better.

Let us assume that each component in our experimental program has not been evaluated prior to deciding to adopt the program *in toto*. Then let us examine the effectiveness of each instructional component (A-E) of the experimental program rather than compare control and experimental programs. We then might raise such questions as: Are program components being implemented as specified?, Does each component elicit the behavior for which it was designed?, and Do these behaviors lead to the kind of performance behaviors expected of program participants at the end of instruction? When these questions are posed before program comparisons, summative evaluations can reveal the general merit of a program as well as provide clues for program revision. If the formative evaluation of program components precedes program comparisons, the developer has the opportunity to record *why* his program performs as it does as well as the level of effectiveness of each program component. Should summative tests indicate either no significant difference or that a competing program is better than the one developed, the developer has data from which to identify those areas of the program where revision is most likely needed. Summative tests, when small and systematic differences between programs are not apparent, provide little basis for deciding *why* a program works. When preceded by formative evaluations, these same tests can be used for directing the course of program improvement.

How Is the Program Working?

Evaluator determines if the program is being implemented according to specifications. Asking how a program works uncovers problems in moving theoretical principles from a planning stage to the field and finding that what was thought feasible in a pilot test may not be so during program operation. Program monitoring and documenting techniques (questionnaires, checklists, and observation schedules) compare the implementation of roles and procedures with specifications called for by the program.

While summative tests attempt to determine overall differences between programs, formative strategies that pose the *how* question provide rationale for outcomes from the summative test. These strategies are applied during program implementation to assure that program participants receive the treatment at the appropriate time and in the specified sequence. Stresses of implementing a large and complex program in an ongoing setting often disrupt even the best-laid plans, and only the most farsighted can determine beforehand how these forces interact with the program to alter its structure and sequence.

Monitoring an ongoing program can reveal that parts of the program are not being implemented in some settings or are implemented poorly in others. These problems are contingent upon the interface between the program and the personnel who will use and work with it. Personalities, attitudes, and professional values of the staff can interact with a finished program, and these interactions are uncovered with strategies that study the implementation of roles and procedures in an ongoing program. While these roles and procedures may be clear on paper, their timeliness and appropriateness to the ongoing program should be questioned during its operation. Strategies that attempt to pose the *how* question monitor and document the interface between program personnel and program content to assure the timely and appropriate implementation of key program components.

The *how* question, contrary to other strategies for program evaluation, is devoid of statistical tests or expected outcomes in the form of hypotheses. Rather, the formative *how* question is a nondirectional strategy that seeks to determine program practices and procedures as they may be altered by real-world contingencies. The *how* question is best posed so that anticipated as well as unanticipated outcomes are recorded. While one attempt to pose a *how* question might take the form: "Does the instructor present the instructional materials at the prescribed time?," another, better phrased, would ask, "What instructional materials does the instructor present at what times?" While the evaluator posing the first question notes that the instructor's activities do or do not correspond to program specifications, the evaluator posing the second question is looking for and recording an array of materials and activities regardless of whether they have been previously specified. The value of posing the second question is that it not only implies an answer to the first question but goes on to record new and perhaps better activities than those that were initially planned for eliciting the desired behaviors.

The formative, *how* question may be familiar to some readers as process evaluation. One process evaluation scheme has been posited by Stufflebeam *et al.* (1971) and another by Stake (1967). Stufflebeam defines process evaluation as a three-step procedure: identifying and monitoring the potential sources of failures in a program, delineating to project staff preprogram decisions and their logistical requirements, and describing what actually takes place. These steps imply noting discrepancies between program procedures and program specifications and searching for unanticipated behaviors that may (for ill or good) upset the program schedule.

Stake offers a process evaluation strategy employing both of the above concepts, in which he suggests a two-stage procedure: the first determines congruence between what is intended and what is actually observed, while the second determines the logical contingency between a program's objectives and its planned activities. The first deals with discrepancies from program specifications and the second with making sure the program has the type and quality of components that its objectives imply. Stake's second stage is an important but often missed ingredient in posing the formative, *how* question; because of its importance to the following question, this will be taken up again later in the chapter.

Why Does the Program Work?

Evaluator determines the need for program revision and refinement during the development process. By identifying instructional variables and intermediate and long-term outcomes, specific program components are evaluated. Correlational techniques establish relationships between degrees of program implementation and behavioral outcomes for the purpose of revising, deleting, or creating new instructional inputs.

While the *how* question focuses upon roles and procedures and the interface between content and implementation, the *why* question centers upon program content and its underlying rationale. Posing the *why* question implies the use of strategies that can guide and direct the course of program development. Techniques that can relate variation in instructional inputs to variation in behavioral outcomes are preferred to those techniques that measure differences between pretests and posttests or differences between experimental and control groups. Individual program components and the conceptual principles upon which they rest are evaluated before the final program is submitted to an overall summative test, at which time only those components that have proved effective are employed in the program.

Among the most crucial differences between determining *what* program is best and *why* the program works is that the *why* question assumes intermediate program outcomes are of primary importance and are far less global than the outcomes used to determine the merit of an entire program. Determining *why* the program works entails identifying a sequence of intermediate behaviors that leads to long-range performance outcomes (i.e., do behaviors elicited by individual program components lead to the kind of performance expected of participants at the end of the program?). Specific program inputs are related to intermediate outcomes and, through the use of correlational techniques, program components are deleted or revised so that program developers know which program components are producing the desired behaviors and to what extent.

Although it is the most complex question, asking *why* the program works is the most rewarding for program improvement. Contrary to raising broad questions about the program's success, the *why* question focuses upon specific instructional transactions defined for measurement purposes as instructional variables, and relates these to expected outcomes. Methodologies that can register progress over time in the development of specific program transactions are preferred to those that test overall differences between programs. Program developers employ results from the formative, *why* question to alter, if necessary, the direction of their development activities and to revise, delete, or create new program transactions. Rather than employ statistical tests that report only levels of significance, the evaluator turns to techniques that can record small increments of improvement from which causal relationships between instructional inputs and behavioral outputs can be inferred. These techniques are based upon the following model for posing the formative, *why* question.

A Model for the Formative, *Why* Question

Evaluations of many complex educational programs fail to recognize the importance of posing the *why* question for directing program improvement. Although this question is integral to program development, it is often passed by for the more traditional but often less appropriate program comparison strategy. Program comparisons when conducted too early ignore the developmental stage of a program and its readiness for a summative test and, therefore, fail to indicate that a "no significant difference" may be to the credit of the developing program. While a premature summative test decreases the likelihood that there will be a difference between competing programs, formative evaluation strategies increase the likelihood that later summative tests will report significant program differences.

The process of developing a complex educational program represents a blend of research, imagination, and intuition, part of which is based upon proven psychological principles and part upon professional judgment. For a developing program it is reasonable to expect that some of its parts will relate to desired outcomes, some will be irrelevant to desired outcomes, and perhaps some will be detrimental to achieving desired outcomes. Many program elements represent the total program and the developer is never sure *a priori* that the best combination of elements has been chosen to produce the intended outcome. Program elements, though often viewed as static, actually represent scalable instructional transactions that can be defined and studied in relation to outcomes. These transactions can be added to or deleted from a program and the frequency of their use increased or decreased. When specific instructional transactions are left unstudied, however, summative tests can indicate that no overall program differences exist even when potent instructional concepts lie beneath this seemingly disappointing result.

The thrust of evaluation activity for a teacher education program has been to develop an evaluation strategy for answering the formative, *why* question. The program is used here for illustrative purposes, but the techniques employed are applicable to virtually every kind of educational program. In order to implement the strategy, however, several activities need to be initiated beforehand. These activities are described below in the sequence in which they should be performed.

Initial Activities

1. With the assistance of program personnel, general program components need to be identified from which instructional transactions can be derived. In a teacher training program, for example, these general components might be: the instructional staff, classroom teacher, college supervisor, and prospective teacher as personalogical components, and individualized, field-based and class-based activities as instructional components. Specific instructional transactions are derived from these general descriptors for the purpose of establishing relationships between program inputs (transactions) and behavioral outcomes. Instructional transactions constitute specific, planned-for activities and materials employed by the developer to bring about desired program outcomes.

2. A second step is to identify potentially high payoff transactions by (a) indicating whether or not developers have specified desirable levels of use for each transaction (yes, no) and (b) estimating the effect of these transactions upon desired performance outcomes (large, small). A four-celled table is constructed as shown in Table 1 for categorizing each instructional transaction by level of specification and by the perceived effect of the transaction upon desired performance outcomes. This second categorization is based upon research and reviews of research that deal specifically with the transactions in question. Thus each instructional transaction is identified by whether a

level of use for it has been specified by developers and by its expected affect upon desired outcomes.

Table 1

Level of Specification by Magnitude of Effect Matrix for Ordering Instructional Transactions According to Their Perceived Effect Upon Desired Outcomes

		Level of Use Specified	
		Yes	No
Magnitude of Effect	Large	Level of use specified, perceived large effect (A)	Level of use not specified, perceived large effect (B)
	Small	Level of use specified, perceived small effect (C)	Level of use not specified, perceived small effect (D)

3. The purpose of the matrix is to construct a priority list of instructional transactions ranging from specified, large effect (high priority), through unspecified, small effect (low priority). Transactions that are unspecified are those for which a range of acceptable quantities had not been stated or decided upon by developers or that need to be redefined so as to exhibit scalable properties from which program developers can choose optimum levels of use. Program developers are then asked to indicate acceptable levels of use for each instructional transaction that previously had not been specified (e.g., *two* micro-teaching sessions, *three* hours of observation, *four* instructor conferences, etc.). After specification, variables that are perceived to have a large effect upon desired outcomes are employed in the following manner.

4. With the assistance of program developers, instructional transactions are categorized according to the extent to which they

approximate "real-life" tasks anticipated at program completion. Program transactions are identified as *low inference* if on face value they are highly related to post-program tasks (i.e., on-the-job performance) and as *high inference* transactions if they are one or more steps removed from these tasks (i.e., preliminary exercises and procedures). The purpose of this categorization is to help program developers identify intermediate (high inference) and terminal (low inference) behavioral outcomes for each instructional transaction that is of interest. For our example program, five classes of transactions emerged, ranging from low inference, which on face value was highly related to teaching (the on-the-job task), to high inference, which was several steps removed from the teaching process (training exercises and procedures). These classes and selected example transactions from low to high inference were:

Class 1: Transactions that involve classroom instruction and management, e.g.,
  (a) full class instruction
  (b) small class instruction
  (c) tutoring

Class 2: Transactions that involve observing classroom instruction and management, e.g.,
  (a) planned observation
  (b) video-tape viewing
  (c) visiting schools

Class 3: Transactions that involve reading, writing, discussing, and planning related to classroom instruction, e.g.,
  (a) instructional modules
  (b) video-tape feedback
  (c) constructing lesson plans and teaching materials

Class 4: Transactions that involve reading, writing, discussing, and planning related to concerns about teaching, e.g.,
  (a) counseling and feedback sessions
  (b) instructor conferences
  (c) faculty discussion of teaching performance

Class 5: Transactions involving personnel with whom the prospective teacher interacts, e.g.,
  (a) faculty contact with college supervising teacher
  (b) faculty contact with classroom teacher
  (c) faculty team meetings.

Conceptual Structure of the Model

Statistically the purpose of an instructional transaction is to produce a stronger relationship with an expected outcome than can be engendered by any concomitant variable, e.g., aptitude, attitude, and personality. The weaker the transaction in engendering the behavior specified for it, the more likely it is that a concomitant variable will be a significant influence upon this behavior. The aim of any transaction (and program) should be to produce behavior that cannot be accounted for solely by variables antecedent to it. The purpose of the formative, *why* question is to confirm relationships between transactions and outcomes that cannot be accounted for simply by the aptitudes, attitudes, and personalities of the program participants. These may be potent forces that interact with a transaction, but they should not in themselves account for the behavior for which a transaction was designed.

Transactions may not always be effective in bringing about desired behavior. It is perhaps misleading to identify activities as transactions if the program has not formally planned these experiences as inputs to the instructional process. To be effective, transactions must have a specific behavioral objective and utilize instructional materials and activities designed to produce specific behavioral outcomes. Table 2 indicates the form these materials and activities might take in a typical teacher training program. Many guides for developing effective transactions are available to program developers. Most suggest the need for a statement of the objective, specific materials and activities for obtaining the objective, opportunities for trying out or practicing activities implicit in the objective, and feedback to the participant concerning his or her performance. Effectively implemented, these characteristics work to strengthen relationships between transactions and expected behaviors.

Depending upon their level of inference, instructional transactions may be designed to produce either intermediate or terminal (end-of-program) behaviors or both. For the purpose of distinguishing intermediate behaviors from those sought at program completion, intermediate outcomes may be defined as factorially simple and terminal outcomes as factorially complex. A factorially simple outcome is one that would be expected to correlate with only a few factors in a large factor matrix comprising many measures of personality, ability, and achievement. *Specific* skills, knowledge, and attitudes can be classified as factorially simple. Outcomes at program completion are

Table 2

The Nature of Program Transactions

	Transaction	Material	Activity
1.	Observing	Flanders' interaction analysis scale	Identifying 10 variations of teacher behavior in the classroom
2.	Tutoring	Filmed example of teacher and pupil working on a tutoring task	Teaching a child a simple task with which he is unfamiliar
3.	Conferencing	Video-tape simulating productive conference between student teacher and classroom teacher	Soliciting feedback on teaching strengths and weaknesses from classroom teacher
4.	Visiting	Register of faculty roles and functions	Visiting school staff
5.	Video-taping	Video-tape lesson of prospective teacher modeling a specific teaching strategy	Practicing the implementation of a specific teaching strategy

more *general* and are expected to correlate with many factors. Therefore these outcomes are classified as factorially complex.

While both intermediate and terminal outcomes are the result of program transactions, the former are specific measures of program objectives while the latter are general measures. Scores on standardized achievement tests, for example, and measures of overall program effectiveness could represent terminal outcomes. A transactional view of an educational program places immediate importance upon specific behaviors that result from instructionally defined transactions and only at a later point upon general measures of program effectiveness. This view suggests an instructional paradigm with intermediate behaviors that are prerequisite to terminal performance. These intervening behaviors form chains or links to general measures of program effectiveness. Table 3 provides several examples of intermediate and terminal outcomes.

The formative evaluation of a complex educational program is a process of validating instructional transactions by measuring their relationship to intermediate and terminal behavior. On the basis of these relationships, effective transactions are emphasized and others are revised or deleted from the program. This process becomes increasingly complex for transactions at high levels of inference where a greater number of intermediate outcomes are expected to link transactions to terminal, "real-life" behavior. For high inference transactions far removed from real-life tasks several intermediate behaviors may be required to establish a relationship between a transaction and terminal performance. For low inference transactions that approximate the terminal task, the link between transaction and terminal behavior may be simple and direct.

Formative, *why* evaluation requires the identification of instructional transactions and their effective implementation. In order to measure relationships between transactions and intermediate outcomes, evaluations determine the degree to which each transaction is implemented by program participants. For our teacher training example, the number of supervisor/student contacts, number of classes observed, minutes of microteaching and hours of student teaching, etc., may be used as indices of the implementation of a transaction and serve to represent the transaction in relationship with intermediate and terminal outcomes. While the degree of implementing a particular transaction often varies across participants, a program can set lower and upper

Table 3

The Nature of Intermediate and Terminal Outcomes

Class of Transaction		Transaction	Intermediate Outcome (Factorially Simple)	Terminal Outcome (Factorially Complex)
	1	Small group instruction	Knowledge of different instructional strategies	Use of different instructional strategies in the classroom
	2	Planned observation	Knowledge of classroom management styles	Implementation of a successful classroom management style in the classroom
	3	Video-tape viewing	Knowledge of methods for determining one's own teaching effectiveness	Knowledge of one's teaching effectiveness in the classroom
	4	Counseling and feedback	Knowledge of self as teacher	Self-confidence, poise, demeanor while teaching
	5	Supervisor's analysis of trainee's performance	Supervisor's knowledge of performance deficiencies	Prospective teacher's classroom behavior *vis a vis* deficiencies

limits, leaving participants to choose from among a prespecified range of alternatives. Natural constraints in a program can create fortuitous variation, or variation can be achieved by specifying beforehand planned variations with a cutoff point below which the transaction would be utilized too infrequently to produce a measurable effect and above which the transaction would be too costly or redundant. Five students, for example, could be randomly assigned to each of 10 levels of use for an instructional transaction, thereby assuring a range of values representing degrees to which the transaction is implemented. Variables for evaluating a transaction, then, might consist of the degree to which a transaction is implemented and either the intermediate or terminal behavior expected from it, the latter measured at or near program completion.

In addition, there are concomitant variables that can influence the relationships between the degree of implementing a transaction and a learning outcome. These sources of influence can be studied by correlating personality, aptitude, and attitude data with outcome behaviors and with degree of implementation. If we designate the degree of implementing a transaction as x, the behavior expected from it as y, and our concomitant variable as z, we can construct the model:

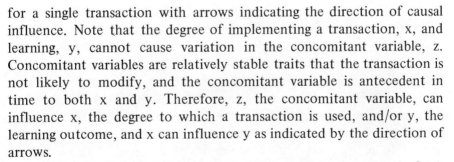

for a single transaction with arrows indicating the direction of causal influence. Note that the degree of implementing a transaction, x, and learning, y, cannot cause variation in the concomitant variable, z. Concomitant variables are relatively stable traits that the transaction is not likely to modify, and the concomitant variable is antecedent in time to both x and y. Therefore, z, the concomitant variable, can influence x, the degree to which a transaction is used, and/or y, the learning outcome, and x can influence y as indicated by the direction of arrows.

While largely overlooked due to a seeming remoteness from traditional statistical techniques, nonexperimental methods based upon the coefficient of correlation offer a useful methodology for posing the formative, *why* question. By determining relationships between an instructional transaction (e.g., hours of on-task practice, x), concomitant variable (e.g., prior familiarity with the content, z), and intermediate or long-term outcomes (e.g., number of concepts learned or used, y), one can depict the effect of a program much as one determines a sequence of events from a PERT chart. Much more valuable to program development than "perting," however, are schematizations of program effects that are empirically confirmed.

Blalock (1964) has made important contributions to a formative, *why* methodology in the context of nonexperimental research. Blalock has shown a way in which evaluators can study relationships between degrees of program implementation, concomitant variables, and intermediate and long-term outcomes by placing critical importance upon the direction of causal relationships among these variables so that the configuration:

can be used to imply a different relationship from

The formative *why* question employs schematizations, such as these, to plot causal relations between transactions and the behaviors they purport to engender. Such schematizations when empirically confirmed may inform the developer that, for example, use of microteaching (x_1), video-tape feedback (x_2) or an instructional module (x_3) are related to concomitant behaviors, e.g., teaching experience (z), and that this variable in turn is related to behavioral outcomes (y) of either an intermediate, e.g., subtask competence, or terminal, e.g., on-the-job performance, nature. Models such as those illustrated above can provide important information to the program developer; the complexity of the method can be expanded and generalized to fit additional concomitant or outcome variables. Table 4 illustrates nine outcomes that are possible

Table 4

Causal Relationships Applicable to the Evaluation of Instructional Transactions

Model	Outcome
(a) $\begin{array}{c} z \\ \cdot \\ x \cdot \quad \cdot y \end{array}$	Learning unrelated to transaction or concomitant variable
(b) $\begin{array}{c} z \\ x \longrightarrow y \end{array}$	Transaction is causing learning
(c) $\begin{array}{c} z \\ \searrow \\ x \quad \quad y \end{array}$	Concomitant variable is causing learning
(d) $\begin{array}{c} z \\ \swarrow \\ x \quad \quad y \end{array}$	Concomitant variable is causing use of transaction
(e) $\begin{array}{c} z \\ \swarrow \searrow \\ x \cdots y \end{array}$	"Spurious" correlation: relationship between transaction and learning is caused by the concomitant variable
(f) $\begin{array}{c} z \\ \swarrow \searrow \\ x \quad y \end{array}$	Concomitant variable is causing both learning and use of transaction
(g) $\begin{array}{c} z \\ \searrow \\ x \longrightarrow y \end{array}$	Both transaction and concomitant variable are causing learning
(h) $\begin{array}{c} z \\ \swarrow \\ x \longrightarrow y \end{array}$	Transaction directly and concomitant variable indirectly is causing learning
(i) $\begin{array}{c} z \\ \swarrow \searrow \\ x \longrightarrow y \end{array}$	Transaction is causing learning but a spurious effect is also present

Note: z and x are antecedent to y and z is antecedent to x. The effect of other variables on z, x, and y is random; arrows indicate causal relationships. A dotted line indicates a significant (but not causal) relationship.

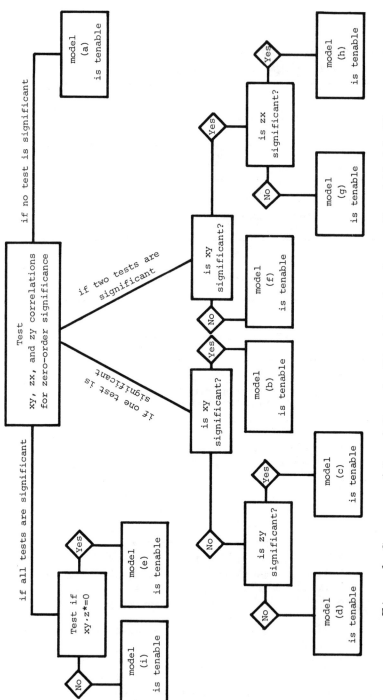

*Figure 1. Sequence of Correlations for Discriminating Among Causal Models.***

*This is the correlation of x and y with the influence of z, the concomitant variable, taken out—hence a partial correlation.

**A computer program for these calculations appears in the appendix to this chapter.

in an evaluation study from the interrelationship of x, y, and z variables and Figure 1 summarizes a procedure that successively eliminates possible outcomes through the use of correlational techniques.

Implementing the Formative, *Why* Model

Because the formative, *how* question logically precedes all others and deals directly with the implementation of instructional transactions, it will be discussed briefly before illustrating the formative, *why* model.

The formative, *how* question can be used to identify "intuitive leaps" made by program developers between objectives and outcomes that lead to missing or poorly implemented transactions. The explication of a program's content should reveal logical contingencies between objectives and outcomes when instructional transactions that are called for are both planned and implemented. Educational programs can fail to plan transactions called for by objectives, or can fail to implement transactions that have been planned.

While failing to plan necessary transactions is an oversight during program development, their failure to become implemented is an oversight during program installation. First, transactions that fail to become implemented may represent an impractical event within the constraints of the field setting, may be implemented, but in a revised or idiosyncratic manner, or may be lost altogether in getting a large and complex program into the field. The congruence between intended and observed transactions is evaluated by monitoring and documenting discrepancies between what is intended and what is actually observed, as is shown by the horizontal arrows in Figure 2. Second, unplanned but needed transactions are uncovered by determining logical contingencies between intended objectives and outcomes. This logical operation links each objective to one or more outcomes via intended program transactions, as is shown by the vertical arrows in Figure 2. Once logical contingencies for each transaction have been identified, the transaction is ready for empirical analyses that study the relationship between the instruction, and the learning, and the aptitude, personality, and attitude traits that can alter this relationship.

To illustrate the formative, *why* model a transaction constructed to acquaint student teachers with a variety of school resources will be evaluated. This transaction emphasizes that "the school contains a

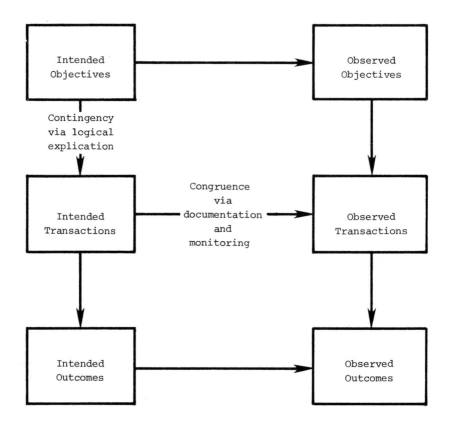

Figure 2. The Process of Identifying Missing or Poorly Implemented Transactions in a Complex Educational Program (after Stake, 1967).

variety of resource personnel and the initiative of the student is needed if she is to make use of members of the school staff as learning resources." Three alternate methods and accompanying materials are provided for learning to identify school staff. A map of the school and a staff list are provided as supporting materials. Having read through the task presented in module format, a student completes a prespecified sequence of activities, one of which is to record the extent to which the transaction has been utilized.

Three types of variables were posited for the transaction: degree of implementing the transaction, outcomes from the transaction, and concomitant variables that can modify the effect of the transaction. The data were analyzed according to the computational procedures outlined in Figure 1 using the set of variables that are listed in Table 5. These variables were subjected to statistical analysis to determine whether it would be reasonable to accept a model that depicts the module and accompanying activities causal to learning or if rival models would be more tenable. Results of the analysis appear below as they were produced for the developer by a computer program that followed the sequence of calculations described in Figure 1. Note that for the following analyses, all concomitant variables (z_1-z_4) are studied for the first outcome, i.e., y_1, before moving to the second outcome, i.e., y_2. Variables may be identified by their subscripts in Table 5. The illustration concludes with a brief discussion placing the results of the evaluation in perspective for the developer.

Table 5

*Implementation, Outcome, and Concomitant Variables
for Evaluating an Instructional Transaction on
Using School Resources*

Degree of Implementation		Outcomes		Concomitants	
x_1	Degree of implementing an instructional task on using school resources (from checklist)	y_1	Attitude toward the instructional task (from attitude scales)	z_1	Student's efficiency
				z_2	Attitude toward authority
		y_2	Knowledge of school resources (from cognitive assessments)	z_3	Attitude toward teaching
				z_4	Grade point average

Formative, *Why* Results

VARIABLE NUMBER (See Table 5)

	1	2	3	4
X MEANS	2.97			
X ST.DEV.	1.39			
Y MEANS	20.87	51.00		
Y ST.DEV.	8.20	24.47		
Z MEANS	31.05	18.05	16.82	2.74
Z ST.DEV.	4.86	3.66	4.42	.80

Results for the Affective Outcome, Y_1

CORRELATIONS

	X(1)	Y(1)	Z(1)
X(1)	1.000	.412*	.501*
Y(1)	.412*	1.000	.405*
Z(1)	.501*	.405*	1.000

ASTERISK INDICATES SIGNIFICANCE AT .05

FOR EACH UNIT OF X, Y INCREASES 2.430 UNITS.
FOR EACH UNIT OF Z, Y INCREASES   .683 UNITS.
FOR EACH UNIT OF Z, X INCREASES   .144 UNITS.

PARTIAL CORRELATION OF X AND Y WITH Z REMOVED IS .265

MODEL E IS TENABLE: SPURIOUS CORRELATION:RELATIONSHIP
BETWEEN INSTRUCTION AND LEARNING IS CAUSED BY THE
CONCOMITANT VARIABLE.

CORRELATIONS

	X(1)	Y(1)	Z(2)
X(1)	1.000	.412*	.209
Y(1)	.412*	1.000	.043
Z(2)	.209	.043	1.000

FOR EACH UNIT OF X, Y INCREASES 2.430 UNITS.
FOR EACH UNIT OF Z, Y INCREASES   .096 UNITS.
FOR EACH UNIT OF Z, X INCREASES   .080 UNITS.

MODEL B IS TENABLE: INSTRUCTION IS CAUSING LEARNING.

```
                  CORRELATIONS
            X( 1)      Y( 1)      Z( 3)

X( 1)    1.000        .412*      .425*
Y( 1)     .412*      1.000       .434*
Z( 3)     .425*       .434*     1.000


FOR EACH UNIT OF X, Y INCREASES  2.430 UNITS.
FOR EACH UNIT OF Z, Y INCREASES   .805 UNITS.
FOR EACH UNIT OF Z, X INCREASES   .134 UNITS.


PARTIAL CORRELATION OF X AND Y WITH Z REMOVED IS   .280
```

```
MODEL E IS TENABLE: SPURIOUS CORRELATION:RELATIONSHIP
BETWEEN INSTRUCTION AND LEARNING IS CAUSED BY THE
CONCOMITANT VARIABLE.
```

```
                  CORRELATIONS
            X( 1)      Y( 1)      Z( 4)

X( 1)    1.000        .412*      .318*
Y( 1)     .412*      1.000       .335*
Z( 4)     .318*       .335*     1.000


FOR EACH UNIT OF X, Y INCREASES  2.430 UNITS.
FOR EACH UNIT OF Z, Y INCREASES  3.444 UNITS.
FOR EACH UNIT OF Z, X INCREASES   .555 UNITS.


PARTIAL CORRELATION OF X AND Y WITH Z REMOVED IS   .342
```

```
MODEL I IS TENABLE: INSTRUCTION IS CAUSING LEARNING BUT
A SPURIOUS EFFECT IS ALSO PRESENT.
```

Results for the Cognitive Outcome, Y_2

```
                  CORRELATIONS
            X( 1)      Y( 2)      Z( 1)

X( 1)    1.000        .265       .501*
Y( 2)     .265       1.000       .339*
Z( 1)     .501*       .339*     1.000


FOR EACH UNIT OF X, Y INCREASES  4.664 UNITS.
FOR EACH UNIT OF Z, Y INCREASES  1.709 UNITS.
FOR EACH UNIT OF Z, X INCREASES   .144 UNITS.
```

```
MODEL F IS TENABLE: CONCOMITANT VARIABLE IS CAUSING BOTH
LEARNING AND INSTRUCTION.
```

```
                        CORRELATIONS
                X( 1)      Y( 2)      Z( 2)

    X( 1)     1,000        ,265        ,209
    Y( 2)      ,265       1,000       -,078
    Z( 2)      ,209       -,078       1,000


    FOR EACH UNIT OF X, Y INCREASES   4,664 UNITS,
    FOR EACH UNIT OF Z, Y INCREASES   -,521 UNITS,
    FOR EACH UNIT OF Z, X INCREASES    ,080 UNITS,
```

> MODEL A IS TENABLE: LEARNING UNRELATED TO INSTRUCTION OR
> CONCOMITANT VARIABLE,

```
                        CORRELATIONS
                X( 1)      Y( 2)      Z( 3)

    X( 1)     1,000        ,265        ,425*
    Y( 2)      ,265       1,000        ,072
    Z( 3)      ,425*       ,072       1,000


    FOR EACH UNIT OF X, Y INCREASES   4,664 UNITS,
    FOR EACH UNIT OF Z, Y INCREASES    ,399 UNITS,
    FOR EACH UNIT OF Z, X INCREASES    ,134 UNITS,
```

> MODEL D IS TENABLE: CONCOMITANT VARIABLE IS CAUSING
> INSTRUCTION,

```
                        CORRELATIONS
                X( 1)      Y( 2)      Z( 4)

    X( 1)     1,000        ,265        ,318*
    Y( 2)      ,265       1,000        ,332*
    Z( 4)      ,318*       ,332*      1,000


    FOR EACH UNIT OF X, Y INCREASES   4,664 UNITS,
    FOR EACH UNIT OF Z, Y INCREASES  10,196 UNITS,
    FOR EACH UNIT OF Z, X INCREASES    ,555 UNITS,
```

> MODEL F IS TENABLE: CONCOMITANT VARIABLE IS CAUSING BOTH
> LEARNING AND INSTRUCTION,

Interpreting Formative, *Why* Results

The developer uses the results of a formative, *why* analysis to revise instructional transactions. Decisions to revise a transaction are based upon the premise that an effective transaction is one that elicits behaviors that cannot alone be accounted for by the aptitude, attitude, and personality of program participants. Interpretation of results focuses upon the effect of these concomitant variables on the relationship between the transaction (x) and learning outcome (y). If either the xy relationship is not significant or the concomitant (z) erroneously causes the xy relationship to be significant, the transaction should be scheduled for revision. Therefore, only causal models that include significant xy relationships should be acceptable. Acceptable models are those indicating that the transaction is causing learning (model b), both transaction and the concomitant variable are causing learning (model g), the transaction directly and the concomitant variable indirectly are causing learning (model h), and the transaction is causing learning, but a spurious effect is also present (model e). When analyses for all concomitant variables exhibit one or more of these causal models, the transaction is ready for inclusion in the program. The occurrence of other models indicates a need to revise the transaction.

The purpose of the formative, *why* analysis is to determine if the concomitant variable influences the relationship between x and y and, if so, to what extent. For the first four analyses in our example (z_1-z_4 for y_1), the nature of the xy relationship is dependent upon student efficiency (z_1), attitude toward teaching (z_3), and grade point average (z_4). These concomitants are shown to affect learning and/or the degree to which students implement the transaction. For z_1 and z_3 the concomitant accounts for a significant portion of the variance in y to the exclusion of x and, therefore, models for z_1 and z_3 indicate that a revision of the transaction is necessary. For z_4 the concomitant accounts for a significant portion of the variance in y but so does x and therefore the model for z_4 is acceptable as is the model for z_2. Generally, however, these data indicate the need to revise the transaction so that when the influences of efficiency (z_1) and attitude toward teaching (z_3) are removed from the xy relationship, the relationship remains significant. Recommendations as to how this might be achieved should be relayed to the developer.

It is important to note that the model for z_2 is tenable but not

Memo _1_   Trial _1_

Variables:

After examining instructional transaction X_1 "Learning School Resources" for your intended outcomes, y_1, attitudinal behavior and y_2, cognitive behavior against four concomitants: z_1 student's efficiency, z_2 attitude toward authority, z_3 attitude toward teaching and z_4 scholastic achievement (GPA), the following results were obtained:

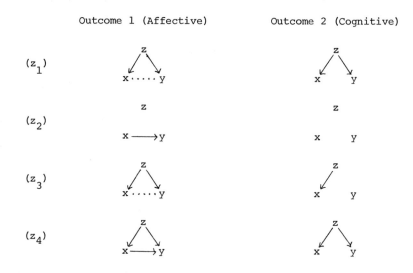

	Outcome 1 (Affective)	Outcome 2 (Cognitive)
(z_1)		
(z_2)		
(z_3)		
(z_4)		

Recommendations:

The materials for the transaction, i.e., school staff list, seem to lack sufficient substance to bring about cognitive outcomes. How about elaborating roles and functions on the list rather than leaving this information for student-teacher contacts. Also, let's require a minimum of 5 student-teacher contacts instead of 2 and provide a page in the module for taking notes during these meetings.

necessarily true. Analyses have already indicated that the xy relationship can be spuriously created by the influence of z_1 and z_3 and therefore these concomitants may be assumed to have an affect upon the xy relationship even when analyses focus upon other concomitants. While the evaluator may want to describe these relationships with a four- or five-variable schematization that takes into account the effect of multiple concomitants, his first priority should be to communicate to the developer the need to revise the transaction in an effort to strengthen the relationship between the transaction and the learning outcome.

For the remaining analyses in which concomitants z_1-z_4 are studied for outcome, y_2, the transaction failed to elicit the expected cognitive behavior. For these analyses the data indicate that the transaction had no effect, thus substantiating the earlier recommendation that a revision for this transaction is in order. The evaluator's work concludes at this stage of the analysis with a memorandum to the developer which takes the form on page 338.

Suggested Readings

Blalock, H.M., Jr. *Causal inferences in non-experimental research.* Chapel Hill, North Carolina: University of North Carolina Press, 1964.
> An important reference for learning how to make causal inferences from evaluative data. An introductory text requiring little sophistication in mathematics.

Borich, G.D. Methodological problems in educational evaluation. In H. Poynor (Ed.), *Problems and potentials in educational evaluation.* Austin, Texas: Southwest Educational Development Laboratory, 1973.
> A survey of six major evaluation problems—two of which ("formative vs. summative" and "units of analysis") relate to concepts discussed in this chapter.

Borich, G.D., and Drezek, S.F. The design of formative evaluations for the Personalized Teacher Education Program. *Memorandum No. 3.* Research and Development Center for Teacher Education, The University of Texas at Austin, 1973.
> A further illustration of the evaluation design for the analyses of data in this chapter. The report provides a list of x, y, and z variables for a large study and information pertaining to their measurement.

Cronbach, L.J. Course improvement through evaluation. *Teachers College Record,* 1963, *64,* 672-682.

A major reference providing the rationale and purpose of formative evaluation. While the author speaks of course evaluation, his concepts are equally applicable to educational programs and products.

Scriven, M. The methodology of evaluation. In *Perspectives of curriculum evaluation: 1.* Chicago: Rand McNally, 1967.

A popular work which underlines the principles of both formative and summative evaluation. Major discussions include process and comparative evaluation.

Yee, A.H., and Gage, N.L. Techniques for estimating the source and direction of causal influence in panel data. *Psychological Bulletin,* 1968, *70,* 115-126.

A technical article outlining several sophisticated techniques following the methods set forth in this chapter.

References

Blalock, H.M., Jr. *Causal inferences in non-experimental research.* Chapel Hill, North Carolina: University of North Carolina Press, 1964.

Stake, R.E. The countenance of educational evaluation. *Teachers College Record,* 1967, *64,* 672-683.

Stufflebeam, D.L., Foley, W.J., Gephart, W.J., Guba, E.G., Hammond, R.J., Merriman, H.O., and Provus, M.M. *Educational evaluation and decision making.* Itasca, Illinois: F.E. Peacock, 1971.

Appendix to
Chapter 12

```
      PROGRAM MODEL(INPUT,OUTPUT)                                            ST
C     PROGRAM MODEL REQUIRES INPUT OF X, Y, AND Z-VARIABLES FOR UP TO        A
C     200 SUBJECTS. IT WILL HANDLE 5 X-VARIABLES OR INSTRUCTIONAL            A
C     MEASURES, 5 Y-VARIABLES OR LEARNING MEASURES, AND 5 Z-VARIABLES        A
C     OR CONCOMITANT MEASURES.  PROGRAM MODEL DECIDES WHICH OF 9 MODELS      A
C     IS APPROPRIATE FOR A PARTICULAR SET OF VARIABLES. THE CORRECT          A
C     MODEL FOR EACH COMBINATION OF X,Y,AND Z VARIABLES IS DETERMINED.       A
C     THE DATA SUPPLIED TO THE PROGRAM IS AS FOLLOWS:  THE FIRST CARD IS     A
C     A PARAMETER CARD WITH THE NUMBER OF SUBJECTS IN COLS.3-5. THE          A
C     NUMBER OF X-VARIABLES IN COL.10, THE NUMBER OF Y-VARIABLES IN          A
C     COL.15, THE NUMBER OF Z-VARIABLES IN COL .20, AND A MISSING            A
C     DATA SIGNAL IN COL.25. IF ALL DATA IS TO BE ANALYZED, PLACE A          A
C     ZERO IN THIS COL. IF BLANKS ARE TO BE IGNORED, PLACE A 1 IN THIS       A
C     COL. IF BLANKS AND ZEROS ARE TO BE IGNORED, PLACE A 2 IN THIS COL.     A
C     IN COLS.26-30, PLACE EITHER 0.05 OR 0.10 FOR THE LEVEL OF              A
C     SIGNIFICANCE DESIRED FOR TESTING CORRELATIONS. THE SECOND CARD IS      A
C     THE FORMAT NECESSARY TO READ THE DATA. THE PROGRAM ASSUMES AN          A
C     X,Y,AND THEN Z-VARIABLE ORDER. THE FORMAT CARD IS FOLLOWED BY          A
C     THE DATA.                                                             A
C     PROGRAMMED IN FORTRAN IV FOR THE CONTROL DATA 6000 SERIES BY           A
C     GARY D. BORICH AND KEN W. WUNDERLICH, UNIVERSITY OF TEXAS.             A
      DIMENSION X(200,5),Y(200,5),Z(200,10),FRMT(8),A(200),B(200),         A
     1          C(200),RXY(5,5),RXZ(5,10),RYZ(5,10),ILL(200),AA(200),      A
     2          BB(200),CC(200),XMEAN(5),XSD(5),YMEAN(5),YSD(5),           A
     3          ZMEAN(10),ZSD(10),NK(5,5,10)                               A
      READ 440, NSUB,NX,NY,NZ,MDATOPT,PL                                   A
      READ 450, (FRMT(I),I=1,8)                                            A
      DO 10 I=1,NSUB                                                       A
      READ FRMT, (X(I,J),J=1,NX),(Y(I,K),K=1,NY),(Z(I,L),L=1,NZ)           A
   10 CONTINUE                                                             A
      PRINT 460                                                            A
      PRINT 470                                                            A
      PRINT 480                                                            A
      DO 20 N=1,5                                                          A
      DO 20 M=1,5                                                          A
      XMEAN(M)=YMEAN(M)=XSD(M)=YSD(M)=0.0                                  A
      RXY(M,N)=0.0                                                         A
   20 CONTINUE                                                             A
      DO 30 M=1,5                                                          A
      DO 30 N=1,10                                                         A
      RXZ(M,N)=RYZ(M,N)=ZMEAN(N)=ZSD(N)=0.0                                A
   30 CONTINUE                                                             A
      DO 70 I=1,NX                                                         A
      DO 70 J=1,NY                                                         A
      DO 70 K=1,NZ                                                         A
      DO 40 L=1,NSUB                                                       A
      A(L)=X(L,I)                                                          A
      B(L)=Y(L,J)                                                          A
      C(L)=Z(L,K)                                                          A
   40 CONTINUE                                                             A
      IF (MDATOPT.EQ.0) GO TO 50                                           A
      CALL AMISOPT (A,B,C,NSUB,MDATOPT,NN)                                 A
      NK(I,J,K)=NN                                                         A
      GO TO 60                                                             A
   50 CONTINUE                                                             A
      NN=NSUB                                                              A
      NK(I,J,K)=NN                                                         A
   60 CONTINUE                                                             A
      CALL CORELAT (A,B,XMEAN(I),XSD(I),RXY(I,J),NN)                       A
      CALL CORELAT (B,C,YMEAN(J),YSD(J),RYZ(J,K),NN)                       A
      CALL CORELAT (C,A,ZMEAN(K),ZSD(K),RXZ(I,K),NN)                       A
```

```
70    CONTINUE                                          A  80
      PRINT 490                                         A  81
      PRINT 500, (XMEAN(I),I=1,NX)                      A  82
      PRINT 510, (XSD(I),I=1,NX)                        A  83
      PRINT 520, (YMEAN(J),J=1,NY)                      A  84
      PRINT 530, (YSD(J),J=1,NY)                        A  85
      PRINT 540, (ZMEAN(K),K=1,NZ)                      A  86
      PRINT 550, (ZSD(K),K=1,NZ)                        A  87
      DO 430 I=1,NX                                     A  88
      DO 430 J=1,NY                                     A  89
      DO 430 K=1,NZ                                     A  90
      R1=RXY(I,J)                                       A  91
      R2=RYZ(J,K)                                       A  92
      R3=RXZ(I,K)                                       A  93
      BYX=R1*YSD(J)/XSD(I)                              A  94
      BYZ=R2*YSD(J)/ZSD(K)                              A  95
      BXZ=R3*XSD(I)/ZSD(K)                              A  96
      T1=R1/SQRTF((1.0-R1*R1)/(NN-2))                   A  97
      T2=R2/SQRTF((1.0-R2*R2)/(NN-2))                   A  98
      T3=R3/SQRTF((1.0-R3*R3)/(NN-2))                   A  99
      DN=NN-2                                           A 100
      T1=T1*T1                                          A 101
      T2=T2*T2                                          A 102
      T3=T3*T3                                          A 103
      P1=PRBF(1,0,DN,T1)                                A 104
      P2=PRBF(1,0,DN,T2)                                A 105
      P3=PRBF(1,0,DN,T3)                                A 106
      S1=1H                                             A 107
      S2=1H                                             A 108
      S3=1H                                             A 109
      NC=N1=N2=N3=0                                     A 110
      IF (P1.LE.0.05) 80,90                             A 111
80    CONTINUE                                          A 112
      S1=1H*                                            A 113
      GO TO 110                                         A 114
90    CONTINUE                                          A 115
      IF (P1.LE.0.10) 100,110                           A 116
100   CONTINUE                                          A 117
110   CONTINUE                                          A 119
      IF (P1.LE.PL) 120,130                             A 120
120   CONTINUE                                          A 121
      NC=NC+1                                           A 122
      N1=1                                              A 123
130   CONTINUE                                          A 124
      IF (P2.LE.0.05) 140,150                           A 125
140   CONTINUE                                          A 126
      S2=1H*                                            A 127
      GO TO 170                                         A 128
150   CONTINUE                                          A 129
      IF (P2.LE.0.10) 160,170                           A 130
160   CONTINUE                                          A 131
170   CONTINUE                                          A 133
      IF (P2.LE.PL) 180,190                             A 134
180   CONTINUE                                          A 135
      NC=NC+1                                           A 136
      N2=1                                              A 137
190   CONTINUE                                          A 138
      IF (P3.LE.0.05) 200,210                           A 139
200   CONTINUE                                          A 140
      S3=1H*                                            A 141
      GO TO 230                                         A 142
210   CONTINUE                                          A 143
```

```
        IF (P3.LE.0.10) 220,230                                          A 144
220  CONTINUE                                                            A 145
230  CONTINUE                                                            A 147
        IF (P3.LE.PL) 240,250                                            A 148
240  CONTINUE                                                            A 149
     NC=NC+1                                                             A 150
     N3=1                                                                A 151
250  CONTINUE                                                            A 152
     PRINT 560, I,J,K                                                    A 153
     PRINT 570, I,R1,S1,R3,S3,J,R1,S1,R2,S2,K,R3,S3,R2,S2               A 154
     IF(I.NE.1) GO TO 255
     IF(J.NE.1) GO TO 255
     IF(K.EQ.1) PRINT 580
255  CONTINUE
     PRINT 600, BYX,BYZ,BXZ                                              A 157
        IF (NC.EQ.0) 260,270                                            A 158
260  CONTINUE                                                            A 159
     PRINT 610                                                           A 160
        GO TO 430                                                        A 161
270  CONTINUE                                                            A 162
        IF (NC.EQ.1) 280,330                                            A 163
280  CONTINUE                                                            A 164
        IF (N1.EQ.1) 290,300                                            A 165
290  CONTINUE                                                            A 166
     PRINT 620                                                           A 167
        GO TO 430                                                        A 168
300  CONTINUE                                                            A 169
        IF (N2.EQ.1) 310,320                                            A 170
310  CONTINUE                                                            A 171
     PRINT 630                                                           A 172
        GO TO 430                                                        A 173
320  CONTINUE                                                            A 174
     PRINT 640                                                           A 175
        GO TO 430                                                        A 176
330  CONTINUE                                                            A 177
        IF (NC.EQ.2) 340,390                                            A 178
340  CONTINUE                                                            A 179
        IF (N1.EQ.1) 360,350                                            A 180
350  CONTINUE                                                            A 181
     PRINT 650                                                           A 182
        GO TO 430                                                        A 183
360  CONTINUE                                                            A 184
        IF (N3.EQ.1) 380,370                                            A 185
370  CONTINUE                                                            A 186
     PRINT 660                                                           A 187
        GO TO 430                                                        A 188
380  CONTINUE                                                            A 189
     PRINT 670                                                           A 190
        GO TO 430                                                        A 191
390  CONTINUE                                                            A 192
        IF (NC.EQ.3) 400,430                                            A 193
400  RXYZ=(R1-R2*R3)/SQRTF((1.0-R3*R3)*(1.0-R2*R2))                     A 194
     TT=RXYZ/SQRTF((1.0-RXYZ*RXYZ)/(NN-3))                             A 195
     TT=TT*TT                                                            A 196
     DM=NN-3                                                             A 197
     PT=PRBF(1.0,DM,TT)                                                 A 198
        IF (PT.LE.PL) 410,420                                           A 199
410  CONTINUE                                                           A 200
     PRINT 680, RXYZ                                                    A 201
     PRINT 690                                                          A 202
        GO TO 430                                                       A 203
                                                                        A 204
```

```
420    CONTINUE                                                          A 205
       PRINT 680, RXYZ                                                   A 206
       PRINT 700                                                         A 207
       PRINT 710                                                         A 208
430    CONTINUE                                                          A 209
440    FORMAT  (2X,I3,2(4X,I1),3X,I2,4X,I1,F5.2)                         A 210
450    FORMAT  (8A10)                                                    A 211
460    FORMAT (*1*,21X,*MODEL A*,28X,*MODEL D*,29X,*MODEL G*,/,23X,*Z*,36 A 212
      1X,*Z*,35X,*Z*,/,23X,1H*,36X,1H*,35X,1H*,/,59X,*.*,37X,*.*,/,58X,*. A 213
      2*,39X,*.*,/,57X,*.*,41X,*.*,/,56X,*.*,43X,*.*,/,55X,*.*,45X,*.*,/  A 214
      3 15X,3HX *,11X,3H* Y,20X,3HX *,11X,3H* Y,19X,17HX *.........* Y,   A 215
      4//,12X,*LEARNING UNRELATED TO*,15X,*CONCOMITANT VARIABLE RELATED*, A 216
      5BX,*BOTH INSTRUCTION AND CONCOMI*,/,12X,*INSTRUCTION OR CONCOMITAN A 217
      6T*,10X,*TO INSTRUCTION*,22X,*TANT VARIABLE ARE CAUSING*,/,12X,*VAR A 218
      7IABLE*,64X,*LEARNING*,////)                                       A 219
470    FORMAT  (21X,*MODEL B*,28X,*MODEL E*,29X,*MODEL H*,/,23X,*Z*,34X,  A 220
      1Z*,35X,*Z*,/,23X,1H*,34X,1H*,35X,1H*,/,57X,*.  .*,33X,*.*,/,56X,*. A 221
      2 .*,31X,*.*,/,55X,*.*,5X,*.*,29X,*.*,/,54X,*.*,7X,*.*,27X,*.*,/,5  A 222
      333X,*.*,9X,*.*,25X,*.*,/,15X,17HX *.........* Y,18X,17HX *-------   A 223
      4-----* Y,19X,17HX *.........* Y,//,12X,*INSTRUCTION IS CAUSING*,/, A 224
      555X,*SPURIOUS CORRELATION*,15X,*INSTRUCTION DIRECTLY AND*,/,12X,*LE A 225
      6ARNING*,64X,*CONCOMITANT VARIABLE INDIREC*,/,84X,*TLY IS CAUSING L A 226
      7EARNING*,////)                                                    A 227
480    FORMAT  (21X,*MODEL C*,28X,*MODEL F*,29X,*MODEL I*,/,23X,*Z*,34X,  A 228
      1Z*,35X,*Z*,/,23X,1H*,34X,1H*,35X,1H*,/,24X,*.*,32X,*.  .*,33X,*. .* A 229
      2,/,25X,*.*,30X,*.   .*,31X,*.   .*,/,26X,*.*,28X,*.     .*,29X,*.  A 230
      3  .*,/,27X,*.*,26X,*.       .*,27X,*.       .*,/,28X,*.*,24X,*.    A 231
      4   .*,/,27X,*.     .*,/,15X,17HX *.........* Y,18X,17HX *          A 232
      5      * Y,19X,17HX *.........* Y,///,12X,*CONCOMITANT VARIAB       A 233
      6LE IS*,13X,*NO RELATION BETWEEN INSTRUCT*,8X,*INSTRUCTION IS CAUSI A 234
      7NG LEARN*,/,12X,*CAUSING LEARNING*,20X,*ION AND LEARNING BUT CONCO A 235
      8MI*,8X,*ING BUT A SPURIOUS EFFECT IS*,/,48X,*TANT VARIABLE EFFECTS A 236
      9 BOTH*,10X,*ALSO PRESENT*,//,1H1)                                 A 237
490    FORMAT  (////,27X,*VARIABLE NUMBER*,//,27X,*1*,8X,*2*,8X,*3*,8X,*4* A 238
      1,8X,*5*)                                                          A 239
500    FORMAT  (12X,*X MEANS*,5X,5(F6.2,3X)/)                            A 240
510    FORMAT  (12X,*X ST.DEV.*,3X,5(F6.2,3X)//)                         A 241
520    FORMAT  (12X,*Y MEANS*,5X,5(F6.2,3X)/)                            A 242
530    FORMAT  (12X,*Y ST.DEV.*,3X,5(F6.2,3X)//)                         A 243
540    FORMAT  (12X,*Z MEANS*,5X,10(F6.2,3X)/)                           A 244
550    FORMAT  (12X,*Z ST.DEV.*,3X,10(F6.2,3X)/,1H1)                     A 245
560    FORMAT  (/////,27X,*CORRELATIONS*,/,20X,*X(*,I2,*)*,5X,*Y(*,I2,*)*, A 246
      15X,*Z(*,I2,*)*)                                                   A 247
570    FORMAT  (/12X,*X(*,I2,*)*,3X,*1.000*,5X,F6.3,A2,3X,F6.3,A2,3X,/,12 A 248
      1X,*Y(*,I2,*)*,2X,F6.3,A2,4X,*1.000*,5X,F6.3,A2,/,12X,*Z(*,I2,*)*,2 A 249
      2X,F6.3,A2,3X,F6.3,A2,4X,*1.000*)                                  A 250
580    FORMAT  (/12X, *ASTERISK INDICATES SIGNIFICANCE AT .05*)          A 251
600    FORMAT  (//,12X,*FOR EACH UNIT OF X, Y INCREASES*,F7.3,* UNITS,*,/ A 256
      1 12X,        *FOR EACH UNIT OF Z, Y INCREASES*,F7.3,* UNITS,*,/    A 257
      2,12X,        *FOR EACH UNIT OF Z, X INCREASES*,F7.3,* UNITS,*)     A 258
610    FORMAT  (//,12X,*MODEL A IS TENABLE: LEARNING UNRELATED TO INSTRUC A 259
      1TION OR*/12X,*CONCOMITANT VARIABLE.*)
620    FORMAT  (//,12X,*MODEL B IS TENABLE: INSTRUCTION IS CAUSING LEARNI A 260
      1NG.*)
630    FORMAT  (//,12X,*MODEL C IS TENABLE: CONCOMITANT VARIABLE IS CAUSI A 261
      1NG LEARNING.*)
640    FORMAT  (//,12X,*MODEL D IS TENABLE: CONCOMITANT VARIABLE IS CAUSI A 262
      1NG*/12X,*INSTRUCTION.*)
650    FORMAT  (//,12X,*MODEL F IS TENABLE: CONCOMITANT VARIABLE IS CAUSI A 263
      1NG BOTH*/12X,*LEARNING AND INSTRUCTION.*)
660    FORMAT  (//,12X,*MODEL G IS TENABLE: BOTH INSTRUCTION AND CONCOMIT A 264
      1ANT VARIABLE ARE CAUSING LEARNING.*)
```

```
 670   FORMAT   (//,12X,*MODEL H IS TENABLE: INSTRUCTION DIRECTLY AND CONC   A 265
      10MITANT VARIABLE INDIRECTLY ARE CAUSING LEARNING.*)
 680   FORMAT   (//,12X,*PARTIAL CORRELATION OF X AND Y WITH Z REMOVED IS*   A 266
      1,F6,3)                                                               A 267
 690   FORMAT   (//,12X,*MODEL I IS TENABLE: INSTRUCTION IS CAUSING LEARNI   A 268
      1NG BUT*/12X,*A SPURIOUS EFFECT IS ALSO PRESENT.*)
 700   FORMAT   (//,12X,*MODEL E IS TENABLE: SPURIOUS CORRELATION:RELATION   A 269
      1SHIP*/12X,*BETWEEN INSTRUCTION AND LEARNING IS CAUSED BY THE*/
      212X,*CONCOMITANT VARIABLE.*)
 710   FORMAT   (1H1)                                                       A 270
       END                                                                  A 271
       SUBROUTINE AMISOPT (A,B,C,NS,MISDATA,NN)                             B   1
       DIMENSION A(200),B(200),C(200),ILL(200),AA(200),BB(200),CC(200)      B   2
       IJK=0                                                                B   3
       DO 10 NQ=1,200                                                       B   4
       ILL(NQ)=0                                                            B   5
       AA(NQ)=0.0                                                           B   6
       BB(NQ)=0.0                                                           B   7
       CC(NQ)=0.0                                                           B   8
 10    CONTINUE                                                             B   9
       DO 60 N=1,NS                                                         B  10
       IF (A(N).EQ.0.0.OR.B(N).EQ.0.0.OR.C(N).EQ.0.0) 20,60                 B  11
 20    CONTINUE                                                             B  12
       IF (MISDATA.EQ.2) 30,40                                             B  13
 30    CONTINUE                                                             B  14
       IJK=IJK+1                                                            B  15
       ILL(IJK)=N                                                           B  16
       GO TO 60                                                             B  17
 40    CONTINUE                                                             B  18
       IF (.NOT.A(N).OR..NOT.B(N).OR..NOT.C(N)) 60,50                       B  19
 50    CONTINUE                                                             B  20
       IJK=IJK+1                                                            B  21
       ILL(IJK)=N                                                           B  22
 60    CONTINUE                                                             B  23
       IF (ILL(1).EQ.0) 120,70                                             B  24
 70    CONTINUE                                                             B  25
       ICOONT=0                                                            B  26
       DO 100 JC=1,NS                                                       B  27
       DO 80 JV=1,IJK                                                       B  28
       IF (JC.EQ.ILL(JV)) 90,80                                             B  29
 80    CONTINUE                                                             B  30
       AA(JC-ICOONT)=A(JC)                                                  B  31
       BB(JC-ICOONT)=B(JC)                                                  B  32
       CC(JC-ICOONT)=C(JC)                                                  B  33
       GO TO 100                                                            B  34
 90    CONTINUE                                                             B  35
       ICOONT=ICOONT+1                                                      B  36
 100   CONTINUE                                                             B  37
       NN=NS-IJK                                                            B  38
       DO 110 JT=1,NN                                                       B  39
       A(JT)=AA(JT)                                                         B  40
       B(JT)=BB(JT)                                                         B  41
       C(JT)=CC(JT)                                                         B  42
 110   CONTINUE                                                             B  43
       GO TO 130                                                            B  44
 120   CONTINUE                                                             B  45
       NN=NS                                                                B  46
 130   CONTINUE                                                             B  47
       RETURN                                                               B  48
       END                                                                  B  49
       SUBROUTINE CORELAT (A,B,AMEAN,ASD,RAB,NN)                            C   1
       DIMENSION A(200),B(200)                                              C   2
```

```
        SUMA=0.0                                                    C    3
        SUMB=0.0                                                    C    4
        SQSUMA=0.0                                                  C    5
        SQSUMB=0.0                                                  C    6
        PRODUCT=0.0                                                 C    7
        DO 10 I=1,NN                                                C    8
        SUMA=SUMA+A(I)                                              C    9
        SUMB=SUMB+B(I)                                              C   10
        SQSUMA=SQSUMA+A(I)*A(I)                                     C   11
        SQSUMB=SQSUMB+B(I)*B(I)                                     C   12
        PRODUCT=PRODUCT+A(I)*B(I)                                   C   13
        CONTINUE                                                    C   14
        AMEAN=SUMA/NN                                               C   15
        BMEAN=SUMB/NN                                               C   16
        ASD=SQRTF(SQSUMA/NN-AMEAN*AMEAN)                            C   17
        BSD=SQRTF(SQSUMB/NN-BMEAN*BMEAN)                            C   18
        RAB=(PRODUCT/NN-AMEAN*BMEAN)/(ASD*BSD)                      C   19
        RETURN                                                      C   20
        END                                                         C   21-
        FUNCTION PRBF (DA,DB,FR)                                    D    1
        PRBF=1.0                                                    D    2
        IF (DA.LE.0.0) RETURN                                       D    3
        IF (DB.LE.0.0) RETURN                                       D    4
        IF (FR.LE.0.0) RETURN                                       D    5
           IF (FR.LT.1.0) GO TO 10                                  D    6
        A=DA                                                        D    7
        B=DB                                                        D    8
        F=FR                                                        D    9
           GO TO 20                                                 D   10
        CONTINUE                                                    D   11
        A=DB                                                        D   12
        B=DA                                                        D   13
        F=1.0/FR                                                    D   14
        CONTINUE                                                    D   15
        AA=2.0/(9.0*A)                                              D   16
        BB=2.0/(9.0*B)                                              D   17
        ZZ=((1.0-BB)*F**0.333333-1.0+AA)/SQRT(BB*F**0.666667+AA)    D   18
        Z=ABS(ZZ)                                                   D   19
        IF (B.LT.4.0)Z=Z*(1.0+0.08*Z**4/B**3)                       D   20
        PRBF=0.5/(1.0+Z*(0.196854+Z*(0.115194+Z*(0.000344+Z*0.019527)))) D 21
       1**4
        IF (FR.LT.1.0) PRBF=1.0-PRBF                                D   22
        IF (ZZ.LT.0.0) PRBF=1-PRBF                                  D   23
        RETURN                                                      D   24
        END                                                         D   25-
```

CHAPTER 13

EVALUATING ONGOING INSTRUCTIONAL PROGRAMS

R. Tony Eichelberger
Learning Research and Development Center
University of Pittsburgh

Much to the chagrin of many researchers and evaluators, the evaluation of educational programs often must take place with little or no manipulation of treatment variables. The failure to manipulate treatment variables is often blamed on the educator's lack of understanding of the research process. Researchers frequently attempt to change an educational program to fit the existing methodology rather than modify the methodology in order to evaluate the program. Although modifications that render traditional experimental design and analysis methods more appropriate are possible, there are often basic inconsistencies between the requirements of the educational setting and those of research methodology. If, after a few months of study, several students in the experimental program are the only students in the school unable to read, they must be given remediation—even if this results in complete loss of internal and external validity for the study.

The thesis of this chapter is that correlational analyses are presently the most appropriate methods for gaining knowledge about the effects of educational programs in natural settings. In the first section of the chapter, the rationale behind these methods is discussed; in the second, appropriate evaluation procedures in a research and development setting are outlined; and in a final section the results that have been obtained using these procedures are illustrated. The following discussion is not meant as an argument against traditional experimental design and statistics when they are applied appropriately; rather, it is an attempt to indicate alternative evaluation procedures for diverse educational settings.

The evaluation strategies outlined and discussed are most useful in a setting where not only the effects of a program must be documented and compared with the effects of other educational programs, but also where different aspects of the program must be investigated with respect to these effects (outcomes). It is much more convincing to have information that allows outcomes to be attributed to program variables than to treat the program as a "black box," reporting only general outcome data.

A Rationale for Correlational Techniques

Historically, educational research has been classified into categories that usually include a major distinction between experimental and correlational studies. Unfortunately, the distinction between the manipulation of independent variables and their non-manipulation has been transferred to the statistics that are typically used in inferential versus descriptive studies (i.e., t or F and r). As a result, many educators and researchers believe that causation cannot be inferred from a correlation coefficient. What these persons fail to consider is that the technique used to analyze data (such as correlation) is not the deciding factor concerning causal inference. For example, if two methods of teaching mathematics are compared with respect to achievement on a math test, either a t-test or a test of significance of the correlation between group membership and math achievement would result in the same level of probability for the obtained result. Various texts show the mathematical equivalence of the two statistical procedures (e.g., Kelley, Beggs, McNeil, Eichelberger, and Lyon, 1969). The manner in which the treatments were implemented, the sequence of occurrence of the variables, the testing instrument, and the makeup of the samples are among the deciding factors in making causal inferences—and not the statistical technique.

Although the example above is a relatively simple one, hopefully it will set the stage for further discussion of correlational procedures. One of the most elementary, yet most thought-provoking, ideas presented by Blalock (1964) is that researchers can make causal inferences with some degree of confidence given appropriate models; but, causality cannot be proven regardless of the extent and quality of the empirical results. This point is best stated by Simon (1971):

> ... the concept of causal ordering employed in this paper does not in any way solve the "problem of Hume" nor contradict his assertion that all we can ever observe are covariations. If we employ an ontological definition of cause—one based on the "necessary" connection of events—

then correlation cannot, of course, prove causation. But
neither can anything else prove causation, . . . (p. 6).

Therefore, regardless of the rigor involved using presently available
inferential procedures, no hypothesis can be proven without some
shadow of a doubt.

Thus, making causal inferences from data is not a binary choice
between unequivocal and ambiguous results as some authors would
indicate (Stufflebeam, Foley, Gephart, Guba, Hammond, Merriman,
and Provus, 1971). Instead, each study lies somewhere along a
continuum with respect to the confidence one has in making causal
inferences. The exact position of any particular study on the
continuum cannot be uniquely determined. It would seem then that the
primary use for data in education is to compile evidence relating to
particular questions of interest and not to report unequivocal results.
From this frame of reference, each new situation must be analyzed so
that the best available methods for collecting and analyzing data are
used *within the constraints of each particular situation.* Evaluation
reports must also be concerned with the appropriateness of the data for
those who will use it.

Evaluations that report only end-of-year results are not convincing
for documenting effects brought about by a program (a primary
function of evaluation). Because of the many problems involved in
evaluating educational programs and the complex nature of the
educational process, there are usually numerous alternative hypotheses
that could account for the results. It has also recently come to the
attention of many educational researchers that differential effects of
two programs cannot be adequately assessed by placing each program in
a given number of classrooms, even when students and teachers are
selected randomly, and analyzing the dependent variables (usually
end-of-year test results). When the classrooms are observed on the
important program (treatment) variables, there is often as much
difference among teachers using the same educational program as there
is among teachers using "different" educational programs on important
implementation variables. This result emphasizes the need to adequately define and to measure differences in the programs actually
experienced by the students, rather than to assume that Method A is
the same method in different classrooms. Researchers and evaluators
have often overlooked this requirement in the past.

Most recent evaluation models, e.g., Lindvall and Cox (1970),

Stake (1967), Stufflebeam (1971), Stufflebeam *et al.* (1971), include some aspect of observing and/or documenting educational activities in the classroom. They refer to this procedure variously as process evaluation, formative evaluation, operations assessment, etc. Even though it is not always stated, each of these models is attempting to define the treatment *post hoc*—admitting that it cannot be done *a priori.* When it is not possible to control the educational process, a traditional experimental design is inappropriate. A useful outcome of describing the treatment as it occurs is that the need for a control group (in this particular aspect of evaluation) is greatly reduced. In those classrooms where the program is "best" implemented, student effects should be largest. The other participating classrooms provide comparison groups at other levels of the implementation variables. These comparison groups allow more adequate investigation of the relationships between educational variables and student learning. If student achievement is highest in classrooms "best" implemented, the data support the positive effect of that program. In addition, the relative effects of different implementation variables can be investigated by using this evaluation procedure.

Formative evaluation, while allowing more realistic study of the teaching-learning process, also needs to be complemented with procedures that compare one program with another. This is often the primary concern of those persons employing evaluators. Funding agencies usually want the best information possible to aid in making difficult decisions. Cronbach (1963) has indicated a need for data about programs, rather than data for deciding which one is best at a particular time. The question should not be what is the "best" at the present time, but: (1) What are the positive and negative aspects of each?; (2) What modifications are needed?; (3) Which program holds greatest promise for the future?; (4) Can the program implementation be replicated? Until changes occur in the "real world," evaluators must present comparative data on programs so that judgments of relative merit with respect to generally accepted criterion variables are possible.

To summarize the rationale, there is no experimental method that allows data to be collected and analyzed so that any hypothesis can be *proven.* The primary value of data, or information, in education is to compile evidence relating to particular questions. The questions of interest in most evaluation efforts usually relate to: (1) documenting the strengths and weaknesses of the program, or product; (2)

identifying important implementation variables and their effects; (3) identifying the educational variables necessary for the program to operate effectively; and (4) comparing the program, or product, with those having similar objectives or purposes.

Correlational analyses can supply useful information for these questions. Correlational procedures allow complexities within the classroom to occur and allow identification of redundancies between implementation variables and outcomes. By repeating the analyses in a number of settings on a longitudinal basis, relationships can be studied and fluctuations observed. Because information about many variables affecting the educational process is needed, multiple correlational methods appear to be the most useful data reduction methods presently available. These include factor analysis, canonical and multiple part and partial correlation, as well as standard multiple linear regression procedures. Other information that is collected systematically, such as supervisory observations, teachers' ratings or self-reports, and developers' knowledge of the curricula, can also be used to help in deciding the confidence we can have in the results obtained and to give direction in selecting the types of variables and analyses needed to more adequately study in following years important questions that are raised.

Program Evaluation Strategies

In a research and development setting, the emphasis of evaluation will differ somewhat from that of school districts, private educational corporations, and publishing companies. The following description of a specific development and implementation procedure is given as background information for the evaluation strategies outlined below. In this setting, basic psychological and educational research knowledge is used for developing and studying individualized education. The procedures developed have been implemented in two developmental schools under the control of local school boards. After individualized educational innovations have been successfully implemented locally (and modified, if necessary) they are then disseminated to specific school districts in the National Follow Through Program. In these classrooms there is much less consultative help than in developmental classrooms, making the situation more like that of typical classrooms.

The evaluation needed for the development and modification of each instructional program is the responsibility of the particular project leader in charge of that development effort, such as reading, math, science, etc. Since each developer must get immediate feedback concerning the applicability and effectiveness of instructional materials, lesson sequences, classroom management, etc., and will be the primary person utilizing the information, it seems imperative that each developer plan, collect, and analyze whatever data are most useful to the development process. These data are best collected in developmental classrooms.

It is difficult for a central evaluation staff to be aware of the intricacies of all programs and the idiosyncracies of each classroom in enough detail so that information useful to the developer for making modifications of specific units or lessons is obtained. A drawback of having a central evaluation staff is that information tends to become more general as data are collected over many programs. The smaller divisions of data that are possible within each curriculum area, such as skill or objective, are extremely expensive to obtain. If one or more persons are hired to evaluate each small project, then other concerns determine whether they are part of a central evaluation staff or attached directly to each project. Some small bits of information are necessary to the development effort, so evaluators working directly in the development process need to expend the resources to obtain them.

In a research and development setting it is reasonable for a central evaluation staff to evaluate educational programs on a broad basis. This type of evaluation is often labeled "summative," but the distinction between formative and summative evaluation (Scriven, 1967) is not a very clear one in the practical setting. For example, information obtained by the central evaluation staff doing "summative" evaluation is often useful in modifying curricula (traditionally the function of "formative" evaluation). Another example is that data collected monthly and used during the year to make changes within the school (formative) can be summarized and analyzed with other data for summative purposes at the end of each school year.

The following describes an evaluation procedure now in use in which three major types of data are collected:

1. student progress data within each curricular area for periodic monitoring of both the instructional program and the students;
2. end-of-year achievement data for discerning longitudinal and comparative effects of the instructional programs; and
3. input, process, and outcome data for in-depth study of

relationships between instructional or environmental variables and changes in students.

1. *Student progress data within each curricular area for periodic
monitoring of both the instructional program and the students.*
Placement and progress data for participating students are collected
monthly and stored in a data bank. Both the last unit completed and
the number of units completed in each area are needed as indicators of
location and progress in the curricula. Other demographic and historical
data on each student, such as number of years in the program,
participation in preschool program, etc., are also collected and stored.

These data can be used by members of each development project
to review student progress in each classroom and in different areas of
each curriculum. General difficulties with aspects of the instructional
program can be observed that might be missed by persons implementing
the programs in the schools. The data might also indicate that a teacher
is having difficulty either in helping certain types of students or in using
specific parts of a curriculum. For example, a teacher may not be using
a part of the perceptual skills program, or a student may be making
uneven progress—high in math, low in reading. Supervisors and
consultants can then use the information for in-service training. These
data are not useful for the daily operation of the school, only for
periodically reviewing academic progress. These data are necessary for
relating student placement or progress in the curricula to other
achievement variables.

At the end of the year, the monthly data can be summarized and
reviewed for making decisions about program revisions, dissemination,
and modifications of the instructional program in the schools. Timing is
important, as decisions for the following September often must be
made during March or April (Mazur, 1971). The placement information
is also useful as input, while progress during the year can be used as
outcome data for in-depth studies of individualized education.

2. *End-of-year achievement data for discerning longitudinal and
comparative effects of the instructional programs.* A useful implementation and evaluation design is outlined in Table 1. Developers usually
start their development effort at a particular grade level and work up or
down from there. It is advantageous to start at the lowest level and
work up. As students progress through school new materials are
developed each year. Both the developmental programs and evaluation
design can then be implemented in a progressive orderly fashion.

Table 1

Longitudinal Evaluation Design (Wang, 1970)

Grade	1968-69	1969-70	1970-71	1971-72	1972-73
Pre	E	E	E	E	E
K	E	E	E	E	E
1	C	E	E	E	E
2	C	C	E	E	E
3		C	C	E	E
4			C	C	E
5				C	C
6					C

E = experimental class
C = control class

In Table 1, for example, during the first year, 1968-69, the instructional program was implemented in preschool (pre: three- and four-year-olds) and kindergarten (k). But testing with the Wide Range Achievement Test (WRAT) (Jastak and Jastak, 1965), was done in preschool through grade 2. In each succeeding year, the program was implemented in one more grade and testing occurred two grade levels above that. This design should be useful regardless of the measures or the criteria variables selected. For most educational programs, some type of generally accepted measure of academic achievement is needed.

Other evaluation efforts reported in the literature tend to show that control groups from other school buildings work to increase rather than reduce the number of alternative explanations of the results (e.g.,

SRI, 1973). Although pupils may be similar on the usual "matching" variables such as socioeconomic status, cultural and ethnic background, and IQ, there are often subtle differences in local neighborhoods with respect to educational attitudes and values that may affect student achievement. Students in different schools are rarely comparable. Each principal has his own way of "running" a school that greatly affects the learning climate. For these and other reasons it is desirable to have comparison groups within the same school. This situation often causes contamination of the control group; but, if there are great differences between traditional classrooms (control) and participating classrooms (experimental) in types of materials used, teacher roles, and classroom control, the contamination may not be extensive. In one developmental school, Cooley (1971) compared control classrooms at each grade level on achievement test scores and found no significant differences, providing further support for the use of the design outlined in Table 1. Decisions about the applicability of the proposed design for a specific evaluation effort depend upon the treatment variables of interest. If the control classes are likely to incorporate important aspects of the program, then this progressive implementation design will not be adequate.

When this design is appropriate, it allows not only comparisons between the new program and the previous program, but also longitudinal trends and the observation of changes within the new program. Since the program being developed is not a final product, some of the concerns that typical curriculum evaluators have, such as deciding which program is best, are not the primary emphasis of the evaluation.

Although the longitudinal implementation and evaluation plan is fairly useful for comparing participating students with previous students in academic achievement, it is neither entirely convincing (regardless of the outcome of the data), nor does it give much information about how student changes were brought about. More in-depth evaluation activities that investigate and attempt to document *how* student changes are brought about are needed.

3. *Input, process, and outcome data for in-depth study of relationships between instructional or environmental variables and changes in students.* These types of study are at the core of most work that should be done by evaluators. The position taken here concerning in-depth evaluation is closely related to Dyer's proposal (1970) for a

"student-change model of an educational system." Dyer calls for four groups of variables for evaluation which are: (1) input, (2) educational process, (3) surrounding conditions, and (4) output. It would appear that all four groups of variables are important, although data are usually collected only on output variables. The example that follows includes input, process, and output (outcome) data on a limited number of classrooms. Some data on physical and psychological conditions in the classroom are also being gathered, but this is considered descriptive of the educational process and not of "surrounding conditions." Dyer's proposal relates more to system-wide or state-wide evaluation rather than evaluation of a particular program or product. Thus, his "surrounding conditions" deal with community, political, and cultural variables, rather than classroom variables.

The variables comprising each group during 1971-72 are listed in Table 2. Input and outcome variables other than standardized achievement tests, such as learning-to-learn, attitude toward subject area, autonomy, problem-solving, and cognitive style should also be used. Keeping in mind the other two types of evaluation taking place concurrently (student progress in the program, and longitudinal and comparative evaluation), the present variables provide sufficient data to study developers' assumptions about their programs.

In delineating the teacher and student variables included under process (degree of implementation), many of the papers and articles written by the developers were studied. The final selection was based primarily on those variables most important to the instructional model under consideration and for which an observable change in student outcome could be expected. For example, in those classrooms in which materials are readily available and students obtained and replaced their own materials, the students would be expected to be more independent (autonomous) than in those classrooms where the teacher distributed materials. Also, in those classrooms where the teacher made more cognitive contacts, students would be expected to have higher academic achievement. These variables were selected because of our interest in studying the process of individualized instruction as well as documenting effects of the program developed.

A useful way for organizing and reporting data is through a number of short reports (Leinhardt and Walker, 1973) followed by the end-of-year evaluation reports. The shorter reports might deal with one variable, such as Fall placement in reading, or with a specific problem,

Table 2*

Input, Process, and Outcome Variables: 1971-72

I.   Input

    A.   Previous year's WRAT scores
    B.   Fall placement in each curricular area
    C.   Cognitive Abilities Test IQ scores

II.   Process (Degree of Implementation)

    A.   Context variables

        1.   Class size
        2.   Teacher's experience in new program
        3.   Teacher and student attendance

    B.   Time and space usage

        1.   Division by subject matter areas
        2.   Use of exploratory activities
        3.   Available square footage per pupil

    C.   Subject matter assignments and pupil assessment

        1.   Prescription practices
        2.   Testing practices

    D.   Classroom management

        1.   Teacher traveling

            a.   Rate
            b.   Distribution

        2.   Teacher-student contact

            a.   Content (cognitive vs. management)
            b.   Affect (positive, negative, or neutral)

    E.   Student self-direction (autonomy)

        1.   Accessibility of exploratory activities
        2.   Selection of learning media
        3.   Obtaining educational materials
        4.   Selection of free time after completing work

III.   Outcome

    A.   Spring WRAT scores
    B.   End-of-year mastery in all curricular areas
    C.   Spring WRAT reading subtest scores

*Variables delineated primarily by Gaea Leinhardt.

such as measurement of individualization or changes in achievement for the last five years. These reports should be completed as soon after the necessary data collection as possible so that everyone is aware of what the actual data are and how they were obtained.

The short reports serve two primary functions in the evaluation scheme, in addition to communicating descriptions of the data to others. First, they are an important documentation and quality control point for the data collected. When data are coded, keypunched, and set up on a computer system, errors occur in every imaginable way. Many errors that cannot be found in normal checking become apparent when unusual results are obtained in calculating summaries of means, standard deviations, skewness, and kurtosis. Skewness is particularly sensitive to unusual scores. The errors are also much easier to correct if found immediately, rather than after the school year.

Secondly, the short reports allow the evaluator to become familiar with the results for each variable in the three groups of variables. When more sophisticated analysis techniques, such as factor analysis and multiple and canonical correlation, are used, the evaluator is in a better position to make an appropriate interpretation of the results. For example, in one study two different process instruments were used and the results were factor analyzed. In addition, canonical correlations of process and residualized outcome variables were computed. Through familiarity with the results for each variable in the analysis, a more appropriate interpretation of the obtained results was possible.

The end-of-year analyses involve covarying the input variables from the outcome variables and analyzing the residuals with the process variables. In this way pupil achievement not accounted for by input can be related to differences among the classrooms on the process variables. Cooley (1971) has previously reported an example of this type of analysis. It is from his initial work that the present evaluation strategy has evolved. When regressions between input and output variables are graphed, classrooms that fall outside some specified range (either above or below expectation) can be identified. Then, characteristics on which these two sets of classrooms differ can be investigated. These investigations need not be strictly statistical in nature. Clinical reports of supervisors and teachers or information on the process instruments not amenable to mathematical representation can be used to differentiate between the two types of classrooms. Much of the best evaluation work should be hypothesis-generating as well as explanatory. As the data collected become more comprehensive and the hypothesized relationships among variables more clearly delineated, techniques such as path analysis should become more useful.

Typical Results from the Evaluation Strategy

It is important that the three types of evaluation information combine into an overall evaluation strategy. Different types of data may be collected and analyzed for different purposes, but all parts must merge together to form a comprehensive evaluation package. A good example of the type of comprehensive evaluation needed is outlined in a tentative manner in the USOE guidelines for the evaluation of ESEA Titles III [Sec. 306], VII, and VIII projects. Process and outcome objectives are *both* evaluated and the two are tied together so that specific outcomes can be attributed to specific processes or combinations of processes. It is difficult to show in a definitive fashion how this is to be done, but the guidelines are certainly worth considering when program or product evaluation is undertaken. In the following examples, progress data used for periodic monitoring of the system are used as input and outcome data in the overall study of the effect of instructional processes on student learning. In addition, data used for end-of-year comparison of the gross effects of the program are also utilized as inputs and outcomes in the in-depth study of the relationships between processes and associated effects of an individualized instructional program.

Student Progress in the Program

Student progress data in each of the curricula areas are collected monthly, and summary sheets are run quarterly for each student. An example of an end-of-year summary sheet is shown in Table 3. Identifying code numbers can be placed in the upper left-hand corner. The curricular areas are abbreviated on the left side, e.g., ERP is early reading program. The beginning and ending units are listed first. Then the number of units completed by the end of each month is printed for every student who has completed work in a particular area. Each student works in only a limited number of areas, as the form is set up for use at all grade levels (K-5). The numbers are cumulative; to calculate the number of units completed in any month it is necessary to subtract the number reported for the previous month. For example, Table 3 shows that the student began in Sullivan book 12 and ended

Table 3

Student Mastery Progress 1971-72

Area	Beg. Unit	End Unit	Cumulative Number of Units								
			Oct.	Nov.	Dec.	Jan.	Feb.	Mar.	Arp.	May	June
ERP											
Sullivan	12	20	2	3	4	6	8	8			
Directed								2	4	6	
Selected								28	40	61	69
IPI Reading	ESA	EVD						1	1	2	2
Library & References	000	000					0	0	0	0	0
KW Spelling		306							1	6	6
CAI Spelling											
Individualized Math	08	26	4	7	12	13	15	17	18	19	19
IPI Math											
CT Multiplication											
Classification											
Visual Motor	F4	I5	0	3	8	8					
Auditory Motor	G6	H9	0	0	0	7	7				
General Motor											
Letters & Numbers											

with book 20 (the last book in the sequence). Two books were completed in October, one in November, one in December, etc., until all eight were completed by the end of February. At that time, this student began work in the IPI Reading skills program (Beck and Bolvin, 1969), completing one unit in March and one unit in May. At the same time, the student completed six Directed Reading books and 69 Selected Reading books. The other information on the summary sheet can be interpreted in a similar manner. Some attempt to make the units comparable is required so that data manipulation is meaningful.

The summary sheets can be used by program directors, developers, and school personnel for studying pupil progress and achievement during the school year and to give direction to planning for the following year. Often the information gained from these sheets is too general for specific program changes, such as modifying particular lessons, but it can give researchers a more global picture of results, initiating questions that then require analysis of the classroom records at the objectives and skills level.

There are two major problems with this monthly data collection procedure. First, it is difficult to obtain fast enough "turn around" for the data to be used by supervisors and teachers for planning on a weekly basis. The second problem is the difficulty in obtaining accurate results in a reasonable amount of time. The data must be coded from sheets the teachers keep in each curricular area. There is usually some lag between a student's classroom performance and the teacher's recording of it on the profiles. Several problems often occur when using records kept by the teacher. For example, inconsistencies among teachers in preparation of the sheets, despite standard directions, often make them difficult to interpret. (Evaluators have difficulty realizing that teachers, and other school personnel, often view evaluation information at the bottom of their priorities.) Then, the general problems associated with transforming the raw data to computer storage bring about additional errors. With experience, many of these errors will be eliminated, but evaluators must be concerned with all possible sources of error in collecting, storing, and analyzing data.

End-of-Year Achievement

The second type of evaluation information (end-of-year achievement data) is used for the longitudinal and progressive implementation and evaluation design. The results obtained in a developmental school

Table 4

Mean Raw Scores on Wide Range Achievement Test (WRAT) for the Longitudinal Evaluation Design

Grade	School Year											
	1968-19			1969-70			1970-71			1971-72		
	Reading	Spelling	Math	Reading	Spelling	Math	Reading	Spelling	Math	Reading	Spelling	Math
Pre	10.1	7.5	10.9				22.1	11.7	15.5	21.0	11.7	13.7
K	17.8*	15.7	16.0	22.0	14.2	18.1	21.4	17.1	16.9	25.4	15.4	17.5
1				34.1*	20.7	22.4	41.3	25.4	23.9	40.1	24.4	23.5
2				41.4	26.5	23.2	50.2*	28.6	25.0	52.3	30.5	26.3
3				51.5	32.7	26.9	50.2	32.7	27.6	55.8*	33.1	27.3
4							60.0	36.6	29.8	56.7	36.2	29.1
5										63.8	40.4	32.0

*Grade levels above the double line participated in the new instructional program.

are indicated in Table 4. The data are reported in raw score form because of inadequacies and misinterpretations of grade equivalents. The raw scores are appropriate for the comparisons and trends being investigated.

The results reported in Table 4 indicate that at each grade level there has been consistent improvement. In the second and third grades improvement occurred during the first year that the new program was implemented. These test results in preschool, kindergarten, and first grade continued at the higher level over at least two years. Grades 1 and 2 (1970-71) are achieving at approximately the same level that grades 2 and 3 (1969-70), respectively, had been achieving previously. It would appear that almost a full grade level improvement had taken place and is continuing. Many evaluators would require a test of significance comparing test results at each grade level with that of the previous years before participation in the program. What would this accomplish? If first graders are scoring as previous second graders, that is convincing evidence. If students improve one additional item on a test and that is statistically significant, has the program had an effect? Before tests of statistical significance are calculated, the evaluator should give much thought to what additional information is being obtained and communicated to the appropriate decision maker. In many instances, information concerning the probability that an observed result is extremely unlikely if an hypothesized condition (such as no difference among groups) were in fact true, is necessary information. But tests of statistical significance have become so ingrained in educational researchers that they are often calculated and reported with little forethought concerning their applicability to a specific evaluation.

Once a positive outcome of the new program is documented, it is important to find out what aspect(s) of the program might be affecting it. Since the data in Table 4 are from a developmental school they may be due to the additional personnel or materials available. Other possible explanations, aside from being an artifact of the test or testing conditions, include: (1) aides were put into each classroom to check papers, collect data, and keep records, (2) program development personnel trained each participating teacher and continued working with every teacher for the entire year, and (3) some students may now spend 25 hours each week on reading rather than 10 hours previously. Data were not collected systematically to investigate these and other alternative explanations.

In order to investigate the important aspects of both the specific instructional program and of individualization in general, the instructional program was implemented in a number of school districts nationwide that are participating in Follow Through. Not only are these settings more like the natural classroom, but differences between the developmental settings and the Follow Through settings are available for investigation. Through longitudinal evaluation many of the alternative hypotheses about the data can be eliminated and the most important implementation variables identified.

An important consideration in the longitudinal evaluation of developmental programs is their dynamic nature. Programs are often categorized as ready for "formative" or "summative" evaluation. This distinction is probably useful in the beginning stages of development, although the development process is not straightforward so that available evaluation models, such as this, fit. Development ordinarily is a process of successive approximations. One program is completed and implemented while work is under way to modify and improve the program or product.

Despite the fact that the results above the double lines in Table 4 are for students participating in our program, the first grade reading materials and methods used in 1971-72 are very different from those in 1970-71 or in 1969-70. Classrooms within first grade are also substantially different in the reading curriculum used. Similar differences occur in other subject matter areas in other grade levels. The longitudinal design enables the evaluator to compare the results of the newest program not only with the control students, but with those who had used the first approximation of the program being developed. When new developmental work is occurring in only one or two classrooms, more in-depth evaluation is required.

Input, Process, and Outcome Evaluation

To investigate those implementation variables most likely to affect student outcomes, the process variables previously listed in Table 2 were measured. Two primary methods for obtaining the information were used. First, observation of the classroom and associated records was carried out on two occasions (Leinhardt, 1972). Second, the teachers completed a questionnaire relating to many of the same variables.

The data obtained from each procedure (instrument) were

analyzed singly and then in combination. First, principal component analysis followed by a varimax rotation was run on each set of data, and an intercorrelational matrix was computed for the process and outcome variables. Next, a selected combination of variables found to be most independent and/or most predictive of outcomes were factor analyzed in order to select the best process variables for continued use. The variables from the observation instrument were also studied in relation to academic change. The outcome residuals, after initial input was partialed out, were related to the observation (process) variables.

The initial evaluation plans assumed that sophisticated techniques, such as canonical correlation and multiple part correlations, would be the primary methods of analysis. But, as additional problems were identified, somewhat less complex procedures were found to be more appropriate. This result is probably due to idiosyncracies of this specific evaluation effort. Many evaluators would feel comfortable using these techniques despite the problems. They might view the judgments discussed in this chapter as too subjective to be useful. That is a decision each evaluator must make for himself. In the present evaluation effort two major problems with canonical and multiple part correlations are: (1) the large number of variables for the number of classrooms, and (2) significant site differences on input variables.

Since the complexities of the educational process are not adequately understood at present, many different types of process information were needed. Information was needed not only to describe each classroom, but also to decide which types of data were most useful to collect. The factor analyses previously described are one way that this decision is aided. If two or three variables relate at $r = .90$ or $.95$, only one of the variables will be needed in the present study. In the first attempt, almost 100 variables were identified for analysis. With only 30 classrooms and 100 variables, statistical procedures will tend to give results of little interpretable value. Regression weights can be obtained that result in accounting for 100 percent of the variance. In order to reduce the number of variables, those with little or no variability or those that failed to replicate on the second observation were dropped. Other procedures were used to further reduce the set of variables to a manageable number. But even with the reduction to about 20 variables, relationships among sets of variables are inflated due to over-fitting of the data. Confidence in the results occurs only when relationships continue to replicate. Tests of significance may be appropriate during any one year of evaluation as indicators of the probability that the relationships will replicate.

A second problem results from significant site differences on variables to be used as covariates in an analysis. For example, all teachers at one site have three years' experience with the instructional model while those at another have no previous experience. Also, one site may be achieving much higher than other sites on input measures. In these situations, not only are the covariate effects extracted from the dependent variable(s), but also other effects, such as systematic differences in implementation of the program among the sites and "real" effects of teacher experience, are extracted. Thus, the initial attempt at in-depth evaluation was more judgmental in nature than planned, but the general procedure is still the same, and valid.

In general, the object of this evaluation procedure is to identify classrooms doing "better" or "poorer" by comparing outcome results with predictions obtained from input information. The process data are then used to indicate possible explanations for the results. The "better" classrooms and "poorer" classrooms are identified by using input and output measures as depicted in Figure 1. Once these classrooms are identified, the process data can be used to differentiate among them.

For those classrooms included in Cooley's study, it was found that the outlyers (those not falling within the confidence interval) were probably an artifact of the Fall testing and placement procedures (the input variable used to predict outcome). Those above the confidence interval were placed too low and thus were under-predicted while those below the interval were placed inappropriately in the Fall and made little progress. These results emphasize the need to adequately describe the educational processes used in each participating classroom. They also point out the importance of appropriate placement in an individualized educational program.

It seems imperative that much additional descriptive data be collected in order to more adequately discriminate among classrooms and their usage of specific instructional products. There may be numerous systematic and non-systematic aspects to a particular site or classroom about which evaluators are not informed. For instance, this year one classroom has been moved three times in the first two months of the school year. Last year some classrooms were flooded. One site has had trouble receiving its grant money and is unwilling to buy necessary materials. The evaluator must remember that he cannot

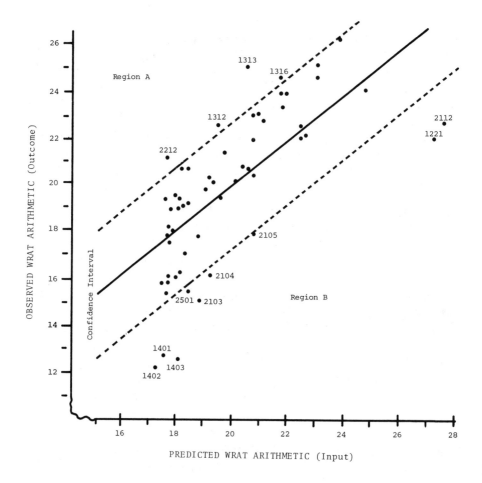

Figure 1. Location of 57 Classrooms Defined by a Linear Function of Four Quantification Measures (Input and WRAT Arithmetic (Output). (From Cooley, 1971.)

simply send out a monthly checklist or observation schedule that includes all possible "unusual" occurrences—especially those of an administrative nature such as funding. Thus, softer data from observers must be used for describing classroom situations. A teacher may be doing an outstanding job, but the class may be working only half the year due to other administrative or physical problems and show relatively low achievement overall. These types of occurrences tend to mask the actual effects of the program and make studying the effects of particular process variables more difficult.

Suggested Readings

Blalock, H.M., Jr. *Causal inferences in non-experimental research.* Chapel Hill, North Carolina: University of North Carolina Press, 1964.
> A short, readable book giving some of the philosophical bases for causal inference, with special emphasis on correlational models.

Blalock, H.M., Jr. (Ed.) *Causal models in the social sciences.* Chicago: Aldine-Atherton, 1971.
> A book of readings dealing with: (1) simple recursive models, (2) path analysis, (3) simultaneous equation techniques, (4) measurement error, and (5) related problems. Indicates present state-of-the-art in path analysis and related causal models. Simon's opening article is a classic.

Cooley, W.W. Methods of evaluating school innovations. Report Number 1971/26. Pittsburgh, Pennsylvania: Learning Research and Development Center, 1971.
> A short paper describing some multivariate evaluation procedures. Results of some of the initial development work in the area of individualized education are reported.

Dyer, H.S. Can we measure the performance of educational systems? *The Bulletin of the NASSP,* 1970, *54* (346), 96-105.
> A short description of the student-change model of an educational system that the author and his colleagues devised in working with the New York State Educational Agency. Helps give meaningful structure for anyone concerned with the effects of an educational system. It is a broader view of the type of evaluation reported in the present chapter.

Stenner, A.J., and Webster, W.J. *Educational program audit handbook.* Arlington, Virginia: Institute for the Development of Educational Auditing, 1971.

> This book was written for auditors and evaluators who are doing evaluation of ESEA Title III [Sec. 306], VII, and VIII projects. It attempts to outline the roles of auditing and evaluating and to describe analysis techniques that might be of value. A selected technical bibliography in the areas of behavioral objectives, measurement, design, and statistics with a rating of required mathematical sophistication needed for using each book is presented. Very useful for someone who wants to know more about the evaluation-audit concept.

USOE Guidelines for ESEA Titles III [Sec. 306], VII, and VIII (Evaluation sections).

> Five elements required for adequate performance objectives are presented and discussed. The evaluation design and necessary analyses are also presented, and the role of the educational program auditor is outlined. This first attempt at explicating a new, more usable, evaluation procedure is a must for persons involved in project evaluation. Some of the ideas presented are somewhat simplistic once a person begins doing an evaluation, but the attempt to evaluate and relate both processes and products to gain useful information for USOE and other interested parties is an important step in the right direction.

Wittrock, M.C., and Wiley, D.E. *The evaluation of instruction: Issues and problems.* New York: Holt, Rinehart and Winston, 1970.

> A report of proceedings of a symposium on evaluation. Many important evaluation concerns are discussed. The editors view evaluation as taking place in the naturalistic setting (little manipulation), and include a useful appendix of articles on path analysis, causal inference from observational data, model building, and causal influence in panel data.

References

Beck, I., and Bolvin, J.O. A model for non-gradedness: The reading program for Individually Prescribed Instruction. *Elementary English,* 1969, *46*(2), 130-135.

Blalock, H.M., Jr. *Causal inferences in non-experimental research.* Chapel Hill, North Carolina: University of North Carolina Press, 1964.

Cooley, W.W. Methods of evaluating school innovations. Invited address to the Seventy-Ninth American Psychological Association Convention, Washington, D.C., 1971.

Cronbach, L.J. Course improvement through evaluation. *Teachers College Record,* 1963, *64,* 672-683.

Dyer, H.S. Can we measure the performance of educational systems? *The Bulletin of the NASSP,* 1970, *54*(346), 96-105.

Jastak, J.F., and Jastak, S.R. *WRAT manual.* Wilmington, Delaware: Guidance Associates, 1965.

Kelley, F.J., Beggs, D.L., McNeil, K., Eichelberger, R.T., and Lyon, J.T. *Multiple linear regression: A behavioral approach.* Carbondale, Illinois: The Southern Illinois University Press, 1969.

Leinhardt, G. The boojum of evaluation: Implementation, some measures. Unpublished doctoral dissertation, 1972.

Leinhardt, G. Observation as a tool for evaluation of implementation. Paper presented at the Annual American Educational Research Association Convention, New Orleans, 1973.

Leinhardt, G., and Walker, A. Mini-reports on evaluation data collected in 1971-72. Unpublished evaluation report, Learning Research and Development Center, 1973.

Lindvall, C.M., and Cox, R.C. *The IPI Evaluation Program.* AERA Monograph Series on Curriculum Evaluation, 1970, No. 5.

Mazur, J.L. Operationalizing educational accountability in public school systems. Paper presented at the Annual American Educational Research Association Convention, New York, 1971.

Scriven, M. The methodology of evaluation. In *Perspectives of Curriculum evaluation.* AERA Monograph Series on Curriculum Evaluation, 1967, No. 1.

Simon, H.A. Spurious correlation: A causal interpretation. In H.M. Blalock, Jr., (Ed.), *Causal models in the social sciences.* Chicago: Aldine-Atherton, 1971, 5-17.

Stake, R.L. The countenance of educational evaluation. *Teachers College Record,* 1967, *68*(7), 523-540.

Stanford Research Institutes. *Follow Through: Interim evaluation report.* U.S. Office of Education, January 1973.

Stufflebeam, D.L. The use of experimental design in educational evaluation. *Journal of Educational Measurement,* Winter 1971, *8*(4), 267-274.

Stufflebeam, D.L., Foley, W.J., Gephart, W.J., Guba, E.G., Hammond, R.J., Merriman, H.O., and Provus, M.M. *Educational evaluation and decision making.* Itasca, Illinois: F.E. Peacock, 1971.

Wang, M.C. Longitudinal evaluation plan for an early learning program. Unpublished paper, Learning Research and Development Center, 1970.

CHAPTER 14

SUMMATIVE EVALUATION:
SOME BASIC CONSIDERATIONS

Keith J. Edwards
Rosemead Graduate School of Psychology

There has been an increasing interest in the development of educational products in the past decade. The federal government has established the system of regional educational laboratories to facilitate such development. Concomitant with this increase in development activities has been a greater emphasis on research and evaluation. However, there is a lack of understanding concerning the relationship of research and evaluation to development. Such misunderstanding has led to a controversy over the roles and methods of research and evaluation in product development.

Guba (1969) has maintained that evaluation is entirely distinct from research and that the use of research paradigms in evaluation is inappropriate. Stufflebeam and others have developed the CIPP model, which delineates the interfaces among evaluation, information, and decision making throughout the development process (Randall, 1969). In discussing the place of experimental design models in evaluation, Stufflebeam (1971) contends that they play a role in only one of the four stages (product evaluation) and thus are of minor relevance to evaluation. Other writers have maintained that experimental design models are the cornerstone of evaluation. Lindvall (1966) suggests the importance of these models by posing the question, "Does this innovation, in the situation with which we are concerned, do what is desired better than alternatives (p. 162)?" It is from the exponents of experimental design models that the term evaluative research has come (Houston, 1972; Porter, 1973; Stanley, 1969, 1972; Suchman, 1967; Welch and Walberg, 1972).

In view of the differences of opinion on the appropriate role and methodology of evaluation, an attempt at specifying analytic strategies must first deal with role definition. Thus, the purpose of this chapter is threefold. First, the role of evaluation is defined in terms of the overall process of educational change and the relationships among research, evaluation, and development within that process. Second, a design strategy for selecting a sample is presented. Third, an analysis strategy for evaluation based upon multiple regression is illustrated. While the first section deals primarily with problem area definitions, it is viewed as a necessary antecedent to the introduction of the analytic models that follow.

Guba (1967) has proposed a paradigm for the educational change process consisting of four major sequential steps: research, development, diffusion, and adoption. Each of the four stages has different objectives and contributes in a different way to change. The four-stage model for change, along with activities that occur in each stage, is depicted in Table 1. The present discussion will focus on the first two stages, research and development.

Table 1

Guba's Model for the Process of Educational Change

Stage	Activities	Objectives	Relation to Change
Research	Depict Relate Conceptualize Test	Advancement of knowledge	One basis for intervention
Development	Depict Invent Fabricate Test	Identify operating problems and solutions	Produce, engineer, package the innovation
Diffusion	Tell–show Help Involve Train Intervene	Create awareness	Make the innovation available
Adoption	Try–test Install Institutionalize	Adapt and install the invention in the school setting	Establish and institutionalize the invention

Research, Development, and Evaluation

Research can be defined as a process of systematic inquiry in a specific area. The basic goal of research is the advancement of knowledge. Its relation to change is to provide one basis for invention. Development, on the other hand, has as its basic objective the identification of operational problems and the formulation of solutions to these problems. The relation of development to change involves production, engineering, packaging, and testing a proposed problem solution or invention. Thus, both in terms of their objectives and their relation to change, research and development are two separate entities.

Many writers attempting to relate research to development have placed them at opposite ends of a continuum. Terms such as basic research, applied research, action research, and development are conceived of as representing varying degrees of scientific control. However, with the present emphasis on research and development in education, the continuum concept is more confusing than helpful. Research and development are distinct activities with different, identifiable objectives.

What may lead people to see research and development as a continuum rather than a dichotomy is the interdependence of these two activities. However, interdependence is not the same as similarity. Development may employ research methodologies and research knowledge, but it is not research. Research may be undertaken to explore new areas brought to light by development, but it is not development.

The importance of the interdependence of research and development cannot be overemphasized. Persons engaged in development activities must be knowledgeable about research and basic research methods if their products are to incorporate empirically valid concepts. When problems arise in an area where little or no research is available, the development specialist must be able to recognize the deficiency and inform the researcher of his needs. This type of interaction between research and development is essential to the advancement of knowledge and its application in problem solutions.

Before discussing the relationship of evaluation to research and development, it is necessary to define evaluation and the roles it plays in the development process. Commonly, evaluation is conceived of as the process of assessing or appraising the value and utility of a program or product. Cronbach (1963) has provided a broader perspective by defining evaluation as the "collection and use of information to make decisions about an educational program." An important aspect of Cronbach's definition is that it draws attention to the full range of functions evaluation serves. In the early phases of development, evaluation is used to identify those aspects of the innovation that need revision. Its purpose is to provide feedback to the developer for revising the new system. Evaluation serving such a role has been called concurrent, formative, or process evaluation (Dyer, 1966; Scriven, 1967).

After an innovation has been developed and its procedures defined, data must be gathered to assess its utility. In such a role, evaluation is concerned primarily with effects the innovation produces in the target population (e.g., students, teachers, administrators). The data gathered serve as input for decision making by the developer. Based upon the evaluative data, he may decide to (a) disseminate, (b) redevelop, or (c) phase out the innovation. In any case, a value judgment concerning the worth of the innovation is made. The type of evaluation that serves this role has been called *ex post facto,* summative, or product evaluation (Dyer, 1966, p. 18; Scriven, 1967, p. 43). Stufflebeam (1971) has defined additional roles for evaluation. However, the formative and summative roles are the ones relevant to distinguishing between research and evaluation.

Evaluation is a definite part of the development process. It is an activity that affects every aspect of development. In the early phases of development, evaluation provides feedback that serves as a guide for revision and improvement. After the product has been developed it must be evaluated to determine its utility. Figure 1 shows the development stage of Guba's change model with both the formative and summative roles of evaluation depicted. The development process begins with depicting the problem, then a solution is invented, the materials are fabricated and evaluation information is obtained. In the formative stages of development the evaluative data are used as feedback to the developer as a basis for improving the innovation. At some point a decision is made that the product is ready for summative evaluation. Subsequent to summative evaluation a decision is made to either diffuse, phase out, or submit the innovation to further development. One important feature of the model is that it conveys the dynamic nature of the development process. In such a process, the flow of information must be precisely defined and well planned if the development activity is to be successful.

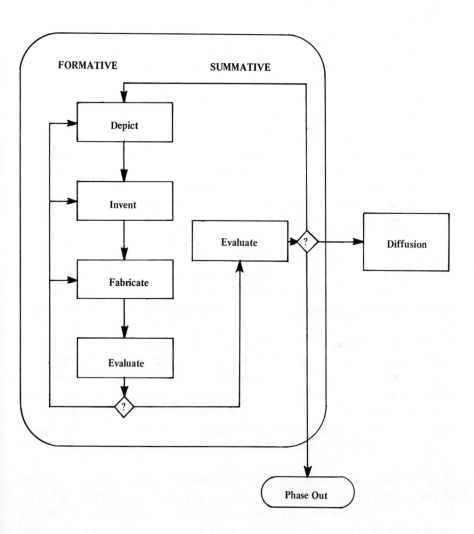

FORMATIVE   SUMMATIVE

Depict

Invent

Fabricate

Evaluate

Evaluate

Diffusion

Phase Out

Figure 1. The Development Stage of Educational Change.

It is recognized that formative and summative evaluations are a part of the development. However, some writers have suggested that the two evaluative roles be performed by separate personnel. Scriven (1967) states that:

> Formative evaluators should, if at all possible, be sharply distinguished from the summative evaluators, with whom they may certainly work in developing an acceptable summative evaluation schema, but the formative evaluators should ideally exclude themselves from the role of judge in the summative evaluation. If this distinction between formative and summative evaluation personnel is made, it becomes possible to retain the advantages of eventual objective professional evaluation without the risks of disrupting the team spirit during development (p. 45).

One danger with such an approach is the tendency of developers not to consider all of the factors necessary for product evaluation before the evaluative data are collected. If summative evaluation personnel are to successfully implement evaluation designs, such designs must at least have been considered in the early stages of development.

A major thesis of this chapter is that research and evaluation are different both in terms of their objectives and their relation to change. Research may be conducted for the purpose of testing theory, expanding concepts, or explaining behavior. Evaluation, on the other hand, is carried out to provide information for decision making. While research is aimed at increasing knowledge, evaluation is aimed at achieving a practical goal with an emphasis on utility. Where research seeks formulations of theoretical abstractions, evaluation deals with highly specific situations and explicit goals. Thus, while evaluation may employ research knowledge *and* research methodology, it is *not* research.

The distinction between research and evaluation in their relation to the change process can be clearly seen in terms of Guba's model. The difference is taxonomic, i.e., research is one of four major stages in the change process, whereas evaluation is an activity within one of the four stages (development). In light of this distinction, the term evaluative research is ambiguous. We should decide what the goals of our inquiry are and then give the inquiry its proper name.

The concept of evaluation as a type of research has decreased the adequacy of evaluation in development in three ways: (a) it has promoted the limited concept of evaluation as a one-shot, judgmental process; (b) it has led to an overemphasis on hypothesis testing and statistical significance and the ignoring of descriptive techniques more relevant to the cost-effectiveness decisions required in evaluating innovations; and (c) terms such as "evaluative research" have tended to alienate developers who properly view research as a function distinct from development. The overall effect of "evaluative research" has been that evaluation merely serves as a stamp of approval or disapproval of an innovation. Development of innovations will become more effective when evaluation is conceived of as a fundamental part of the developmental process, not simply an appendage to it.

Experimental Models in Evaluation

Given that evaluation is an essential step in the process of development, the question arises, "What is the appropriate methodology for evaluation?" In attempting to present a partial answer to this question, it goes without saying that there is no one methodology that is appropriate for all phases of evaluation. At the same time, the experimental and quasi-experimental designs advocated by Campbell and Stanley (1963) are more useful than evaluators have acknowledged in either theory or practice. Houston (1972), Stanley (1972), and Welch and Walberg (1972) have noted that although experimental design techniques have existed for many years they remain largely untried in the area of curriculum evaluation. Welch (1969) reported that only four evaluation projects out of 46 government-sponsored curriculum projects used experimental models. Thus, controlled field evaluation studies using experimental models have not failed but rather remain largely untried.

Educational evaluators cannot continue to avoid using experimental models with the justification that such models involve doing research. Research must be distinguished from evaluation on the basis of objectives and not on the basis of method. The logic of comparative judgment inherent in experimental models is directly relevant to the relative effectiveness of innovations. Also, it is not very useful for evaluators to disparage experimental models by minimizing their information yield in the decision-making milieu of educational development. Whether or not an innovation works and does a better job than alternatives is admittedly only one of many relevant questions in development. But it is clearly the most crucial question from the consumer's viewpoint.

Experimental design and statistics should be viewed as neutral fields with respect to the research-evaluation distinction made earlier. Statistics represents a discipline whose methods are equally relevant to research and evaluation. Historically, statistics and experimental research have developed simultaneously and the methods are interrelated. Developers and evaluators are in a sense educational engineers and should employ the methodological rigor that such a term connotes. In part, this means being aware of the strengths and weaknesses of experimental models and thus being able to implement optimally efficient designs in field settings.

Randomization:
Cornerstone or Stumbling Block

There are a variety of experimental design models relevant to evaluation, but a characteristic that is common to all is the random assignment of subjects to various innovations. Assignment of a unit (e.g., students, classrooms, schools, etc.) to an innovation is random when the probability of a unit receiving a given treatment is equal for all subjects. For example, suppose one wanted to evaluate the effects of two questioning strategies on students' comprehension and retention of math concepts. An experimental model for the evaluation would begin by assigning each of the students to be involved to one of the two groups on the basis of a flip of a coin or a series of random numbers matched to student I.D. numbers.

A stumbling block to the use of randomization in evaluative designs is the attitude of administrators and developers toward the concept. The argument against its use is based on the premise that randomization is important for research; and, since evaluation is not research, randomization is not appropriate in evaluation. The conclusion is faulty for two reasons. As emphasized earlier, just because a technique has been primarily identified with research does not mean it is inappropriate for other activities. Second, and most important, there is a confusion as to the goal of random assignment. Critics of the experimental model argue that random assignment is necessary for generalizing experimental results to a larger population. The fact of the matter is that random assignment of subjects to groups has little to do with generalizability of results or external validity. Its major goal is to provide a situation in which internally valid causal inferences can be made. The goal is accomplished by creating groups that are equal (in theory) on all variables prior to the experiences being compared. In practice, the extent to which groups are actually equal depends on the number of experimental units (subjects) involved. If the number of units is large, then randomization is efficient. If the number of units is small, then matching or forming subgroups on the basis of relevant variables (e.g., achievement) prior to random assignment is desirable (see Stanley, 1967). In either case, random assignment maximizes the likelihood that causal inferences attributing outcome differences to differences among treatments will be valid. This is an important consideration in evaluative studies, where one objective is to determine the relative efficacy of alternative innovations.

Given that randomization is desirable for internal validity, the question is, "How can it be used in school settings?" Cooley (1971) has suggested that the only feasible approach is to treat classrooms as the unit of analysis, with random assignment of classes to treatments. One large evaluative project of a new physics curriculum employed such an approach (Welch and Walberg, 1972). However, the technique requires that a large amount of resources be allocated to the evaluation effort in order to involve a sufficient number of classrooms. It is well known that evaluation efforts have been weak primarily because of lack of funds. Thus, implementation of Cooley's plan is unlikely at any stage of product development other than a large summative evaluation.

Evaluators should be aware of a more serious shortcoming of the use of classrooms as the unit of analysis. It has been shown that results of analysis at the group level may not apply to the individuals in the group. For example, Robinson (1950) has shown that a correlation between two variables based upon group averages can differ in sign from the correlation between the same two variables using individuals. The present writer contends that the individual should always be included as a unit of analysis for an evaluation study. Only when students are included as units of analysis can the effects of innovations on students with varying traits be examined. Investigating such traits is an essential part of an evaluation since it is usually the case that a given innovation is not universally better than the standard program for all students. Regression analyses are best suited to investigating interactions between student traits and instructional treatments.

Some Techniques for Evaluating School Innovations
Choosing the Sample

The key to successfully implementing randomization in an evaluation study is to identify a cluster of students from which the evaluation groups can be randomly organized. An example of one such cluster that occurs in most schools involves two or more classes of a subject meeting during the same period of the day. The cluster consists of all the students in the classes meeting at the same time. The evaluative groups are formed by drawing students randomly without regard to the original class they attended. The only limitation is that the number of random groups will be equal to or less than the number of classes meeting during the same period. However, special circumstances could overcome this limitation, such as the hiring of additional personnel to teach more groups (which would have to be smaller than the original classes).

Any set of classes meeting during the same period of the day cannot be assumed to be equal. The goal of randomly reassigning students is to make the groups equal. In most school settings the assignment process can be made more efficient by first grouping (blocking) all students in the cluster into achievement levels (e.g., low, medium, high) and then assigning them to evaluate groups within achievement levels.

In addition to creating an evaluative design with high internal validity, assigning students to new groups creates an initial Hawthorne Effect for all groups. Since all groups experience something new, the chances of differential group performance resulting from special attention given one or two classes is diminished.

The primary pitfall of such a design is that the various evaluative groups must be taught by different individuals, since the groups all meet at the same time. If the techniques being compared are auto-instructional, the effect of different group monitors will be minimal. However, if the teacher is involved in the technique, as is most often the case, then group differences may emerge as a result of differential teacher effects. In such a situation, the teacher effect is confounded with the effect of the innovation. That is, we cannot tell how much of the observed group differences are attributable to the teacher versus the innovation. A way to circumvent this confounding is to rotate teachers among the various groups during the study. The disruptive potential of rotating instructors can be minimized by extending the study over a relatively long period of time and using only as many rotations as seem logically necessary. For example, if half of the teachers are males and the other half females, but they are generally similar on other dimensions, only one rotation of instructors would be needed to cancel out the teacher-sex effect. While changing instructors midway through a course is an atypical experience, the fact that it happens in all groups preserves the validity of comparisons among those groups.

An example of a study using the approach outlined above is one conducted by the author and a colleague comparing the individual and combined effects of a learning game and student teams on student attitude and achievement in mathematics (Edwards and DeVries, 1972). Four groups in a 2 x 2 factorial design were used. With the cooperation of school personnel and the students, students from four first-period math classes were randomly assigned to one of the four treatment groups within subgroups of math achievement (high, middle, and low). In this manner, what is technically known as a 2 x 2 x 3 randomized-block design involving 120 students was successfully implemented in the context of the ongoing school program. The teachers involved were two males and two females, who rotated among groups so that each group was taught by one male and one female.

In addition to controlling for teacher-sex differences, rotation of teachers was beneficial in another way. All the teachers involved in the study had to be trained in all of the techniques being evaluated, since during the study each teacher used both the games and teams techniques. Thus, no group of teachers was "stuck" with the control group.

Sometimes it is not possible to find a school with enough classes meeting during the same period of the day to use the cluster technique described above. In that case the following modification may be possible. The classes of two teachers with parallel schedules can be used to form clusters of students within a given period. The evaluative groups could then be formed randomly within a period. Figure 2 shows an example of two teachers with parallel schedules for four periods. Note that the ability levels of the classes occur in such a manner as to produce clusters of students with equal average ability. In the example, each teacher could conduct comparisons among alternative techniques. Whereas the classes for a teacher were initially different on ability, the

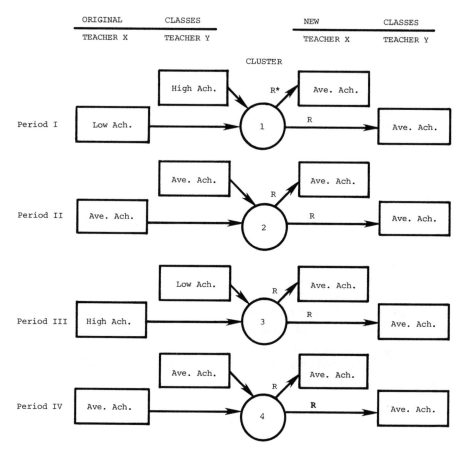

ORIGINAL   CLASSES

TEACHER X   TEACHER Y

CLUSTER

NEW   CLASSES

TEACHER X   TEACHER Y

High Ach.   R*   Ave. Ach.

Period I   Low Ach.   1   R   Ave. Ach.

Ave. Ach.   Ave. Ach.

Period II   Ave. Ach.   2   R   R   Ave. Ach.

Low Ach.   R   Ave. Ach.

Period III   High Ach.   3   R   Ave. Ach.

Ave. Ach.   Ave. Ach.

Period IV   Ave. Ach.   4   R   R   Ave. Ach.

*R indicates random selection from the cluster.

Figure 2. Using The Classes of Teachers with Parallel Schedules to Form Equivalent Evaluative Groups.

newly formed groups are quite comparable. If no two teachers have parallel schedules, then the classes of the participating teacher can be balanced across periods by drawing students within periods from any other available class for that subject. The principle involved here is that when students are randomly reassigned to groups within a period for a given subject very little change in scheduling is required. The student is simply asked to go to a different classroom for the duration of the evaluation study.

It should be noted that when groups are formed, as in Figure 2, the confounding factor is no longer the teacher but the period of the. day. While many teachers maintain that period of the day makes a difference in learning, there is no evidence to indicate that this is so. All the same, it is probably best to avoid using classes from the last period of the day.

The advantage of the cluster techniques described above is that they can be employed at any time during the school year. If the evaluation study is to be implemented at the beginning of a school year, it is possible to form larger clusters of students from which evaluative groups can be drawn. In most junior high schools and some upper elementary schools, the students are administratively organized into small groups to promote more intimate settings for student-student and student-teacher interactions. Each group may consist of 150 to 200 students who are all taught by the same group of teachers (one from each subject-matter area). These groups can be treated as the clusters from which evaluative groups can be formed. Again it will usually be more efficient to classify the students by achievement levels in the relevant subject areas before assignment to groups is carried out. It should be noted that groups formed in this manner are usually more heterogeneous in ability than teachers are used to handling. If this is likely to cause problems, a compromise can be to assign all the lowest achieving students to one class and not involve this class in the evaluative study.

Three examples for using the cluster idea to form evaluative groups have been presented. In each case the objective was to create groups that could be considered equal on relevant variables at the beginning of an evaluative study. There are undoubtedly other clusters that resourceful evaluators can identify and use.

One prerequisite to successful implementation of such designs is the support and cooperation of the school administration and staff. The author has found school personnel to be quite receptive and flexible; much more so than anticipated. However, there are some steps one can and should take to insure such reception. First, start small with a project that is likely to succeed. This will help the evaluator and his agency to establish credibility and create a positive image. Second, the evaluator should provide all necessary materials and aid required by the innovation being evaluated. Third, the evaluator should get to know what the students in the schools are like. For example, some weeks prior to a study conducted by the author, he substituted for the teachers so they could observe the innovation being pilot tested in another classroom. Other steps are possible, but these are sufficient to illustrate the point. If evaluators are to implement sound designs in field settings, they must be able to combine a creative use of methods with a sensitivity to the values and attitudes of school personnel.

Analyzing the Data

After an evaluative study has been conducted, one is faced with the problem of analyzing the data. A point often ignored by evaluators is that plans for data analysis should be made before the study is implemented. This is necessary to insure that all the data required by the analytic model are obtained in the course of the study. But, even if the evaluator is thorough enough to plan his data analysis prior to actually gathering the data, he is still faced with the problem of selecting the best method. The usual choice of evaluators is some variant of analysis of variance (ANOVA) or covariance (ANCOVA). Both ANOVA and ANCOVA are discussed elsewhere in detail. (See, for example, Glass and Stanley, 1970; Myers, 1966; Winer, 1962.) Another method that has been discussed recently in the research literature as an alternative to ANOVA and ANCOVA is regression analysis.

Technically, analysis of variance and regression analysis (RA) are not different but are both based on what statisticians refer to as the general linear model. However, in the minds of most practitioners, ANOVA and RA are quite different. ANOVA is associated with experimental psychology, hypothesis testing, and research. RA, on the other hand, is viewed as a descriptive technique used in survey or field studies. Both techniques can be used for either purpose, but RA offers more possibilities for the comprehensive analysis of data. Thus, it is the author's position that RA is the preferred method for analyzing evaluation data. An illustration of how RA can be applied in a common evaluation design is provided below. Further details on how to extend the model to include more complex designs can be found in Cohen (1968) or Walberg (1971).

It is frequently the case in evaluative studies that information on the subjects is available or can be obtained prior to implementation of the innovation. The information may be in the form of a pretest on relevant variables (Case A) or may be scores on some closely related variables (Case B). In either case the design can be represented as

$$O \quad X_1 \quad O$$
$$O \quad X_2 \quad O$$

where time passes from left to right, O indicates a variable was measured pre or post and X indicates exposure to a particular program. This is often referred to as a pretest-posttest design (Campbell and Stanley, 1963). Most evaluative designs are variations on this basic scheme. Analysis of data for this design using RA would proceed as follows. First, calculate descriptive statistics (e.g., mean, median, standard deviation) within groups for each variable. Second, calculate the regression of the posttest on the pretest within each treatment group. Third, visually display the regression lines for all groups on one graph and compare the regression lines statistically. The visual graphs and the descriptive statistics will provide a detailed picture of how each group has performed. The statistical comparisons will aid in interpretation. A graph of two regression lines based on data from a study conducted by the author and his colleagues is shown in Figure 3. One group used an academic game with team competition in learning math and the other one did not. The regression equation for each group is written below the respective line. These lines specify the posttest scores estimated from the pretest. For example, in group 2 a subject's estimated posttest score (symbolized Y) will be 1.56 units times his pretest score (X) plus 4.70 units.

Given the information in Figure 3, one can compare posttest performance within each group by examining the slope (1.56) of the regression line. The degree to which posttest performance is dependent on the pretest score is best measured by the correlation coefficient squared (r^2). This figure multiplied by 100 gives the percent of variance on the posttest score explained by the pretest within each group. The

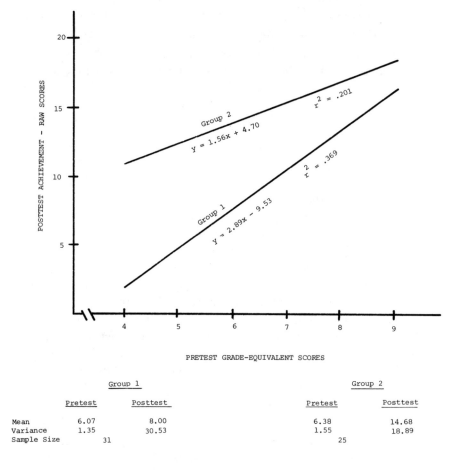

	Group 1				Group 2	
	Pretest	Posttest			Pretest	Posttest
Mean	6.07	8.00			6.38	14.68
Variance	1.35	30.53			1.55	18.89
Sample Size		31				25

Figure 3. Within-group Regressions of Posttest Achievement on Pretest Grade Equivalent Achievement for Two Groups in a Mathematics Evaluation Study.

statistical significance of the relationship can be examined using the statistic

(1)
$$F = \frac{r^2}{(1 - r^2) / (N - 2)}$$

which is compared to the critical values of the F-distribution with 1 and N - 2 degrees of freedom where N is the number of individuals used to calculate the regression equation. For the example in Figure 3, the F statistic was significant beyond the .001 level.

Between-group comparisons using regression equations can be made at two levels. The first involves comparing the distance between regression lines for the two groups, assuming that the lines are parallel. Statistically, this is analogous to comparing the treatment means of subjects who have the same pretest score, hence the effect of the pretest on the posttest is held constant across groups.

For Figure 3, the difference between means is significant beyond the .01 level of confidence. Assuming the two regression lines are parallel, one would conclude from this result that for students with the same pretest scores, those in group 2 do significantly better on the posttest. If assignment to groups was random (as it was in this case), then one can conclude that program 2 is more effective than program 1.

If the regression lines are not parallel, then comparison of means is not very meaningful, since the distance between the lines is not constant. The statistical procedure used to determine if two regression lines are parallel involves comparing the slopes of the regression lines. Two examples of groups with non-parallel regression lines are given in Figure 4. In both cases, it is clear that differences between the two groups on posttest scores is a function of pretest level. In terms associated with ANOVA we would say that pretest interacts with the treatments. In Figure 4, the first situation is referred to as an ordinal interaction and the second as disordinal. Both conditions are examples of what are referred to generally as trait-treatment interactions (TTI) where the pretest is the measured trait (see Berliner and Cahen, 1973). For Figure 3, the difference between the two slopes is not significantly different.

A regression model for testing slope differences includes variables that indicate group membership. Variables used for this purpose are called "dummy" variables and are the key to using the regression model with evaluative designs involving multiple groups.

In an example involving two groups, group membership can be indicated by a single "dummy" variable, D, where

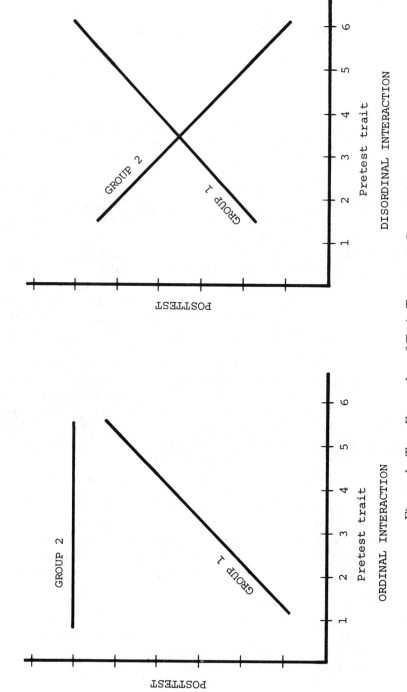

Figure 4. Two Examples of Trait-Treatment Interactions.

D = 1 if student is in group 1, or
D = 0 if student is in group 2.

Note that, while there are two groups, only one dummy variable is necessary to indicate group membership. The regression equation in a study involving two groups including both the pretest and the dummy variable is

(2) $$Y = a_0 + b_0 X + b_1 D$$

in which a statistical test on b_1 would be analogous to a comparison of group means holding the effect of X on Y constant. When the design involves three groups, then two "dummy" variables are needed to identify group membership. For three groups, the dummy variables can be coded as

$D_1 = 1$, $D_2 = 0$ for subjects in group 1,
$D_1 = 0$, $D_2 = 1$ for subjects in group 2,
$D_1 = 0$, $D_2 = 0$ for subjects in group 3.

Again note that only two dummy variables are needed to uniquely identify membership in one of the three groups. In general, when there are g groups involved, only g - 1 dummy variables are necessary to identify group membership. The regression equation for evaluation involving three groups which would include a pretest variable (x) is

(3) $$y = a + b_0 x + b_1 D_1 + b_2 D_2$$

in which b_0 is the regression coefficient for the posttest on the pretest (x) for the total sample. A statistical test on b_1 and b_2 would be analogous to comparing the means for groups 1 and 3 and groups 2 and 3, respectively. An examination of how D_1 and D_2 are coded will help in understanding why this is so. Note that D_1 distinguishes between subjects in group 1 and those not in group 1, and D_2 between subjects in group 2 and those not in group 2. Thus, group 3 with the dummy variables coded (0,0) is the group against which the other two are compared.

The contribution of a pretest or dummy variable to variance on the posttest can be tested for significance by calculating

(4)
$$t = \frac{b_j}{\sqrt{S^2 b_j}}$$

where b_j is the regression coefficient for the variable of interest and $S^2 b_j$ its variance. Both quantities are commonly available from the printouts of computer programs. The t-statistic has $(N - k)$ degrees of freedom where N is the total sample size and k is the number of terms in the regression equation.

At this point the analogy between the regression approach specified by equation 3 and ANOVA/ANCOVA is of interest. Inclusion of the pretest (X) is analogous to the covariate in ANCOVA, and testing the regression coefficients of the dummy variables for significance is analogous to multiple comparisons in ANOVA. It is also possible to obtain the ANCOVA F-statistic for the treatment effect using the regression model in equation 3 and the squared multiple correlation coefficient.

In using RA to test whether or not the treatment groups are significantly different, we let $R^2_{y.x}$ denote the squared multiple correlation for the regression of the posttest on the pretest for the entire sample and $R^2_{y.x,D}$ denote the squared multiple correlation for equation 3. The difference between these two values $(R^2_{y.x,D} - R^2_{y.x})$ is the percentage of variance in the posttest explained by the treatment differences controlling for differences among subjects on the pretest. The significance of this increment in R^2 caused by including the dummy variables and thus the significance of the treatment group difference can be tested by calculating

(5)
$$F = \frac{(R^2_{y.x,D} - R^2_{y.x})/d}{(1 - R^2_{y.x,D})/(N - k)}$$

where F has d and N - k degrees of freedom; d is the number of dummy variables and N and k are as defined above. It will always be the case that d is one less than the number of treatment groups which corresponds to the degrees of freedom for the treatment effect in ANOVA.

As was noted in the first example, the above tests are meaningful only if the regression lines are parallel. The general regression model, as shown in equation 3, does not give any information on the equality of regression slopes between groups. Additional terms must be included to compare regression slopes and the fact that such comparisons involve trait-treatment interactions gives a clue as to what those terms should be. Using the dummy variable and the pretest, two new variables are created by simply multiplying each dummy by the pretest score (x.Dj) for each subject. When D_1 is coded as above, the new variable xD_1 contains the pretest scores for all members of group 1 and zeroes for everyone else. Table 2 illustrates the complete data matrix for a hypothetical three-group study. Including these terms in the regression model yields

(6) $y = a + b_0 x + b_1 D_1 + b_2 D_2 + b_3 (xD_1) + b_4 (xD_2)$.

When all terms are calculated in a single regression equation and the D's are coded as shown in Table 2, b_3 and b_4 are measures of the interactions of pretest with treatments. The contribution of b_3 and b_4 to the variance of the posttest can be tested for significance using equation 4. The significance test for the overall interaction effect is given by

(7) $$F = \frac{(R^2_{y.x,D,(xD} - R^2_{y.x,D)}/d}{(1 - R^2_{y.x,D,(xD)})/N - k)}$$

where $R^2_{y.x,D,(xD)}$ is the squared multiple correlation for equation 6 and with $k = 6$.

The regression technique illustrated here with three groups can be extended to include more groups by simply including more dummy variables (see Cohen, 1968, for further examples). But the reader may wonder why RA should be used when it seems to yield the same information as the more familiar ANOVA/ANCOVA techniques. There are a number of reasons why RA is superior, especially for evaluation studies. One reason mentioned earlier, which bears repeating, is that RA is descriptively oriented while ANOVA emphasizes hypothesis testing. Almost all computer programs reflect these distinctions in that all RA programs report R^2 but not the F-statistics of equations 5 and 7. In the cost-effectiveness decisions inherent in evaluation studies, R^2 is the more relevant information.

Another advantage of RA over ANOVA is that its use requires the evaluator to define explicitly the structure of his data analytic model.

Table 2

*Data Matrix for Evaluation Study Using Regression
Analysis and Dummy Variables to Identify
Group Membership*

	Posttest y_i	Pretest x_i	Dummy Variables D_1	D_2	Interaction Terms x_iD_1	x_iD_2
Group 1	89	71	1	0	71	0
	85	70	1	0	70	0
	82	65	1	0	65	0
	91	76	1	0	76	0
	87	72	1	0	72	0
Group 2	82	71	0	1	0	71
	80	73	0	1	0	73
	77	65	0	1	0	65
	75	73	0	1	0	73
	81	76	0	1	0	76
Group 3	73	72	0	0	0	0
	71	71	0	0	0	0
	70	68	0	0	0	0
	76	75	0	0	0	0
	69	65	0	0	0	0

Users of the ANOVA technique rarely question whether the full model specified by the design is appropriate. The model-building nature of RA is both conceptually more appealing and often statistically more efficient. The latter is especially true when trait-treatment interactions are of major interest. To investigate such interactions in ANOVA, the trait variable (e.g., pretest achievement), which is almost always a continuous variable, must be broken down into categories. Unless five or more categories can be formed, with adequate sample sizes in each, the procedure results in a loss of potentially valuable information concerning individual differences inherent in the pretest. The regression model of equation 6 provides a test of the trait-treatment interaction using each student's actual score. Additionally, using the continuous variable in RA results in a loss of only one degree of freedom from the denominator of equation 7, whereas in ANOVA more degrees of freedom are lost when three or more categories are formed. Thus, using the pretest as a continuous variable in RA rather than as a factor in ANOVA, insures that all variation on the posttest associated with the pretest will be accounted for and it makes more efficient use of the sample size.

In summary, using the RA approach to data analysis is a more efficient and comprehensive way to treat evaluation designs involving ANOVA or ANCOVA. Any study using RA should include the treatment groups by using dummy variables as illustrated in equation 6 as well as plotting the regression lines and tabulating descriptive statistics.

Conclusion

This chapter has included three major points. The first dealt with the role of evaluation in development. Evaluation is distinguished from research on the basis of objectives and not methods. The statistical and design methodology traditionally associated with research can serve certain key objectives of evaluation involving comparative judgment. The second major point was that random assignment of subjects to treatment groups increases the internal validity of designs which is a vital concern in evaluation studies. The use of clusters for forming random groups was illustrated by using classes meeting in a school during the same period of the day. The third point was that regression analysis provides a more efficient model for data analysis involving pretests than either analysis of variance or covariance. The key to using

RA in evaluative studies is to create "dummy" variables to identify group membership and to include the pretest to investigate trait-treatment interactions. Evaluative studies that attempt to optimize internal validity by using randomization and that make efficient use of the data by performing the analysis with RA models are more likely to serve their information-producing function in development and thus lead to improved innovations.

Suggested Readings

Campbell, D.T., and Stanley, J.C. *Experimental and quasi-experimental designs for research.* Chicago: Rand McNally, 1966.

> This monograph has become a classic and is important reading for all who conduct evaluation studies. The emphasis in the text is on the logic of comparative experimentation. The material is technical but easy to read.

Cohen, J. Multiple regression as a general data-analytic system. *Psychological Bulletin,* 1968, *70,* 426-443.

> This is the major article in the research literature on the use of regression for analyzing data from multiple groups. While the material is technical, much of it is presented in an understandable, intuitive way with examples. A basic knowledge of analysis of variance and correlation techniques is helpful.

Popham, W.J. *An evaluation guidebook: A set of practical guidelines for the educational evaluator.* Los Angeles: Instructional Objectives Exchange, 1972.

> This is a useful handbook which deals with a number of topics related to educational evaluation. The material is up to data and includes discussions of criterion-referenced measurement and matrix sampling. The major points are summarized in a series of short guidelines. It is nontechnical reading.

Suchman, E.A. *Evaluative research: Principles and practice in public service and social action programs.* New York: Russell Sage Foundation, 1967.

> The first two words of the title are an unfortunate combination of terms in light of the distinctions made in the beginning of the present chapter. The book, however, is quite

useful and draws upon the author's extensive experience in evaluating social programs. Many of the principles he discusses have application in education. The material is all nontechnical.

Tuckman, B.W. *Conducting educational research.* New York: Harcourt Brace Jovanovich, 1972.

While this is an introductory textbook on how to do research, most of the methods are relevant to evaluation studies also. The book is very readable and comprehensive. There is a separate chapter devoted to evaluation. Most of the material is verbal; only the two chapters dealing with statistics and design are technical.

References

Berliner, D.C., and Cahen, L.S. Trait-treatment interaction and learning. In F.N. Kerlinger (Ed.), *Review of research in education.* Itasca, Illinois: F.E. Peacock, 1973.

Campbell, D.T., and Stanley, J.C. Experimental and quasi-experimental designs for research on teaching. In N.L. Gage (Ed.), *Handbook of research on teaching.* Chicago: Rand McNally, 1963.

Cohen, J. Multiple regression as a general data-analytic system. *Psychological Bulletin,* 1968, *70,* 426-443.

Cooley, W.W. Methods of evaluating school innovations. Pittsburgh: Learning Research and Development Center, 1971.

Cronbach, L.J. Course improvement through evaluation. *Teachers College Record,* 1963, *14,* 672-683.

Dyer, H.L. Overview of the evaluation process. In *On evaluating Title I programs.* Princeton: Educational Testing Service, 1966.

Edwards, K.J., and DeVries, D.L. Student teams and instructional games: Their effects on students' attitudes and achievement. Technical Report Number 147, December 1972, Johns Hopkins University, Center for Social Organization of Schools.

Glass, G.V., and Stanley, J.C. *Statistical methods in education and psychology.* Englewood Cliffs, New Jersey: Prentice-Hall, 1970.

Guba, E.G. The basis for educational improvement. Paper presented at the National Seminar on Innovation, Honolulu, July 1967.

Guba, E.G. Significant differences. *Educational Researcher,* 1969, *20*(4), 4-5.

Houston, T.R. Behavioral science impact-effectiveness model. In P. Rossi and W. Williams (Eds.), *Evaluating social programs.* New York: Seminar Press, 1972.

Lindvall, C.M. The task of evaluation in curriculum development projects: A rationale and case study. *School Review,* 1966, Summer, 156-167.

Myers, J.L. *Fundamentals of experimental design.* Boston: Allyn and Bacon, 1966.

Porter, A.C. Analysis strategies for some common evaluation paradigms. Paper presented at the meeting of the American Educational Research Association, New Orleans, February 1973.

Randall, R.S. An operational application of the CIPP model for evaluation. *Educational Technology,* 1969, *9,* 40-44.

Robinson, W.S. Ecological correlations and the behavior of individuals. *American Sociological Review,* 1950, *15,* 351-357.

Scriven, M. The methodology of evaluation. In R.W. Tyler, R.M. Gagne, and M. Scriven, *Perspectives on curriculum evaluation.* Chicago: Rand McNally, 1967.

Stanley, J.C. Elementary experimental design: An expository treatment. *Psychology in the Schools,* 1967, *4,* 195-203.

Stanley, J.C. Principles of scientific research are not pertinent to educational evaluation? *Educational Researcher,* 1969, *20*(5), 8-9.

Stanley, J.C. Controlled field experiments as a model for evaluation. In P. Rossi and W. Williams (Eds.), *Evaluating social programs.* New York: Seminar Press, 1972.

Stufflebeam, D.L. The use of experimental design in educational evaluation. *Journal of Educational Measurement,* 1971, *8,* 267-274.

Suchman, E.A. *Evaluative research: Principles and practice in public service and social action programs.* New York: Russell Sage Foundation, 1967.

Walberg, H.J. Generalized regression models in educational research. *American Educational Research Journal,* 1971, *8,* 71-91.

Welch, W.W. Curriculum evaluation. *Review of Educational Research,* 1969, *39,* 429-443.

Welch, W., and Walberg, H. A national experiment in curriculum evaluation. *American Educational Research Journal,* 1972, *9,* 373-384.

Winer, B.J. *Statistical principles in experimental design.* New York: McGraw-Hill, 1962.

CHAPTER 15

SELECTING UNITS OF ANALYSIS

Hugh Poynor
Educational Systems Associates

Inappropriate statistical analyses occur all too frequently in evaluation. While many evaluators perform sophisticated tests of significance, not all of them are able to identify proper units of data for their statistical analyses. A proper unit of analysis is the smallest source of data that is both logically and statistically defensible. A single pupil's test score and the average of test scores for a class of pupils are two of the most common units of analysis. In the first case, there may be 30 units per class in the analysis, while in the second case, only one unit per class. Therefore, units of analysis are usually an average of scores or the individual scores themselves. Before examining methods for identifying proper units of analysis, brief mention must be made of the consequences of employing improper units.

Among the possible consequences of selecting improper units of analysis are rejection of the evaluation report in whole or part, wholly erroneous conclusions, or both. Whenever such a mistake is made, report findings cannot be credible. A case in point is the several hundred evaluation reports that were recently reviewed by the American Institutes for Research (AIR) (1971). Ninety-seven percent of the reports did not stand up under careful scrutiny and many of these employed improper units of analysis.

Many of us are uncomfortably aware that current evaluation reports are not subjected to the intensive technical review that is commonplace for research reports submitted for journal publication. An important distinction exists between the usual prepublication review and review by the funding source. The latter review might more appropriately be considered a milestone examination, while the former could be considered an intensive critique. Had the offending 97 percent of the AIR sample been afforded an intensive critique, the number of unacceptable reports surely would have been reduced.

Purpose

The problem to be discussed in this chapter is the identification of the smallest proper evaluation unit, either pupil scores or classroom averages. The proper unit of analysis can be identified either logically or statistically. Both approaches separate pupil units from classroom averages, although to different degrees. Hopefully, the reader who is easily led to favor pupil units at the outset may be persuaded in some circumstances to favor classroom units. The statistical argument for classroom units will be developed through a series of computer simulated empirical demonstrations. By examining the extent to which erroneous conclusions are produced by inappropriate statistical tests, these simulations will reveal the importance of choosing the proper unit of analysis.

Logical Unit of Analysis

Social psychologists generally agree that people behave differently when in groups than when alone. Therefore, pupils in classrooms are not mutually exclusive individuals. This case can be supported, since independent knowledge of discrete pupils does not add up to knowledge of the classroom as a whole. Classroom experience affects pupils, and as such it may be considered a treatment. Confusion arises when these "treatments" alter the outcome of an evaluation effort designed to reveal the effect of a new program or product that is intended to be the principal treatment of interest.

Glass (1967) reviewed the use of pupil test scores as the smallest proper unit of analysis. He argues that pupil units first must satisfy the requirement that (1) pupils respond independently of other pupils, and (2) pupils be randomly assigned to treatments. While the latter requirement addresses the ever-present selection bias problem of compensatory educational research, the former requirement addresses the issue of classrooms as treatments. If classroom conditions differentially influence pupil test scores, then the classroom may be termed a treatment, since it systematically affects scores within treatments. In this case, pupils are disqualified as proper statistical units, since they did not respond independently of other pupils. When pupils fail to qualify as proper analysis units because of unique conditions among the classrooms, class averages may serve as the statistical unit. However, in research and evaluation settings it is generally not advantageous to reduce the sample size from the number of pupils to the number of classrooms. Taking 30 as a typical class size, this reduction may be as great as 97 percent.

Sample size is an extremely influential determinant of whether or not a given treatment difference is considered reliable or statistically significant. A particular treatment difference, say 12 points on an achievement test, may be judged significant or nonsignificant depending upon class variations and sample size. Since size can be more directly controlled than variation, it is selected by the evaluator as the dimension through which he may maximize the detection ability of his statistical tests. These tests may not indicate that a 12-point difference between treatment groups is significant for a small sample size, whereas with a large sample size the test may indicate statistical significance. Whether the evaluator selected a small sample or sample size was reduced through disqualifying individual pupils as proper units, his statistical detection power is less than with large samples.

Such loss can be avoided through early identification of the proper evaluation unit. During the planning stage of evaluation, these units must be logically derived. Rules for logical derivation are provided below to aid in developing a sound rationale for use of either pupil test scores or classroom averages as the proper evaluation unit. It should become clear that there is not general agreement on which unit is proper, nor on the method of logically deriving the units. Several perspectives are reviewed to provide an overview of some current controversies. Some of these controversies will then be resolved through a series of empirical studies.

Classroom units. Glass (1967) has questioned pupils as the proper unit of statistical analysis unless they respond independently of other pupils. Glass calls attention to classes as treatments if pupils within a class are systematically responding to unique class stimuli. Whether because of the presence of different teachers, "troublemakers," or unusual physical conditions, complete independence of pupil responses within a classroom is usually doubtful. Everyone can remember the influence of a "loudmouth" and how the rest of the pupils' activities depended on his behavior. If the "loudmouth" were somehow rapidly shuttled among classes so that his influence on pupil behavior was equally present across classes, then his effect would be controlled. Similarly, the poorest teacher in an experimental setting might be imposed on all classes and the room with the poorest heat, light, and noise conditions equally assigned to all classes.

Good evaluation designs control sources of confusion by eliminating disruptive sources or by balancing sources of influence across treatment conditions. In either manner, management of treatment conditions and data-gathering activities must occur before one can feel certain that the experimental treatment is uncontaminated. Unfortunately, many times evaluation practices do not include these steps. It is largely for this reason that the class mean may be the proper unit of analysis. This might be the case where there was no reason to conclude that pupils were independent replications of the experiment because of unmanaged classroom conditions. Usually, it is safe to assume that classes are independent replications of a study, but occasionally even classes must be aggregated if conditions among school buildings are not balanced.

The particular treatment itself serves as an indication of the appropriateness of class means whenever it involves the teacher rather than the pupil. Teacher training or teacher counseling programs evaluated through pupil test results have classrooms as their proper units. This is almost certainly the case in all evaluations investigating the influence of these programs. Pupils are simply not proper units if the treatment is given to the teachers.

Where pupil measures are collected as evidence of the influence of teacher programs, it is necessary to mention that the mean and variance of the class are based on pupil scores, but these scores do not serve as independent replications. They serve merely as sample statistics that ultimately provide the basis for computing the mean and variance. It is these latter values that are to serve as independent replications. For instance, pupil values are seen as acceptable descriptive statistics, but as unacceptable inferential statistics.

Careful consideration of *who* receives an experimental treatment, on the one hand, and consideration of the extent to which extraneous influences are present in a research setting, on the other hand, will allow one to logically determine whether classrooms or pupils are proper analysis units. Thus, it is maintained that *classrooms as units are proper in either of the two following conditions*: (1) the class as an entity, the social climate, the teacher, or the physical environment is the recipient of the treatment, or (2) an evaluation design places different teachers in different treatments or otherwise permits unbalanced influences to occur.

Pupil units. In the end, one's analysis is based on pupil test scores and it is this single fact that often leads one to use pupils as the unit of analysis. Since pupils receive treatments and take tests, it is argued that they must reflect the treatment's effect. In a discussion of the unit of analysis issue, Harris (Wittrock and Wiley, 1970) contends that you cannot separate the performance of a class of pupils from the performance of individuals who make up the class. Harris is right so far as descriptive distribution statistics are concerned and so far as a proper evaluation design is concerned. Those who follow his advice are likely to report analyses that are up to his high standards only if they do everything else he would do in an experiment, and this includes proper control of the experimental conditions. When these precautions are not taken, pupils may not be the best analysis units, but may be used only as the basis for the class mean and variance to be employed in later analyses.

The use of class means as analysis units is not always compelling since many times they also do not reflect the treatment unit. As Glaser (Wittrock and Wiley, 1970) states:

It is still true no one has ever taught a class. You teach an individual in the context of a class (p. 285).

Taking Harris and Glaser's view, the value of pupil units resides in the fact that pupil units relate directly to the ultimate beneficiaries of the treatment. Furthermore, the individual is a logistically stable sampling unit. Pupils come and go, changing a class, thereby changing the analysis unit. It is virtually impossible to expect a class unit to remain intact across school years, thereby inhibiting longitudinal research based upon classroom units. As Wittrock (Wittrock and Wiley, 1970) points out:

If I can talk about individuals in a class and still have some basis for assuming that the errors are independent within that class, I am on a better basis to make generalizations than if I have to work with the class as a unit (p. 285).

There are, then, some reasons for wanting pupils to be the unit of analysis. If they qualify as independent replications of the effects produced by a treatment, they are likely to qualify as proper units. This condition occurs in educational evaluation through well-planned designs that balance unique class-related conditions across treatments. Where pupils qualify as independent replications of treatment effects, this condition also occurs through closely monitored, well-managed treatment conditions. Without these steps, however, it is doubtful that pupils in different treatment classrooms will provide two sets of data that can be classified as differing only because of the treatment conditions. Other influential conditions may be preventing independent pupil responses.

Conclusions: Logical Units

Pupils are always proper analysis units in research and evaluation settings that have both of the following characteristics: (1) the pupil is the recipient of a treatment being investigated, and (2) the experimental conditions have been designed and actively managed to balance teachers and physical conditions among experimental and control classrooms so that these influences are held constant. Unfortunately, lack of management has promoted classroom means as the proper units of analysis under improperly controlled research conditions. One is left wondering what could be proper given an improper research situation. Evaluation studies are often below commonplace standards for research and, therefore, class means may be more appropriate than pupil scores.

While the proper unit may at times be the pupil, this must be verified by a statistical test that eliminates classroom effects as systematic influences of pupil responses. Preparation for the statistical test may include sampling within classrooms only a portion of the pupils rather than all of the pupils, thereby avoiding the loss in statistical detection power for treatment effects by holding the size of the pupil sample constant while increasing the size of the class sample. Simply stated, this amounts to testing fewer pupils per class, but testing more classes.

Prudent use of resources would guide the evaluator to this same strategy when classes are the proper units of analysis, namely, when (1) the class as a social entity or the class teacher is the recipient of the treatment, or when (2) *post hoc* evaluation designs or natural school settings form the conditions surrounding a treatment. Pupils are the logically proper units if *both* the previous pupil conditions are satisfied, whereas classes are the proper units if *either* of these conditions is satisfied. A large number of studies fall under condition (2) even though the pupil was chosen as the analysis unit. As seen earlier, care should be taken with semantics so that class treatments are not confused with pupil treatments that occur in class settings. Although the class mean is a more accurate estimate of degree of treatment influence, it is more expensive to obtain and it has less payoff value in terms of practical detection power per unit of effort. Thus, evaluation questions concerning social climate, group behavior, teacher personality characteristics, and so on are more expensive and typically produce fewer significant findings than those concerning pupil performance. Good research designs, of course, overcome these deficiencies if they are planned early in the life of a project.

Early queries about proper units of analysis allow evaluators to determine the proper unit. Coupled with good management during the treatment phase, it can be insured that the proper unit is secure and need not be submitted to debate or critical discussion that may diminish findings at the point when they are publicly reported. Still, a final step must be taken in addition to the logical development and careful management of a proper unit. In the pupils' unit, this amounts to a necessary confirmation of the independence of pupil responses.

Statistical Units of Analysis

The statistical procedures for determining proper units of analysis presented in this chapter assume one has identified pupils as the logical unit for analysis, rather than classroom means. Should means be appropriate, however, the influence of several statistical techniques and various sample sizes upon a means analysis are provided to guide the reader to the most cost-effective use of his efforts. It will be recalled that sample size itself is a determinant of the detection power of statistical tests and this will be demonstrated through a series of empirical studies.

Logically identifying the proper units of analysis is a necessary antecedent for entering into statistical computations. There is also an antecedent computing step that must precede the final statistical test of treatment differences. Statistical analysis techniques are adopted as decision rules in order to provide an indication of the reliability of differences found between treatment groups. The more reliable these differences are, the more confident one is that his decision regarding a treatment difference is accurate. The proper statistical analysis procedure involving pupil units depends heavily on prior statistical verification of the pupils as independent sources.

The statistical procedure used in this verification step involves what several texts (Kirk, 1968; Winer, 1962) refer to as hierarchical analysis of nested factors. Initially, classrooms are considered to be "nested" within their respective treatments (e.g., experimental or comparison) and appear in the statistical analysis as variables. Steps include accurately locating classrooms in the statistical analysis, and then verifying the independence of pupil responses with a statistical test of the classroom's variable.

Once these steps have been taken, the evaluator may be in a position to determine the logically and statistically valid sample size. If the statistical test reveals that classrooms are homogeneous (nonsignificant classroom effect) then pupils are acceptable as independent replications. If the classroom effect produces a significant test result, pupils within the classrooms are disqualified as proper analysis units and the evaluator is left with class means for the analysis. When classes are found to be significantly different, they differ simultaneously within their respective treatment assignments. That is, within the experimental treatment, classrooms are not homogeneous, or classrooms within the comparison treatment are not homogeneous, or both. One should be alerted that many unique conditions may be operating in an experimental setting whenever classrooms differ significantly. Consequently, pupils cannot be used as units of analysis since it is doubtful that their test responses are free of systematic nontreatment influences.

Evaluation design. Often the evaluator is unable to control his conditions to the point of balancing teachers in both treatments; that is, having all teachers serve in both roles as experimental and as comparison instructors. Teachers are usually found specializing in one curriculum or the other, so their classroom is assigned accordingly to that curriculum treatment. At this point, pupils may be questionable as the logical unit of analysis since different teachers are likely to provide unique conditions for the pupils. Recall that pupil units must qualify on both the curriculum recipient condition and the balanced design condition. Through careful management, however, the evaluator may effect a condition that is acceptably near to balanced teachers by manipulating the selection and placement of teachers into their treatment conditions in a pair-wise fashion. By finding two nearly matched teachers and placing one in each treatment, some degree of balancing is achieved.

Virtually all evaluators have cast their data-gathering schedules in a pre-post (before-after) design. Such an arrangement, when employed with a comparison group, allows the relative influence of a treatment to be determined, since it contrasts the gains following pretesting of the experimental pupils with those gains of the comparison pupils. This basic design arrangement is depicted in Table 1 and will serve as the model for the present discussion.

Table 1

Evaluation Design Having Two Treatment Groups and Classrooms Nested Within Each Treatment Group

Treatment/Classroom Assignment		Pretest	Posttest
Experimental Group	Class 1 (Teacher 1)	Pupil 1 Pupil 2	Pupil 1 Pupil 2
	Class 2 (Teacher 2)	. . .	. . .
Comparison Group	Class 3 (Teacher 3)	. . .	. . .
	Class 4 (Teacher 4)	. Pupil N	. Pupil N

Statistical analysis. Two procedures are typically employed to analyze pre-post data: Repeated Measures Analysis of Variance (ANOVA) and Analysis of Covariance (ANCOVA). These techniques are not identical in their computations nor in the information they provide. Discussion of their differences is outside the scope of this chapter since thorough treatments of each technique can be found in virtually every advanced statistics text. It will suffice to say that both are used frequently and serve to provide the evaluator with decision rules concerning treatment differences.

Both the ANOVA and ANCOVA nested analyses permit use of either a pupil-based or classroom-based statistical test. A pupil-based test is acceptable if the preliminary test for significant classroom effects has been made and classroom effects been found to be nonsignificant. Otherwise, a classroom means-based test must be employed to determine treatment differences. The latter test uses fewer analysis units (the number of classrooms in the evaluation) and therefore has less detection power than a test using more analysis units. The reader will recognize the number of units that are statistically analyzed as essentially the number of degrees of freedom (df) that appear in most statistical tables. Employing the larger df pupils test requires one to use ANOVA to test for significant classroom differences. This is the statistical step verifying pupils as independent sources. ANCOVA statistics employ statistical models (Poynor, 1972; Ward and Jennings, 1973) that use a df different from the ANOVA statistics. If use of the class difference test is significant, the evaluator must retreat to the classroom means-based model.

The nested design is appropriate in the vast majority of evaluations, especially when mature programs or products are being tried in a variety of school settings and under natural classroom conditions. It has also been found that the nested design is generally unused, perhaps for lack of knowledge about it or because it has never been clearly taught to evaluators as a useful statistical tool. Not employing one of the various nested designs for any reason, however, can many times result in error.

Simulation evidence. In a series of studies conducted by the author, evidence was found indicating the importance of decision rule statistics based upon proper analysis units. Analysis of inappropriate units was found to yield either underpowered tests of significance, or greatly inflated tests that indicated treatment differences where none existed. The evidence for these statements will be discussed after an explanation of the computer simulation procedures that were employed to provide such evidence.

A sample of 1,000 evaluations was provided through a data-generating computer program that effectively produced results that would have been found by carrying out the same amount of testing but at a greatly increased cost. In all, 600,000 pre- and posttests were analyzed according to the pupil- and classes-based ANOVA and ANCOVA analyses. All scores conformed to the normal distribution requirements for the statistical tests, and a procedure was employed that permitted classrooms to differ without disturbing experimental/comparison treatment differences and vice versa. This procedure is essential if the influence of classroom differences upon evaluation outcomes (i.e., treatment differences) is investigated (see Veldman, 1971).

The data base was submitted to ANOVA and ANCOVA statistical analysis in order to produce a large sample of evaluation findings. The 1,000 analyses were performed for each of several different class sizes, classes per group, treatment variances, and class variances. Analysis results were cast in the form of frequency of significant ($p \leq .05$) findings for each test under the optional pupil unit and class mean unit conditions. These frequencies were then transformed into percentages since the relative advantages and disadvantages of each unit of analysis must be examined even though the marginal frequency of significant findings under these analyses are different. Thus, percentage data permit comparison of pupil-based analyses with classes-based analyses when each is proper but when the opportunity for either analysis is not equally frequent.

Sample size had a pronounced effect on significant findings, as expected. Table 2 reveals the influence of adding pupils and adding classrooms to an evaluation design. Results such as these may be used as empirical demonstrations of cost-effective sampling so that the least expensive amount of testing can be done with assurance that adequate detection power will result.

Within any sample size, group difference values (expressed in standard deviations, σ) had a high impact on findings. This serves mainly as verification that the simulation is in proper working order, and as an aid in distinguishing between the four analysis columns. That is, the more powerful analyses are those that had pronounced rates of increase in significant findings for the range of group differences. For instance, those analyses that would yield 80 percent significant results for a $.5\sigma$ difference are preferred to those analyses that would require a $.75\sigma$ difference to yield 80 percent significant evaluations. Given a fixed experimental/comparison test score difference, the likelihood that the difference will be declared "statistically significant" depends upon whether or not ANOVA or ANCOVA is employed and whether the analysis is classes- or pupils-based. Differences between ANOVA and ANCOVA were anticipated by Ray (1960), who derived ratios expressing the relative advantage of ANCOVA over ANOVA for fixed values of pretest-posttest correlation.

Table 2 also provides dramatic evidence as to the influence of

Table 2

Percent of Significant (p ≤ .05) Group Differences for
Several Degrees of Group Difference and Sample Size

Sample Size	Difference Between Groups	Analysis of Variance		Analysis of Covariance	
		Classes	Pupils	Classes	Pupils
Class size = 15 / 2 Exp./2 control	0	0%	4%	5%	5%
	.25σ	0	12	5	20
	.50σ	0	24	5	62
	.75σ	0	41	9	92
	1.00σ	0	58	9	99
	(df)	(1,2)	(1,56)	(1,1)	(1,57)
Class size = 30 / 2 Exp./2 control	0	0	6	0	6
	.25σ	0	15	0	36
	.50σ	0	37	5	85
	.75σ	0	62	6	99
	1.00σ	4	82	11	100
	(df)	(1,2)	(1,116)	(1,1)	(1,117)
Class size = 30 / 8 Exp./2 control	0	0	6	2	7
	.25σ	6	34	8	50
	.50σ	42	87	68	97
	.75σ	97	99	94	100
	1.00σ	100%	100%	98%	100%
	(df)	(1,8)	(1,290)	(1,7)	(1,297)

Note. Analysis of variance statistic is groups by trial interaction term from a nested analysis using the classes or pupils' error term. Analysis of covariance statistic is group difference model comparison using class averages or pupil scores as the basis of models.

classroom differences on the detection of significant treatment differences. Once classes are found to differ significantly, one must conclude that pupils are improper evaluation units, and the evaluator is reduced to performing ANOVA or ANCOVA significance tests based upon class means. Comparison of the detection powers of class and pupil columns in Table 2 suggests that the classes-based test (smaller df) is greatly weaker in all cases except those of very large experimental/comparison treatment differences.

Pupil units have these detection advantages when used under appropriate analysis conditions, so they provide for efficient evaluation of the degree to which a program or product changes pupil test performance. Efficiency and sensitivity to performance differences are desirable features of all analysis activities, especially when a heavy investment has been made in the treatment being evaluated and analysis results are to be used as evidence to continue funding. Employing pupil units under these conditions can make a vital difference.

But what if one employs pupils as the analysis units under all circumstances? Even though this is the case for some evaluations, it has been an issue in this chapter to acknowledge both classroom mean units and pupil units as proper under the conditions that the unit was (1) logically derived and (2) statistically tested before declared proper as a unit of analysis. Ignoring logical development of the unit permits critics to uncover illogical designs, if such is the case, and discredit the testing or analysis procedure as illogical and irrelevant. Ignoring statistical verification of the pupil unit under conditions where the evaluator was right, of course, has no effect since pupils were proper anyway. Ignoring statistical verification of the pupil unit under conditions where the evaluator was wrong, however, does pronounced damage to findings. This error creates artificial significant differences between treatment groups.

The extent to which these erroneous significant differences guide the allocation of funds is an indication of misspent funds. The percentage of erroneous findings ranges from 39 to 59 percent incorrect as can be noted from Table 3 under conditions where the pupil unit is the unit of analysis, but pupils do not meet the qualifications as independent replications of the experiment. In other words, if the pupils fail to meet qualifications as appropriate units in the preliminary test of the classrooms variable, then at least 39 percent of the time the evaluator will have statistically significant but wholly untrue treatment

Table 3

Percent of Erroneous Results Under Conditions that
Classrooms Are Significantly Different, But the
Difference Between Experimental/Comparison
Treatments Is Zero

No. Classes	No. Pupils per Class	Pupils	
		ANOVA	ANCOVA
2/2	15	39%	43%
2/2	30	52%	59%
8/2	30	53%	56%

Note. Class means within the two groups were (on
the average) .5 standard deviations apart and constituted statistically significant effects, while the
means of the two groups were identical.

differences to report. This result should provide considerable support
for determining the proper unit of analysis *before* evaluation is begun.

Suggested Readings

Campbell, D.T., and Stanley, J.C. *Experimental and quasi-experimental
designs for research*. Chicago: Rand McNally, 1967.
> A design and analysis source book that approaches issues
> from a verbal rather than mathematical perspective. Specific
> attention should be directed to their designs for social
> research—which can be translated directly to the types of
> problems addressed in this chapter.

Cox, D.R. *Planning of experiments*. New York: John Wiley, 1958.
> A useful treatment of design and analysis issues emphasizing
> written explanations and examples rather than mathematical
> expressions. Specific attention is called to his treatment of
> precision (pp. 7-9, 165-175), which directly relates to
> consideration of sampling units.

Glass, G.V., and Stanley, J.C. *Statistical methods in education and
psychology*. Englewood Cliffs, New Jersey: Prentice-Hall, 1970.

An exceptionally clear presentation of nested classrooms as experimental units. Taking probability as the starting point, the authors build a good case for separating by definition the units of statistical analysis from the experimental units. See pages 501-509, especially.

Kirk, R.E. *Experimental designs: Procedures for the behavioral sciences.* Belmont, California: Brooks/Cole, 1968.

Perhaps the best treatment presently available to the researcher wishing to perform statistical analysis of his data. Use of three-dimensional figures and a broad repertoire of examples provides an excellent introduction to computational aspects of analysis of variance of nested (hierarchical) designs. (See Chapter 7, especially.)

Winer, B.J. *Statistical principles in experimental design.* New York: McGraw-Hill, 1962.

An advanced statistics text covering an array of variations in types of analysis of variance designs. The text is recommended because of its variety and coverage in depth of nested designs.

References

American Institutes for Research. *Evaluation of the impact of educational research & development products* (interim report). Palo Alto, California: AIR, 1971.

Glass, G.V. The experimental unit and the unit of statistical analysis. Paper presented at the American Educational Research Association Convention, 1967.

Kirk, R.E. *Experimental designs: Procedures for the behavioral sciences.* Belmont, California: Brooks/Cole, 1968.

Poynor, H. Detection of curriculum treatment differences: Excluding teacher variance in hierarchical analysis of variance designs. Unpublished doctoral dissertation, The University of Texas at Austin, 1972.

Ray, W.S. *Introduction to experimental design.* New York: Holt, 1960.

Veldman, D.J. *Empirical tests of statistical assumptions.* RMM-9R. Austin, Texas: Research and Development Center for Teacher Education, The University of Texas at Austin, 1971.

Ward, J.H., and Jennings, E. *An introduction to linear models.* Englewood Cliffs, New Jersey: Prentice-Hall, 1973.

Winer, B.J. *Statistical principles in experimental design.* New York: McGraw-Hill, 1962.

Wittrock, M.C., and Wiley, D.C. (Eds.), *The evaluation of instruction.* New York: Holt, Rinehart and Winston, 1970.

CHAPTER 16

SELECTING ANALYSIS STRATEGIES

Andrew C. Porter and Thomas R. Chibucos
Michigan State University

We attempt to provide in this chapter information which can be used by a variety of individuals such as project evaluators and administrators to make informed decisions regarding the appropriateness of several alternative analysis strategies for several common evaluation paradigms. The mathematical developments which underlie our recommendations are kept to a minimum. Individuals interested in such mathematical considerations, however, are referred to Porter's (1973) article.

For purposes of discussion, we divide evaluation paradigms into two categories or cases. Case I designs are those in which random assignment is employed, whereas Case II designs are characterized by a lack of random assignment. In both Cases I and II, the evaluator's main interest is in determining whether or not treatments or programs cause differences in some outcome measure. The two categories or cases of designs may be illustrated diagrammatically for a two-group design as follows:

Case I	*Case II*
R O X O	O X O
R O O	O O

where time passes from left to right, O indicates a variable was observed, X indicates exposure to a product or program, R in front of each line of X's and O's indicates random assignment to groups, and a dashed line separating the rows of X's and O's indicates that there was not random assignment to groups (Campbell and Stanley, 1963). Further, we distinguish between two situations characterized by type of antecedent information. Situation A is represented whenever the variable observed antecedent to treatment is measured by a pretest that is the same test or a parallel form of the test used for measuring the variable following the treatment. On the other hand, if the variable observed antecedent to treatment is any variable except a pretest, Situation B is represented. There are, therefore, four Case-Situation combinations, each representing a particular evaluation design. Although we consider only these four very basic designs in this chapter, our comments concerning choices of analyses apply directly to more complex designs which have one of the four designs as a basic component.

For each of the four evaluation paradigms presented in the chapter, four alternative analysis techniques are considered, and recommendations are made for choosing among these techniques for each Case-Situation combination. The four analysis techniques discussed are: (1) analysis of covariance (ANCOVA) with a random rather than fixed covariable; (2) estimated-true-score ANCOVA; (3) analysis of variance (ANOVA) using an index of response as the dependent variable, of which analysis of gain scores is a special case; and (4) repeated measures ANOVA, where one measure is the variable observed prior to program participation and the other measure is the outcome variable. All analysis strategies are discussed only in terms of a single antecedent variable and a single posttest.

The criteria for comparing the four analysis techniques for each of the evaluation paradigms are: (1) the hypothesis tested; (2) the statistical power for testing the hypothesis; and (3) the assumptions made. Regarding the last criterion, those assumptions which are strategy-specific, rather than those which are common across analysis techniques, are emphasized. Readers interested in the consequences of violating the assumptions associated with statistical tests are referred to an excellent review by Glass, Peckham, and Sanders (1972), since this topic is not covered in the present chapter.

Throughout the chapter, numerical examples are presented to provide concrete illustrations of important points. We hope the examples will facilitate a working understanding of the analysis strategies discussed. For readers not familiar with ANOVA and ANCOVA computational procedures, the correctness of the numerical results will probably need to be taken on faith; however, readers familiar with the computational procedures may also use the examples as exercises to check and sharpen their computational skills.

The designs for most of the summative evaluations currently being conducted represent some extension and/or combination of the four paradigms discussed in the present chapter. Choosing among analysis strategies for evaluation designs has been, of course, an important educational research problem for a long time, but there seems to be increasing interest in the problem and a concomitant increase in confusion about the advantages and disadvantages of alternative solutions. At present, the Office of Education's National Follow Through Program involves evaluations at the national, sponsor, and individual site levels. All three levels of evaluation use pretest and other antecedent variables (i.e., variables observed prior to the introduction or occurrence of a program) in designs that sometimes employ random assignment (Case I), but more frequently do not involve random assignment (Case II). Head Start Planned Variation represents a similar large-scale national evaluation. Further, local insistence on evaluation seems to be increasing. For example, Title III projects in Michigan have recently been required to use five to ten percent of their budgets for evaluation, and Title I projects are headed in the same direction. It is clear, therefore, that criteria for choosing among analysis strategies and recommendations for such choices are of interest and value to a wide range of individuals and are relevant to a variety of educational evaluation situations.

Preliminary Issues

Unit of Analysis

Prior to getting into comparisons of the various analysis strategies for the four evaluation paradigms, there are two preliminary issues that need to be discussed. One of the most basic issues is the question of what the unit of analysis should be. Unit of analysis refers to the "thing" which is observed to yield the basic data for statistical analysis. In educational evaluations of child performance, should the unit of analysis be the individual child, a classroom of children, a school, or a location? One answer to this question which is very relevant to the emphasis on analysis in the present chapter is that when one wishes to generalize the results of an evaluation, the unit of analysis should be the same as the experimental unit (i.e., the smallest number of individuals that receive the treatment or program experience *independent* of other individuals). This answer is based on the assumption of independence which underlies the analysis techniques considered in this chapter, and, in fact, which underlies all inferential statistical procedures. To the extent that the units of analysis in a study are not independent of each other, the probabilities associated with tests of significance and confidence intervals are questionable.

The answer to the question of choice of unit of analysis is complicated in educational evaluations, however, where there are usually degrees of independence. For example, students in a single classroom are more independent of each other when classroom discussion is discouraged than when discussion is encouraged. As another example, in the national Follow Through evaluation, classrooms in a school are probably more independent of each other than students in a classroom. Still, schools in a location are probably more independent of each other than are classrooms in a school, and locations or projects are probably even more independent than schools in a location. In general, if the conglomerate of students is large, then it is more likely that there will be independence among the units of analysis. But there will also be fewer units to analyze. Thus, some compromise choice frequently must be made. For example, schools might represent the best choice using independence as the criterion for selecting units, but the choice of schools might yield a sample size that is too small for analysis. On the other hand, choosing individual students as the unit of analysis would give the evaluator a larger sample size, but might very well violate the assumption of independence. Classrooms would then be a compromise unit of analysis, providing greater independence than the use of individual students, and also providing a sufficient number of units to support the analysis.

If classrooms are to be the units of analysis, then the testing plan should focus on testing in as many classrooms as possible. Using classrooms as the unit of analysis, an observation on a classroom could be based on only a *sample* of the children in each classroom. If the samples were taken randomly, no bias would be introduced into the data. Sampling children from classrooms might not represent much of a savings in testing dollars for group administered tests, but it could represent a considerable savings for individually administered tests. Perhaps the dollars saved by not testing all children in a classroom could be used to do testing in additional classrooms.

Correct identification of the *experimental unit,* and thus the unit of analysis, is also relevant to the question of whether it is the program or some alternative factor, which is causing differences among groups. Consider a program that is designed to help children improve their ability to read. Let the program be one that is group administered by a teacher and one in which the teacher plays a rather central role in implementing the program. A program director might employ an evaluation design which compares the program as it is implemented with a group of children by one teacher, to the usual classroom reading program, implemented with another group of children by a different teacher. Treating students as the units of analysis, one might well be tempted to compare the reading achievement of the two groups of children to provide information about program effectiveness. Recognition that both programs are oriented to groups of children or to the classroom as a whole and that each program is administered by a single teacher, however, leads to the conclusion that children do not receive a program independently of each other. The experimental unit and thus the unit of analysis is the *group* of children. There is one unit of analysis for the program being evaluated and one unit of analysis for the comparison program. An evaluator is much less likely to try to make sense out of a comparison that involves only one observation on each of the two things being compared. Such a reluctance to interpret the comparison is warranted, since any difference or lack of difference between the two program groups might just as likely be due to individual teacher differences, or to any other unique group experience, as to program effects. For example, perhaps the program would only look good with an "excellent" teacher assigned to it, but not with other teachers.

One-Group Pretest-Posttest Design

The second preliminary issue concerns what probably has been the most frequently used design for evaluation of programs or other innovations, i.e., the design characterized by the administration of a pretest and a posttest to only one group of program participants. The analysis of such a one-group design is performed to determine whether or not there was a reliable change from pretest to posttest. Many evaluators are aware of the difficulties of attributing change (or lack of change, for that matter) to the program being evaluated. Campbell and Stanley (1963) have done an excellent job of describing alternatives to program as explanations of why change did or did not occur: history effects, maturation, testing effects, instrumentation, regression, and perhaps even mortality. These methodological weaknesses alone make Case I or Case II designs preferable to the one-group design.

Assume for a moment, however, that all of these alternative explanations were somehow argued away, i.e., assume we can state that the program caused the change or lack of change in the dependent variable. The question remains, does the design address an interesting question from a program director's point of view? We are not convinced that it does; in fact, we believe that the question posed by an internally valid pretest-posttest design with all subjects receiving the program is generally not of interest. Should we conclude that a program is effective if children profit more than if they were in no program at all? If the children were not in the program being evaluated, they would probably be in some other program. Thus, the question of interest is not whether a program is better than nothing at all, but rather whether a program is more effective than a specific alternative program. A pretest-posttest design might demonstrate that children make substantial gains but begs the question of whether these gains are greater than gains attributable to the program's alternatives. We, therefore, argue that a program evaluation should involve a comparison group of children who participate in a reasonable alternative program, i.e., Case I and II designs. The general evaluation question becomes "Is the program better than the alternative?" Such a design addresses a more interesting question, and has fewer methodological weaknesses.

Case I–Situation A

We will now consider the first of the four evaluation paradigms which are the major focus of this chapter. Recall that Case I designs are those which have as a basic component the random assignment of experimental units to programs, and that Situation A indicates the use of a pretest as antecedent information. Case I designs are considered prior to Case II designs despite our realization that the majority of past and current evaluation designs have not been characterized by random assignment. First, we believe that, other things being equal, a design in which random assignment is employed provides the best means of determining whether or not programs cause differences on the posttest. Second, we believe that a strong commitment to the importance of random assignment, as well as to the use of experimental units which are conglomerates of students (e.g., classrooms or schools), will result in a greater number of evaluation designs which employ random assignment (Bock, 1971; Campbell and Erlebacher, 1970; Porter, 1969). Third, given random assignment, the problems of statistical analysis are much more straightforward for Case I than for Case II. Thus, starting with Case I will allow the analysis techniques to be considered in situations that are relatively less complex. Finally, with the exception of the hypothesis tested, the criteria we use for selecting among the analysis strategies are not greatly changed from Case I to Case II designs. Therefore, some of our comments about Case I designs transfer in a fairly straightforward fashion to Case II designs.

Analysis of Variance

In order to provide a base of comparison for the analysis strategies which use antecedent information, first consider an analysis strategy that does not. An ANOVA of the posttest only tests the hypothesis of interest to the evaluator. The null hypothesis about programs is that there are no differences in the population means on the posttest, Y. Since random assignment is a characteristic of Case I designs, the evaluator need not be concerned about change. That is, when experimental units have been randomly assigned to treatments, differential change may be inferred from differences in the posttest measure. This is because the assumption is made that the treatment groups started the study, on the average, equal on all possible variables.

Consider an example in which students are divided into two equal groups of ten each on the basis of sex, and are then randomly assigned to one or the other of two treatments. The data matrix presented in Table 1 represents the design with the second column of scores being the individual scores on the posttest. The two treatments are denoted T_1 and T_2, and the two sexes are denoted S_1 and S_2. I_1 through I_{20} represent the twenty individual students in the study. Note that there are four cells in the design, each cell being defined as a treatment-sex combination $(T_1 S_1, T_1 S_2, T_2 S_1, T_2 S_2)$. The hypothesis of no treatment effects can be stated formally $\mu_{Y_{1..}} = \mu_{Y_{2..}}$, where $\mu_{Y_{1..}}$ denotes the population mean on the posttest for treatment one, and $\mu_{Y_{2..}}$ denotes the population mean on the posttest for treatment two. Sex has been included as an independent variable in the design to afford the evaluator a test of whether treatment differences are the same for each sex (i.e., to test whether or not there is a treatment by sex interaction). This reflects our belief that evaluators should be concerned with whether treatments have the same effect for all students or whether there may be groups of students across which treatments have differential effects. This has been popularized as concern for "aptitude" by treatment interactions; however, we wish to emphasize the potential value of considering treatment by "characteristics of experimental units" interactions in general.

A two-way ANOVA can be used to test the hypotheses of interest, i.e., that there is no treatment effect, and that there is no treatment by sex interaction. A two-way ANOVA of the data presented in column two of Table 1 is provided in Table 2. The F test of the treatment by sex interaction is equal to zero. There is, therefore, no reason to believe that a treatment by sex interaction is present. Further, the F test of no treatment effect equals 2, which does not exceed the tabled value of 4.49 for a significance level of $\alpha = .05$ with 1 and 16 degrees of freedom. The data provide no reason to conclude that the treatment caused different effects on the posttest, Y. It might be noted that the F test for sex is significant, but this was not a hypothesis of direct interest to the evaluator. Further, there was a small difference between sample treatment means as suggested in the second column of Table 3. The mean across sexes for treatment one is 11 and the mean across sexes for treatment two is 10, giving a one-point difference between sample treatment means. Had the statistical power of the ANOVA F test been greater, this small difference might have been statistically significant. One of the most important factors in determining the power of the ANOVA F test is the magnitude of the population variance (σ_Y^2) within sex by treatment combinations. This is the expected value of the denominator of the F test, and the smaller the magnitude of this variance, the greater the statistical power of the ANOVA (Cox, 1957).

The assumptions underlying the ANOVA are: (1) equal population variances within sex by treatment combinations, (2) the posttest is normally distributed in the population, and (3) independence of units of analysis. It also is assumed that other independent variables, not included in the design, do not interact with treatments. The last assumption is sometimes called the assumption of additivity (Cox, 1958) and is not required for a valid F test but is required to avoid misinterpretation of results. If an interaction is present in the data, but is overlooked, the evaluator might conclude that there are no

Table 1

Data Matrix for a Case I Evaluation

Treatments	Sexes	Individuals	X	Y	Y-X	$\hat{X}$
T_1	S_1	I_1	8	9	1	8
		I_2	10	10	0	9.6
		I_3	6	8	2	6.4
		I_4	9	11	2	8.8
		I_5	7	7	0	7.2
	S_2	I_6	11	11	0	11.2
		I_7	14	14	0	13.6
		I_8	10	12	2	10.4
		I_9	13	15	2	12.8
		I_{10}	12	13	1	12
T_2	S_1	I_{11}	6	7	1	6.4
		I_{12}	8	8	0	8
		I_{13}	10	9	-1	9.6
		I_{14}	7	6	-1	7.2
		I_{15}	9	10	1	8.8
	S_2	I_{16}	12	12	0	12
		I_{17}	14	13	-1	13.6
		I_{18}	10	11	1	10.4
		I_{19}	13	14	1	12.8
		I_{20}	11	10	-1	11.2

X: Antecedent Information (covariable)
Y: Posttest or Outcome Variable
Y-X: Gain Score
$\hat{X}$:   Estimated True Score on X

Table 2

Analysis of Variance of the Posttest Data in Table 1

Sources	d.f.	SS	MS	F*
T	1	5	5	2
S	1	80	80	32
TxS	1	0	0	0
I:TS	16	40	2.5	

*F-value required for statistical significance at $\alpha = .05$ with 1 and 16 degrees of freedom is 4.49.

Table 3*

Means for the Data Presented in Table 1

	S	X	Y	Y-X	$\hat{X}$
T_1	S_1	8	9	1	8
	S_2	12	13	1	12
T_2	S_1	8	8	0	8
	S_2	12	12	0	12

*See legend for Table 1.

differences among treatments when in fact there are treatment effects. The treatment effects may simply be different across types of subjects and might, therefore, average to zero when considered over all subjects.

Analysis of Covariance

The analysis of covariance (ANCOVA) using a random covariable is an analysis strategy that can be used to test the same hypothesis as ANOVA but, hopefully, with greater statistical power. ANCOVA requires information on an antecedent variable, and the null hypothesis for ANCOVA is stated in terms of no difference among adjusted population means. Again consider the example presented in Table 1. This time, however, the statistical analysis uses the data in column one (the scores on the pretest) as well as the posttest data in column two. The ANCOVA null hypothesis can be stated formally

$$\mu'_{Y_{1..}} = \mu'_{Y_{2..}},$$

where $\mu'_{Y_{1..}}$ is the adjusted mean of the posttest for treatment one and $\mu'_{Y_{2..}}$ is the adjusted mean on the posttest for treatment two. An adjusted treatment mean is defined

(1) $$\mu'_{Y_{T..}} = \mu_{Y_{T..}} - \beta_{Y.X}(\mu_{X_{T..}} - \mu_{X...}),$$

where $\mu_{Y_{T..}}$ is a treatment population mean on the posttest, $\mu_{X_{T..}}$ a treatment population mean on the pretest, $\mu_{X...}$ is the grand population mean on the pretest and $\beta_{Y.X}$ is the population slope for predicting posttest from pretest within each cell of the design. It is important to realize that random assignment results in population treatment means on the pretest being equal to each other and to their grand mean. The result is that for Case I designs in general $\mu_{X_{T..}} - \mu_{X...} = 0$ and so the adjusted treatment means on the posttest are equal to the unadjusted means on the posttest. Thus, the ANCOVA and ANOVA analysis strategies test the same null hypothesis about treatments. By parallel arguments it is also true that, for Case I designs, ANOVA of the posttest and ANCOVA test the same null hypothesis regarding the treatment by sex interaction.

Sample adjusted means are calculated by substituting sample estimates of the population parameters in the definition of population adjusted means. Note in Table 3 that the treatment means of the pretest were exactly equal. By using equation (1) above and the means in Table 3 it follows that $\overline{Y}'_{1\,..} = 11$ and $\overline{Y}'_{2\,..} = 10$, i.e., the adjusted posttest means equal the unadjusted posttest means. This equality also holds for the treatment by sex interaction, but it must be emphasized that neither equality holds for every Case I set of sample data, since random assignment results in chance treatment differences or interactions in the covariate data. These chance differences have mild effects on the adjusted main effects or interactions in ANCOVA.

Since both ANOVA and ANCOVA test the hypothesis which is of interest to the evaluator, it is of interest to compare the two procedures on the criterion of statistical power. Consider a two-way ANCOVA of the data in Table 1. The results of the ANCOVA are presented in Table 4 and indicate again that F = 0 for interaction. But now the F test for treatments is 5.21 which exceeds the tabled value of 4.54 for $\alpha = .05$ with 1 and 15 degrees of freedom.

Recalling that ANOVA and ANCOVA tested the *identical* treatment effect, it is seen that ANCOVA was more powerful since the treatment effect was significant when analyzed by ANCOVA, but not when analyzed by ANOVA. Again the sex effect is not of direct interest to the evaluator, but note that it is no longer statistically significant. The conclusions from ANCOVA of the data are that there is no reason to believe a treatment by sex interaction is present, but that there is a treatment effect. Although one must be careful to generalize from a particular example to the general case, our example suggests that the statistical power of ANCOVA can exceed that of ANOVA. A comparison of the mean square error for ANOVA (2.5) to the mean square error for ANCOVA (.96) suggests that the improvement in statistical power is due to a decrease in the mean square error despite the loss of one degree of freedom from 16 to 15.

The general relationship between the expected value of the mean square error for ANOVA, σ_Y^2, and that for ANCOVA, $\sigma_{Y.X}^2$, is

$$(2) \qquad \sigma_{Y.X}^2 = \sigma_Y^2 \, (1 - \rho_{XY}^2) \, [1 + \frac{1}{fe - 2}] \, ,$$

where ρ_{XY} denotes the within cell population correlation between pretest and posttest and fe denotes the degrees of freedom for error. In

Table 4

Analysis of Covariance of the Posttest Data
in Table 1 Using X as the Covariate

Sources	d.f.	SS_X	SS_Y	SS_{XY}	SS_Y'	d.f.'	MS_Y'	F*
T	1	0	5	0	5	1	5	5.21
S	1	80	80	80	1.07	1	1.07	1.11
TxS	1	0	0	0	0	1	0	0
I:TS	16	40	40	32	14.4	15	.96	

*F must equal or exceed 4.54 to be statistically significant at $\alpha = .05$, for 1 and 15 d.f.

general, it can be shown that the larger the pretest-posttest correlation, the smaller the mean square error for ANCOVA.

The assumptions on which ANCOVA is based are: (1) for a given value of the covariate, X, the posttest is normally distributed with equal variance across values of X; (2) the observations are independent of each other; (3) the slope, $\beta_{Y.X}$, is the same for the populations of all cells; and (4) X and Y have a linear relationship. The assumptions are the same as those made for classical ANCOVA with a fixed covariable, except that the covariable is random and may be measured with error. When errors of measurement are present, the above assumptions are made on the observed variables rather than the latent *error-free* variables, except for the assumption of equal slopes across treatments which should be met for both latent and observed variables. The assumption of equal slopes, (3) above, is discussed more fully in Special Note A.*

In summary, ANCOVA and ANOVA test the same hypothesis for Case I–Situation A. If one is willing to roughly equate the assumptions of normality, equal variance, and independence for the two procedures, although they are not exactly identical, ANCOVA requires the additional assumptions of a linear relationship between X and Y, and equal reliability of X across treatment conditions (see Special Note A). To the extent that the pre-post correlation is different from zero, and degrees of freedom are large, however, ANCOVA will test the hypothesis with greater statistical power than ANOVA. Elashoff's (1969) comments to the effect that for pre-post correlations smaller than ±.3 the improvement in statistical power associated with AN-COVA is negligible should be kept in mind.

ANOVA of Index of Response
One of the most popular analysis strategies for using information on a pretest is to form an index of response and use the index as a new dependent variable in ANOVA. The index is most familiar when it is referred to as a gain score. An index of response is defined $Z = Y - KX$, where Z is the index, Y is the posttest, K is any constant, and in Situation A, X is the pretest. When $K = 1$, Z is a gain score, though the definition of an index makes it clear that a gain score is only one of an infinite variety of indices that might be formed.

---

*Special Notes are found at the end of this chapter. These notes are intended for readers who wish to go more deeply into matters raised in the chapter.

When using ANOVA of an index of response the null hypothesis about treatments can be stated as no difference among the treatment population means on the index of response. Again consider the data in columns one and two of Table 1. These data are used to form an index of response. The null hypothesis about treatments is stated formally as $\mu_{Z_{1\,..}} = \mu_{Z_{2\,..}}$ where $\mu_{Z_{1\,..}}$ is the population mean of treatment one on the index Z, and $\mu_{Z_{2\,..}}$ is the population mean on the index of treatment two. To facilitate understanding of the hypothesis being tested, population means on Z can be restated in terms of the original variables X and Y,

$$(3) \qquad \mu_{Z_{T\,..}} = \mu_{Y_{T\,..}} - K(\mu_{X_{T\,..}} - \mu_{X...}) .$$

The only difference between these means and the ANCOVA adjusted means is that $\beta_{Y.X}$ has been replaced by K. By arguments identical to those given for ANCOVA, for Case I designs in general the population treatment means on the index, Z, are identical to the population treatment means on the posttest, Y. Therefore, use of an index of response with Case I designs tests the treatment hypothesis of interest to the evaluator which is identical to the null hypothesis for ANOVA of Y and ANCOVA. It is important to realize that this statement is in no way dependent upon the value of K.

Since ANOVA of index of response tests the hypothesis of interest, it is reasonable to consider the statistical power of the procedure. Consider a two-way ANOVA of the gain score index defined on the data in Table 1. The gain scores are presented in column three of Table 1 and the results of the analysis are presented in Table 5. Again, there is a zero F for interaction, and this time F = 5 for treatments, which is larger than the tabled F of 4.49 with 1 and 16 degrees of freedom, and a .05 level of significance. The conclusions drawn from the analysis are that there is no reason to believe that a treatment by sex interaction exists, but that there is reason to believe that treatments bring about different levels on the posttest. The treatment means for the gain scores are directly obtainable from column three of Table 3. The mean for treatment one is 1 and the mean for treatment two is 0. Again, since there were no treatment differences on X in our example the treatment difference is identical to that for ANOVA. The total disappearance of the sex effect is indicated by the zero F for sex in Table 5 but for the present is of no direct interest to the evaluator.

Table 5

Analysis of Variance of the Gain Scores
Presented in Table 1

Sources	d.f.	SS	MS	F*
T	1	5	5	5
S	1	0	0	0
TxS	1	0	0	0
I:TS	16	16	1	

*Required $F \geq 4.49$ (d.f. 1, 16; $\alpha = .05$)

A comparison of the treatment F's in Tables 2, 4, and 5 indicates that the F is smallest and not significant for ANOVA of Y, bigger and significant for ANOVA of the gain scores index of response, and largest for ANCOVA. Again one must be careful in overgeneralizing from a single example but the results suggest that at least for some situations, use of an index of response can result in greater statistical power than ANOVA of the posttest but less statistical power than ANCOVA. To see more clearly the relationship between the power of the three statistical procedures presented thus far, consider the relationship between the expected values of the mean square errors for ANOVA of Y, σ_Y^2, and ANOVA of an index of response, σ_Z^2,

$$(4) \qquad \sigma_Z^2 = \sigma_Y^2(1 - \rho_{XY}^2) + a^2 \sigma_X^2 ,$$

where $a = K - \beta_{Y.X}$. It follows directly that the expected value of the mean square error for an index of response is smallest when $K = \beta_{Y.X}$. Since the smaller the expected value of the mean square error, the greater the statistical power, the evaluator should attempt to use an index of response where $K = \beta_{Y.X}$. Unfortunately $\beta_{Y.X}$ is a population parameter and its value is in general unknown. At least for Case I designs, however, the evaluator has the reassurance that although an incorrect choice of K may decrease statistical power, as shown earlier the hypothesis of interest will still be tested.

When $K = \beta_{Y.X}$, σ_Z^2 reduces to $\sigma_Y^2(1 - \rho_{XY}^2)$. Further, recalling that the expected value of the mean square error for ANCOVA is $\sigma_Y^2(1 - \rho_{XY}^2)[1 + \frac{1}{fe - 2}]$, and further noting that ANCOVA had one less degree of freedom error, it follows that ANOVA of index of response can be more powerful than ANCOVA. This is particularly true when degrees of freedom are small since that is when $[1 + \frac{1}{fe - 2}]$ is largest and when the loss of one degree of freedom is most dear. Further, it can be shown that whenever $0 < K/\beta_{Y.X} < 2$ ANOVA of index of response has a smaller expected mean square error than ANOVA of Y (Cox, 1957). In our example of gain scores, $K = 1$. By using the ANCOVA intermediate results reported in Table 4, it is possible to estimate $\beta_{Y.X}$:

$$b_{Y.X} = \frac{SS_{XY_{I:TS}}}{SS_{X_{I:TS}}} = \frac{32}{40} = .8.$$

For the example $K \neq b_{Y.X}$ and, therefore, the mean square error for ANCOVA reported as .96 in Table 4 is less than the mean square error for ANOVA of gains reported as 1 in Table 5. Also, since $0 < K/\beta_{Y.X} = 1.25 < 2$, the mean square error of 1 for ANOVA of gains is less than the mean square error for ANOVA of Y reported as 2.5 in Table 2. Had the index $Z = Y - .8X$ been used in place of gain scores, the expected value of the mean square error for ANOVA of the index would have been .9, which is smaller than the .96 reported for ANCOVA.

Although the assumptions of normality, equal variance, and independence are made on the dependent variable Z when using ANOVA of index of response, these assumptions can be shown to be identical to the parallel three assumptions made for ANCOVA. Further, for ANOVA of index of response certain assumptions are involved in using the model for defining the dependent variable as

$$Z = Y - KX.$$

First, since the model for the dependent variable is linear, the assumption is made that for each cell of the design, X and Y are linearly related. Second, since error variance is at a minimum when $K = \beta_{Y.X}$, ANOVA of index of response has $K = \beta_{Y.X}$ as an additional assumption.

In summary, ANCOVA and ANOVA of an index of response test the same hypothesis. Given the one additional assumption that the *a priori* chosen value of K equals $\beta_{Y.X}$, use of the index of response has a slightly smaller expected value for its mean square error and one more degree of freedom than ANCOVA, and thus, has greater statistical power than ANCOVA. The problem, of course, is how to select a value of K which is close enough to $\beta_{Y.X}$ to make the procedure more powerful than ANCOVA which estimates $\beta_{Y.X}$ from the data in the study. Arguments for setting the value of K for Case I–Situation A designs are discussed further in Special Note B.

We conclude that gain scores are almost never appropriate for Case I–Situation A designs, but when some rather restrictive assumptions are met, use of the index

$$Z = Y - \rho_{XX}X,$$

where ρ_{XX} denotes the test-retest reliability of the pretest, can result in better statistical power than ANCOVA. An important warning, however, is that ρ_{XX} is the *reliability* of the pretest for the populations of *units of analysis.* If the units of analysis are classrooms, the reliability for a test is frequently higher than the same test for a population of students. We feel the index has some practical merit since evaluators frequently have good knowledge of the reliability of their pretest.

Repeated Measures ANOVA
Another procedure that has been suggested for analysis of Case I–Situation A designs is the repeated measures ANOVA, where the pretest is one measure and the posttest is the other. As we understand it, the prime motivation for use of a repeated measures ANOVA has been that the use of an index of response, and in particular the use of gain scores, results in an analysis using a dependent variable of notoriously low reliability. Although we agree that an index of response typically has low reliability, we wish to point out that repeated measures ANOVA does not offer a better alternative. Further attention is given in Special Note C at the end of this chapter to the reliability of

indices of response and the affect of reliability on their use as a dependent variable.

Stanley (1966) has shown that for Case I designs, the main effect for treatments, T, and the treatment by measures interaction in a repeated measures ANOVA, test identical hypotheses. More importantly, Jennings (1972) and Bock (1971) have pointed out that the F test of the treatment by measures interaction in a repeated measures analysis is identical to the F test of the treatment main effect in ANOVA of gain scores. The example in Table 1 can be used as an illustration of the equivalence of the two analysis strategies. The results of a repeated measures ANOVA of the data presented in columns 1 and 2 of Table 1 are given in Table 6. The results of interest are those for the test of the treatment by measures interaction. In particular, the mean square for the treatment by measures interaction is one half the mean square for the treatment main effect reported in Table 5. Further, the mean square error for testing the treatment by measures interaction, IM:TS, is one half the mean square error for testing the gain score treatment main effect labeled I:TS in Table 5. Therefore, the treatment by measures F of 5 is numerically equal to the gain score F-ratio for treatments reported in Table 5. Further, since the number of measures is two, both F tests have identical degrees of freedom. Similarly, the test for a treatment by sex by measures interaction in Table 6 is identical to the gain score treatment by sex test in Table 5. Although the sex by measures interaction is not of direct interest to the evaluator, its test is identical to the test for a sex main effect using gain scores. The results for the first four sources listed are not included in the table, since they are of no direct interest to the evaluator.

Since the test statistics are identical, it follows that the repeated measures ANOVA and the ANOVA of gain scores test the same hypothesis, with identical assumptions, and identical statistical power. If either analysis is to be used, ANOVA of gain scores seems preferable, since the hypothesis can be presented as a main effect rather than an interaction. Interactions are more difficult to present, and where there are more than two treatment groups, require more difficult *post hoc* comparisons. Because of its equivalence to gain score analysis, the repeated measures ANOVA will not be mentioned further. Comments about gain score analysis should be applied directly to the repeated measures ANOVA strategy.

Table 6

Repeated Measures Analysis of Variance
Using Pretest and Posttest as Measures

Sources	d.f.	SS	MS	F*
T	1			
S	1			
Error (I:TS)	16			
M	1			
TxM	1	2.5	2.5	5
SxM	1	0	0	0
TxSxM	1	0	0	0
Error (IM:TS)	16	8	.5	

*$F \geq 4.49$ required for significance at $\alpha = .05$, with 1 and 16 d.f.

Analysis of Covariance Using Estimated
True Scores as the Covariate

The final analysis strategy to be considered is ANCOVA using estimated true scores as the covariate (Porter, 1967). Although the procedure was originally proposed for analyzing data from Case II designs, we have included it here for logical consistency. The procedure is described in terms of the data presented in Table 1. The first step is to replace the pretest data with estimated true scores, where an estimated true score for the design is defined:

$$(5) \qquad \hat{X}_{TSI} = \bar{X}_{TS.} + \rho_{XX}(X_{TSI} - \bar{X}_{TS.}),$$

where $\hat{X}_{TSI}$ denotes an estimated true score for an individual subject, $\bar{X}_{TS.}$ denotes a cell mean on the pretest, ρ_{XX} denotes the reliability of the pretest within cells, and X_{TSI} denotes the score of an individual subject on the pretest. Estimated true scores, where $\rho_{XX} = .8$, are presented in column four of Table 1. Following the replacement of pretest scores with their estimated true scores as the covariate, the analysis strategy is computationally identical to classical ANCOVA.

The null hypothesis about treatments is identical to that shown previously for classical ANCOVA,

$$\mu'_{Y_{1..}} = \mu'_{Y_{2..}},$$

where $\mu'_{Y_{1..}}$ is the adjusted mean of the posttest for treatment one and $\mu'_{Y_{2..}}$ is the adjusted mean of the posttest for treatment two. For estimated true score ANCOVA, an adjusted treatment mean is defined

(6) $$\mu'_{Y_{T..}} = \mu_{Y_{T..}} - \beta_{Y.\hat{X}}(\mu_{\hat{X}_{T..}} - \mu_{\hat{X}...}).$$

It is easily shown that $\mu_{X_{TS.}} = \mu_{\hat{X}_{TS.}}$ from which it follows that estimated true score pretest means equal their corresponding original pretest means. Numerical examples of this point are given in Table 3 where it can be seen that $\hat{X}$ means in column four are identical to the X means in column one. Therefore,

$$\mu'_{Y_{T..}} = \mu_{Y_{T..}} - \beta_{Y.\hat{X}}(\mu_{X_{T..}} - \mu_{X...})$$

which is identical to the adjusted mean for ANCOVA using X as the covariate except $\beta_{Y.\hat{X}}$ replaces $\beta_{Y.X}$. By arguments identical to those used earlier $\mu'_{Y_{T..}} = \mu_{Y_{T..}}$ for Case I designs. For Case I designs, the null hypothesis for treatments, tested by estimated true scores ANCOVA, is identical to the null hypothesis tested by the four analysis strategies previously described and is the one of interest to the evaluator.

Since the hypothesis tested is of interest, other properties of the procedure need to be explored. The results of estimated true scores ANCOVA for the data in Table 1 are presented in Table 7. The F test of no treatment differences equals 5.21 and is identical to the F test for treatment when using the observed pretest as the covariate, as reported

Table 7

Analysis of Covariance of the Posttest Data in Table 1 Using $\hat{X}$ as the Covariate

Sources	d.f.	$SS_{\hat{X}}$	SS_Y	$SS_{\hat{X}Y}$	SS_Y'	d.f.'	MS_Y'	F*
T	1	0	5	0	5	1	5	5.21
S	1	80	80	80	0	1	0	0
TxS	1	0	0	0	0	1	0	0
I:TS	16	25.6	40	25.6	14.4	15	.96	

*Required $F \geq 4.54$ with 1 and 15 d.f. and $\alpha = .05$.

in Table 4. Again the F test of a treatment by sex interaction is zero. The F test for sex is also zero as was the case for ANOVA of gain scores. The sex effect is of no direct interest to the evaluator for Case I designs but will be discussed further under Case II.

For our contrived example, the sample adjusted means using $\hat{X}$ as the covariate are identical to those using X as the covariate. This is not true in general, however, despite the fact that the population adjusted means are equal for Case I. The reason is that for any set of sample data the pretest means on the covariate can differ by chance.

The within cell population slope using estimated true scores as the covariable is

$$\beta_{Y.\hat{X}} = \frac{1}{\rho_{XX}} \beta_{Y.X} .$$

This can be illustrated by the example in Table 7

$$b_{Y.\hat{X}} = \frac{SS_{\hat{X}Y_{I:TS}}}{SS_{\hat{X}_{I:TS}}} = \frac{25.6}{25.6} = 1 .$$

Since ρ_{XX} was given as .8 and since $b_{Y.X}$ equaled .8 it is seen that $b_{Y.\hat{X}} = (1/\rho_{XX}) b_{Y.X}.$

Also of interest is the observation that the mean square error is equal to .96 for both ANCOVAs. This can be proven to be generally true for both Case I and Case II designs. Also, both ANCOVAs use identical degrees of freedom. Since the ANCOVA is still the basic model of analysis and since, within treatment groups, $\hat{X}$ is a linear transformation of X, ANCOVA using estimated true scores has as a minimum all of the assumptions of ANCOVA using X as a covariable. As noted earlier, both ANCOVA procedures test with identical mean square errors the same null hypothesis about treatments for Case I designs. The use of $\hat{X}$, however, requires knowledge of the reliability of the covariable whereas the use of X does not require such knowledge. Therefore, ANCOVA using X as the covariable is preferred to ANCOVA using $\hat{X}$ as the covariable in Case I—Situation A designs.

Summary: Case I—Situation A

In summary, all four analysis strategies considered for Case I—Situation A designs were shown to test the same null hypothesis. It was shown that ANOVA of index of response represents the alternative with most statistical power if the slope, $\beta_{Y.X}$, of the within treatment group regression line is known. ANOVA of gain scores was shown to be an index of response with $K = 1$, and repeated measures ANOVA was demonstrated to be identical to ANOVA of gain scores. It was argued that for Case I–Situation A designs, $\beta_{Y.X}$ will almost never equal one and so gain scores or repeated measures ANOVA will generally result in poorer power than necessary. Given that the pretest and posttest measure the same dimension with equal reliability, and that there is no true differential change in subjects on the dimension measured (Special Note B), the index $Z = Y - \rho_{XX}X$ was argued to represent a strategy having good statistical power. At least for short-term programs, when there is not a floor effect on the pretest or a ceiling effect on the posttest, the assumptions seem likely to be met satisfactorily. The advantage in terms of the statistical power of an index of response over ANOVA seems particularly likely for studies having very small sample sizes, where both a loss of one degree of freedom for each covariate and an inflation of the error term due to estimating $\beta_{Y.X}$ are most severe. An advantage for the index also seems particularly likely when there are multiple outcome measures, each with a pretest. In such a case, a separate index can be formed for each outcome measure, whereas multivariate ANCOVA would use all pretests as covariates for all outcome measures with a considerable loss of degrees of freedom.

The pretest and posttest, however, do not necessarily measure the same dimension, and even if they do, they are not necessarily equally reliable. Further, information on the test-retest reliability of the instrument is not always available. In such cases, ANCOVA using X as the covariable generally represents a more powerful strategy than use of the index $Z = Y - \rho_{XX}X$.

The assumptions underlying use of ANOVA of an index of response were shown to be the same as those for ANCOVA. ANCOVA using estimated true scores as the covariable was shown to be identical to classical ANCOVA except that it requires knowledge of the reliability of the covariable. Since it requires additional information and has no compensating advantages, ANCOVA using estimated true scores as the covariable should not be used for Case I designs.

Various statistical analysis strategies which assume a linear relationship between the antecedent information and the dependent variable (i.e., a linear model) are considered in detail in this chapter. We would be remiss, however, if we failed to at least mention a *design* technique that can be of use to the researcher. The technique known as randomized blocking can be as powerful as the analysis strategies we discuss in this chapter when a linear model is appropriate (see Cox, 1957, and Feldt, 1958, for informative considerations of blocking). The main advantage of blocking, however, is that it is a good procedure when a linear relationship does *not* exist. Since the analysis strategies based on a linear model are simpler from a design point of view, i.e., they require simple random assignment to programs rather than stratified random assignment, and since they are more powerful techniques relative to blocking when ρ_{XY} is moderate to large, we favor the best linear model-based strategy for a particular design. If a nonlinear relationship between the antecedent information and the posttest is suspected, randomized blocking is clearly a preferable strategy to strategies that assume an underlying linear model.

Case I—Situation B

Case I—Situation B is identical to Case I—Situation A except that the antecedent variable, X, is not a pretest. Usually Situation B results when: (1) concern for statistical power occurred after the study had been conducted, or (2) the evaluator feared that use of a pretest would be reactive and thus limit external validity (Campbell and Stanley, 1963). If neither of the above is true, then a pretest should probably be used, since a pretest is the variable most likely to have a high correlation with the posttest. As shown earlier the higher the correlation between the antecedent variable and the posttest the greater the statistical power.

Most of the comparisons of analysis strategies for Case I—Situation A did not make use of the restriction that X was a pretest, and they, therefore, apply equally well to Case I—Situation B. When X is not a pretest, the assumptions necessary to make ANOVA of $Z = Y - \rho_{XX}X$ a useful procedure are almost certainly not met. ANOVA of index of response is still the best strategy when $\beta_{Y.X}$ is known, but when X is not a pretest the likelihood of knowing $\beta_{Y.X}$ seems considerably small. Therefore, ANCOVA using X as the covariable will most generally be the best analysis strategy to use for Case I—Situation B designs.

Case II—Situation A

We will now consider the Case-Situation combination that is characterized by a lack of random assignment of subjects to programs, and by the use of a pretest as the antecedent information or covariable. It should be noted that, when random assignment has not been employed, the typical procedure in summative evaluations is to use a pretest in order to establish a baseline which can be used at a later point to aid in interpreting the results on the outcome measure. Therefore, Case II–Situation A represents the most prevalent class of evaluation designs.

The most important criterion when comparing analysis strategies for Case II designs is the hypothesis tested. The evaluator undoubtedly wishes to test the null hypothesis of no differences among treatment groups on the outcome measure. Because of non-random assignment, however, there are likely to be many variables confounded with treatments or programs. Therefore, the interpretation of comparisons made among treatment groups is not straightforward, i.e., differences (or lack of them) among treatment groups may be attributable to factors other than the treatments. For this reason, ANOVA of the posttest is no longer as useful a base for comparison as it was in Case I, and, therefore, it is not presented for Case II designs.

Two useful categories of potential confounding variables (Porter and Chibucos, 1972) are:

(1) systematic difference in the dependent variable dimensions that are present in the units of analysis at the outset of program participation, and

(2) systematic differences that occur in the dependent variable dimensions during program participation, and which are not a function of program participation.

The question of interest is which, if any, analysis strategy controls for the two types of confounding variables *and* tests the hypotheses of interest?

There are two basic positions with regard to the utility of Case II designs. One position is characterized by the viewpoint that data gathered in Case II designs are of little use. Relevant to that position, Lord (1967) has stated that "there is no logical or statistical procedure that can be counted on to make proper allowances for pre-existing differences between (treatment) groups" (p. 305). The second opinion concerning this question (and we align ourselves with this opinion) is that the results of carefully analyzed Case II designs do supply useful evaluation information. Harnquist (1968) stated:

Even if the initial standing of the subjects is controlled by means of a number of relevant variables, there will always be room for uncontrolled differences that may be important. The investigator, who because of the nature of his problem cannot use random or systematic assignment of subjects to treatments, has to live with an insecurity in that respect—and try to behave intelligently within the limitations of his design—or leave the scene of non-experimental research (p. 57).

We agree totally with the position that random assignment is a worthwhile goal which should be pursued diligently in each evaluation. Nevertheless, even when random assignment is accomplished, the researcher is not "home free." There must still be vigilance and concern about confounding variables which belong to the second category of confounding variables described above. The "insecurity" Harnquist refers to is only quantitatively not qualitatively different when random assignment has been employed. Random assignment represents a "long run" solution to the category of confounding variables due to systematic between-treatment differences at the outset of the study, but it does not insure, even in the long run, that all systematic differences between treatment groups during the study are due to program differences. An obvious example is a design where students are randomly assigned to treatment groups, but then one instructor administers a treatment to one group and another instructor administers a different treatment to the other group. Despite random assignment and thus control over potential confounding variables at the outset of the study, numerous confounding variables can enter the design while the study is being conducted, e.g., instructors are confounded with treatments. Our earlier concern for correct identification of the experimental unit helps to avoid but does not rule out such possibilities. While we feel random assignment is an important goal when designing evaluation studies, even once accomplished, there is no logical or statistical procedure that can be *counted on* to make proper allowance for all confounding. Therefore, the interpretation of results from designs lacking random assignment requires a quantitative, rather than a qualitative, increase in tentativeness above and beyond what would have been required had random assignment been employed. Finally, we are not in any way trying to say or even imply that any known statistical adjustment is an adequate substitute for random

Table 8*

Data Matrix for a Case II Evaluation

Treatments	Sexes	Individuals	X	Y	Y-X	$\hat{X}$
T_1	S_1	I_1	8	14	6	8.4
		I_2	11	17	6	10.8
		I_3	12	16	4	11.6
		I_4	9	13	4	9.2
		I_5	10	15	5	10.0
	S_2	I_6	10	15	5	10.0
		I_7	9	13	4	9.2
		I_8	8	14	6	8.4
		I_9	12	16	4	11.6
		I_{10}	11	17	6	10.8
T_2	S_1	I_{11}	20	20	0	20.0
		I_{12}	18	19	1	18.4
		I_{13}	19	18	-1	19.2
		I_{14}	21	22	1	20.8
		I_{15}	22	21	-1	21.6
	S_2	I_{16}	19	18	-1	19.2
		I_{17}	22	21	-1	21.6
		I_{18}	20	20	0	20.0
		I_{19}	21	22	1	20.8
		I_{20}	18	19	1	18.4

*See legend for Table 1.

assignment. We are, however, saying that some statistical adjustments are useful in ruling out, or at least diminishing, some factors which are rivals to treatments in explaining between treatment group differences.

Analysis of Covariance

One of the most frequently used analysis strategies for Case II–Situation A designs is ANCOVA with the pretest as the random covariate. The assumptions for the analysis are unchanged from Case I to Case II designs; however, the hypothesis tested and the statistical power must be reconsidered.

Consider a new example presented in Table 8. The design is identical to the design for the earlier example, but whereas there were no treatment differences on the pretest in the earlier example, the data in the new example reflect a treatment difference on the pretest as shown by the means reported in column one of Table 9. The 10-point pretest treatment difference is meant to be illustrative of the type of confounding that can occur when random assignment of units to treatments is not an aspect of the design.

The null hypothesis about treatments can be stated formally for the example as $\mu'_{Y_{1..}} = \mu'_{Y_{2..}}$ where $\mu'_{Y_{1..}}$ and $\mu'_{Y_{2..}}$ are the same adjusted means as reported in the Case I discussion of ANCOVA. Recalling that an adjusted population treatment mean is defined

Table 9*

Means for Data Presented in Table 8

	S	X	Y	Y-X	$\hat{X}$
T_1	S_1	10	15	5	10
	S_2	10	15	5	10
T_2	S_1	20	20	0	20
	S_2	20	20	0	20

*See legend for Table 1.

$\mu'_{Y_{T..}} = \mu_{Y_{T..}} - \beta_{Y.X}(\mu_{X_{T..}} - \mu_{X...})$ it no longer follows that the adjusted means reduce to their unadjusted counterpart, since for Case II designs there is no reason to believe that population treatment means on the covariate are equal to each other. Thus, the null hypothesis no longer is in agreement with the null hypothesis associated with ANOVA of posttest. The null hypothesis of interest to the evaluator is that there are no differences among population treatment means on the posttest after having adequately adjusted for the population treatment mean differences on the pretest. The key word in the last sentence is the word "adequately." The definition of an adjusted mean makes clear that ANCOVA using a pretest as the covariate addresses the question of whether or not treatment posttest means are equal after first subtracting $\beta_{Y.X}$ of treatment group differences on the pretest. The hypothesis tested is of interest given the following two assumptions:

(1)   the within treatment group relationship, $\beta_{Y.X}$, is predictive of the between treatment group differences in the posttest that are due to initial differences in the pretest (Evans and Anastasio, 1968; Linn and Werts, 1969), and

(2)   the pretest measures the effect of all confounding variables that also affect the posttest.

Although neither the first nor the second assumption is likely to be completely true for a summative evaluation, to the extent that they are valid assumptions, ANCOVA more closely tests the evaluator's hypothesis of interest than does ANOVA of the posttest. In the event the pretest is not perfectly reliable, however, results from ANCOVA are in general misleading for Case II designs as is shown in Special Note D at the end of this chapter.

Our conclusion thus far is that ANCOVA using X as the pretest for Case II designs should only be used when X is perfectly reliable (Special Note D). Although we feel that a perfectly reliable pretest is rarely available to the evaluator, if one is available, the statistical power of ANCOVA is of interest. It can be shown that the expected value of the mean square error for ANCOVA of Case II designs is identical to that for Case I designs. The adjusted mean square associated with the hypothesis being tested, however, is depressed to the extent that there are differences on the pretest for the hypothesis being tested and to the extent that the within cell variance on the pretest is small. These points are discussed in Special Note E at the end of this chapter.

Analysis of Variance of Index of Response

ANOVA of an index of response represents another commonly employed analysis strategy for Case II—Situation A designs, particularly when gain scores are not used as the index of response. Using the example provided in Table 8 the null hypothesis for treatments can be stated

$$\mu_{Z_{1..}} = \mu_{Z_{2..}},$$

where the μ's denote population treatment means on the index Z for treatments one and two. Recall that a population treatment mean on the index can be stated in terms of the pretest and posttest means as

$$\mu_{Z_{T..}} = \mu_{Y_{T..}} - K(\mu_{X_{T..}} - \mu_{X_{...}}).$$

It follows from the discussion of ANCOVA for Case II designs (Special Note D) that if K equals $\beta_{T_Y.T_X}$, the slope defined on the latent true variables, ANOVA of index of response more closely tests the hypothesis of interest than either ANCOVA using a less than perfectly reliable pretest as the covariate or ANOVA of the posttest.

Similar to Case I, the problem for the evaluator is to determine the value of $\beta_{T_Y.T_X}$ so that it can be used as K in the definition of the index of response. If the pretest and the posttest measure the same dimension with equal reliability, and if there is no true differential change in subjects on the dimension measured, it can be shown that $\beta_{T_Y.T_X}$ equals one. It follows that gain scores are the index which tests the hypothesis of interest to the evaluator. It should be noted that the assumptions are identical to those previously asserted as being necessary for ρ_{XX} to be the best value of K for Case I—Situation A designs (Special Note B).

A greater degree of caution is necessary when using index of response for Case II designs than for Case I designs. Recall that for Case I designs, ANOVA of index of response tested the hypothesis of interest to the evaluator regardless of the choice of K, and a whole range of values around the best value would improve statistical power over that of ANOVA of the posttest. For Case II designs, however, the *exact* correct choice of K is necessary to test the hypothesis of interest.

Referring to Figure 1 in Special Note E and realizing that K must equal the population slope defined on the latent true variables, the larger the between group difference on the pretest due to lack of random assignment, the larger the extrapolation associated with use of the index, and therefore, the greater the error in the hypothesis tested for even small discrepancies between K and $\beta_{T_Y \cdot T_X}$. For this reason we recommend the use of ANOVA of gain scores for Case II—Situation A designs only when the evaluator is certain that the underlying assumptions are met exactly. In our opinion, the assumptions are rarely, if ever, met exactly.

The examples presented in Tables 1 and 8 can be used to illustrate the use of gain scores for Case II—Situation A designs since the data were contrived to exactly fit the assumptions stated above. The results of an ANOVA of gain scores for the data in Table 8 are presented in Table 10. The F test for the treatment by sex interaction is zero and the F test for treatment is 125.00 which is statistically significant beyond the .05 level. It should be noted that the significant treatment effect is not in agreement with the potentially misleading ANCOVA results discussed previously. Further, it is important to see that the gain score means for treatments one and two, as calculated via the means reported in column three of Table 9, are 5 and 0, respectively. The

Table 10

Analysis of Variance of Gain Scores
Presented in Table 8

Sources	d.f.	SS	MS	F*
T	1	125	125	125.0
S	1	0	0	0
TxS	1	0	0	0
I:TS	16	16	1	

*Required $F \geq 4.49$ for $\alpha = .05$ and d.f. = 1, 16.

five-point difference between treatments is identical to the five-point difference between the corrected adjusted treatment means reported earlier, in the discussion of ANCOVA, as the real treatment differences.

For the example in Table 8, ANCOVA has not found true treatment differences that were found by the correct index of response. By referring to the sex effect for ANOVA of gain scores and ANCOVA analyses of the data reported in Table 1, it could be concluded further that ANCOVA can find spurious treatment effects which are eliminated by ANOVA of the correct index.

The assumptions for ANOVA of index of response are identical to those for Case I designs except that K should equal $\beta_{T_Y.T_X}$ rather than $\beta_{Y.X}$. The implications of this exception are presented in Special Note F.

Estimated True Scores Analysis of Covariance

Estimated true scores ANCOVA is an analysis strategy which was developed specifically to correct for the bias in ANCOVA for Case II designs where the covariable is less then perfectly reliable. Using the example presented in Table 8 the null hypothesis for treatments is $\mu'_{Y_{1..}} = \mu'_{Y_{2..}}$ where the μ's are the population adjusted treatment means for treatments one and two. As stated in Case I, population adjusted treatment means for estimated true scores ANCOVA are defined as

$$\mu'_{Y_{T..}} = \mu_{Y_{T..}} - \beta_{Y.\hat{X}}(\mu_{X_{T..}} - \mu_{X...}) .$$

Since
$$\beta_{Y.\hat{X}} = (1/\rho_{XX}) \beta_{Y.X} ,$$

and
$$\beta_{T_Y.T_X} = (1/\rho_{XX}) \beta_{Y.X} ,$$

estimated true scores ANCOVA tests for equality of adjusted means on the latent true variables, which is the hypothesis of interest to the evaluator. In other words, substituting estimated true pretest scores for observed pretest scores as the covariate in ANCOVA adjusts for the less than perfect reliability of the covariable.

The results of an estimated true scores ANCOVA for the data

Table 11

Analysis of Covariance on the Posttest Data in Table 8 Using $\hat{X}$ as the Covariable

Sources	d.f.	$SS_{\hat{X}}$	SS_Y	$SS_{\hat{X}Y}$	SS_Y'	d.f.'	MS_Y'	F*
T	1	500	125	250	6.1	1	6.1	6.34
S	1	0	0	0	0	1	0	0
TxS	1	0	0	0	0	1	0	0
I:TS	16	25.6	40	25.6	14.4	15	.96	

*Required F $\geq$ 4.54 for α = .05 with d.f. = 1, 15.

presented in Table 8 are reported in Table 11. The estimated true scores for use as the covariable are also reported in Table 8 and as before were calculated by the formula

$$\hat{X}_{TSI} = \overline{X}_{TS.} - \rho_{XX}(X_{TSI} - \overline{X}_{TS.}),$$

where ρ_{XX} equals .8 to be consistent with the gain scores analysis. Several of the results in Table 11 are of interest. First, the conclusions for all three hypotheses are consistent with the correct ANOVA of gain score results presented earlier. Second, the within cells slope of the regression line is

$$b_{Y.\hat{X}} = \frac{SS_{\hat{X}Y_{I:TS}}}{SS_{\hat{X}_{I:TS}}} = \frac{25.6}{25.6} = 1.$$

This is consistent with the use of K equal to one for gain scores and is also consistent with $\beta_{Y.\hat{X}} = (1/\rho_{XX})\beta_{Y.X}$, since $b_{Y.\hat{X}} = (1/.8).8 = 1$, where .8 is both the value of ρ_{XX} and the value of $b_{Y.X}$ previously calculated for the data in Table 8 (Special Note D). The adjusted treatment means are calculated using the formula

$$\overline{Y}_{T..}^{\textstyle*} = \overline{Y}_{T..} - b_{Y.\hat{X}}(\overline{X}_{T..} - \overline{X}_{...}),$$

and the means via Table 9 are 20 and 15 for treatments one and two, respectively. As should be for this special problem, these means are identical to those reported for gain scores. It should be noted that parallel arguments hold for the treatment by sex interaction and the sex main effect. Third, the mean square error for estimated true scores ANCOVA is identical in value to the mean square error for ANCOVA using observed pretest scores as the covariate.

Although the estimated true scores ANCOVA and the ANOVA of gain scores tested the same hypotheses and reached the same conclusions for the example, it must be pointed out that their F test results were not identical. The treatment F test for gain scores reported in Table 10 was 125.0 and had 16 degrees of freedom for error, while the estimated true scores ANCOVA treatment F test was only 6.34 with 15 degrees of freedom error. Clearly the ANOVA of gain scores procedure had, and has in general, greater statistical power when K is correctly set equal to $\beta_{T_Y \cdot T_X}$. Recall, however, that ANOVA of an index of response only tests the correct hypothesis when the evaluator knows the value of $\beta_{T_Y \cdot T_X}$, i.e., the slope defined on the latent true variables, and that this is rarely if ever the case. Further, small discrepancies between K and $\beta_{T_Y \cdot T_X}$ can cause big errors in the hypothesis tested. On the other hand, estimated true scores ANCOVA estimates the slope defined on the latent true variables from the data and, therefore, tests the hypothesis of interest to the evaluator even when the value of $\beta_{T_Y \cdot T_X}$ is unknown. Special Note G provides further consideration of the statistical power of estimated true scores AN-COVA.

The assumptions for estimated true scores ANCOVA are identical to those for ANCOVA when the reliability of the covariate is known. This is because estimated true scores are a linear transformation of the pretest within a cell of the design, and the procedures are computationally identical once the estimated true scores are substituted for the original observations.

The need to know, or at least estimate, the reliability of the covariable necessitates a choice of what type of reliability coefficient to use. This problem has been considered by several researchers but as yet there is little agreement. Our belief is that the reliability should be a parallel forms estimate, or if that is impossible, a short time lapse test-retest estimate. We recommend, when there is doubt as to the correct value of the reliability coefficient to use in calculating estimated true scores, that a range of likely values be considered. Then two estimated true scores ANCOVAs should be done, one using the largest and one using the smallest reliability coefficient in the range. If the results are the same for both analyses of covariance, the dilemma is avoided. If the results differ, conclusions must be more tentative, but a range of values of the reliability might be determined for which program effects are significant.

It should be realized that, when an estimate of the reliability rather than the parameter is used, ANCOVA using estimated true scores provides an approximate rather than exact test. The quality of the approximation has been investigated for a variety of situations (Porter, 1967) and has been found to be well within the bounds necessary for the procedure to have practical utility. Use of multiple covariates is a problem that is currently being considered. At present the solution is believed to be known, if population reliabilities are known, and work is now concentrating on the quality of the test when reliabilities are estimated. The solution is not, however, a straightforward substitution of estimated true scores for each covariate as it is in the single covariate case.

Summary: Case II–Situation A

In summary, for Case II–Situation A designs, ANOVA of the posttest is seriously affected by initial differences due to lack of random assignment and, therefore, is not a viable analysis strategy. The usual procedure of using ANCOVA with a pretest as the covariate is only appropriate for a perfectly reliable pretest. ANOVA of index of response tests the hypothesis of interest to the evaluator when K is set to equal the slope of the regression line for predicting latent true posttest from latent true pretest. In the rare event that the value of the population slope defined on the latent true variables is known exactly, ANOVA of index of response will generally provide the most powerful test of the hypotheses of interest. The evaluator is warned, however, that even minor discrepancies can cause major alterations in the hypothesis tested.

ANCOVA using estimated true scores as the covariate was shown to test the hypothesis of interest to the evaluator without requiring knowledge of the population slope. Thus, of the analysis strategies considered for Case II–Situation A, ANCOVA using estimated true scores is the analysis of greatest applicability.

Our presentation for Case II designs relied completely on analysis strategies for controlling confounding variables which are reflected in the covariate, and made the assumption that within cell regression lines are accurate predictors of between cell confounding. The procedure of matching units in treatment groups is a design strategy which might also be considered (Porter and Chibucos, 1972). Campbell and Erlebacher (1970) have demonstrated that matching on less than perfectly reliable antecedent information results in the same kinds of misleading conclusions that we noted for ANCOVA of Case II designs. It can be shown (Thorndike, 1942) that matching on estimated true scores, however, avoids the problem. As noted for Case I, matching does not require a linear relationship between the covariate and the dependent variable. Further, since use of matching does not rely on the within cell regression line for predicting the posttest from the covariable, it does not require that the regression line be predictive of posttest differences.

Case II—Situation B

Case II—Situation B is identical to Case II—Situation A except that the antecedent variable, X, is not a pretest. Frequently, when random assignment has not been employed and no pretest was given, it is because formal program comparisons were not originally planned. There are at least two reasons why such a situation seems unlikely to provide interpretable data on the relative merits of the program being evaluated. First, it is generally believed that information on a pretest is the best single source of information about potential confounding effects reflected in the posttest. Second, unless evaluation was a prominent concern from the outset, it is likely that obvious non-program related differences that occurred during the initial phases of program implementation will have been forgotten by the time of data interpretation. Such differences represent the source of potentially important confounding variables which, if overlooked when interpreting the results of the evaluation, might completely reverse the conclusions reached. Probably the most notorious example of a Case II—Situation B evaluation design is the Westinghouse—Ohio University study of the national Headstart program (Campbell and Erlebacher, 1970; Porter, 1969).

There is another possibility as to why Case II—Situation B designs arise in evaluation studies. It is sometimes true that the same test cannot be used as both pretest and posttest. For example, the Follow Through program typically starts in kindergarten and extends through third grade. An achievement test appropriate for beginning kindergarten students would hopefully have a serious ceiling effect when given to students at the end of their third grade.

Most of the comparisons of analysis strategies for Case II—Situation A did not require that X be a pretest and to that extent those arguments apply equally well to Situation B. The arguments necessary for concluding that gain scores test the desired hypothesis were dependent upon some rather restrictive assumptions that seem unlikely to be met unless the antecedent variable is a pretest. The conclusion is that ANCOVA using estimated true scores as the covariable is the best procedure for Case II—Situation B designs except in the rare event where the slope defined on the latent true variables is known. If the slope is known, ANOVA of index of response is the preferred analysis strategy.

Chapter Summary

Four general classes of designs typically used in evaluation studies were identified and for each the following analysis strategies were considered: analysis of covariance using a random covariate, analysis of variance of an index of response including gain scores as a special case, repeated measures analysis of variance, and analysis of covariance using estimated true scores as the covariate. The criteria used to compare the analysis strategies were the hypothesis tested, the assumptions made, and the statistical power of the analyses for testing the hypothesis.

Repeated measures ANOVA with pretest as one measure and posttest as the other measure, and ANOVA of gain scores were shown to be identical in all respects. Because of a relatively large expected mean square error, use of gain scores for Case I designs should be avoided; however, the index $Z = Y - \rho_{XX}X$ was argued to have utility for some Case I–Situation A designs. The reliability of indices of response was considered and an argument made that despite their generally low (sometimes zero) reliability, their use can result in greater statistical power than would be obtained by ignoring the antecedent information. When information is not available for forming an index of response, classical ANCOVA is the preferred analysis strategy for Case I–Situations A and B.

For Case II designs, classical ANCOVA should only be used when the covariable is measured with perfect reliability. For some Case II–Situation A designs gain scores were seen to test the desired hypotheses, but some rather restrictive assumptions must be met exactly. Therefore, estimated true scores ANCOVA was the preferred analysis strategy. It was argued that Case II–Situation B designs are not desirable, but may be necessary for longitudinal studies. When they are necessary, ANCOVA using estimated true scores provides the best strategy of those strategies considered in detail.

For Case II designs, both the analysis strategies discussed in detail and matching on estimated true scores have unique advantages and weaknesses. Since we do not feel that any one strategy can be relied on to control all confounding variables we recommend a multiple strategy approach. Where results are invariant across strategies the evaluator can be more firm in his conclusions. Where different strategies result in different conclusions the evaluator is appropriately warned as to the tentativeness of his conclusions.

An evaluator conducting a summative evaluation must take the position that there is no design and/or analysis strategy which can be counted on to garner unimpeachable evidence as to a program's success or lack of success relative to an alternative. Certainly there are the elements of chance which are reflected in making statistical errors. There may be, however, far more important factors at work, which are labeled confounding variables, i.e., factors which are not defined as part of the program, but which distinguish the experiences of program participants from those in the comparison group. Although we have argued that confounding variables are far less likely for designs employing random assignment, they are not ruled out. When such factors are recognized at the conclusion of an evaluation they must be taken into account during the interpretation of results. Common sense and vigilance are the best remedies we know, both for guarding against the intrusion of confounding variables and for dealing with them when they are present.

Special Note A

Assumption of Equal Slopes

The assumption of equal slopes is a special case of the assumption of additivity made to facilitate interpretation in ANOVA. In particular, if there is no treatment by covariable interaction, then the assumption of equal slopes across values of T is met. Since the hypothesis of interest is in terms of the latent variables, we assume that the slopes of Y on X for latent variables are equal across T; however, since the hypothesis is tested using the observed variables, it is also required that the slopes defined on the observed variables be equal. Given equal slopes for the latent variables, and that the reliability of X is equal across all values of T, it follows that the slopes for the observed variables must be equal. Therefore, the assumption "$\beta_{Y.X}$ is a constant across all values of T" could be restated better that: (a) the slope of the latent variables is a constant across all values of T; (b) the reliability of X is a constant across all values of T.

We should note that in practice we would have preceded the ANCOVA tests of hypotheses with a statistical test of the equality of within cell slopes (see Winer, 1971). Our example data, however, were contrived to exactly meet the assumption that $\beta_{Y.X}$ is constant across all levels of the treatment. It is very important to emphasize that concern for meeting this assumption should be just as great for ANOVA as for ANCOVA. In either case, if the assumption is violated, then the conclusion is that a treatment by covariable interaction exists. The difference between ANOVA and ANCOVA in this regard is that for ANCOVA, the evaluator deliberately tries to select a covariable that meets the assumption, whereas in ANOVA the choice of a covariable is not made. Rather, with the latter procedure, the evaluator attempts to argue on a logical basis, from related research for example, that treatment by potential covariable interactions are not present in the data. For both ANOVA and ANCOVA the evaluator needs to understand treatment by "other potential independent variable" interactions prior to interpreting main effects. The fact that ANOVA of the posttest only does not provide a test for the interaction in no way implies that such interactions are not present in the data.

Special Note B

Defining K for Index of Response in Case I–Situation A

Assume that the pretest and the posttest measure the same dimension and that there is no true differential change on the dimension in the units of analysis between the time of the pretest and the time of the posttest. The two assumptions seem likely for short-term studies, but merit carefully scrutiny for long-term studies (Bereiter, 1963; Lord, 1958). Further, assume that the reliability of the pretest is equal to the reliability of the posttest. Given classical measurement theory it follows that $\sigma_X^2 = \sigma_Y^2$ and since

$$\beta_{Y.X} = \rho_{XY} \frac{\sigma_Y}{\sigma_X},$$

it further follows that

$$\beta_{Y.X} = \rho_{XY},$$

i.e., the slope for the regression of the posttest on the pretest equals the correlation between pretest and posttest. Again considering the assumption of additivity, treatment effects should make the latent true posttest a linear transformation of the latent true pretest within each cell of the design. Since linear transformations do not affect the magnitude of a linear correlation, ρ_{XY} is like a test-retest reliability coefficient, ρ_{XX}, where the time lag is the period of time between the pretest and the posttest. Since it has been argued that the slope, $\beta_{Y.X}$, should equal the test-retest reliability, ρ_{XX}, given the additional assumptions described above, the index of response can be defined

$$Z = Y - \rho_{XX}X .$$

Special Note C

Reliability of Indices of Response

Although indices of response can be shown in general to have relatively low reliability, the low reliability is not a valid reason for rejecting their use in analyzing Case I designs. The earlier statement that the expected value of the mean square error for an index of response is less than the expected value of the mean square error for ANOVA of the posttest when $0 < K/\beta_{Y.X} < 2$ still stands.

The apparent contradiction between low reliability and good statistical power can be explained by considering the definitional formula for the reliability of an index,

$$\rho_{ZZ} = \frac{\sigma^2_{T_Z}}{\sigma^2_{Z}} ,$$

where ρ_{ZZ} is the reliability of the index Z, $\sigma^2_{T_Z}$ is the variance of the index defined on the latent true pretest and posttest variables (i.e., the pretest and posttest free from errors of measurement), and σ^2_Z is the variance of the index defined on the observed pretest and posttest. Given the earlier described assumptions of no true differential maturation of units during the study, that the pretest and posttest measure the same dimension and that any true treatment effects are the same for all units in a cell of the design, it can be shown that $\sigma^2_{T_Z} = 0$ when $K = \beta_{Y.X}/\rho_{XX}$. It follows directly that the reliability of Z is then zero. Further, given the same assumptions, ρ_{XY} is as high as the reliability of the pretest and posttest will allow. The same assumptions that make the reliability of an index zero are the assumptions that facilitate large values of ρ_{XY}. The larger ρ_{XY}, the smaller the expected value of the mean square error for an index of response and the better its statistical power. Given $K = \beta_{Y.X}/\rho_{XX}$ and thus $\rho_{ZZ} = 0$, it can be shown that when $.5 < \rho_{XX} < 1$, the expected mean square error for ANOVA of Z is less than the expected mean square error for ANOVA of the posttest. Thus, even an index having zero reliability can provide a more powerful test for treatment effects than ANOVA of the posttest only.

Special Note D

ANCOVA With an Unreliable Covariable

The evaluator's hypotheses are always in terms of the latent true variables which are free from errors of measurement. Given classical measurement theory assumptions, a population mean of a latent true variable is equal to the population mean of the observed variable which almost always contains error of measurement. Since the hypotheses associated with the analysis strategies for Case I designs were in terms of population means only, errors of measurement in the observed variables in no way compromised the hypotheses tested. For Case II the null hypothesis for ANCOVA involves $\beta_{Y.X}$, the slope of the regression line for predicting posttest differences from pretest differences. It can be shown that $\beta_{TY.TX} = (1/\rho_{XX}) \beta_{Y.X}$ where ρ_{XX} denotes the reliability of the pretest and $\beta_{TY.TX}$ denotes the slope of Y on X for the latent true variables. Since in general ρ_{XX} is less than one, in general $\beta_{Y.X}$ is less than $\beta_{TY.TX}$. The conclusion is that since the hypotheses are in terms of the latent true variables, ANCOVA using a pretest as the covariate removes from the posttest mean differences too little of the pretest mean differences, and thus does not test the hypothesis of interest to the evaluator (Lord, 1960; Porter, 1967; Smith, 1957). Parallel arguments apply for the treatment by sex interaction null hypothesis.

The example presented in Table 8 can serve to partially illustrate some of these points. The results from ANCOVA using X as the pretest are reported in Table 12 where it is seen that the F tests for sex and treatment by sex interaction are zero, and that the F test for treatment is 3.47 which is not significant at the .05 level. The conclusion is that there are no significant differences anywhere in the design. The sample estimate of the slope used to calculate adjusted treatment means can be calculated from the data in Table 12

$$b_{Y.X} = \frac{SS_{XY_{I:TS}}}{SS_{X_{I:TS}}} = \frac{32}{40} = .8 .$$

The sample adjusted treatment means are then calculated by the formula

$$\overline{Y}'_{T..} = \overline{Y}_{T..} - b_{Y.X}(\overline{X}_{T..} - \overline{X}...)$$

and, via Table 9, are 19 and 16 for treatments one and two respectively. As indicated earlier, however, $\beta_{Y.X}$ is too small if the reliability of X is less than one. Correcting $b_{Y.X}$ for the unreliability of X (multiplying it by $1/\rho_{XX}$) results in a corrected sample slope of 1. Using the corrected sample slope the sample adjusted means are 20 for treatment one and 15 for treatment two, the *reverse* of unadjusted means shown in Table 9. The corrected difference of five points between treatments is two points larger than the ANCOVA three-point difference and may

Table 12

Analysis of Covariance of Posttest Data Presented in Table 8 Using X as the Covariable

Sources	d.f.	SS_X	SS_Y	SS_{XY}	SS_Y'	d.f.'	MS_Y'	F*
T	1	500	125	250	3.4	1	3.4	3.47
S	1	0	0	0	0	1	0	0
TxS	1	0	0	0	0	1	0	0
I:TS	16	40	40	32	14.4	15	.96	

*F must be ≥ 4.54 to be statistically significant at $\alpha = .05$, for 1 and 15 d.f.

be statistically significant. The conclusion is that if the reliability of the pretest were .8 rather than 1, ANCOVA tested the wrong null hypothesis and for that reason may have been insensitive to a true treatment effect.

Special Note E

The Power of ANCOVA for Case II Designs

Using treatments as an example, inspection of Figure 1 may shed some light on why the initial differences on the pretest should depress the adjusted mean square for treatments and so decrease the statistical power of the ANCOVA F test. In Figure 1, the lines labeled T_1 and T_2 denote the population within cell regression lines for each treatment and the line labeled "a" is a point on X where the population adjusted means are calculated. The distance from "d" to "e" represents the difference between the population-adjusted treatment means. The central point to be made is that calculation of adjusted treatment means requires extrapolation on X using the regression lines. Since ANCOVA estimates the slope of the regression lines from the sample data, the estimate may by chance be either too high or too low. When the extrapolation is made using the sample regression lines, the adjusted means may, therefore, be either too close or too far apart. The greater the initial differences on the pretest, the further the extrapolation must be, and the greater the sampling error of the differences between adjusted means due to sampling error in estimating the slope of the regression lines.

Special Note F

The Power of ANOVA of Index of Response
for Case II Designs

The expected value of the mean square error is the same as given for Case I,

$$\sigma_Z^2 = \sigma_Y^2 (1 - \rho_{XY}^2) + a^2 \sigma_X^2 \,,$$

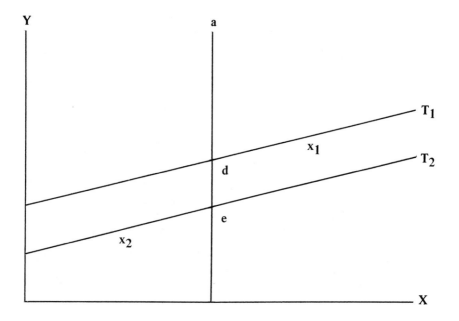

Figure 1. Population Regression Lines for Two Treatment Groups.

X: Covariable

Y: Posttest

T_1 and T_2: Treatments one and two

x_1, x_2: The point of the population means for treatments one and two

The vertical line denoted "a" defines the point on X where T_1 and T_2 are compared.

where $a = \beta_{Y.X} - K$. Unfortunately when X is not perfectly reliable $\beta_{Y.X}$ is not equal to $\beta_{TY.TX}$ which is the necessary value of K in order that the analysis strategy test the hypothesis of interest to the evaluator. It follows that the mean square error is inflated to the extent that the reliability of X is less than one.

The same relationship between the expected mean square errors of ANCOVA and ANOVA of index of response holds for Case II as for Case I when the antecedent information is perfectly reliable. The mean square for treatments in ANOVA of index of response, however, is not depressed by the factors which were noted to depress the adjusted mean square for treatments in ANCOVA since the extrapolation does not vary with the estimate of the slope. The conclusion is that for Case II designs with a perfectly reliable pretest the statistical power of ANOVA of the correct index of response is greater than that for ANCOVA. The evaluator must remember, however, that ANOVA of index of response tests the wrong null hypothesis except when $\beta_{TY.TX}$ is known exactly, but ANCOVA with a perfectly reliable covariable tests the correct hypothesis of interest even when the value of $\beta_{TY.TX}$ is not known.

Special Note G

Statistical Power of Estimated True Scores ANCOVA

The lower power of estimated true scores ANCOVA can be understood by recalling the earlier discussion of the statistical power of ANCOVA using a perfectly reliable covariate in Case II designs. In that discussion it was pointed out that the adjusted mean square for treatments is depressed by two factors, i.e., the extent of initial differences on the covariate and the within cell variance of the covariate. Since estimated true scores ANCOVA and ANCOVA using a pretest as the covariate are computationally equivalent, given the substitution of covariables, the same factors depress the adjusted mean square for treatments for both ANCOVA procedures. As seen earlier the initial differences are identical whether estimated true pretest scores or observed pretest scores are used. The adjustment which causes estimated true scores to test the hypothesis of interest does so, however, by reducing the within cell variance of the covariate by a factor equal to the reliability of the covariate. This causes a further depression to the adjusted mean square for treatments. All of this may be misleading since ANCOVA using observed pretest scores as the covariate only tests the correct hypothesis when the covariate is perfectly reliable. It follows from the above arguments that when the covariate is perfectly reliable the two procedures have identical power.

Suggested Readings

Campbell, D.T., and Stanley, J.C. *Experimental and quasi-experimental designs for research.* Chicago: Rand McNally, 1966.

> This classic is a must for anyone interested in educational research and evaluation. Campbell and Stanley's treatment of internal validity serves as an excellent introduction to categories of potentially confounding variables for Case II designs.

Cox, D.R. *Planning of experiments.* New York: Wiley, 1958.

> The first seven chapters are most relevant to the issues addressed in the present chapter. Cox deals with such topics as the importance of comparative studies, experimental unit, assumption of additivity, factorial designs, random assignment, and use of ANCOVA, ANOVA of index of response and blocking to increase statistical power.

Elashoff, J.D. Analysis of covariance: A delicate instrument. *American Educational Research Journal,* 1969, *6,* 383-401.

> A thorough discussion of analysis of covariance.

Kerlinger, F.N. *Foundations of behavioral research.* (2nd ed.) New York: Holt, Rinehart and Winston, 1973.

> Chapters 14, 15, and 21 are most relevant to the issues addressed in the present chapter, although chapters 17-20 and 22 might also be considered. Kerlinger's coverage of topics is at an elementary level and avoids detail.

Winer, B.J. *Statistical principles in experimental design.* New York: McGraw-Hill, 1971.

> Chapters 5 and 10 are particularly relevant for those interested in analysis of variance and covariance computations.

References

Bereiter, C. Some persisting dilemmas in the measurement of change. In C.W. Harris (Ed.), *Problems in measuring change.* Madison, Wisconsin: University of Wisconsin Press, 1963.

Bock, R.D. Multivariate statistical methods in behavioral research. Unpublished manuscript, Statistical Laboratory, Department of Education, University of Chicago, 1971.

Campbell, D.T. and Erlebacher, A. How regression artifacts in quasi-experimental evaluations can mistakenly make compensatory education look harmful. In J. Hellmuth (Ed.), *Compensatory education: A national debate.* Vol. III. *The disadvantaged child.* New York: Brunner/Mazel, 1970, 185-210.

Campbell, D.T., and Stanley, J.C. Experimental and quasi-experimental designs for research on teaching. In N.L. Gage (Ed.), *Handbook of research on teaching.* Chicago: Rand McNally, 1963, 171-246.

Cox, D.R. The use of a concomitant variable in selecting an experimental design. *Biometrika,* 1957, *44*, 150-158.

Cox, D.R. *Planning of experiments.* New York: Wiley, 1958.

Elashoff, J.D. Analysis of covariance: A delicate instrument. *American Educational Research Journal,* 1969, *6*, 383-401.

Evans, S.H., and Anastasio, E.J. Misuse of analysis of covariance when treatment effect and covariance are confounded. *Psychological Bulletin,* 1968, *69*, 225-234.

Feldt, L.S. A comparison of the precision of three experimental designs employing a concomitant variable. *Psychometrika,* 1958, *23*, 335-353.

Glass, G.V., Peckham, P.D., and Sanders, J.R. Consequences of failure to meet assumptions underlying the analysis of variance and covariance. *Review of Educational Research,* 1972, *42*, 237-288.

Harnquist, K. Relative changes in intelligence from 13 to 18. *Scandinavian Journal of Psychology,* 1968, *9*, 50-82.

Jennings, E. Linear models underlying the analysis of covariance, residual gain scores and raw gain scores. Paper presented at the meeting of the American Educational Research Association, 1972.

Linn, R.L., and Werts, C.E. Assumptions in making causal inferences from part correlations, partial correlations, and partial regression coefficients. *Psychological Bulletin,* 1969, *72*, 307-310.

Lord, F.M. Further problems in the measurement of growth. *Educational and Psychological Measurement,* 1958, *18*, 437-454.

Lord, F.M. Large-sample covariance analysis when the control variable is fallible. *Journal of American Statistical Association,* 1960, *55*, 307-321.

Lord, F.M. A paradox in the interpretation of group comparisons. *Psychological Bulletin,* 1967, *68*, 304-305.

Porter, A.C. *The effects of using fallible variables in the analysis of covariance.* Doctoral dissertation, University of Wisconsin, Madison, Wisconsin, 1967.

Porter, A.C. Comments on some current strategies to evaluate the effectiveness of compensatory education programs. Paper presented at the meeting of the American Psychological Association, 1969.

Porter, A.C. Analysis strategies for some common evaluation paradigms. Paper presented at the meeting of the American Educational Research Association, 1973.

Porter, A.C., and Chibucos, T.R. Some design and analysis concerns for quasi-experiments such as Follow Through and Head Start. Paper presented at the meeting of the American Psychological Association, 1972.

Smith, F.H. Interpretation of adjusted treatment means and regressions in analysis of covariance. *Biometrics,* 1957, *13*, 282-307.

Stanley, J.C. Analysis of variance of gain scores when initial assignment is random. *Journal of Educational Measurement,* 1966, *3*, 179-182.

Thorndike, R.L. Regression fallacies in the matched groups experiment. *Psychometrika,* 1942, 7, 85-102.

Winer, B.J. *Statistical principles in experimental design.* New York: McGraw-Hill, 1971.

EPILOGUE

EPILOGUE: SHIFTING EDUCATIONAL REALITIES AND THE LEARNER VERIFICATION OF INSTRUCTIONAL MATERIALS

P. Kenneth Komoski
Educational Products Information Exchange

A number of long-standing realities related to development, evaluation, selection, and use of instructional materials have been undergoing important and far-reaching changes in recent years. Together, these shifting realities will work profound changes during the 1970s in the nature of instructional materials. What follows is an attempt to describe these shifts and the changes they portend—particularly for those involved in product development and evaluation.

First of all, it is important to recognize that during the first three years of the 1970s, the standard textbook, the once universal omnibus of American public instruction, has begun losing considerable ground economically and pedagogically to other instructional media. In many school systems, the central textbook repository, with its large inventory of hardcover volumes distributed annually in September for daily prescribed use by teachers and students, is slowly being replaced by decentralized instructional materials centers (IMCs) where teachers and even in some cases students themselves select instructional resources from many hundreds of books, tapes, films, "kits," and multimedia materials. Of course, the book is far from dead, but its instructional role in relation to other media is being redelineated.

A shift considered by some educators to be long overdue from textbook-centered, standardized instruction toward student-centered, less standardized, more individualized learning, is well underway. As it gathers force, it will lead to a future filled with a greater and greater variety of instructional media—of increasingly "optionized," "individualized," and "personalized" curriculum programs. This multimediated future, which seems not simply achievable but inevitable, is viewed as both desirable and refreshingly profitable by educational publishers faced with the important reality shift which results from recent demographic and economic developments.

The salient movement within that shift is the leveling off of elementary and secondary school enrollments in response to decreases in birthrate. Thus, textbook publishers who have been part of a growth industry (with reasonable per-unit profit enhanced by guaranteed annual increases in total unit sales) during the last quarter century must now try to sell a larger number of products each year to a market in which the number of product users becomes smaller each year. The projected industry-wide sales figures for 1973 is over $500,000,000 for the first time in history, but that is very misleading. It is based on increased costs and prices rather than on significant increases in sales or profits, which do not in fact exist.

A number of solutions to current profit problems are being pragmatically pursued by the education industry and, needless to say, increasing interest in individualized instruction and personalized curriculum programs using multimedia materials is highly compatible with these product development and marketing "solutions."

One solution is to market more audio-visual products, which can be produced more quickly than books and with a higher profit margin. A partial (but more cumbersome) solution is to construct all products of consumable components which offer a high rate of replacement sales. Both these strategies are now comparatively common within the education industry. Another more risky, and therefore less usual, strategy is to sell a variety of products that cater to specialized markets within education: products targeted for use by teachers and learners with differing capabilities and styles, products designed for use in distinctively different educational contexts, products for the "home market," etc. Unfortunately, the producers really do not know which of these solutions to bet on, or whether to hedge their bets by pursuing them all simultaneously. More than that, their instincts tell them that the textbook is far from finished as a useful market item. They suspect that it is about to become the "loss leader" for the education industry (i.e., the product on which one makes very little, if any, profit, but which encourages the purchasers to buy more of one's other, more profitable, merchandise). Thus, once a school system buys a given textbook, it is a prime market for the publisher's "correlated," "individualized," "multimediated" materials. The fact that many school systems tend to confine their buying in a given curriculum area to one publisher bodes well for short-term solutions based on this assumption.

A radical and commercially more risky alternative to the textbook-plus-correlated-materials approach is the development of generated-from-scratch comprehensive instructional systems. They can produce high profits because the often enormous product development costs are usually underwritten by federal or foundation funds. But unless federal dollars for such product development centers are increased enormously, or granted jointly or outright to commercial producers wishing to share in or to undertake on their own the in-house development of such comprehensive systems, this does not look like an industry-wide solution. Many companies will be reluctant to undertake such development completely on their own, without the built-in market that tends to accompany federally-funded materials development. But, given recent statements issued by the National Institute of Education, such federally subsidized product development by private industry is a real possibility, and one which would produce another significant shift within the educational marketplace.

Another long-standing reality in connection with instructional materials which has begun to undergo change during the seventies has to do with purchaser expectations and demands. This shift is occurring more slowly than most others, perhaps because it is more fundamental and in the long run will have a more profound effect on the marketplace and on the ultimate educational consumer, the learner. Also, it relates more directly to product evaluation than do some of the others. For these reasons, it deserves a longer look.

Traditionally, the expectations and the demands of most school purchasers regarding instructional materials have centered on factors such as the product's physical construction, its costs, and its content, rather than on its direct effects and discernible affects on learners and teachers. A survey of materials selection practices conducted by the Educational Products Information Exchange Institute in 1969 for eight sponsoring state education departments revealed that, after carefully examining construction and cost factors, local and state selection groups invested most of their prepurchase time and energy in checking the content (i.e., validity for and compatibility with the local curriculum, educational philosophy, and social values) of materials under consideration, sometimes demanding that producers add or delete specific content in order to insure acceptability. The larger the potential purchase, the greater the chance that such demands would be answered with action by the producer. The study also indicated, however, that purchasers neither demanded nor expected to find available evidence regarding the direct instructional effects and indirect motivational effects of materials under consideration. In only one case did the survey uncover a school system which systematically gathered empirical evidence of product effectiveness based on limited local classroom use. A recent follow-up to this study concluded that as of 1972 most local and state systems were still concentrating their selection efforts on judging the content of the materials and deciding whether they would hold up under year-long daily use by students (i.e., How good is its coverage? How good is its cover?).

Once those matters have been decided in the affirmative and a material has been chosen, then it is simply assumed that any teacher should be able to see to it that students learn the content of the material in question. It also seems to be assumed that if the selectors like the materials, the students and teachers will like them too. In other words, nobody seems to feel it necessary to measure either the effects or the affects resulting from the actual use of the materials.

There is, of course, a long tradition which assumes that teachers will be able to teach effectively and with positive affect, no matter what materials they may be required to use. But this tradition, like most, contains its share of mythology. The reality has always been that even teachers who are quite worthy of the name have not succeeded in teaching all learners very well using traditional textbooks. The tacit understanding has been that a good many learners would fail to learn no matter what materials were used. This has been accepted as a reality in American public education ever since the first textbooks and the first dropouts who failed to learn from them.

This reality became firmly institutionalized during the second half of the nineteenth century, when state legislatures made America the first country to guarantee (indeed, require) universal schooling for all children. Certainly that guaranteed universal schooling did not guarantee universal learning. All children were sent to school to learn, but it was not expected that all had the capacity or the motivation to learn—no matter how good the teacher and the teaching materials.

Evidence of this long-held view is found in the fact that until very recently no teacher has ever been held accountable for achieving a specified level of learning for each and every student within a class. Similarly, no textbook publisher has ever been actually *required* to provide evidence that his materials have measurably helped teachers and learners achieve such a specified level of learning.

Today, however, the interrelated demands for equal educational opportunity, educational accountability, and individualized instruction, are in the process of making such demands and expectations a part of the shifting realities which are affecting all aspects of education and not least the instructional materials field.

Within the last year the California legislature has passed two laws that reflect the new view. The first of the laws does, in effect, hold teachers accountable for individual student learning at legislated state-wide levels. The second law holds instructional materials producers accountable for gathering "learner-verification" evidence that can be used by educators to judge the extent to which instructional materials contribute positively to student achievement. The implications of these two laws have been underscored in a current California court case in which a school system is being sued for failing to instruct a student successfully in fundamental curriculum areas such as reading and mathematics.

Clearly, these legislative and legal actions have implications so great that in time no aspect of development, marketing, selecting, buying, and use of instructional materials will remain unaffected. Already, in California, teachers have begun to maintain that they cannot be held accountable for specific levels of achievement with particular learners if they are required to teach with materials which are not, in their judgments, appropriate for the learners and targeted to the specified learning objectives. Implicit in such a stand is the fact that teachers want more of a say in selecting the materials to be used by each student for whose learning they are accountable. This would constitute a major shift in the way materials are selected for student use by many schools. Also implicit in this position is the fact that teachers are demanding that producers of the materials used in their classrooms be willing to bear a fair share of the total instructional responsibility.

The California legislators have, as noted earlier, stolen a march on the teachers and passed a law requiring producers of educational materials to "learner-verify" their products. If accurately interpreted and applied, this law will see to it that producers provide schools with empirically obtained descriptions of the performance of specific materials with learners, under specific teaching-learning conditions, and within a variety of educational contexts. They also must make it clear that they use the empirical findings to improve or maintain at a high level the future performance of their materials.

The major immediate implication of the two laws for producers is that those who do not gear up for complete learner-verification processes will not have their materials approved for purchase and use in California schools. A longer run implication, for the market in general, is that learner-verification requirements set in California, which constitutes more than 10 percent of the national school market, are bound to affect that market. Thus, product effectiveness and product improvement may, in California at least and probably much more widely, become as important selection and purchasing criteria for instructional materials as construction, content, and cost.

But let's look at the pitfalls. Let's assume that "Murphy's Law" preempts the California learner-verification law and "everything that can go wrong does go wrong." The State Department of Education guidelines for industry's compliance to the learner-verification requirement are either too stringent or too loose; the industry rejects the idea of the legislation and lobbies for the repeal of the learner-verification requirement, maintaining that—like the automobile industry—it cannot comply because the increased costs of producing "verified" products will price them out of the market; and/or the logistics for gathering learner-verification data and the procedures for monitoring and auditing the process become so complicated for schools and producers alike that the learner-verification requirement is dropped as unworkable.

Of course, all these things could happen. Indeed, one or more of them may very well happen in the short run in California. But in the long run, throughout the country, it seems inevitable that some reasonable approximation of the learner-verification concept as described in the present California law will become accepted and used by purchasers and producers. A cynical response might be that the inertia of long-standing habits and attitudes of people in schools, in state education departments, and in the education industry will hold the movement back. A few years ago, one would have had to acknowledge such cynicism not as cynicism at all but as an accurate reading of the current time. But the shift which new factors and forces have started is very likely to be irrevocable. At some future date it will be possible to look back and see the present as the beginning of a transformation that, in time, affected every aspect of the instructional materials process: materials design, development, marketing, and revision [producers]; materials selection, purchase, installation, and use [purchasers]. This transformation may come about slowly and even fitfully. It may also come more swiftly than many suspect. The signs of the transformation are easy to spot:

Teachers refusing to be held accountable for student achievement, unless, in their judgment, the materials assigned to them meet the needs of their students and are compatible with their particular teaching style.

Schools becoming increasingly reluctant to buy materials which are not supported by some objective evidence of their probable success with learners.

Increasing demands by parents and minority groups that the materials a school uses be geared to meet the learning needs of each child who is expected to learn from them, whether handicapped, normal, or gifted—irrespective of ethnic, social, or racial background.

In view of the long-range potential implicit in the adoption of the learner-verification concept by producers and users, other questions arise. What about the present research and development base upon which learner-verification must be built? Where is the solid ground? Where are the soft spots? Are there some established constructs that can be incorporated into this new concept? Are there some that ought to be struck down? modified? Are there totally new techniques and components to be developed? It is to these important questions that we now turn.

The questions are important, that is, if one accepts the concept of learner verification as having face validity. It seems reasonable to expect a producer to take time to investigate, regularly and systematically, whether his objectives for his materials are being achieved by learners who use the products. Further, he should be expected, having engaged in such verification, to use the verification data to make whatever improvements are necessary as long as the product remains on the market.

To date, verification activities such as "field tests," "tryouts," or other forms of "formative evaluation" to measure the results of product use have been used only during a product's prepublication or developmental life. A more comprehensive concept of learner verification, however, calls for a continued gathering of data on both cognitive and affective results of a product's use before and after publication, for as long as the product has a "market life."

Such cradle-to-grave verification and revision becomes increasingly necessary in an educational system committed to instructing each and every individual. It is a practical means of developing and refining materials so that they can make it possible for teachers and learners to do their jobs. Lacking a hard science of learni..g and motivation and a thoroughly scientific technology for instructional material development, the practical empiricism implicit in the concept of learner verification seems a reasonable way to proceed. It is more than possible that, in time, increasingly scientific principles of product development will emerge from observable trends in the sorts of internal product changes and external product adaptations resulting from the continuous verification of products. If such general principles are forthcoming, the process of learner verification, which is essentially an empirically-based corrective feedback device, will also become the basis of a much needed scientifically-based collective feed-forward mechanism.

Another closely related shift is that from what used to be a fairly stable educational and societal ground to one which continuously shifts. The most obvious example of this shifting ground is the way in which television has subtly but irrevocably expanded the scope of information which youngsters bring with them to school. More important, perhaps, is its effect on values and attitudes of the young. It seems likely that materials developed as recently as five years ago for pre-*Sesame Street* first graders today are causing very different reactions and are having very different effects and affects on regular viewers of *Sesame Street*. It seems likely also that, in a society in which change has become a constant, educators and educational producers deal more effectively with these shifts. A comprehensive approach to instructional materials must for this reason include the continuous verification of both effective and affective results of using specific products with learners.

A welcome side effect of this recognized, accepted, and expected continuous verification may be to render obsolete the currently fashionable phrase "validated materials," a misleading way of describing materials which have been through *some* testing before being put on the market. Those who use the term have invested it with the connotation that validated materials are ones on which the purchaser may rely, confident that, if used as directed, they will produce predictable instructional outcomes. Even if this sort of instructional predictability were true for "validated materials," it would be more properly called reliability, and we would find ourselves talking about reliable materials, *not* validated materials. The idea that materials can be validated (guaranteed to produce specified results) is indeed a soft spot in the research base upon which the work of creating more reliable materials must be built.

It is reliable materials that educational purchasers are looking for, and it is reliable materials that they need. But progress is slow and the number of materials published to date that might be called reliable is minuscule. The idea of holding a teacher who has used a particular set of materials—or the company which has produced them—accountable for not having produced predicted results with those materials is far from a present reality for any but the simplest objectives. Achieving high levels of reliability in teaching more complex objectives will require, among other things, a good deal more expertise in the analysis of the complex behaviors to be learned, and a good deal more hard empirical work in instructional design. The task for the seventies is to see how much progress can be made toward achieving reliable results with a given set of materials when used in different and similar instructional settings, particularly when the two major variables in those settings, learners and teachers, are very much alike. The task must also include a move for progress toward the goal of maintaining a product's reliability over time, given our society's continually changing educational ground. The educational research and evaluation community has given educational producers many of the evaluation and analytical tools they could be using to carry out the learner-verification process. True, many useful tools are still lacking, but the lack is not so great that any conscientious developer of instructional materials cannot set about using learner verification and revision to improve the quality of the products he now has on the market and those he is currently developing.

Much of the initial work on the available tools was done during the sixties by research and development projects funded federally or by foundations and more recently by the few commercial producers who have used some approximation of the development processes designed by such projects. As most of these projects originally were part of, or in some way an extension of, either the curricular reform or the programmed instruction movements that flourished during the early sixties, the instructional materials resulting from these efforts have certain characteristics in common:

(1)   the presence of clearly stated objectives expressed in operational or behavioral language;

(2)   the sequential development of learning activities based on an overall organizational scheme;

(3)   articulated or easily identifiable means and methods for carrying out those learning activities; and

(4)   some intrinsic or extrinsic evaluation procedures for measuring the outcomes of the learning activities and achievement of the initially stated objectives.

Each of these characteristics contributes to the empirical base from which the process of learner verification emanates. But the most important, if not always present, characteristic of such materials is their being subjected to what has been variously called classroom tryouts, field trials, field testing, developmental testing, and more recently, formative evaluation. All of these phrases refer to the rather simple, common-sensical ideal that when materials have been especially designed to instruct learners toward the achievement of particular learning objectives, it is wise to take time and trouble to verify the extent to which those objectives are actually being achieved, by means of such measures as pre- and posttests of mastery of those objectives. One of the most valuable aspects of this process is the use of "fine grain" data produced by the testing to identify specific shortcomings and to attempt to eradicate these shortcomings by revising those portions of the materials which are identified as inadequate. This, of course, means putting all materials through such pre- and posttesting with learners and teachers from schools that will eventually become the primary market for the materials under development. The average layman finds it hard to believe that such testing has not always been done with material used in schools. It seems so reasonable to expect that materials developed for use by poor readers will actually be tried and revised on the basis of trials with poor readers during development, that the materials designed for use by gifted youngsters will be developmentally shaped by testing with such youngsters, and that materials aimed primarily at center-city youngsters will be shaped during development through formative evaluation based on use and testing in center-city schools. This simple developmental procedure is one of the footings on which the emerging concept of learner verification might build.

Even so, in 1971, when EPIE Institute took stock of the situation in connection with the then 200,000 or so commercially available print and nonprint instructional materials, it was estimated that only one percent of the 200,000 had been put through anything resembling learner verification during their prepublication development. In 1973, an unprecedented survey conducted by a trade association in the education industry asked producers how many of their recently-launched products had been undergoing field testing. The fact that the industry as a whole has only begun to ask this question simply underscores the newness of the idea of prepublication learner verification. It also underscores how radical a departure from traditional practice the demand for both pre- and postpublication learner verification of materials is.

Suppose that, due to this demand and to mounting pressures resulting from the various shifts under discussion, more and more educational companies begin to adopt the concepts and the process of pre- and postpublication learner verification. How are they likely to proceed? How firm an operating base must they have? Is simple pre- and posttesting, using a criterion reference, enough? The answer is probably "yes" if the material being developed is a 10- or 20-frame filmstrip designed to transmit factual knowledge. But the answer is an emphatic "no" if the product is a 10- or 20-lesson video-tape course or a textbook designed for year-long use.

A short filmstrip with limited factual objectives, a limited role in the curriculum, and limited developmental budget may be learner-verified and revised using the simplest techniques of data gathering and analysis. Furthermore, given the relatively uncomplicated technology of filmstrip production, the mechanics of revision amount to a relatively simple procedure. Yet, despite this readily available revision opportunity, producers of filmstrips have not yet begun to gather the verification data that would enable them to continuously upgrade and update their materials as needed.

The task of gathering data and revising a video-taped course of 10 to 20 lessons is more complicated and expensive than learner-verifying a filmstrip, particularly if the series is designed to teach a higher level of learning than simple, factual knowledge. First of all, since it is extremely important to measure the effect on students and teachers of any course-length mediated instruction, simple pre- and posttesting is not likely to be a sufficient means of verification though it should be used to measure instructional effect. As verification data accumulate and fine grain analysis identifies particular shortcomings of the series, once again as with filmstrips, the technology of video-tape makes it relatively simple and inexpensive to revise as needed—a task that is do-able but not often done.

The continuous verification and revision of single filmstrips and video-tape courses is relatively uncomplicated, when compared to standard textbooks. As indicated at the outset, the textbook is still the central instructional material used by learners. And because many textbooks are used in a series covering a number of years of instruction, their verification with learners and subsequent revision is both crucially important and difficult to accomplish. Nevertheless, it must be done. Any materials that carry as much of the responsibility for structuring the day-to-day, hour-by-hour activities of hundreds of thousands of teachers and millions of learners, as textbooks do, must be as instructionally effective and as positively affective as possible. But the task of making the textbook responsive to the changing needs and attitudes of learners as well as continuously improving its instructional effectiveness by means of specific modification, is more difficult than upgrading a single film or video-taped series of lessons. Yet it can be done and must be done because, if the textbook industry is to be a responsible member of the educational community, it must learn how to become more responsive to the ultimate educational consumer, the learner.

There are a number of quite effective ways in which this can be done, given current evaluation and production technologies. There are also potentially much more effective ways of accomplishing continuous responsiveness through learner verification, given the further development of newly emerging evaluation techniques and production technologies. Using simple pre- and posttesting procedures during a textbook's development, and then after its entry into the school market, a producer can regularly gather empirical feedback for revision on: (1) how well the major objectives of his materials are being achieved by learners; (2) how teacher and student attitudes and feelings are affecting the performance of the materials.

While such simple procedures may not always satisfy the tenets of formal research and evaluation, they would be a marked improvement over what for many years has been accepted by the industry as adequate market feedback on which to base textbook revisions once every three years or so. Witness the following statements based on interviews conducted in 1971 by EPIE Institute with executive editors from major textbook companies:

We have about one hundred salesmen and consultants who report back what they pick up in the field; that's really our field testing.

A couple of years ago, we wanted to do some field testing, but scheduling wouldn't allow it . . . it takes too much time and we wouldn't have gotten the books out . . . it wasn't a question of money, but just scheduling.

Clearly, any systematic data-based feedback would be a more reliable basis for revising materials than informal reports "picked up" in the field by salesmen and consultants whose ego involvement with the products that they have sold and recommended to schools is apt to make them rather selective in what they hear from school people and even more selective about what they report back to company headquarters.

This is not to say that uninvolved field consultants cannot be found and trained to conduct structured interviews and make systematic observations of product use in order to gather data on which to base the development and revision of products, but too few educational producers now make this sort of systematic effort. Nevertheless, the techniques of pre- and posttesting and in-depth interviewing and observation, as developed by the educational research community, are readily available to all educational producers. In addition to these techniques, there are others as well. Many of these techniques have been developed by market researchers, some of whom are among the most able applied social scientists in the country, and who have specialized in the measurement of motivation and of the effectiveness of written and pictorial messages.

Of course, it may be necessary, in fact desirable, to develop new techniques of data gathering specifically geared to the task of learner-verifying and revising instructional materials or, as some suggest, to adapt existing research techniques from disciplines outside of educational research. Both of these developments may well begin to occur on a large scale in the near future.

As much as these available and newly emerging techniques of

product evaluation have to contribute to the changing nature of instructional materials, there are also some important developments taking place in the technologies of materials production, reproduction, and distribution that may make equally important contributions to the inevitable acceptance of the concept of learner verification by producers and purchasers alike. Typical of these developing technologies are:

(1) the production technology employed by The Center for Individual Instructional Systems (a division of the National Laboratory for Higher Education in Durham, North Carolina), through which the producer prints instructional materials on plastic-coated pages which are ring-bound together, making it possible for the purchaser to replace pages, chapters, or sections of chapters sent to him by the producer who has improved portions of the materials on the basis of learner-verification feedback;

(2) photographic "typesetting" and printing which enables a publisher to change type, pictures, or charts anywhere on any page of printed material because "type" in the traditional sense is never used—the photographic display and memory make it unnecessary. Nor is it necessary, with photographic typesetting and printing, to make any sort of permanent metal or plastic plates from which to print. This technology could, in time, revolutionize the printing of instructional materials in that most textbooks represent a heavy investment in metal plates which are very expensive to change. Therefore, most producers settle for superficial "plate patches" even during a so-called major three-year textbook revision; and

(3) the various technologies of photo-copying, magnetic tape duplication, microform reproduction, and electronic dissemination of information in all forms.

Such representative technological developments as these are bound, in the long run, to solve the problems currently related to production, revision, redesign, reproduction, and dissemination of instructional materials—and to solve them in economically attractive ways, from the standpoint of both the producer and the purchaser.

In the short run, however, these and related technologies are presenting rather formidable economic, psychological, legal, and ethical problems which must be solved. If producers need new techniques of systematic data gathering in order to carry out learner verification, both producers and purchasers need new ways of dealing with each other in order to focus on the task of putting continually improved and up-dated materials of instruction into the hands of teachers and learners.

For example, state and local schools, bound either by legal statute or purchasing habit, are going to have to change in order to open themselves to the possible benefits that may accrue from such things as easily up-datable, loose-leaf, plastic-paged materials—or local "instant (re)production" of needed materials.

Producers who are frightened by the implications of duplication by local schools of all types of copyrighted instructional media must figure out simple, sensible ways to allow any school to reproduce such material without jeopardizing the producers' profit from direct sales. Any solution is bound up in an ethical-legal-economic issue. One possible solution would be to legally require schools that wish absolute freedom to reproduce copyrighted materials at will to drop a pre-addressed record-of-reproduction form in the mail to the producer whose materials they have just copied. Then, at the end of the school year, the producer would simply bill the school on the basis of the number of copies made of each of his materials. The more copies made, the smaller the unit price, perhaps.

The point is simply that each new and yet-to-emerge production and reproduction technology presents as much potential for progress as it does for producing anxiety. The potential in each of these production technologies, as well as in the techniques of learner verification, depends on the development of a new type of producer-purchaser relationship, a relationship in which mutual concern and cooperation are manifest not only in rhetoric but in practical, productive solutions to the problems inherent in today's shifting educational society.

Inevitably, of course, as shifts continue to occur, solutions to the problems created by them will inevitably be forthcoming. What is not inevitable, however, is the quality of those forthcoming solutions. That quality depends in turn on the quality of the decisions made by many people in schools, state education departments, federal agencies, and last, but hardly least, the educational industry. Poor decisions can open pitfalls which limit the progress that is already being made. The greatest dangers are:

(1) the shift away from the standard textbook toward the increasing proliferation of multimedia materials may flood schools with endless arrays of mediocre options rather than supply them with high quality alternatives for meeting the needs of individual learners;

(2) the shift toward legislated demands for the achievement of measurable, behaviorally stated objectives may drastically skew all classroom teaching and instructional materials development in the direction of the easily measurable rather than the educationally desirable; and

(3) the shift toward learner verification of materials may be made more in an effort to persuade purchasers to buy rather than to help learners learn and teachers teach (thus, data will be gathered to prove how good a product is, rather than to improve it, and make it what it could be).

If these pitfalls are not avoided, the end result is very likely to be an irreversible shift toward the trivialization of education led by materials producers and reinforced by purchasers who will make the mistake of assuming that by simply producing or buying more of the latest materials, by gathering or supplying more data, by making more sales or lobbying for more money for materials purchases, they will end up with more effective learning. All these things cannot of themselves automatically add up to more effective learning. There is a crucially important factor missing from that equation—commitment to the development and use of effective techniques for improving our rather rudimentary instructional tools.

An important part of that commitment is going to have to be made in the form of dollars. The education industry is going to have to redirect some of its resources to what for many companies will be an entirely new dimension of product development. But, unfortunately, these reallocated dollars will not be sufficient to pay the full cost of improving the tools of learning. State and local school systems will have to bear a good portion of the cost of learner verification in the form of higher prices paid for better materials. But there is a serious question as to whether they are prepared to do this. The legislation in California related to learner verification, for all of its forward looking character, takes a step backward by appropriating an annual per pupil expenditure for instructional materials which is substantially under the national average expenditure.

There is no question that schools could spend substantially more for improved instructional materials without spending what would amount to substantially more money in relation to a school's overall budget. This seeming anomaly is possible because of the very small amount of this country's educational dollars put into the purchase of instructional materials. Most Americans do not realize it, but many schools spend less than one percent of their annual budget on materials, and even the most affluent spend less than two percent. Yet the materials purchased with this money structure more than 75 percent of pupils' study time in school and at home.

Many critics of education like to point out that education is a labor intensive sector of the economy, meaning by this that some 70 percent of the country's educational dollars are spent on teachers' salaries.

But teacher-labor represents only a minute portion of the total labor expended during a school day in the average classroom. With all due respect to the teaching profession, the aggregate labor of learning expended by 20 to 30 students in the course of a school day is far greater than that expended by their classroom teacher. Such heavy labor intensity is inevitable in education, but isn't it time we seriously looked to improving the tools that the laborers are required to use? Even if that improvement is apt to double or even triple the present cost of these tools, at most this would mean increasing that portion of our educational budgets spent for learning materials from one to two, or possibly, three percent. Translated into dollars, this would require a commitment to increase a current national expenditure of about one billion dollars to two billion, about the same amount spent each year by American smokers on tobacco.

Clearly, such an increase would hardly put inordinate pressure on state and local education budgets. And even more clearly, it would be sufficient to pay for the cost of increasing the learning effectiveness of 50 million American children.

INDEX